The "Inequality" Controversy

The

'INEQUALITY"
Controversy:

Schooling and Distributive Justice

Donald M. Levine
& Mary Jo Bane

Basic Books, Inc., Publishers

New York

Library of Congress Cataloging in Publication Data
Main entry under title:

The "Inequality" controversy.

Includes bibliographical references and index.
1. Educational equalization—United States.
2. Education—Economic aspects—United States.   I.   Levine, Donald M.   II.   Bane, Mary Jo.
LC213.2.I43   370.19   74-25910
ISBN 0-465-03243-5
ISBN 0-465-03244-3 pbk.

© 1975 Basic Books, Inc.
Printed in the United States of America
DESIGNED BY VINCENT TORRE
75 76 77 78 79   10 9 8 7 6 5 4 3 2 1

CONTENTS

III

Equality, Equity, and Equal Opportunity

IV

Conclusions

CONTRIBUTORS

HARVEY A. AVERCH is Deputy Assistant Director for Analysis and Planning, Research Application Directorate at the National Science Foundation. He is co-author of *The Matrix of Policy in the Phillipines* (1971) and *How Effective Is Schooling?* (1974).

MARY JO BANE, associate director of The Women's Research Center and assistant professor of education at Wellesley College, is a co-author of *Inequality: A Reassessment of the Effect of Family and Schooling in America* (1972).

JAMES S. COLEMAN is professor of sociology at the University of Chicago. He is co-author of *Equality of Educational Opportunity* (1966) and chairman of the President's Panel on Youth.

GODFREY HODGSON, formerly a correspondent for *The London Observer* and *The London Sunday Times*, is now a free-lance writer. He is a frequent contributor to *The Atlantic Monthly*.

CHRISTOPHER LASCH, professor of history at the University of Rochester, is the author of *The Agony of the American Left* (1969) and *The World of Nations* (1973).

DONALD M. LEVINE is associate professor in the Department of Educational Administration at Teachers College, Columbia University, and a Consultant to the New York City Board of Education, the New Jersey State Department of Education, and the Rand Corporation. He edited *Performance Contracting in Education—An Appraisal (1973)*.

JACOB MINCER, professor of economics at Columbia University, is the author of *Schooling, Experience, and Earnings* (1974). He edited *Economic Forecasts and Expectations: Analysis of Forecasting Behavior and Performance* (1969).

DANIEL P. MOYNIHAN, professor of government at Harvard's Kennedy School of Government, is a former Ambassador to India and Presidential advisor on urban and other public policy issues. He is the author of *The Politics of a Guaranteed Income* (1973) and co-author of *Beyond the Melting Pot* (1963).

ROBERT NOZICK, professor of philosophy at Harvard University and a member of the board of editors of *Philosophy and Public Affairs,* is the author of *Anarchy, State, and Utopia* (1974).

JOHN RAWLS, John Cowles Professor of Philosophy at Harvard University, is the author of *A Theory of Justice* (1971).

T. PAUL SCHULTZ, professor of economics at the University of Minnesota, is the author of *Structural Change in a Developing Economy* (1971).

LESTER C. THUROW is professor of economics at the Massachusetts Institute of Technology. He is co-author of *The Economic Problem* (1974) and author of *Generating Inequality* (to be published in 1976), *Poverty and Discrimination* (1969), and *Investment in Human Capital* (1970).

BURTON A. WEISBROD, professor of economics at the University of Wisconsin, is the co-author of *American Health Policy: Perspectives and Choices* (1974) and co-editor of *The Daily Economist* (1973).

WALTER A. WEISSKOPF is a professor in the Graduate Division of Economics at Roosevelt University. He is the author of *The Psychology of Economics* (1955) and *Alienation and Economics* (1971).

The "Inequality" Controversy

INTRODUCTION

OUR ATTITUDES toward poverty present a confused picture. Since the Depression, public interest has focused intermittently, but increasingly, on the deprived lives of the poor and the unequal distribution of income that defines poverty. Political action has produced an ever-broader range of public assistance programs, from the WPA to Medicaid. None of these programs have been designed to eliminate poverty by the most direct route—by giving enough cash to the poor to push their incomes over some relative poverty line. None have openly taken up the cause of distributive justice. Instead, we have created a host of ingenious programs to alleviate poverty indirectly. We have spent money to make the poor more employable, to find them jobs, and even to employ them publicly. As a last resort, we have used limited transfers in cash (Aid to Families with Dependent Children [AFDC]) and in kind (food stamps) to disprove the adage that "the poor are always with us." Despite commitments like the War on Poverty—which sought to eradicate the problem, not simply to ameliorate it—the poor are still here, so it is hard to call our approach an unqualified success. But we continue to avoid the alternative of eliminating poverty *ipso facto* by a simple and direct redistribution of income. No matter how sincerely and expensively Americans care for the poor and yearn for distributive justice, they shrink from the idea of outright cash grants.

Of all indirect policies in effect during the last ten years, education has received the most attention. But the explicit idea of education as a weapon against poverty is a recent development. It has strong roots in the traditional conception of education as the key to social integration and mobility, a notion apparently justified by the assimilation of successive waves of immigrants through the schools. It was reinforced after World War II by the theorists of human capital, who showed that investments in schooling yielded ample returns in the form of higher lifetime earnings streams. And it had inherent attractions because of its very indirectness. Publicly supported education, it seemed, could give

3

the poor the tools they needed to escape from poverty by dint of their own efforts. It would not oblige Americans to violate the work ethic by creating a dole.

The catalyst in the development of education as an antipoverty policy was the 1954 Supreme Court ruling in the case of *Brown v. The School Board of Topeka, Kansas*. In holding that "separate but equal" schools for blacks were unconstitutional, the Court did not base its argument only on the denial of fundamental freedoms. It also ruled that even if expenditures (school inputs) were equal, segregated schools were unacceptable because the very fact of segregation produced unequal results (school outputs). As James Coleman points out,[1] this was the first time that concern with the *results* of education had been formalized. Equality of educational opportunity thenceforth would have to mean *effective* equality, in terms of some measure of school output. From this concern it was but a short step to compensatory education, the Elementary and Secondary Education Act (ESEA) of 1965, and an explicit belief in the lifetime results of schooling that gave education a leading role in antipoverty policy.

During this same period, however, the significance of education in the economic status system was subject to closer scrutiny and growing doubt. The Supreme Court ruling had stimulated social scientists to begin tracing the immediate and longer-term effects of schooling. By the time they were finished, educators were left with only the hope that schools might make a measurable difference to children.

The most important revelations came in the 1966 Equality of Educational Opportunity Survey (EEOS), conducted by Coleman. Essentially, EEOS showed that differences in existing school inputs made relatively small differences in school outputs. Subsequent analyses of EEOS data generally verified this conclusion. In addition, the rise of compensatory education led to evaluations of alternative schooling strategies. But these studies suggested that new applications and levels of school inputs were just as ineffective as the old ones. Nothing the schools could do, it seemed, made much difference to the cognitive achievement of their pupils.

Despite initial attempts to downplay this research, the results had enormous impact on the educational establishment. Taxpayers began to resist rising school costs and to demand that school systems quantify and report student outcomes achieved by spending public money. The federal government insisted that school systems demonstrate how effectively they had used funds received under ESEA of 1965. The burning debate about the effects of schooling was further fanned in the 1970s by a series of civil suits which argued, somewhat belatedly, for more equal expenditures among school districts in the name of more equal educational results.

Controversy about antipoverty policy and the role of education came to a head in late 1972 with the publication of *Inequality: A Reassessment of the Effect of Family and Schooling in America.*[2] The product of more than five years of study by Christopher Jencks and seven colleagues, *Inequality* reanalyzed an enormous body of prior research in an attempt to discover the roots of social and economic inequality and the effects of education on inequality. The general conclusion was: "Neither family background, cognitive skill, educational attainment, nor occupational status explain much of the variation in men's incomes."[3] In other words, variations in income cannot be explained by any of the factors with which we have conventionally associated such variations. Conversely, Jencks and his associates concluded, economic success is largely the product of luck and peculiar competencies (e.g., the ability to pitch a baseball) over which government has no control. The social policy recommendation seemed obvious: since all indirect antipoverty programs are doomed to failure, the only way to eliminate poverty is to redistribute income directly. *Inequality*'s conclusions for educational policy were similarly radical. Given: a) that differences in schooling have only minor effects on cognitive achievement, and b) that equalizing opportunity is almost impossible without reducing the absolute inequalities that lead to unequal opportunities, we must abandon the notion of education as a means to some noneducational end. Rather, we should view education in the context of the internal life of schools and try to equalize distribution of those resources that affect the immediate experience of schooling, forgetting entirely the idea of long-term benefits.

Reactions to *Inequality* have been disparate, violent, and frequently negative. The book threatened numerous vested interests, from social workers to the scions of wealth. It raised disturbing questions about the depth and effects of America's commitment to equality of opportunity and to equality of results. The furor it created was only aggravated by the authors' avowedly political objectives—to publicize the problem of income inequality and to state the case for socialism. (Some readers, though, felt that *Inequality* pointed the way to a new, and less benign, neglect of the underprivileged.) Much of the reaction was tinged with confusion about the book's analysis and purpose, for *Inequality* is a complex work with many broad implications.

The goal of this collection is to help dispel the confusion by providing some perspective on the issues of schooling and distributive justice. The articles speak to the *Inequality* controversy; they should foster continued thinking about what education can and should do, and about how education fits into the longer-term goals and structures of our society. It is on such thinking that more sensible policies for education and better approaches to distributive justice will depend.

The readings are divided into four parts. The first part—"Schools and Society"—deals with a range of issues that will impinge on educational policy making after *Inequality:* How can we use existing research to develop policies that will fulfill the ideal of equal educational opportunity without undermining the ideal of economic equality? What kinds of goals are relevant to and useful for education? How can we improve future research to make it more useful for policy formation? The answers to these questions will form the structure of education in the future.

While it is important that educational policies rely on correct interpretations and elaborations of data about the effects of education, interpretation inevitably reflects the researcher's bias. Obviously, the interpretations reported in *Inequality* are geared to the book's view of education-as-determinant-of-income. Just as obviously, a number of interpretations can come from the same data Jencks and his associates used. Some scholars, for example, have used the EEOS and other data to assert that integration is the key to educational achievement.[4] This divergence of interpretations becomes wider and harder to resolve when we turn to the crucial questions of how—and how much—money should be spent for schooling. In light of *Inequality,* Jencks contends that more money should be spent to make schooling equally enjoyable for all children; Moynihan's interpretation is that money spent on education (and any other social program) increases short-run income inequality. As Godfrey Hodgson puts it, "Is a glass half-empty, or is it half-full?" It's a matter of interpretation.

It is also, of course, a matter of goals, since one's ideas about the ends of education condition one's opinions about the means. *Inequality* assumed that Americans want schools to prepare children for society, not just by giving them some general acquaintance with the liberal arts, but by equipping them with specific tools for success in the social and economic structure. But there are other goals for education, and they must be reconciled with the goal of social and economic competence. We support schools, for example, because universal schooling helps to socialize and politicize children in essentially similar ways, and this homogenization is important in such a heterogeneous country. We also pay for education because basic literacy seems essential to a form of government—like democracy—that depends on an informed and articulate citizenry. Some parents find schooling useful because schools act as caretakers for their children. Others believe in the value of education *per se*—i.e., acquaintance with the liberal arts. Attitudes like these are partly a product of the history of education in America. They vary by class and ethnic group; they may change across the board as works like *Inequality* diffuse through our culture. So it is dangerous to make exclusive generalizations about the purposes of education, especially at a time when the bulk of research on school effectiveness is forcing us to reassess policy in a very basic way. Only after we have considered alternative goals and understood their interrelationships can we begin to sketch future policies.

In addition to an understanding of goals and some agreement about interpretations of the available data, effective policy making requires more viable types of educational research than presently exist. We will have to develop methods of evaluating educational programs that can be used to improve future decisions. This is a question of research strategy. Because current research usually fails to reveal the ways in which education affects children, we may have to develop other modes of research. Moreover, changes in the role of education will require corresponding changes in our methods of study. To some extent, data interpretations, goals, and research strategies are circularly related: interpretations help determine goal structures, which set the dimensions of research strategies, and these strategies may reveal data that lead us to reassess our original interpretations. The point at issue now, though, is that as long as research strategy remains clouded, the success or failure of programs will elude measurement, and the policy-making process will have to rely as much on luck as on analysis.

The second part—"What Determines Income?"—deals with a particular formulation of the role of education and the utility of schooling: the argument that education is positively related to economic success, and that a more equal distribution of education will therefore lead to a more equal distribution of income. A major justification of education has been provided by the human capital economists, who argue that education increases a person's productivity and hence his wages, the marginal value of his productivity. Human capital theorists, using highly aggregated data, have supported their view in many ways, among them by showing that real per capita income in the United States (and some other countries) has increased beyond the explanatory power of investments in physical capital, and by demonstrating that income distribution has become more equal despite the unchanged (and very unequal) distribution of wealth. The obvious implication is that workers themselves have become more productive by making ever-greater investments in education and training, by augmenting their human capital.

If *Inequality* is correct about the absence of any strong and rational education-income nexus, how can the human capital theorists also be right? The problem may lie in interpreting the data: Jencks concentrated on income differences *within* groups of people, but most economic analyses focus on differences *among* groups. Average returns to education for a particular group may be satisfactory, while individual returns

7

vary widely. As Thurow has noted, "Education might be a profitable but risky investment." [5] The data are similar, but the interpretations differ. Once again, is the glass half-empty or half-full?

It seems more likely, though, that differences between Jencks and the human capitalists arise from problems in measuring income inequality and in conceptualizing the structure of the labor market. In the first place, as T. Paul Schultz notes,[6] differences in defining the data base can lead to very different conclusions about the extent of income inequality and its relation to education. If the sample is limited to fully employed men, 25 to 64 years old, income inequality has remained remarkably stable from 1939 to 1967. But if the sample is enlarged to include all men and women in this age group, there appear to have been real reductions in inequality. The difference may be attributed to an increased number of hours worked per capita, and the economic effect of education therefore may be to increase the extent or duration of a person's employment rather than his wage rates. As full and partial unemployment decline, so does inequality.

Secondly, education may function not to upgrade the labor supply, but as a way to regulate labor demand. Wages are determined institutionally—by union contracts, minimum wage laws, and so on—but access to the jobs that yield those wages depends on educational attainment. The driving principle of the labor market is job competition rather than wage competition. This explanation supports the finding of *Inequality* that wages *within* occupations vary with little respect to educational attainment, although years of schooling may be a prerequuisite for access to a particular type of job.

On the other hand, even if we accept the human capital model, there are important questions about the form of investments. Investments in schooling beyond a certain level may not be as remunerative as investments in work experience made by taking a job at a very low wage rate for the sake of future payoffs. It may be possible to realize higher returns by shifting the balance of investments away from education and toward work experience or on-the-job-training. Yet calculating the costs and benefits of such a strategy is impossible at this time because we have yet to establish input-output models for education that would tell us what types and levels of educational investments produce the desired skills at the lowest costs. Nor have we been willing to make the educational and social experiments that might foreshadow such a model. Only with reliable input-output information can we make meaningful comparisons among different investment plans. If it is a mistake, as *Inequality* suggests, to see education in terms of the input-output model, we may never be able to develop the needed data; again, new approaches to educational research seem necessary.

Although the articles of the second part are inconclusive, they teach a valuable lesson for the future: analyses of educational policy must consider the dynamics of the education-employment-income sequence, for only an understanding of these dynamics can enable us to predict what will happen when we change things. Moreover, to understand these dynamics, and to make reliable predictions, we will have to analyze data collected across cultures and over time. Some of these data already exist and can be brought together. A great deal of information, though, remains to be collected before we can speak with any assurance of education's impact on economic equality.

The third part—"Equality, Equity, and Equal Opportunity"—explores some of the philosophical questions that lie at the heart of the controversy about inequality and Inequality. These are crucial questions because their answers dictate the educational goals that future policies will have to accommodate. Any close examination of goals inevitably leads us back to broad and basic philosophical problems—as soon as we start trying to decide whether education should promote equality of results and/or equality of opportunity, we must define the various types of equality, and our definitions necessarily will refer to some notion of the equitable (just) society. The articles in this section attempt to clarify the conflicts among the various concepts of equality that have been applied to education, and to point out root divergences in our ideas of the just society.

The first philosophical problem we encounter in policy making is the definition of "equality of educational opportunity." Historically, that concept involved supporting free schools with a common curriculum and educating children of different backgrounds in the same local school. (This concept was related to some of the alternative goals of schooling we mentioned before, including sociopolitical homogenization and basic literacy.) Given equal educational opportunities, students were responsible for making the best of them. Both the short- and the long-term effects of schooling, according to this model, were the consequences of the student's efforts and abilities, and the schools had little responsibility for the resulting cognitive, social, or economic inequalities.

By the 1950s the passive view of educational opportunity had begun to be modified by an increasing concern for unequal results at the lower ends of the income and social status distributions. This led to a more active approach, which underlined the school's responsibility for the results of schooling, and to the revolutionary belief that equal educational opportunity should be measured not only in terms of the input factors that characterize educational opportunity—money, facilities, curriculum, teachers—but also in terms of educational outputs, usually reported as scores on standardized achievement tests. This was not to say that all

9

differences in educational outputs were evidence of unequal educational opportunities, but that if the educational achievement of certain groups differed consistently from the achievement of other groups, it was the school's fault. The principle was formalized in Coleman's fifth definition of equal educational opportunity,[7] which used as its criterion the production of equal educational results for children from different backgrounds (in practical terms, for socioeconomically different *groups* of children).

Ironically, by showing that differences in school resources made such small differences in cognitive achievement for different groups of children, the Coleman report left advocates of equal educational results in a quandary. Granted the criterion of equal results, it had seemed sensible to allocate school resources unequally in an effort to compensate for cultural disadvantages. But if results remained basically unchanged by manipulations of school resources, perhaps the proper egalitarian posture was a return to the traditional focus on an equal distribution of resources, regardless of the cognitive outcomes. At least this approach would assure an equal distribution of the consumer benefits of education.

A more problematical version of the debate among educational egalitarians has taken place recently, as policy makers have grappled with equality of economic opportunity versus equality of economic results. The argument is somewhat similar: Equality of economic opportunity means very little—and certainly fails to achieve anything—unless it leads to more equal economic results. So if we believe that income inequality has changed little, relative to our efforts to equalize income opportunities, we must forsake the idea of opportunity and turn toward direct income redistribution. Such an extension of the education argument makes a hash of the distinction between opportunity and results. It removes from the opportunity-results sequence all those factors of individual merit—talent, will, perseverance—that seem to make the difference between success and failure, and that Americans traditionally have valued. In short, it replaces the notion that people should be rewarded according to their performance with the idea that worldly goods should be distributed more or less equally among all people. No individual really deserves anything; all individuals deserve something fairly similar.

This development is a profoundly uncomfortable one for people living in a capitalist and ostensibly meritocratic society, for it implies that the inequalities so long accepted as proper are, in fact, unjust. Why pay the chairman of ITT almost a million dollars unless he can be said to have earned it in some way? The only remaining justification for income inequality is that income serves as an incentive, that rich rewards are needed to motivate people to allocate and employ national resources as efficiently as they can. In that case, though, we need a motivational model that will indicate how much reward is enough. Without such a model, a million dollars seems like overkill, especially in light of the benefits we might reap by redistributing most of that money among the (not necessarily deserving) poor. On the other hand, as an incentive for running ITT with maximum efficiency, that sum may be exactly what is necessary, and redistributing it may actually injure the poor by imperiling the economic performance of the country.

Strong contradictions persist even when we resort to the incentive argument. If we change the rationale for economic inequality from one of deserving to one of incentives, we probably will have a lot of income to redistribute. But if we simply proceed to appropriate this "illegitimate" money for redistribution, we flaunt sacrosanct ideas about private property. How do we explain to somebody who is entitled, under the common law, to a certain amount of income (or property) that the new dispensation has voided his entitlement and historic rights to that property? Similarly, if we seek to equalize results, we will have to limit severely the individual's present liberty to make choices and engage in activities that maximize his economic returns at the expense of others. Few stronger *disincentives* to economic efficiency can be imagined. It seems, then, that a principle of justice that envisions a fair *pattern* of economic results must conflict with the existing principle of justice, which envisions a fair set of *procedures* for determining those results, and thus gives scope for individual or peculiar preferences and motivations.[8]

These problems affect educational policy directly and indirectly. At the most general level, if we decide that the just society must go beyond fair competition (fair procedures) to include a generation and distribution of income that is to the greatest good of the least privileged (a fair pattern), we will have to design educational policies that trade off a more equal distribution of educational resources against any growth in aggregate benefits that schooling may encourage. At some point, for example, the effort to give all children a fair share of school resources will reduce the resources available to the brightest children, who may be able to generate, in later years, the most income for redistribution. What blend of resource equality and investment in potentially high wage earners will yield the greatest good for the least advantaged over time? Further, if future social policy includes some sort of aftertax income redistribution, will the poor gain more from an educational policy that concentrates on developing the talents of relatively few very promising children, or from a policy that involves broader but less concentrated developments of economic potential? (Or is the problem academic because education is only a way to ration jobs and does not improve labor productivity?)

More particularly, if current research and philosophy lead us to concentrate on equalizing the quality of school life, how far should we go? We may want to compensate rural children for their "unpleasant" schools by giving them proportionately more money than suburban and core-city children get. But almost all of that extra money will come out of the pockets of suburban taxpayers, who may be quite justified in protesting that this radical transfer violates their historical rights (besides wiping out any school quality advantages bought with the rich suburban tax base). Should we include private schools in our equalization efforts? If so, how do we distribute their resources for the greatest good of children in low-quality public schools, and yet avoid unacceptable property violations or restrictions on a parent's liberty to buy his child a high-quality education? The answers to these and other thorny questions about educational policy lie in the resolution of the philosophical problems.

The importance of the first three parts of this book to any discussion of national policy should be clear. Policy analysis—the means by which we develop and test future policies—depends on defining the problem (Part I), considering existing research and analysis (as exemplified in Part II), and evaluating alternatives in light of accepted goals and restraints (as debated in Part III). These three parts also advance policy analysis by demonstrating that social, economic, and educational policies are intricately interrelated. In thinking about the future, we must analyze these areas simultaneously and watch for unsuspected interactions.

The concluding essays show how the various empirical and analytic perspectives of the preceding parts can be brought together to suggest new policies. The first paper draws on sociological surveys, Rawls' work, and the *Inequality* data to speculate about economic policies that will accommodate both Rawlsian notions of fairness and American political realities. The conclusions are both more and less than we might hope for, since they indicate that some income redistribution is both necessary and possible, but probably only under the guise of charity or insurance. The second paper closely scrutinizes the philosophical, economic, and educational arguments of *Inequality* in an attempt to adduce the book's lasting impact on educational policy. Again, the conclusions are mixed: although it is premature to abandon interest in the short- and long-term effects of education (both cognitive and economic), present methods of analysis are inadequate. Only a more rigorous approach that combines measures of educational cost with innovative research on educational effectiveness can reveal promising policies that will fit into a larger framework of social and economic policies.

In general, what kinds of perspectives on *Inequality* and inequality do these readings provide? First of all, there seems to be concurrence about the disappointing implications of research on school effectiveness. Despite significant statistical disagreements, most researchers would agree with Jencks and others that variations in levels of school resources have little effect on variations in children's scores on standardized achievement tests. Such a conclusion must lead us to abandon attempts to improve traditional school outputs simply by increasing the level of inputs. We certainly seem to have reached that "flat area" of a theoretical educational production function where outputs diminish severely with each input increment.

But this is no news—taxpayers have suspected all along that more money alone cannot solve educational (or social) problems. More interesting inferences can be drawn from *Inequality* by looking at the limitations of the book's conclusions about education. First, those conclusions should not be read to mean that schools make no difference. Differences in years of schooling do make cognitive and economic differences for students, though the precise degree of those differences is hard to measure in the absence of adequate control groups. In most cases, therefore, we should probably encourage students to stay in school and avoid policies that have an opposite effect. True, for many students it may seem that work experience is a more than adequate substitute for school; but unless sweeping changes are made in America's social and economic structure, the lack of at least a high school and probably a college education will continue to be a significant and fairly rational barrier to economic advancement.

Second, *Inequality's* conclusion about the effects of schooling are limited to cognitive results. Noncognitive outcomes—which may be more important to long-term success than cognitive ones—have not been dealt with mainly because of measurement problems. Affective outcomes of schooling must be assessed before we can abandon absolutely the factory model of education in favor of the family life model.

Finally, current research deals mostly with existing arrays and uses of school resources. Lacking any dynamic model for the educational process —and any reliable evaluations of educational experiments—we cannot know what will happen if we alter the process itself, i.e., the ways in which resources are used. The possibility of significant shifts in the curve of diminishing returns should not be dismissed.

Perhaps the most interesting perspective on the role of education that emerges from these readings is the evident need to rethink educational goals. There is a clear conflict between those who maintain that education should be a means to economic ends and those who feel that education should limit itself to providing basic literacy and, in the case of higher education, to training professionals. One group focuses on our manpower needs (sometimes through legislation like the

National Defense Education Act) and on earnings streams; the other concentrates on minimum levels of cognitive achievement and, in the egalitarian variation, on the equalization of the quality of school life. Although any major shift in educational goals is likely to evolve through disillusion with the existing goal-set, instead of being determined through policy debates, we still must ask ourselves whether we are prepared to accept a largely noneconomic rationale for education, and whether any new rationale should take a starkly egalitarian approach to the allocation of school resources. If we favor egalitarianism, we must go several steps further to ask who should pay for schooling, what levels of government should be responsible for equalization, and how any additional funds will be spent within the school system. These questions are important because school funding is itself a significant channel of income distribution and redistribution.

The issues of income inequality and of the connections between education and income seem less clear than those of school effects and educational goals. Measurement of income inequality is an ambiguous task because available data usually are not the ones we should be analyzing. They often ignore establishment of separate households by people who used to live in large family groups (mainly the young and the old), unrecorded transfers, aftertax redistribution, and variations in time worked. Generally, it seems true that income inequality has not changed dramatically since World War II. Any statement more informative than that—and any plan for direct redistribution of income—will have to await more reliable data, or at least more agreement about the existing data and their implications.

The case is similar with the issue of education and income: while there is convincing evidence in *Inequality* and other studies that the human capital model is of limited usefulness, we have yet to reconcile the contradictory implications of existing data, or to assess recent elaborations of the model. Mincer has suggested,[9] for example, that postschool investments in human capital may be very important, and this line of reasoning supports *Inequality*'s speculations about the major role on-the-job training may play in labor productivity. And if educational attainment increases one's propensity to make such investments, education may influence income indirectly.

If we accept the more likely explanation—that education affects income by giving people a range of credentials that can be used to ration jobs—we still have to decide whether or not credentialism is rational. Almost no work has been done that can tell us if the more educated are in general the more trainable, and therefore worth preference in a job queue. Even less attention has been paid to developing better rationing devices and ways to select the more trainable employee.

Furthermore, even if educational credentials are part of an irrational rationing system, and we conclude that equalizing education will not equalize income, education may still make sense as a "defensive necessity" [10] (i.e., a basic weapon in job competition). Only sweeping changes of our industrial system and of our methods of managing labor demand can change this situation. The outlook is even gloomier if we turn to reducing inequality on the job, since that reform would seem to require improbably massive shifts in American attitudes toward hierarchy and free competition. Nonetheless, it seems desirable to relate employment more directly to actual skills, and a shift of employer emphasis from educational attainment to work experience may be the most feasible first step in that direction.

As the readings in Part III indicate, a philosophical evolution is the basis and framework for the whole inequality controversy, whether it relates to education, to employment, or to income. There is little disagreement among philosophers or sociologists that Americans generally endorse the principle of fair competition, of equal opportunities and fair procedures in all forms of competition. But how much further are we willing to go? Most Americans will go along with ostensible efforts to equalize opportunity (e.g., through education, job training, placement centers) and with a limited amount of direct aid to those who cannot work, or cannot work enough. Greatly increased direct aid is another matter, especially if it is openly designed to narrow income differentials, which many Americans prize as proof of their own success, and if it is available even to those who can work but choose not to, in flagrant violation of the work ethic. A program of that sort, which is what we really mean by "income redistribution," is sure of defeat unless and until people's attitudes change radically. The evolution of those attitudes thus far presages abandonment of the meritocratic approach to equality that rests on beliefs in desert and entitlement. But many unforeseeable developments lie between the death of the equal opportunity panacea and general acceptance of outright equality, of the idea that justice is both fair procedures *and* a relatively equal distribution of worldly goods. Until that idea becomes the definition of social justice in America, we will continue to investigate and employ indirect means of alleviating poverty in preference to frontal attacks.

N O T E S

1. See James Coleman, "The Concept of Equality of Educational Opportunity," pp. 199–213 of this book.

2. Christopher Jencks, Marshall Smith, Henry Acland, Mary Jo Bane, David Cohen, Herbert Gintis, Barbara Heyns, Stephan Michelson, *Inequality: A Reassessment of the Effect of Family and Schooling in America* (New York: Basic Books, 1972).

3. Ibid., p. 5.

4. See Godfrey Hodgson, "Do Schools Make a Difference?," pp. 22–44 of this book.

5. Lester Thurow, "Proving the Absence of Positive Associations," *Harvard Educational Review* 43, no. 1 (1973): 107.

6. See T. Paul Schultz, "Long-Term Change in Personal Income Distribution," pp. 147–169 of this book.

7. See Coleman, "The Concept of Equality of Educational Opportunity."

8. See John Rawls, "A Theory of Justice," pp. 228–251 of this book, and Robert Nozick, "Distributive Justice," pp. 252–273 of this book.

9. See Jacob Mincer, *Schooling, Experience, and Earnings* (New York: National Bureau of Economic Research, 1974).

10. See Lester Thurow, "Education and Economic Equality," pp. 170–184 of this book.

I

Schools and Society

INTRODUCTION

SCHOOLS TODAY stand at a crossroads, unsure of what direction to take. The bulk of research indicates that schooling does relatively little of what it always claimed to do—foster the cognitive abilities of students and thus assure them a productive niche in the economy. The decline of this particular set of educational goals has yet to be counterbalanced by the growth of a new set. Understandably, educators are confused, baffled, and even angry. In the absence of traditional justifications, they have few notions about the kinds of schools America needs, the ability of schooling to affect children in any way, or the means by which schools should be financed. In the search for appropriate goals and justifiable patterns of finance, as Christopher Lasch puts it, educators are forced "to struggle with questions they have spent most of their careers avoiding." This part deals with that struggle by presenting a variety of views on the evolution of the current uncertainty and the possibility of developing new goals and forms of schooling. The last two pieces explore future educational policies from the viewpoints, respectively, of research strategy and political economy.

Godfrey Hodgson's article, "Do Schools Make a Difference?," details the fallout from Coleman's 1966 study of differences in schooling and achievement for black and white children. As Hodgson rightly observes, Coleman was staggered to find the lack of differences in schooling for blacks and whites. What made Coleman's data the "bedrock and foundation" of subsequent analyses, however, was the finding that what differences did exist made negligible differences in children's achievement. Widely diverging attempts were made to explain the reasons behind Coleman's conclusions: Jensen, Herrnstein, and others argued that genetic factors were mainly responsible for differences in black and white achievement test scores, so schools were relatively unimportant. Pettigrew held that the key to educational achievement for blacks was integration, while Armor's study of busing flatly contradicted that contention. Extensive debate centered on the supposed technical inadequacies of Coleman's study. The net result, though, has been a growing consensus that equal educational opportunity has little to do with the equality of results it was thought to encourage.

Granted that schools have little power to influence cognitive achievement and earning power, we must resort to income redistribution if we have a genuine concern for economic equality. But where does that leave the schools? How much money should they receive, and to what end? Those questions, according to Hodgson, are still very much up in the air.

In "Inequality and Education," Christopher Lasch takes a much more positive approach. He begins by stating his own view of the significance of *Inequality*, which is that Jencks has destroyed the assumption "that there is a close connection between opportunity and result, between the distribution of advantages and the distribution of income." Lasch takes the stance of a credentialist, stressing: a) that the amount of schooling rather than its quality gives some people better jobs than others, b) that educational credentials are distributed largely by class because of the importance of cultural attitudes to educational attainment, and c) that credentials affect income only because income is partly a function of occupational status, which is mainly determined by educational attainment. These findings lead Lasch to conclude that education may have to be justified in and of itself, that we shall have to turn from extrinsic rationales to intrinsic ones. But his examination of the history of American public schools reveals no tradition of education for education's sake. Instead, our schools have persisted in trying to serve political ends (egalitarianism) and intellectual ones at the same time. The result has been failure on both fronts. As a response to *Inequality* and a remedy for decades of confusion about educational goals, Lasch urges a return to a staunchly utilitarian system of education very much like European models: education for everybody to encourage literacy, "the bulwark of democracy against tyrants and demagogues"; higher education only for those who intend to enter the learned professions. In short, since equal educational opportunity is both pointless and subversive of the true ends of schooling, we should ignore it. Instead, educational policy should be restructured to serve indisputable societal needs.

Harvey Averch and his associates' "How Effective Is Schooling?," on the other hand, implies that some important evidence about the effects of schooling is not yet in, so conclusions as definite as Lasch's (or Jencks') are premature. Averch summarizes the research on school effectiveness and notes our failure to find any variant of the existing educational system that is consistently related to educational outcomes. Considering the evidence from a management standpoint, he suggests that only sweeping changes in the organization, structure, and conduct of education are likely to improve both cognitive and noncognitive outcomes. Moreover, since spending more money in the same old ways is pointless, Averch ventures an idea likely to be anathema to the educational establishment: we probably can redirect and *reduce* educational expenditures without undermining educational outcomes. Yet there are reservations. We cannot be sure of having reached the point of diminishing returns because input-output studies are basically flawed. All of them assume a "black box" that transforms inputs into outputs and fail to trace the process of this transformation. Input-output studies like Coleman's also are suspect because they cannot analyze "true experiments" that incorporate adequate controls on variables, and because they deal with such highly aggregated data that differences in the deployment of the same levels of resources are obscured. The result of these deficiencies is an inability to find relationships even if they exist. So far, our research methods have been grossly inadequate, according to Averch. In order to assess the deficiencies of current policy more reliably—and to develop meaningful future policies—we first must create a research strategy that incorporates inputs, outputs, process, and noncognitive effects.

In "Equalizing Education: In Whose Benefit?," Daniel P. Moynihan assesses the evidence on educational effectiveness from the standpoint of political science. He asks of educational policy the classic political question—*Cui bono?*—and answers that teachers rather than students are the immediate beneficiaries of increased school expenditures. Perhaps too cynically, he sees the research on schooling as a stimulus to ever-increasing educational funding, since the diminishing returns to schooling allow vested interests to take "a posture of demanding more [which] is never endangered by fulfillment." Citing the phenomenal growth in recent years of educational expenditures—and the even more impressive growth of teachers' wages—he predicts that any additional funds for education will have the short-run effect of aggravating our lopsided distribution of income. In light of education's entry into national politics and the fact that increased funding is of such dubious value, Moynihan urges that school finance and educational policy be decided by legislative action, and not by the courts that presently have so much power over the allocation of educational resources. Still, Moynihan feels, as Averch does, that concerted new research efforts are the prerequisites of educational policy for the future. If we are going to spend more money for education, let it be for educational research like that going on at the National Institute for Education. Only in this way can we achieve a firm grasp of educational goals and the best ways to attain them.

(1)

Do Schools Make a Difference?

Godfrey Hodgson

THE DAY Daniel Patrick Moynihan arrived at Harvard in the spring of 1966, he met some of his new colleagues at the Faculty Club in Cambridge. One of those present that evening was Professor Seymour Martin Lipset of the Harvard government department. "Hello, Pat," said Lipset, "guess what Coleman's found?"

"Coleman" was James S. Coleman, professor of social relations at Johns Hopkins, who had been charged by the Johnson Administration with conducting an extensive survey of "the lack of availability of equal educational opportunities" by reason of race, religion, or national origin. And what the Coleman survey had found, as Lipset paraphrased its voluminous findings, could hardly have come as more of a surprise. He had found, as Lipset told Moynihan excitedly, that "schools make no difference; families make the difference."

Some six years later, Moynihan arrived a few minutes late for lunch with a friend at the same club, in a mood of jubilant intellectual pugnacity unusual even for him. Both the delay and the mood, he explained, resulted from a demonstration he had run into on his way across Harvard Yard from a class. Some students were handing out leaflets. It was their content which had produced Moynihan's mood of sardonic amusement. "Christopher Jencks," they said, "is a tool of reactionary American imperialist capitalism."

Christopher Jencks a tool of capitalism? In the dozen years since he graduated from the Harvard Graduate School of Education, where he is now an associate professor, Sandy Jencks (as he is called) had moved perceptibly from the liberal toward the radical position. While an editor of *The New Republic* he began working with the distinctly New Left Institute for Policy Studies in Washington. He got into the neighborhood community control thing, and he helped to found the Cambridge Institute, which looks for "alternative visions of the American future": decidedly one of the rising intellectual reputations on the American left. Now he has written a book, *Inequality*, in association with other researchers, working in large part from the same Coleman report data which, in Lipset's words, showed that "schools make no difference."

Pat Moynihan had started on the left, too. Trained as an orthodox social scientist, he grew up among liberals, and then discovered a most unorthodox flair for polemical prose and persuasive speech. After a political apprenticeship working for Governor Averell Harriman of New York, he took office as a liberal intellectual in good standing as an Assistant Secretary of Labor in the Kennedy Administration, and stayed on for a period under Johnson.

For some years now, however, he could hardly have been called a man of the left. His intellectual voyage can be dated from the publication of his report on the Negro family in 1965. Many liberals and blacks reacted with outrage to his dour assessment of the likelihood that orthodox liberal policies could eliminate the problems of the black under-class. He was outraged in turn by what he perceived as the liberals' dishonest and antiintellectual refusal to follow where social science led. And by the time he returned to Washington in 1969 to serve Richard Nixon as a Cabinet-rank counselor, he could no longer be called a man of the left at all. In recent years he has in fact established himself as the shrewdest strategist and most flamboyant impresario of an intellectual movement which can perhaps be called neoconservative—though Moynihan maintains that it is radical. Whatever the label, it is almost contemptuously skeptical of the New Left and of conventional liberal shibboleths alike.

Moynihan's amusement at seeing his colleague Jencks leafleted in Harvard Yard was not due to malice or *Schadenfreude*. On the contrary, it seemed to him to confirm that the argument between him and his friends and the left was over: that he had won. "Jencks ends up," he told me, "where Richard Nixon was in 1969."

Christopher Jencks does not see it that way. In fact, it is a strange kind of argument: one in which the participants largely agree about the Coleman survey, greatly as it surprised them when they first grasped it, but disagree, sometimes vehemently, on what it implies. The fight calls into question certain propositions which, until the Coleman report, few social scientists and few liberals dreamed of doubting: principally, that one of the main causes of inequality in American life has been inequality in education; and that education could be used as a tool to reduce inequality in society. The crucial role which education has been assigned in the United States is under heavy challenge. Is there now to be a retreat from the traditional faith in education as a tool of social change in America?

Since the days of Horace Mann and John Dewey—indeed since the days of Thomas Jefferson, that child of the Enlightenment—education has occupied a special place in the optimistic vision of American progressives, and of many American conservatives, for that matter. As the historian David Potter pointed out in *People of Plenty*, the American left, encouraged by the opportunities of an unexhausted continent and by the experience of economic success, has always differed sharply from the European left in that it has generally assumed that social problems could be resolved out of incremental growth: that is, that the life of the have-nots could be made tolerable without taking anything from the haves. Education has always seemed one of the most acceptable ways of using the national wealth to provide opportunity for the poor without offending the comfortable. As a tool of reform, education had the advantage that it appealed to the ideology of conservatives, to that ethic of self-improvement which stretches back down the American tradition through Horatio Alger and McGuffey's *Readers* to Benjamin Franklin himself. This was particularly true in the age of the Great Migration. The public school systems of New York and other cities with large immigrant populations really did provide a measure of equality of opportunity to the immigrant poor. By the time the New Deal coalition was formed (and educators of one sort and another were to be a significant part of that coalition), these assumptions about education were deeply rooted. And they were powerfully reinforced, and virtually certified with the authority of social science, by the Supreme Court's 1954 desegregation decision in *Brown* v. *The School Board of Topeka*. *Plessy* v. *Ferguson*, the 1896 Supreme Court decision by which statutory and customary segregation in the South were reconciled with the Thirteenth, Fourteenth, and Fifteenth Amendments, was not a school case. (At it happens, it concerned segregation on a Lake Pontchartrain ferry steamer.) But when, in the late 1930s and the 1940s, the NAACP, its lawyers, and its allies began to go to court to lay siege to segregation, they deliberately, and wisely, chose education as the field of attack. This was not accidental; they well knew that education was so firmly associated with equality in the public mind that it would be an easier point of attack than, say, public accommodations or housing. Not coincidentally, they worked their way up to the main citadel of the 1954 *Brown* decision by way of a series of law school cases: lawyers would find it hard to deny that segregation in law school was irrelevant to success in professional life.

In *Brown,* the NAACP's lawyers deployed social science evidence in support of their contention that segregated education was inherently unequal, citing especially work done by psychologists Kenneth and Mamie Clark with black children and black and white dolls. The Clarks' conclusions were that segregation inflicts psychological harm.

The historical accident of the circumstances in which school segregation came to be overthrown by the Supreme Court contributed to the currency of what turned out to be a shaky assumption. The great majority of American liberals, and this included large numbers of judges, Democratic politicians, and educators, came to suppose that there was incontrovertible evidence in the findings of social science to prove not just that segregated education was unequal but that if you wanted to achieve equality, education could do it for you. Or, to put the same point in a slightly different way, the prominence given to footnote 11 in the *Brown* judgment, which listed social science research showing that education could not be both separate and equal, had the effect of partially obscuring the real grounds for overthrowing segregation, which were constitutional, political, and moral.

Then a contemporary development put education right at the center of the political stage. President Johnson's "Great Society" was to be achieved without alienating the power structure and, above all, the Congress. Education was an important part of the Great Society strategy from the start, but as other approaches to reducing poverty and racial inequality, notably "community action," ran into political opposition, they fell apart, and so the proportional emphasis on educational programs in the Great Society scheme grew. In the end, the Johnson Administration, heavily committed to reducing inequality, was almost equally committed to education as one of the principal ways to do it.

Each of the events and historical developments sketched here increased the shock effect of the Coleman report—once its conclusions were understood. A handful of social scientists had indeed hinted, before Coleman, that the effect of schools on equality of opportunity might have been exaggerated. But such work had simply made no dent in the almost universal assumption to the contrary.

James Coleman himself has confessed he does not know exactly why Congress, in section 402 of the Civil Rights Act of 1964, ordered the Commissioner of Education to conduct a survey "concerning the lack of availability of equal educational opportunities for individuals by reason of race, color, religion or national origin." The most likely reason is that Congress thought it was setting out to document the obvious in order to arm the administration with a public relations bludgeon to overcome opposition. Certainly James Coleman took it for granted that

25

his survey would find gross differences in the quality of the schools that black and white children went to. "The study will show," he predicted in an interview more than halfway through the job, "the difference in the quality of schools that the average Negro child and the average white child are exposed to. You know yourself that the difference is going to be striking."

He was exactly wrong. Coleman was staggered—in the word of one of his associates—to find the *lack* of difference. When the results were in, from about 600,000 children and 60,000 teachers in roughly 4,000 schools, when they had been collected and collated and computed, and sifted with regression analysis and all the other refinements of statistical science, they were astonishing. A writer in *Science* called them "a spear pointed at the heart of the cherished American belief that equality of educational opportunity will increase the equality of educational achievement."

What did the figures say? Christopher Jencks later picked out four major points:

1. Most black and white Americans attend different schools.
2. Despite popular impressions to the contrary, the physical facilities, the formal curricula, and most of the measurable characteristics of teachers in black and white schools were quite similar.
3. Despite popular impressions to the contrary, measured differences in schools' physical faculties, formal curricula, and teacher characteristics had very little effect on either black or white students' performance on standardized tests.
4. The one school characteristic that showed a consistent relationship to test performance was the one characteristic to which poor black children were denied access: classmates from affluent homes.

Here is how James Coleman himself summed up the 737 pages of his report (not to mention the additional 548 pages of statistical explanation):

Children were tested at the beginning of grades 1, 3, 6, 9 and 12. Achievement of the average American Indian, Mexican American, Puerto Rican, and Negro (in this descending order)[1] was much lower than the average white or Oriental American, at all grade levels . . . the differences are large to begin with, and they are even larger at higher grades. Two points, then, are clear: (1) these minority children have a serious educational deficiency at the start of school, which is obviously not a result of school, and (2) they have an even more serious deficiency at the end of school, which is obviously in part a result of school.

Coleman added that the survey showed that most of the variation in student achievement lay within the same school, and very little of it was between schools. Family background—whatever that might mean—

must, he concluded, account for far more of the variation in achievement than differences between schools. Moreover, such differences as *could* be attributed to the schools seemed to result more from the social environment (Jencks' "affluent classmates," and also teachers) than from the quality of the school itself.

This was the most crucial point. For if quality were measured, as it had tended to be measured by administrators and educational reformers alike, in material terms, then the quality of the school, on Coleman's data, counted for virtually nothing.

When other things were equal, the report said, factors such as the amount of money spent per pupil, or the number of books in the library, or physical facilities such as gymnasiums or cafeterias or laboratories, or even differences in the curriculum, seemed to make no appreciable difference to the children's level of achievement. Nothing could have more flatly contradicted the assumptions on which the administration in Washington, and urban school boards across the country, were pouring money into compensatory education programs.

As we shall see, the report exploded with immense force underground, sending seismic shocks through the academic and bureaucratic worlds of education. But on the surface the shock was not at first apparent. There were two main reasons for this. The first was that the report was, after all, long, tough, dry, and technical. It had been written in five months in order to comply with a congressional deadline, and it therefore made no attempt to point a moral or adorn a tale: it was essentially a mass of data. All of these characteristics militated against its being reported in detail by, for example, the Associated Press, the source from which most American newspapers get most of their out-of-town news.

The Office of Education, which realized all too clearly how explosive the report was, didn't exactly trumpet the news to the world. The report was released, by a hallowed bureaucratic stratagem, on the eve of July 4, 1966. Few reporters care to spend that holiday gutting 737 pages of regression analysis and standard deviations. And to head off those few who might have been tempted to make the effort if they guessed that there was a good story at the end of it, the Office of Education put out a summary report which can only be described as misleading. "Nationally," it said, to take one example, "Negroes have fewer of some of the facilities that seem most related to academic achievement." That was true. But it was not the significant truth.

The point was that the gap was far smaller than anyone expected it to be. To take one of the summary report's own examples, it was true that Negro children had "less access" to chemistry labs than whites. But the difference was that only 94 percent of them, as compared to 98 percent of whites, went to schools with chemistry labs. That was hardly the kind of difference which could explain any large part of the gap

27

between white and black achievements in school, let alone that larger gap, lurking in the back of every educational policy maker's mind, between the average status and income of blacks and whites in life after they leave school.

A few attempts were made to discredit the survey. But the Coleman findings were in greater danger of being ignored than of being controverted when, at the beginning of the academic year in the fall of 1966, Pat Moynihan began to apply his talents to make sure that the report should not be ignored. He and Professor Thomas Pettigrew of the Harvard School of Education organized a Seminar on the Equality of Educational Opportunity Report (SEEOR). The seminar met every week at the Harvard Faculty Club, and by the end more than 80 people had taken part.

Moynihan had taken the precaution of getting a grant for expenses from the Carnegie Corporation, some of which was laid out on refreshments, stronger than coffee or cookies. "It was quite something, that seminar," says Jencks, reminiscing. "Pat always had the very best booze and the best cigars." But if Moynihan is a connoisseur of the good things in life, he also knows how to generate intellectual excitement, or to spot where it is welling up.

"When I was at the School of Education ten years ago," Jencks says, "almost nobody who was literate was interested in education. The educational sociologists and psychologists, the educational economists, they were all pretty near the bottom of the heap. Suddenly that's changed."

"That seminar taught me something about Harvard," Moynihan says. "People here are not interested in a problem when they think it's solved. There are no reputations to be made there. But when something which people think was locked up opens up, suddenly they all want to get involved." People started coming up to Moynihan in Harvard Yard and asking if they could take part: statisticians, economists, pediatricians, Professor Abram Chayes from the Law School (and the Kennedy State Department). Education had become fashionable. Jason Epstein of Random House and Charles E. Silberman from *Fortune* magazine started coming up from New York.

Harvard had seen nothing quite like it since the arms control seminars of the late 1950s, at which the future strategic policies of the Kennedy Administration were forged and the nucleus of the elite that was to operate them in government was brought together. In the intervening decade, domestic social questions had reasserted their urgency. Education had emerged as the field where all the agonizing problems of race, poverty, and the cities seemed to intersect.

If schools, as Seymour Martin Lipset paraphrased Coleman, "make no difference," what could explain the inequalities of achievement in school and afterwards? One school of thought was ready and waiting in the wings with an answer. In the winter of 1969, the following words appeared in an article in the *Harvard Educational Review:*

> There is an increasing realization among students of the psychology of the disadvantaged that the discrepancy in their average performance cannot be completely or directly attributed to discrimination or inequalities in education. It seems not unreasonable, in view of the fact that intelligence variation has a large genetic component, to hypothesize that genetic factors may play a part in this picture.

The author was Professor Arthur Jensen, not a Harvard man, but an educational psychologist from Berkeley with a national reputation. He had jabbed his finger at the rawest, most sensitive spot in the entire system of liberal thinking about education and equality in America. For after more than a generation of widespread IQ testing, it is an experimental finding, beloved of racists and profoundly disconcerting to liberals, that while the average white IQ is 100, the average black IQ is 85. Racists have seen in this statistical finding confirmation of a theory of innate biological inferiority. Conservatives have seen in it an argument against heavy expenditures on education, and against efforts to desegregate. And liberals have retorted that the lower average performance of blacks is due either to cultural bias in the tests used or to unfavorable environmental factors which require redoubled efforts on the part of social policy makers.

Jensen marched straight into the fiercest of this cross fire. He argued two propositions in particular in his article: that research findings suggest that heredity explains more of the differences in IQ between individuals than does environment, and that heredity accounts for the differences between the average IQs of groups as well as between those of individuals.

The article was scholarly in tone. In form it was largely a recital of research data. And it was tentative in its conclusion that perhaps more of the differential between blacks' and whites' average IQs was due to heredity than to environment. That did not stop it from causing a most formidable rumpus. It became a ninety days' wonder in the press and the news magazines. It was discussed at a cabinet meeting. And Students for a Democratic Society rampaged around the Berkeley campus chanting "Fight racism! Fire Jensen!"

Two years later, a long article in *The Atlantic* by Professor Richard Herrnstein on the history and implications of IQ provoked a reaction which showed that the sensitivity of the issue had by no means subsided. Herrnstein touched only gingerly on the racial issue. "Although there are scraps of evidence for a genetic component in the black-white difference," he wrote, "the overwhelming case is for believing that Amer-

29

Godfrey Hodgson

ican blacks have been at an environmental disadvantage . . . a neutral commentator (a rarity these days) would have to say that the case is simply not settled, given our present stage of knowledge."

Neutral commentators certainly proved rare among those who wrote in to the editor. Arthur Jensen wrote to say that Herrnstein's essay was "the most accurately informative psychological article I have ever read in the popular press"; while a professor from the University of Connecticut said: "This is not new. Hitler's propagandists used the same tactics in the thirties while his metal workers put the finishing touches on the gas ovens."

If Herrnstein—understandably enough—tiptoed cautiously around the outskirts of the black-white IQ argument, he charged boldly enough into another part of the field. The closer society came to its ideal of unimpeded upward social mobility, the closer he predicted it would come to "meritocracy," a visionary state of society described by the British sociologist Michael Young. A new upper class composed of the descendants of the most successful competitors with the highest IQs would defend its own advantage far more skillfully and successfully than did the old aristocracies. Herrnstein did not welcome this trend; he merely argued that it might be inevitable. "Our society may be sorting itself willy-nilly into inherited castes," he concluded gloomily. Or, as his Harvard colleague David K. Cohen neatly epigrammatized Herrnstein's long article in a rejoinder in *Commentary*, "His essay questioned the traditional liberal idea that stupidity results from the inheritance of poverty, contending instead that poverty results from the inheritance of stupidity."

Cohen went on to disagree with Herrnstein's prediction. "America is not a meritocracy," he wrote, "if by that we mean a society in which income, status, or power are heavily determined by IQ. . . . Being stupid is not what is responsible for being poor in America."

But that still left the original question open.

If differences in the quality of schools, as measured by money, facilities, and curricula, don't explain inequality, because the differences between the schools attended by children of different racial groups are simply not that great in those respects, then what does? Genetic differentials in IQ, perhaps, says Jensen. Nonsense, says a majority of the educational community; the explanation is more likely to be integration —or rather the lack of it.

"I'm a Southern liberal," says Tom Pettigrew. "There are only about thirty of us, and my wife says we all know each other." Pettigrew comes from Richmond, Virginia, but his father immigrated from Scotland, and there is something about him that strikes one as more typically Scots

30

than Southern. He is a shy man with a passion for methodological precision: "I really believe that data can free us," he says. He also has a deceptive, because quiet, commitment to the liberal faith.

The Coleman report gave only three pages to the effects of desegregation, and Pettigrew didn't think that was enough. At Jim Coleman's explicit insistence, the data bank of the survey was to be made generally available for the cost of the computer tapes. Pettigrew persuaded the Civil Rights Commission to take advantage of this and to reanalyze the data to see what light it cast on the effects of desegregation. David Cohen and Pettigrew were the main authors of the resulting survey, which came out in 1967 as *Racial Isolation in the Public Schools* and gave the impression that the Coleman data supported desegregation. This was true up to a point. Coleman had concluded that desegregation did have an effect. But his report also showed that social class had a greater effect. Pettigrew is not much troubled by this, because of the close connection between race and social class in America. "Two-thirds of the whites are middle-class," he says, "and two-thirds of the blacks are working-class."

Pettigrew also draws a sharp distinction between desegregation and integration. By integration he means an atmosphere of genuine acceptance and friendly respect across racial lines, and he believes that mere desegregation won't help blacks to do better in school until this kind of atmosphere is achieved. He is impressed by the work of Professor Irwin Katz, who has found that black children do best in truly integrated situations, moderately well in all-black situations, and worst of all in "interracial situations characterized by stress and threat."

Pettigrew believes, in other words, that integration, as opposed to mere desegregation, will be needed to bring black children's achievement up to equality with whites'. And he argues that no one can say that integration hasn't worked, for the simple reason that it hasn't been tried.

"The U.S. is going through a period of self-flagellation," he said to me. "I dispute the argument that Moynihan is forever putting out. He says liberalism was tried and didn't work." This, as we shall see, misstates Moynihan's views. The difficulty is partly semantic. Moynihan believes that past policies, which can be called "liberal," have "worked" in the sense that they have produced a surprising degree of equality in terms of all the resources that go into schools, without, however, achieving equality of outcome. "I say liberalism hasn't been tried," Pettigrew goes on. "Racial integration has yet to be tried in this country." Desegregation proceeded so slowly, Pettigrew says, that the courts "got mad and started ruling for busing in 1969 and 1970." Until desegregation is achieved, he argues, we won't know whether integration works.

Godfrey Hodgson

The Civil Rights Commission's report on racial isolation did recommend that the federal government set a national standard that no black children should go to a school that was more than 50 percent black. In practical terms, that meant busing. And, in fact, Pettigrew argues that some busing will be needed to achieve desegregation—and thus to produce the physical circumstances in which integration as he understands it can take place. He has been actively involved as a witness in several desegregation suits in which he has advocated busing.

It is, therefore, as Pettigrew himself wryly remarks, an irony that he should have suggested to one of his junior colleagues at the Harvard School of Education that he do a study on busing. The colleague's name was David Armor, and Pettigrew's idea was that it would be interesting to take a look at Project Metco, a scheme for busing children out of Roxbury, the main Boston ghetto, into nearby white suburban schools.

That was in 1969. Three years later, a paper by David Armor called "The Evidence on Busing" was published in The Public Interest. Armor said he had concentrated on the question of whether "induced integration"—that is, busing—"enhances black achievement, self-esteem, race relations, and opportunities for higher education." In a word, Armor maintained that it did not.

The article used data not only from Project Metco but from reports of four other Northern programs for induced integration: in White Plains, New York; Ann Arbor, Michigan; Riverside, California; and New Haven and Hartford, Connecticut. And on the basis of this data,[2] Armor maintained that "the available evidence . . . indicates that busing is not an effective policy instrument for raising the achievement of blacks or for increasing interracial harmony."

"None of the studies," said Armor, "were able to demonstrate conclusively that integration has had an effect on academic achievement as measured by standardized tests." Aspirations, indeed, were high among the black children in Project Metco. But they might be too high, in view of the fact that, while 80 percent of them started college, half of them dropped out. As for race relations, Armor found the bused students not only more militant but actually more hostile to integration than the study's "control group," which was not bused. Militancy, as measured, for example, by sympathy with the Black Panthers, seemed to be particularly rife among those children who had high aspirations (such as going to college) but were getting C grades or below in competitive suburban high schools.

But Armor did not limit himself to reporting the results of his own Metco study and the other four studies. His article was a sweeping, slashing attack on the whole tradition of liberal social science. He described what he called the "integration policy model," based on social science research going back to the time of John Dollard and Gunnar Myrdal. Though the "real goals of social science and public policy are not in opposition," Armor said, he claimed that almost all of the "major premises of the integration policy model are not supported by the data" —by which he meant the studies he quoted.

It was a frontal assault on the liberal tradition in the social sciences for a generation: on "forty years of studies," as one of his opponents put it. At one point Armor came close to accusing his opponents of deliberate dishonesty: "There is the danger that important research may be stopped when the desired results are not forthcoming. The current controversy over the busing of schoolchildren affords a prime example."

It was not likely that such an attack would go unanswered, and, in fact, the response was both swift and severe. Pettigrew and three colleagues fired back a critique which called Armor's article "a distorted and incomplete review." To back up their charge, they argued that the studies Armor had cited as "the evidence on busing" were highly selective. Armor had not discussed seven other studies which they said met his own methodological criteria—from New York, Buffalo, Rochester, Newark, Philadelphia, Sacramento, and North Carolina—surveys which had reported positive achievement results for bused blacks. The integrationists also found what they claimed were disastrous weaknesses in Armor's own Metco study. For one thing, they said, he compared the bused children with a control group which included children who were also attending desegregated schools, though not under Project Metco. "Incredible as it sounds," Pettigrew and his colleagues commented, "Dr. Armor compared children who were bused to desegregated schools with other children many of whom were also bused to desegregated schools. Not surprisingly he found few differences between them."

"We respect Dr. Armor's right to publish his views against mandatory busing," they said. "But we challenge his claim that those views are based on scientific evidence." (Armor is replying to the critique in *The Public Interest*, the journal which published his paper.)[3]

If the tone of the public controversy sounds rough, it was positively courtly compared to the atmosphere inside William James Hall, the new Harvard high-rise where Pettigrew and Armor had their offices, two doors apart.

Armor, too, started out on the left. He was president of the student body at Berkeley in 1959–1960, and head of SLATE, a forerunner of the radical Free Speech Movement there. He was also a protégé of Pettigrew's at Harvard, and indeed a close friend. But by the spring of 1972, Pettigrew realized that Armor had become vehemently opposed to mandatory busing.

Both men became very bitter. Armor failed to get tenure at Harvard, and has now moved to a visiting professorship at UCLA. Armor accused one of Pettigrew's assistants of breaking into his office to steal his Metco data. Pettigrew wrote to the New York *Times:* "There is no evidence beyond the allegation itself for the charge, much less any link between the paper's critics and the alleged intrusion." Armor accused Pettigrew of suppressing his paper; Pettigrew does concede that he told Armor that he had done "incomparable harm" by publishing it.

Tempers, in short, were comprehensively lost over the Armor affair. Much of the bitterness, no doubt, must be put down to personal factors. But it would be wrong to dismiss the episode as a mere squabble between professors. For it shows just how traumatically a world where consensus reigned half a dozen years ago has been affected by the pressure to abandon certain cherished premises. And the issue, after all, is the interrelationship of education, race, and equality in America, which is not exactly a recondite academic quibble.

To an unbiased eye ("a rarity these days," as Richard Herrnstein might say), Armor's paper has been rather seriously impugned. It does not follow that his central thesis is entirely discredited. Even Pettigrew was quoted, at the height of the row, as saying that "nobody is claiming that integration has been a raving success." "That's not what they were saying before," says Moynihan. And Christopher Jencks, who can hardly be accused of conservative prejudice, has summed up the evidence in the most cautious and equivocal way. Blacks, he says, might do much better in "truly integrated schools, whatever they may be." Failing that consummation, devoutly to be wished, the benefits of desegregation appear to be spotty, and busing can be expected to yield contradictory results.

Jencks' position is easily misunderstood. In an interview, he drew some distinctions for me. He reminded me that he had himself written that the Coleman report "put the weight of social science behind integration." It was not until Armor's article was published, he said, that social scientists began to argue that desegregation itself might not work. Jencks personally feels that Armor's data were shaky, and that the effect of Armor's paper came from its review of other studies—a review which, as Pettigrew pointed out, does not refer to all the available studies. Jencks himself thinks that desegregation is probably necessary, simply in order to meet the constitutional requirements of the Fourteenth Amendment, in virtually every urban school district in the country. He does, however, have personal reservations about mandatory busing, on libertarian grounds. The furthest he would go was to say, "I think that a case can be made out that busing might be a useful part of an overall strategy of desegregation." That is not to say that he has any tenderness toward segregation. On the contrary, he rejects it as absolutely as any of the "integrationists." The difference is that Jencks does not think that segregation explains nearly as much of existing inequality as the integrationists think it does.

But with Armor's paper and its reception, we are getting ahead of the story. The Coleman report came out in 1966. It was not until 1972 that two major books appeared, each an attempt to reassess the whole question of the relationship between education and equality in America in the light of the Coleman data. Each was collaborative.

The first of these two books was the Random House collection of papers arising out of the SEEOR seminar, which was published as *On Equality of Educational Opportunity*, with Frederick Mosteller (professor of mathematical statistics at Harvard) and Daniel Patrick Moynihan as coeditors. Most of the leading participants in the debate contributed chapters, Pettigrew *and* Armor, Coleman, David Cohen, and Christopher Jencks among them. The introductory essay was signed jointly by Mosteller and Moynihan. If much of the technical analysis and of the drafting were Mosteller's, the essay's style and conclusions are vintage Moynihan.

Later in the year, Christopher Jencks and seven of his colleagues (two of whom, Marshall Smith and David Cohen, had also contributed to the Mosteller-Moynihan volume) published an only slightly less massive book: *Inequality: A Reassessment of the Effect of Family and Schooling in America*. This work displays considerably more intellectual cohesion than the Mosteller-Moynihan book, presumably because Jencks actually wrote his group's text himself from start to finish and, according to the preface, it "embodies his prejudices and obsessions, and these are not shared by all the authors." But again, though the book draws upon data from dozens of other large- and small-scale surveys, the data from the Coleman survey are the bedrock and foundation.

The enormous body of analysis and reinterpretation in these two books represents the completion of the first stage of the reaction to Coleman. I began by quoting Professor Lipset's hasty shorthand for Coleman's central discovery: "schools make no difference." Professor Pettigrew draws an important distinction. "Never once was it said that schools make no difference. The belief that Coleman hit was the belief that you could make a difference with money." (He added: "Americans are crazy in the head about money; they think you can do everything with money.") However that may be, the nub of the discovery that has set off the whole prolonged, disturbing, confusing, sometimes bitter debate can be expressed as a simple syllogism:

1. The "quality" of the schools attended by black and white children in America was more nearly equal than anyone supposed.

2. The gap between the achievement of black and white children got wider, not narrower, over twelve years at school.

3. Therefore there was no reason to suppose that increasing the flow of resources into the schools would affect the outcome in terms of achievement, let alone eliminate inequality.

Among the social scientists, the central ground of debate about the meaning of those findings now lies between Jencks and Moynihan. It is a strange debate, for the two protagonists have much in common, even if one does have New Left loyalties, and the other served in Nixon's White House and now as Nixon's Ambassador to India. Both use the same data. Indeed, the spectacle of social scientists reaching into the same data bank for ammunition to fire at each other is sometimes reminiscent of war between two legs of the same octopus. Both agree on many of the implications of the data, and on many of the conclusions to be drawn from them. Yet those who lump the two professors together, as many practical educators and civil rights lawyers do, as "Moynihan and Jencks and those people up at Harvard," could hardly be more wrong. The two men are divided by temperament and ideology in the preconceptions they bring to the data, and ultimately in the policy prescriptions they draw from that data.

Perhaps the very heart of their disagreement, after all, comes down to a matter of temperament. Is a glass half-empty, or is it half-full? A pessimist will say it is half-empty when an optimist says it is half-full. Pat Moynihan (and his coauthor Mosteller—but I should be surprised if these particular thoughts were not Moynihan's contribution, since they coincide with so much that he has said and written elsewhere) looked at the Coleman data and made the very reasonable inference that if the differences in quality between the schools attended by different groups of children in the United States were so much smaller than everyone had expected to find them, then the United States had come much closer to realizing the goal of equality of educational opportunity than most people realized. He then chose to relate this to the general question of social optimism versus social pessimism. At the time of the Coleman report's publication, "a certain atmosphere of 'cultural despair' was gathering in the nation," they wrote, "and has since been more in evidence. Some would say more in order. We simply disagree with such despair."

One of the specific recommendations of the Mosteller-Moynihan essay is optimism. The electorate should maintain the pressure on government and school boards, the essay urges, "with an attitude that optimistically expects gains, but, knowing their rarity, appreciates them when they occur." Yet on examination this is a strange use of the word "optimism." For optimism normally connotes an attitude toward the future. But the emotion that is being evoked here has more to do with the past: it is not optimism so much as pride. "The nation entered the middle third of the twentieth century bound to the mores of caste and class. The white race was dominant. . . . Education beyond a fairly rudimentary point was largely determined by social status. In a bare third of a century these circumstances have been extensively changed. *Changed!* Not merely a sequence of events drifting in one direction or another. To the contrary, events have been bent to the national will." True, the essay concedes, the period ended with racial tensions higher than ever before, and with dissatisfaction with the educational system approaching crisis. Nevertheless, say Moynihan and Mosteller, we should accentuate the positive. "It is simply extraordinary that so much has been done. . . . No small achievement! In truth, a splendid one. . . . It truly is not sinful to take modest satisfaction in our progress."

Swept along by the dithyrambic rhythm of these tributes to past policies, it would be easy to conclude that Moynihan thinks they should be pressed to the utmost. But he does not. When I asked him why not, he replied promptly, if cryptically: "Production functions." In an article in the Fall, 1972, issue of *The Public Interest*, he spells out what he means. The argument is characteristically simple, forceful, and provocative.

Proposition 1: "The most striking aspect of educational expenditure is how large it has become." It has now reached $1,000 per pupil per annum, and it has been rising at 9.7 percent annually for the last ten years, while the GNP has risen 6.8 percent.

Proposition 2 (the Coleman point): Maybe not much learning takes place in a school without teachers or a roof. But "after a point school expenditure does not seem to have any notable influence on school achievement."

There are, Moynihan concedes, considerable regional, class, racial, and ethnic variations in achievement, and he would like to see them disappear. "But it is simply not clear that school expenditure is the heart of the matter."

This is where the production function, or what is more familiar to laymen as the law of diminishing returns, comes in, according to Moynihan. The liberal faith held that expenditure of resources on education would produce not merely a greater equality in scholastic achievement, but greater equality in society. On the contrary, says Moynihan, additional expenditure on education (and indeed on certain other social policies) is likely to produce greater *inequality*, at least of income.

The day the students leafleted Christopher Jencks in Harvard Yard, Moynihan said to me: "They're defending a class interest." What he meant was that as future teachers, or social workers, or administrators of education or social policies, left-wing students had a vested economic interest in the high-investment "liberal" policies they defended.

"Any increase in school expenditure," Moynihan wrote in *The Public Interest*, "will in the first instance accrue to teachers, who receive about 68% of the operating expenditure of elementary and secondary schools. That these are estimable and deserving persons none should doubt"— Brutus is an honorable man—"but neither should there be any illusion that they are deprived." With teachers earning some $10,000 a year on the average, he argues, and with many of them married women with well-paid husbands, "increasing educational expenditures will have the short-run effect of income inequality."

As a matter of statistical fact, that may be literally true. But it is a peculiar argument nonetheless, for several reasons. For, leaving aside the matter of their spouses' incomes, teachers are not, relatively, a highly paid group. Marginal increases in their salaries have an imperceptible effect on inequality in the national income distribution.

Whatever its merits, however, Moynihan's position is plain. But it is worth noting that this position fits oddly with an exhortation to optimism. There is indeed nothing sinful about taking satisfaction in past progress; but when this attitude is combined with skepticism about the benefits to be expected from future public expenditure, it is usually called not optimistic but conservative.

Like Moynihan, Christopher Jencks is concerned with equality, not only in the schools but also in the world after school. The essence, and the originality, of his thinking lie in the use he makes of two crucial, though in themselves unoriginal, distinctions.

The first distinction is between equality of opportunity and equality of condition. Most Americans say they are in favor of equality. But what most of them mean by this is equality of opportunity. What we have learned from the Coleman report, says Jencks, and from the fate of the reforms of the 1960s, is that contrary to the conventional wisdom, you cannot have equality of opportunity without a good deal of equality of condition— now and not in the hereafter.

This is where the second of Jencks' distinctions comes in. Where the Coleman survey, and most of the work published in the Mosteller-Moynihan volume, looked at the degree of equality between *groups*, Jencks is more interested in inequality between individuals. Coleman's conception of equality looked at the distribution of opportunity between two groups. For Coleman, as Marshall Smith puts it, if you laid the distribution curve of one group over the distribution curve of the other, and they coincided exactly, then you could say that the two groups were equal. And Coleman found that between white and black Americans, this was closer to being true than most people had suspected. "Sandy Jencks is saying that though this may apply as between groups, this approximate equality disappears when you look at individuals."

It is cause for shock, he says in the preface to his book, "that white workers earn 50 percent more than black workers." But it is a good deal more shocking "that the best-paid fifth of all white workers earns 600 percent more than the worst-paid fifth. From this point of view, racial inequality looks almost insignificant"—by comparison with economic inequality.

Is the glass half-empty, or half-full? If Moynihan's instinct is to emphasize the real progress that has been made toward reducing inequality in America, Jencks stresses how much inequality remains, not only in educational opportunity, in learning skills, and in educational credentials but also in job status, in job satisfaction, and in income.

The trouble is, he points out—and here I am summarizing an argument which is based, step by step, on mountains of statistical data—that whatever measure you take—income, socioeconomic status, or education— there is plenty of inequality among Americans. But the same people by no means always come out at the same point on each measure. In the social scientists' terms, these different kinds of inequality don't "correlate" very closely. It follows that school reform is not likely to effect much greater equality outside the school. The "factory model," which assumes that the school's outcome is the direct product of its inputs, must be abandoned, says Jencks. For him, a school is in reality more like a family than a factory.

This idea underlies a surprising strand in Jencks's thought. If there is no direct correlation between expenditure on schools and effects on society—for example, in producing greater equality between racial groups —some would draw the lesson that it is not worth spending more than a (possibly quite high) minimum on schools. (That is something like Moynihan's theoretical position, as we have seen.) No, says Jencks, spend more money; not because of the benefits it will bring in some sociological hereafter but simply because people spend something close to a fifth of their life in school, and it is better that they spend that time in a pleasant and comfortable environment.

"There is no evidence," Jencks writes, "that building a school playground will affect the students' chances of learning to read, getting into college, or earning $50,000 a year when they are fifty. Building a playground may, however, have a considerable effect on the students' chances of having a good time during recess when they are eight." And in a recent statement protesting the use of the conclusions which *Inequality* reaches "to justify limiting educational expenditures and abandoning efforts at desegregation," Jencks writes that "educators will have to keep struggling," and that "they need more help than they are currently getting." But he concludes that the egalitarian trend in American education over the last 30 years has not made the distribution of either income or status outside the schools much more equal. He writes: "As long as egalitarians assume that public policy cannot contribute to economic equality directly, but must proceed by ingenious manipulation of marginal institutions like the schools, progress will remain glacial."

"Marginal institutions like the schools"! The phrase sets Jencks every bit as far outside the old liberal orthodoxy as Moynihan's suggestion that spending money on schools may actually increase inequality. Fourteen words from the end of his book Jencks unfurls a word which startles many of his readers. "If we want to move beyond this tradition, we will have to establish political control over the economic institutions that shape our society. That is what other countries usually call socialism. Anything less will end in the same disappointment as the reforms of the 1960s." [4]

Norman Drachler was superintendent of the huge, tormented Detroit public school system from 1966 to 1971. When I talked to him recently, he was going through the anguish of liberal educators who had the intellectual honesty to try to reconcile the new teachings of the social scientists with the working assumptions of a lifetime of effort.

He showed me a headline from the New York *Times* of December 4, 1966, which perfectly summed up the pre-Coleman orthodoxy. WHEN SPENDING FOR EDUCATION IS LOW, it said, ARMY INTELLIGENCE TEST FAILURES ARE HIGH. And he showed me figures to prove that when federal money under Title I of the Elementary and Secondary Education Act of 1965 was concentrated on the schools with the greatest need in Detroit, reading scores improved by two months from 1965 to 1971, while the city-wide average declined by two months. "In the worst schools, Title I helped to arrest a disastrous fall," says Drachler. "Where we spent more money, we did do better."

How did he square this with the Coleman report?

"I think Coleman is basically correct. With better schools we can only make a small difference. But it is worth that investment."

The post Coleman challenge to the case for spending money on education is beginning to echo through the halls of Congress, ominously for the supporters of federal aid to education, who include both Representative John Brademas, Democrat of Indiana, the chairman of the House Select Subcommittee on Education, and one of his Republican colleagues, Representative Albert Quie of Minnesota. In a recent speech Quie has made it plain that he remains to be convinced that compensatory education makes no difference. John Brademas is afraid that the social science findings, misunderstood or deliberately misrepresented, will be used to justify savage cuts in federal aid to elementary and secondary education and to make opposition to such programs respectable. He is deeply skeptical of the case against the efficacy of educational spending, pointing out not only that federal aid still amounts to only 7 percent of the cost of elementary and secondary schooling but also that in many cases funds intended under Title I for compensatory education for underprivileged children have been indiscriminately spent for political reasons on middle-class children, so that few valid conclusions can be drawn from the experience of Title I. He feels adrift without adequate information, while the opponents of educational spending are able to use the social scientists' evidence, often disingenuously. In his own reelection campaign in Indiana last fall he was amused, but not happy, to find his Republican opponent quoting what he called the "Colombo report" (meaning the Coleman report) at him.

Education lobbyists claim that the "Jencks report" has been freely cited by the Nixon administration's Office of Management and Budget on Capitol Hill in justification of the cuts in the fiscal 1974 budget. And even in some of the more conservative governors' offices, one lobbyist for elementary and secondary education told me there is a widespread feeling that "Coleman and Jencks" have the effect of giving education a low priority.

Money is one issue; integration is another. Although, as Christopher Jencks put it to me, "the impact both of Coleman and of the Moynihan-Mosteller book is to put the support of social science behind integration," and even though a majority of the social scientists who have spoken up remains integrationist, there is no mistaking the chill which the Armor paper, supported as it has been to some extent by various influential figures in the intellectual community, has sent down the spines of the integrationists. Last November, for example, Harold Howe, U.S. Commissioner for Education in the Johnson administration (he is now with the Ford Foundation), conceded that "the lively researches of statistically oriented social scientists have cast some shadows on conventional assumptions about the benefits of integration, particularly in the schools."

The first place where those shadows would fall is in the courts, which are now jammed with cases arising from the tough desegregation orders made by federal judges in all parts of the country since 1969. Integrationists insist that the law requires school desegregation under the Fourteenth Amendment, wholly independent of social science data regarding its effect. As former Chief Justice Earl Warren put it in a recent interview with Dr. Abram Sachar of Brandeis, Brown was a race case, not an education case. And so far the judges have upheld the principle that the requirement of desegregation in the law is independent of evidence about its effect.

But already the courts have begun to hear social science evidence about the equality of achievement in schools. In Keyes (the Denver school desegregation case which the Supreme Court has already heard, but on which it has not yet handed down its opinion), Judge William Doyle, in the district court, asked for evidence about the achievement of 17 schools which he found to be segregated, though not as a result of public policy. James Coleman himself was one of the witnesses, and he testified that while compensatory education had proved disappointing, desegregation might be helpful.

David Armor was a witness on the other side in one of the Detroit desegregation hearings. But in the Memphis case, where his paper was produced in evidence, the court of appeals gave it short shrift. Judge Anthony Celebrezze (a former Democratic secretary of HEW) dismissed it as "a single piece of much criticized sociological research," and said "it would be presumptuous in the extreme for us to refuse to follow a Supreme Court decision on the basis of such meager evidence."

Judicial reaction generally, says Louis Lucas, a Memphis lawyer who appeared for plaintiffs in both the Detroit and Memphis cases, "has been to say 'a plague on both your houses' to the social scientists. They have noticed how much criticism of the new findings there has been, and they say in effect, 'We are not going to retry *Brown.*'"

But that is exactly what less sanguine integrationists are afraid the Supreme Court will do, with respect to the most difficult Northern desegregation cases: not frontally, but by erosion. Norman Drachler, for example, told me he thought it very probable that the Burger Court would find some way to retry *Brown* without seeming to do so. Nick Flannery, of the Harvard Center for Law and Education, told me that "the Burger Court will almost certainly be looking for distinctions to draw that will narrow the scope of *Brown.*"

Flannery suggested some possibilities. The Court could adopt Judge Doyle's argument (in the Denver case) that not all segregation results from public policy. Or it could adopt the Justice Department's contention that the wrong to be remedied is not segregation itself, but discrimination, so that the plaintiff can get relief only when he can show not merely generalized segregation but particular instances of discrimination. In the *Swann* case, in 1971, having to do with Charlotte, North Carolina, Chief Justice Warren Burger laid down the principle that the scope of the remedy need not exceed the scope of the violation. That might seem to lay the groundwork for limiting *Brown* in this way. Alternatively, the Court might reverse the integrationist doctrine that has been developing in the lower courts, by imposing burdens of proof on the plaintiffs which would make the process of bringing a school desegregation case even lengthier and more expensive than it is already.

Some years ago, the great historian of the South, C. Vann Woodward of Yale, compared the civil rights movement of the 1960s to the Reconstruction period after the Civil War and said that he thought this second Reconstruction was ending. There is a parallel in the intellectual world that Woodward did not draw. The 1870s—the years of "reunion and reaction," when the nation wearied of the political impasse created by white resistance to the Radicals' drive for Negro equality—were also the years when America's intellectual life was swept by the ideas of Herbert Spencer and his followers, the Social Darwinists. Their enthusiasm for ruthless competition that would drive the weakest to the wall, for "anarchy with a policeman" as the type of society most likely to produce the highest evolution of man, did much to rationalize and to justify public indifference as white supremacy reasserted itself after Reconstruction. The skepticism about the efficacy of social reform which seems to be emerging from the social science of the Nixon era in itself, of course, bears no resemblance to the harsh Social Darwinism of the age of the Robber Barons. The only parallel would lie in the danger that this new skepticism which is eroding the confident liberal assumptions could be distorted and used to rationalize a second period of indifference in a nation once again weary of the stress of reform.

What can be said, at the end of the first stage of the reception of the Coleman doctrine, is that—whether you believe with Daniel Patrick Moynihan that liberal education policies of the last few generations have succeeded so well that they have run into diminishing returns, or with Christopher Jencks that they have proved disappointing—those policies, and the intellectual assumptions on which they were built, are in bad trouble. They have lost support in the ranks of the social scientists who provided America, from Roosevelt to Johnson, with a major part of its operating ideology.

NOTES

1. Coleman oversimplified his own report slightly on this point: In the first grade blacks did better than Puerto Ricans, while in the twelfth grade Mexican Americans did better than American Indians.

2. Armor mentioned three orther studies: one from Berkeley, California, one from Evanston, Illinois, and one from Rochester, New York.

3. Armor, David J., "The Double Double Standard: A Reply." *The Public Interest* (winter, 1973), pp. 119–131.

4. In one sense, Moynihan is closer to Jencks than is generally supposed. When he went to work for President Nixon, both he and the president were fully aware of the Coleman conclusions. At that point, in February, 1969, two documents arrived on Moynihan's desk within 72 hours. The first was Arthur Jensen's article, which started

from the proposition that compensatory education wasn't working. The second document, the Ohio Westinghouse report, was a gloomy appraisal of one major experiment with compensatory education, Project Headstart. Moynihan says that the conception of his Family Assistance Plan was directly influenced by the social science findings about education and equality. "The argument was put to the president," he says, "that enormous expectations had built up that you could achieve racial equality through compensatory education, and it was not working. Point two: a proposition had been put forward by Dr. Jensen which the democracy could not live with. Therefore, point three: you had to move directly to income redistribution." There is an ironic parallel here—if a distant one—to the way in which Christopher Jencks concludes his book *Inequality*.

(2)

Inequality
and Education

Christopher Lasch

THE MOST important finding of Christopher Jencks's much discussed
study can be stated simply. There is little correlation between income and
the quality of schooling, and school reform can no longer be regarded,
therefore, as an effective means of equalizing income. To put the matter
more broadly, equalizing opportunity will not guarantee equal results.
If we wish to reduce inequality, we should adopt policies designed to
equalize income instead of attempting to equalize opportunity in education, the goal of so much liberal reform in recent years.

Some of the widespread criticism of Jencks' book rests on misunder-
standing. His findings became familiar long before his evidence was published, and they were presented in a way that made them seem to be
part of a conservative reaction against the meliorism of the 1960s. It
appeared that Jencks was saying that schools "are no longer important,"
in the words of one of his critics—an argument that would presumably
contribute, whatever the author's intention, to a new social policy of benign neglect. Together with Edward Banfield, Daniel Moynihan, and
Arthur Jensen, Jencks was seen as leading a "new assault on equality."
Not only did he argue that schooling is unimportant, his study, it was
said, gave support to the idea that IQ is largely hereditary. *Inequality*
appeared also to stress the role of luck in economic success, thereby
reviving the "Horatio Alger myth." The entire study, it appeared, was
pervaded by an "air of resignation." [1]

By this time the misunderstandings surrounding the book—not noticeably dispelled by its publication—may be too widespread to be countered

Reprinted with permission from the *New York Review of Books*. © 1973 NYREV, Inc.

by further explanation. It is quite likely, moreover, that the real source of these misrepresentations is a determination to discredit the book by carrying its argument to absurd extremes. To many people—to professional educators in particular but also to many critics of the educational system—Jencks' findings are inherently unpalatable. Not only do they undermine the popular belief that schooling is an avenue of economic advancement, they also undermine the progressive version of this national mythology—namely that progressive educational policies can be used to promote social justice and a new set of social values: cooperation, spontaneity, and creativity.

Jencks' evidence strongly suggests that the school does not function in any direct and conscious way as the principal agency of indoctrination, discipline, or social control, and he therefore tends to challenge the progressive critique of the school that has recently reappeared in the form of demands for "open classrooms," "schools without walls," etc. The book thus offends both liberals and many radicals as well; while for conservatives, Jencks' advocacy of equal rights (as distinguished from equal opportunity) doubtless identified him as a proponent of the "new equality."

As Irving Kristol has explained, the slogan of equality is used by alienated intellectuals and pseudointellectuals as a battle cry in their struggle to seize power from the bourgeoisie (just as the bourgeoisie once used equality as a rallying cry against the aristocracy). Fortunately the slogan does not have to be taken seriously, since "a society that does not have its best men at the head of its leading institutions," in the comforting words of Daniel Bell—comforting because they imply that this objective is well served by our present arrangements—"is a sociological and moral absurdity." [2]

Jencks' intentions are far more modest, and his conclusions stated more tentatively, than this angry debate might lead one to expect. In the first place, he does not argue that schools "are no longer important" or even that schooling is irrelevant to economic success. On the contrary, his study confirms the widespread impression that people with academic credentials get better jobs than people who lack these credentials. It adds two qualifications to this impression, however; here lies the book's importance.

It is the amount of schooling rather than the quality of schooling, according to Jencks, that explains why some people get better jobs than others. Even the amount of schooling, moreover, does not account for the great disparities of income within those occupations—disparities that are as important in explaining inequality as the disparities between different kinds of work. Educational credentials, in other words, do not fully explain why some people have much higher incomes than other people. Indeed they do not even account for all disparities in occupational status. Both these lines of argument need to be followed in some detail.

Jencks and his associates found that although the distribution of educational opportunity varies widely, these variations appear to have little influence either on occupational status or on income. In themselves neither intelligence, grades, nor the quality of schools people attend explain why some people end up as doctors and lawyers and others as janitors and mail carriers. Still less do they account for differences in income. What matters is the level of educational attainment—the achievement of academic credentials. What determines the distribution of these credentials?

The answer, in so far as it can be inferred from statistical evidence, seems to be that some people find schooling less painful than others and/or have reconciled themselves to staying in school for a long time for the sake of the rewards to which it presumably leads. There is little correlation between the amount of schooling people end up with and the quality of the schooling to which they are subjected. Neither the great disparity in school expenditures among various districts, curriculum placement (tracking), racial segregation, nor the socioeconomic composition of the school seems to have much to do with the level of education students finally attain.

Statistically the distribution of credentials is determined partly by the distribution of "cognitive skills"—ability to use language and make logical inferences, to use numbers easily, and to absorb and retain miscellaneous information—and partly by family background. Since family background influences cognitive skills, it is difficult to estimate their relative weight. Nor is it easy to distinguish between the influence of heredity and the influence of environment on the development of cognitive skills. "An individual's genes can and do influence his environment." A child who begins with a small genetic advantage may find it easier to attract the sympathetic attention of his parents and teachers. The important point is that schooling does almost nothing to equalize the distribution of cognitive skills. In general, "the character of a school's output depends largely on a single input, namely the characteristics of its entering children. Everything else—the school budget, its policies, the characteristics of the teachers—is either secondary or completely irrelevant."

This information points to the conclusion, in itself surprising perhaps only to professional educators, that the distribution of educational credentials is largely a function of class. Not that economic advantages are automatically transferred from parents to their children in the form of educational credentials. Only about "half the children born into the upper-middle class will end up with what we might call upper-middle

Christopher Lasch

class educational credentials," while "about half the children born into the lower class will end up with what we might call lower-class credentials."

The influence of family background depends only partly on socioeconomic status. It also includes cultural influences that are by no means strictly dependent on socioeconomic status. Jencks' data seems to show that "cultural attitudes, values, and taste for schooling play an even larger role than aptitude and money." If middle-class children are likely to "average four years more schooling than lower-class children," this outcome seems to derive largely from the fact that "even if a middle-class child does not enjoy school, he evidently assumes that he will have to stay in school for a long time."

This data helps to remind us that culture is an important component of class; that class, in other words, is much more than a matter of social and economic standing.[3] The middle class perpetuates itself not by handing down its economic advantages intact but by implanting in the young attitudes that help to keep them in school until they have acquired the credentials necessary for middle-class jobs (if not always for middle-class incomes).

Having established a connection between credentials and class, Jencks traces what happens to people who have acquired these credentials. Do people with college degrees end up with better jobs? Do they make more money than people without degrees? As we would expect, Jencks finds that although "there is a great deal of variation in the status of men with exactly the same amount of education," occupational status is "quite closely tied to . . . educational attainment."

On the other hand, his figures show little correlation between educational credentials and income. Intangibles, it appears, have more effect on income inequality than we had supposed—luck, differences of competence that can by no means be put down to education, and the cumulative effect of initial differences in competence, whereby those who have skills often get a chance to develop them more fully, while those who lack them are discouraged from aspiring to more interesting and rewarding work. "Once people enter a particular occupation, those with additional education do not make appreciably more money than others in the occupation." Of two men working in the same insurance firm, the more highly paid is by no means certain to be the one who went to the better school, got better grades, or even finished more years of schooling.

Even if it were possible to give everyone the same amount of schooling, Jencks concludes, this would have little effect on the distribution of income. A direct political attack on inequality therefore makes more sense than an attempt to equalize educational opportunities. Jencks suggests that the government might provide incentives to employers to rotate jobs, giving employees the chance to develop a variety of skills.

48

Again, it might legislate incomes directly. Whatever the particular measures, the point is "to establish political control over the economic institutions that shape our society," in short to adopt "what other countries usually call socialism." [4]

Some of Jencks' critics on the left, as noted, have accused him of reviving the myth that virtue is rewarded with economic success. "We are asked to believe in Lady Bountiful," writes Colin Greer; "we are asked to believe—strange as it sounds—in the rule of luck over the exploitative affairs of men, women, and children in their society." [5] But the Harvard study shows quite clearly that middle-class children start life with enormous advantages; that these advantages enable them to acquire college degrees; and that college degrees in turn have an important bearing on occupational status and even on income, at least to the extent that income is a function of occupational status.

The study also seems to indicate, however, that middle-class children are by no means assured of economic success simply by virtue of their socioeconomic status. Jencks goes so far as to say that "there does not seem to be *any* mechanism available to most upper-middle class parents for maintaining their children's privileged economic position." Stephan Michelson has suggested that Jencks' strategy is to convince "higher status adults" that they have nothing to lose from an egalitarian income policy, since they cannot transfer their economic standing to their children. Whether or not this is Jencks' intention, his findings about mobility are quite consistent with his general purpose, to destroy the assumption that there is a close connection between opportunity and result, between the distribution of advantages and the distribution of income.

His study seems to show that there is a fair amount of social mobility in America, both upward and downward over small degrees of the social scale, but little equality. Some of the not-so-rich, it seems, get slightly poorer, while some of the not-so-poor get somewhat richer, but the gulf between wealth and poverty remains as wide as ever. Only by confusing equality with mobility, however, can we see these conclusions as reaffirming the "Horatio Alger myth."

In one respect, it must be said, Jencks' picture of American society is highly misleading. It omits the upper class, a class so tiny that it altogether escapes Jencks' statistical filter. Some people do pass on to their children all the perquisites of great wealth and power. They are not numerous, and their influence cannot easily be measured. A limitation of social science, as it has come to be defined, is that it simply ignores what it cannot measure. Another limitation is that it tends to confuse correlations with causes, or at least to encourage this confusion in the reader. One therefore has to insist that Jencks' study tells us nothing about the

Christopher Lasch

way class power is exercised in America, about the connections between money and power, about the underlying sources of inequality, or even about the role of the school system in perpetuating inequality. It merely examines a number of statistical correlations between income and schooling.

In order to understand how the school system really works, we have to examine its historical origins. There now exists a considerable body of historical writing on the development of the American public school, much of it prompted by recent criticism of the schools. Out of this writing —to which the recent books by Katz, Spring, and Greer are important contributions—it is possible to construct the following interpretation.[6]

The principle of universal compulsory education won general acceptance in the middle of the nineteenth century largely because reformers like Horace Mann and Henry Barnard convinced influential portions of the public that the schools could perform tasks far more important than instruction in academic subjects. They insisted that the school could become an agent of social reformation and/or social discipline.

In soliciting public support, these reformers appealed to the belief that schools under proper professional leadership would facilitate social mobility and the gradual eradication of poverty or, alternately, to the hope that the system would promote order by discouraging ambitions incommensurate with the students' stations and prospects. The latter argument was probably more appealing to wealthy benefactors and public officials than the first. Both led to the same conclusions: that the best interests of society lay in a system of universal compulsory education which would isolate the student from other influences and subject him to a regular regimen, and that the system must be operated by a centralized professional bureaucracy.

The ideology of school reform contained a built-in, ready-made explanation of its own failures. Once the principle of the common school had been generally accepted and the memory of earlier modes of education had begun to fade, critics of the new system found it difficult to resist the logic of the position put forward by educators: that the admitted failures of the system could be attributed to lack of sustained and unequivocal public commitment, particularly in the matter of funds, and that the only remedy for these failures, therefore, lay in bigger and better schools, better professional training, more centralization, greater powers for the educational bureaucracy—in short, another dose of the same medicine.

Toward the end of the nineteenth century the school system came under heavy public criticism. The schools were inefficient and costly; mo-

50

notonous classroom drill failed to engage the pupils' enthusiasm; too many of the pupils failed. This criticism, however, in no way questioned the underlying premises of universal compulsory education; its upshot was a concerted drive to make the schools more "efficient."

Joseph Mayer Rice, who had inaugurated the muckraking attack on the school system with a series of articles in the *Forum* in 1892, published in 1913 a tract called *Scientific Management in Education.* Here as in his earlier writings he stressed the need to remove education from political control. The application of this commonly held idea to education had the same consequences as its application to city government in the form of civil service reform, the city manager system, and other devices intended to end political influence and promote the introduction of "business methods." It encouraged the growth of an administrative bureaucracy not directly responsible to the public and contributed to the centralization of power.

The political machines which the new system displaced, whatever their obvious shortcomings, had roots in the neighborhoods and reflected—although with many distortions—the interests of their constituents. The new educational bureaucrats, on the other hand, responded only to generalized public demands for efficiency and for an educational policy that would "Americanize" the immigrant—demands the educators themselves helped to shape—and therefore tended to see their clients as so much raw material to be processed as expeditiously as possible.

In 1909, Ellwood P. Cubberley voiced a widespread concern when he referred to the new immigrants from southern and eastern Europe as "illiterate, docile, [and] lacking in self-reliance and initiative" and argued that the task of the public schools was "to assimilate and amalgamate these people as a part of our American race, and to implant in their children, so far as can be done, the Anglo-Saxon conception of righteousness, law and order, and popular government, and to awaken in them a reverence for our democratic institutions and for those things in our national life which we as a people hold to be of abiding worth." Charles William Eliot of Harvard, in a speech to the National Educational Association in which he urged fuller use of the "public school plant" as "the only true economy," insisted that educational reform "means a larger and better yield, physically, mentally, and morally, from the public schools."

The high rate of failure provoked the usual outcries of alarm. One of Colin Greer's sharpest ideas—an idea, incidentally, that is consistent with the drift of Jencks' study—is that the unacknowledged function of the common school system is to fail those whom the higher levels of the employment structure cannot absorb; whose class and ethnic origins, in other words, consign them to a marginal economic position. Failure in school thus reconciles a certain necessary part of the population to failure in life. (On this analysis, the current crisis in public education derives from the fact that failure is no longer functional. Since the number of unskilled jobs is rapidly diminishing, those who fail have no place to go and become permanent charges on the state. Many of them also become discontented and rebellious.)

The debates of the progressive period, beginning around the turn of the century, furnish support for Greer's interpretation. Critics of the schools attacked the high rate of failure while urging reforms that would inevitably perpetuate it. The continuing high rate of failure then served as the basis of renewed appeals to the public, both for money and for additional powers for the educational bureaucracy.

In response to the outcry about failure, systems of testing and tracking were now introduced into the schools, which had the effect of relegating academic "failures" to programs of manual and industrial training (where many of them continued to fail). Protests against genteel culture, overemphasis on academic subjects, "gentleman's education," and the "cultured ease in the classroom, of drawing room quiet and refinement," frequently coincided with an insistence that higher education and "culture" should not in any case be "desired by the mob."

The demand for "educational engineering" and the elimination of "useless motions" led to the adoption of an "index of efficiency" of the kind expounded in 1909 by Leonard Ayres in his *Laggards in Our Schools,* whereby a school's efficiency would be measured by the children's progress through the grades. "If we can find out how many children *begin* school each year we can compute how many remain to the final elementary grade. Such a factor would show the relation of the finished product to the raw material." Adoption of this principle reinforced the class bias of the educational system. Since children of immigrants and of rural migrants to the city commonly entered school at a later age, the number of "overage" children did not necessarily reflect their failure to make satisfactory academic progress. Failure henceforth would be tied more firmly than ever to class and ethnic origin.

Even the more liberal ideas of the progressive educators were turned to the purposes of "efficiency"; when this proved impossible, they were ignored. John Dewey and his followers revolted against unimaginative classroom methods, against the authoritarianism that was built into the school system in so many ways, and against the school's inability to make modern life intelligible. Their ideas were worked out in such experiments as the Laboratory School in Chicago (1896–1914), the Gary Plan in Indiana (1908–1915), the Dalton Plan in Massachusetts (1919). Except in private schools for the very rich, their good intentions have left few imprints on the educational system. Instead the rhetoric and ideas of progressivism were appropriated by educational bureaucrats for their own purposes.

Ambiguities in progressivism itself facilitated this process. Like the advocates of efficiency, the progressives attacked impractical academic instruction, demanding what would be called today a more "relevant" education. They too exaggerated the influence of the school as an agent of social reform, seeing education as a panacea for all the evils of industrial society. Sharing with the advocates of efficiency a deep antipathy to genteel culture and perhaps to culture in general, the progressives had no secure philosophical basis from which to resist the perversion of their ideas in the practice of the public schools.

Progressivism in education helped to ease the transition from the backward and already outmoded version of the gospel of industrial efficiency promoted by F. W. Taylor and his disciples to the newer version, which stressed "cooperation" in the classroom as opposed to the factorylike drill. Joel Spring shows how many debates about education closely paralleled and were influenced by debates in corporate circles between Taylorites and advocates of "cooperation." The former wanted to speed up production by means of a crude system of incentives and rewards. The leaders of the "cooperative" movement, on the other hand—industrial innovators like John H. Patterson of the National Cash Register Company, the department store magnate E. A. Filene, and the managers of the H. J. Heinz Company—proposed to "humanize" the factory by introducing suggestion boxes, company newspapers, more "personal contact," pension programs and welfare plans, social activities, athletics, libraries, schools, training programs, and other integrative devices.

Part of the impetus for educational reform in the progessive period came from manufacturers who wished simply to shift the more costly of these programs, especially the training programs, to the schools. But the more imaginative educators saw that the school itself could become a miniature factory, a "workplace" in which the habits of cooperation could be "learned through doing." In addition they argued that the schools had to assume functions formerly performed by the extended family, now defunct.

Perhaps the most important effect of these reforms was that they gave rise to a pervasive belief that there is a close connection between education and industry and between schooling and status. Educators insisted that a highly rationalized society, in which arbitrary distinctions between persons were increasingly giving way to the more functional principle of merit, would depend more and more heavily on an efficiently organized system of compulsory education in order to select the right people for the right jobs.[7] Employers came to prefer educated workers because they assumed that education instilled orderly habits and a "cooperative" disposition. Their hiring policies in turn appeared to give substance to a growing popular belief that economic advancement depends on aptitude for schooling.

Those who hoped to enter high-status occupations came to take it for granted that they had to submit to 16 years of schooling and in many cases to extended professional training as well. Those who had no aptitude for school, who could not afford it, or who merely hated it, tailored their expectations accordingly. In this way the school system came to serve the function described by Jencks in one of the most arresting passages in his book, that of limiting the number of aspirants to high-status jobs—jobs that are widely believed (not without reason, but with less reason than is commonly supposed) to depend on schooling. Educational credentials came to serve as "a legitimate device for rationing privilege" in a society "that wants people sorted and graded but does not know precisely what standards it wants to use."

If there were general agreement on standards, a simpler system of certification could easily be devised—a system of examinations, for instance. In the absence of such agreement, schooling has the advantage not only that it is vague but that in some ways it replicates conditions on the job, providing employers, in Jencks' words, with something like "direct observation of an individual 'at work.'" The fact that a young person has attained a certain level of schooling, because it is believed to indicate submission to a discipline not unlike that of a job itself, matters more to prospective employers than the skills acquired along the way.

The American educational system, it would seem, rests on one of those illusions that acquire a certain validity simply because they are so widely shared—in this case, the illusion that schooling is an indispensable precondition of economic success. Because "the myth that schooling is synonymous with status [to quote Jencks again] is . . . even more widespread than the reality," the illusion is self-validating, like "confidence" in the stock market. So long as people believe in the myth and act accordingly, it has some semblance of reality. If events were to shatter the illusion—for instance, prolonged unemployment among a high proportion of college graduates and people with advanced degrees—the entire structure might gloriously collapse.

I have said that revisionist histories of education seem to suggest the foregoing interpretation. The authors themselves, however, would probably reject the two conclusions I draw from their work (as well as from Jencks')—that inequality can be reduced only by economic and political action, not through educational reform, and that the merits of the present school system therefore have to be discussed without counting on the system's putative influence on economic success, social mobility, and the eradication of poverty. Educators themselves, these authors still retain a "fragile faith in the schools," as Herbert Gans puts it in a perceptive introduction to Greer's *The Great School Legend*.

Whereas Gans reads Greer's study as supporting the view that "an overall strategy" against poverty "must be mainly economic," Greer himself clings to the hope of school reform. Instead of changing the class structure, he proposes to change the school. He recognizes that "the actual educational power of public education" has been "vastly overestimated" and that in view of this fact, "we should really consider the school to be a symbolic mechanism that holds a diverse, highly competitive society together." Yet he cannot bring himself to relinquish the hope that under proper conditions "schools could be an agent for major change"— for example, by discouraging "hostile competitiveness." In his recent assault on Jencks, Greer retreats completely from his perception that education is a "symbolic mechanism" and insists that the content of schooling really matters—from which it follows that progressive educators, by changing this content, can change the direction in which society is moving.

Katz's book ends on a similarly indecisive note. On the one hand, Katz believes that radical critics of education "oversimplify" when they describe the school's function as the inculcation of "middle-class attitudes." Indeed he suggests that the newly fashionable educational radicalism, infatuated with creativity, spontaneity, and other neoprogressive slogans, "is itself a species of class activity," since it is only the affluent who can afford to worry about whether the school encourages children to "express themselves." The poor may well prefer a school system that teaches their children how to read and write, and Katz himself thinks that it might be a good idea "to take the schools out of the business of making attitudes."

At the same time, however, he describes the radical criticism of the schools as "profoundly true." Like Greer, Katz is unwilling to admit that recent educational radicalism is merely an updated version of progressivism. Yet this radicalism not only adds little to the progressive indictment of the schools, it reaffirms the very belief it claims to criticize, namely that schooling is a powerful instrument of social policy. Instead of disposing of the "great school legend" once and for all, it merely gives it a radical disguise.

The confusion surrounding the revisionist history of education is most clearly illustrated by Joel Spring's book on the progressive period. In many ways this is the best of the three historical accounts at hand. It both complements and corrects Raymond Callahan's earlier study, *Education and the Cult of Efficiency*, which identified the efficiency movement too narrowly with Taylorism and thereby missed the congruence between "efficiency" and progressivism.

Spring's analysis of the ideology of "cooperation" is shrewd and perceptive, not least because it exposes some of its inner inconsistencies. Thus the reformers of the progressive period introduced vocational guidance in order to channel people into careers appropriate to their "abilities," only to find that tracking systems divided the school along class lines, giving rise to tension and hostility instead of "cooperation." Another series of "reforms" then had to be introduced in order to overcome or to paper over these divisions, the same integrative devices previously tried out in the factory—clubs, extracurricular activities, homerooms and assembly, student government, "school spirit," and above all athletics.

Spring's study might have led him to conclude that educational reformers have never really succeeded in turning the school into a smoothly functioning machine that molds the human "raw material" into a single pattern. For one thing, this objective is inconsistent with the need to reinforce existing class distinctions. For another, the school has to compete with the family and the street, influences on the child which it has never managed to supersede. The intentions of educational reformers, therefore, have been consistently thwarted in practice; one cannot take their intentions as an accurate description of the system as it actually operates.

In his concluding chapter, however, Spring does just that, crediting the "cooperative" movement with having made the school into a controlled environment that destroys man's "ability to create his own social being." Like the reformers themselves, Spring forgets that the life of the child, indeed the social life of the school itself, is shaped only in part—often in very small part—by the school.

Quite apart from the family, we have to reckon with the influence of a youth culture that is at least partially self-created and autonomous, a culture created on the streets but having a large, perhaps decisive influence on the school. Judging the results of educational reform by its intentions, Spring assumes that the school has succeeded in its drive to produce well-adjusted individuals who fit smoothly "into the institutional organization." But if this is true, how can we account for the present chaos in the schools? Far from generating uniformity, the schools are plagued by boredom, disruption, violence, drugs, and gang warfare. The educational reforms of the progressive period may have subjected vast numbers of people to schooling, but this is not the same thing as bringing "a greater part of the population under institutional controls." It is precisely the collapse of those controls that those who live and work in the schools are now experiencing as a daily reality—the crumbling of authority and the replacement of authority with violence.

The great contribution of the Jencks study, it has been said, is that it forces us to consider proposals for educational reform on their merits, without regard to their economic effects.[8] The proper conclusion to be drawn from *Inequality* and from recent historical writing on the school is not that schools are "no longer important" but that they are important in their own right. Why have most of the contributors to the debate been so reluctant to draw this conclusion? The idea that education is valuable in itself makes educators uncomfortable because it forces them to struggle with questions they have spent most of their careers avoiding. Why *should* education be valued? What are the proper objectives of educational policy? Does the present system promote them?

The founders of this country, whose ideas about education are still worth at least a passing glance, believed that the most important objects of public education were to provide for intellectual leadership and to make people effective guardians of their own liberty, in Jefferson's phrase. Jefferson thought that the study of history, in particular, would teach the young to judge "the actions and designs of men . . . to know ambition under every disguise it may assume; and knowing it, to defeat its views." [9]

The ideal citizen of Jefferson's republic was the man who cannot be fooled by demagogues or overawed by the learned obfuscations of professional wise men. Appeals to authority do not impress him. He is always on the alert for forgery, and he has the worldly wisdom of men's motives, enough understanding of the principles of critical reasoning, and sufficient skill in the use of language to detect intellectual fraud in whatever form it presents itself. In the poltical theory of early republicanism, the ideal of an enlightened electorate thus coincides with the goals of liberal education.

It is interesting to see how Jefferson proposed in practice "to diffuse knowledge more generally through the mass of the people." His bill establishing public education in Virginia (never enacted) entitled everyone to three years of free schooling (more if they wanted to pay) in reading, writing, and arithmetic. A handful of the most promising scholars were to be sent at public expense, along with the children of parents who could afford such schooling, to the grammar schools, where they would learn Greek, Latin, geography, and "the higher branches of numerical arithmetic." Half of the state-supported grammar school students would be discontinued at the end of six years (some of them becoming grammar-school teachers), while the rest would be sent to college for three years—once again, along with the children of the rich.

The ultimate result of the whole scheme of education would be the teaching all the children of the state reading, writing, and common arithmetic; turning out ten annually, of superior genius, well taught in Greek, Latin, Geography, and the higher branches of arithmetic; turning out ten others annually, of still superior parts, who, to those branches of learning, shall have added such of the sciences as their genius shall have led them to; the furnishing of the wealthier part of the people convenient schools at which their children may be educated at their own expense. The general objects of this law are to provide an education adapted to the years, to the capacity, and the condition of every one, and directed to their freedom and happiness.

In the first stage of this program, Jefferson continued, "the principal foundations of future order will be laid." Here students will imbibe the first principles of morality, together with "the most useful facts from Grecian, Roman, European and American history." In the next stage—for children roughly between eight and fifteen, whose minds are "most susceptible and tenacious of impressions" but "not yet firm enough for laborious and close operations"—foreign languages are to be emphasized, a form of study that will contribute to the mastery of one's own language. The highest stage is to be devoted to "science," the special blend of liberal and professional training that Jefferson later tried to build into his plan for the University of Virginia.

Later generations would find these proposals curiously casual and offhand, indifferent to the "needs" of the young, insufferably elitist. The reformers of the mid-nineteenth century regarded the old-fashioned curriculum as much too restricted. Overly intellectual, it paid too little attention to the moral development of the child and to the possibility that a program of compulsory education could inculcate habits of industry, thrift, and obedience—qualities essential to the nation's economic development and to the maintenance of public order.

Educational theorists of the progressive period were even harsher in their condemnation of the Jeffersonian concept of education. Not only did it ignore the need to educate the "whole child," not only did it ignore the connection between "learning and life," but it left nothing to the initiative of the child, content merely to drum a dead culture into the young by means of memorization and drill.

In our own time, early republican ideas appear downright undemocratic. Jefferson's system assumes that education is largely a prerogative of wealth; nor are we reassured by his promise that "twenty of the best geniuses will be raked from the rubbish annually" and instructed at public expense. Yet in the light of what we have recently learned about our own educational system, these objections no longer carry quite the overwhelming force they might once have had. Our own system, it appears, also perpetuates existing class distinctions. It ensures that those who start life with the advantages of money and birth will go further than those who don't. But at the same time—here is the most important point of all—the prevailing system manages to make this education increasingly worthless. As job training, education is largely irrelevant to the skills actually required by most jobs.[10] As intellectual training, American education is half-baked at best.

In short, our school system neither levels nor educates. We could more easily accept its intellectual failures, though we could not forgive them, if we knew that at least the system was an effective instrument of egalitarian social policy. Since it is not, the time has surely come to insist that the two objectives, egalitarianism and intellect, be separated, and that the schools be left free to address themselves to intellectual concerns while the state attacks inequality more directly and effectively through economic policies designed to equalize income.

I do not mean to argue that the entire drift of educational policy for the last 150 years has been an unqualified disaster. Whatever the merits of eighteenth-century educational ideas, they led in practice to a pedagogy that was often narrow and stifling. The best educators of the progressive period and their successors in recent years—Paul Goodman, Herbert Kohl, Colin Greer himself—revitalized classroom practice by appealing to the natural curiosity of the child instead of locking him into dogmatic formulas. Far from advocating a return to McGuffey, I wish to preserve and expand what is valuable in this pedagogy while stripping away the social ideology that has so often been attached to it—the ideology of school reform as the motor of social progress.

It is as a social theory of education that eighteenth-century ideas still have something to teach us. True, they assumed that a close connection between wealth, political leadership, and education was both inevitable and proper. Nevertheless they stated, with a clarity and candor subsequently lost, the two objectives a democratic system of education might reasonably expect to accomplish.

The first of these ends is to give everybody the intellectual resources—particularly the command of language—needed to distinguish truth from public lies and thus to defend themselves against tyrants and demagogues. Is it necessary to insist that this object is more urgent than ever?

The second purpose of education is to train scholars, intellectuals, and members of the learned professions. The eighteenth century saw no other reason for higher education. Neither do I. The dream of bringing culture to the masses, by making higher education widely available, has failed; mass higher education has only facilitated the spread of mass culture, impoverishing popular culture and higher culture alike. Higher education is necessarily "elitist" if it is to mean anything—an education for people with a pronounced taste for intellectual matters, who plan to spend their lives in intellectual pursuits; an education, it goes without saying, that should be made available to men and women of all classes, but only to those who are qualified for it and completely committed to it.

Christopher Lasch

Because any higher education worth the name is unavoidably restrictive in this sense, it should be an object of policy to ensure that higher education is meagerly rewarded in worldly goods. Professionals should be underpaid; scholars should live on the edge of austerity. This will discourage people from seeking higher education because they see it as a means to wealth and power. A democratic society needs intellectual leadership as much as any other kind of society does, but it has a special stake in seeing that an intellectual elite does not become also a political elite, that it carries on its work in the critical spirit necessary to serious inquiry of any sort.

An egalitarian income policy is quite consistent with the type of educational reform that seeks to restore the intellectual value of education. Indeed these aims are mutually dependent. Equality of incomes would deprive education of its cash value (thereby completing a process that market conditions may already, inadvertently, have set in motion). If incomes were roughly equalized, the demand for extended education would diminish drastically; the overdeveloped educational bureaucracy would wither at its source. Is it possible to imagine a fairer prospect?

NOTES

1. For these criticisms see Maurice R. Berube's review in *Commonweal,* January 19, 1973, pp. 353–354, and the essay by Kenneth E. Clark and Lawrence Plotkin in *Christopher Jencks in Perspective,* a pamphlet published by the American Association of School Administrators (Arlington, Virginia, 1973), p. 35.

2. Note the American conservative's penchant, illustrated again in these observations by Kristol, for a simplified pseudo-Marxism: equality is merely a slogan in the class warfare between the bourgeoisie and the "new class" of alienated intellectuals and half-intellectuals

In the United States, where Marxism remains officially taboo and therefore unstudied, even conservatives draw freely on "Marxism"—probably because liberalism has become increasingly vacuous and remote from reality, absorbed as it is in purely technical approaches to the world; while conservatism itself is, obviously, unpopular, resting in religious assumptions that can be taken seriously only at the risk of ridicule.

Note also the familiar antiintellectual gambit used by both sides in the current debate on equality. For Kristol, the new egalitarianism is a disease of the intellectuals. For Jencks' critics on the left, *Inequality* is a typical product of the academy. True, the book *seems* to have provoked disagreement in the academy, but this controversy itself is only a form of capitalist competition. "Just as capitalists compete in production, but unite to preserve the production system . . . so the presence of an 'intellectual class interest' is not contradicted by the presence of debate" (Stephan

Michelson, "The Further Responsibility of Intellectuals," *Harvard Educational Review*, February 1973, p. 94).

3. Accordingly terms like "upper-middle class," "lower-middle class," etc., are misleading. Such terms do not really refer to classes but simply to income groups. A superficial reading of Jencks' book might lead to the conclusion that the distribution of educational credentials has little to do with class, since it seems to be influenced by cultural considerations more than by socioeconomic status. It is more accurate to conclude, however, that class is a cultural as well as socioeconomic phenomenon, and that as such it has a great deal to do with the distribution of educational credentials. The concept of class used by academic sociologists, which Jencks has unfortunately borrowed for the admittedly limited purposes of his analysis, is static, rigid, abstract, and hierarchical; whereas in reality classes are the product of a specific series of historical events, cultural and political as well as social and economic. The American middle classes, both the "old" middle class of propertied wealth and the "new" middle class of salaried employees, still shows many of the cultural characteristics of a class devoted to accumulation as opposed to leisure and display, including an emphasis on schooling as a means of getting ahead.

4. Stephan Michelson, whose radical gamesmanship I criticized in note 2, above, complains ("Further Responsibility," p. 105) that Jencks trivializes the idea of socialism, which implies a change in the nature and relations of work and in the distribution of political power, by narrowing it to income equality. This time I think he is on firm ground. An egalitarian income policy is not necessarily "socialist" (although that is obviously no reason to reject it), and I do not see why Jencks unnecessarily alienates potential support for such a policy, and provides ammunition to its critics, by calling it socialist. One such critic complacently predicts that "his chief recommendation—that the country turn to a vast socialistic overhaul of its economic institutions as the only way to guarantee equality—will get little support" (Paul B. Salmon, foreword to *Christopher Jencks in Perspective*, p. v.).

5. Text of a radio broadcast by Greer, station WBAI, September 26, 1972.

6. The following account draws also on Michael B. Katz, *The Irony of Early Educational Reform* (1968); Lawrence A. Cremin, *The Transformation of the School* (1961); Raymond E. Callahan, *Education and the Cult of Efficiency* (1962); and Edward A. Krug, *The Shaping of the American High School* (1964).

7. This tenet of the professional educators' creed finds typical expression in a recent criticism of Jencks by the Nevada state commissioner of education, Kenneth H. Hansen. "The position taken by Jencks seems to divorce the schools from the needs of society, overlooking the seemingly inescapable relationship between changes in the social order and changes in education. In a society constantly demanding higher levels of skill to cope with new demands, in a society in which technological obsolescence makes career development and training a lifelong responsibility of the educational institutions, in a society where almost no one can satisfactorily perform any meaningful job (despite the income he might be awarded) without some mastery of the cognitive skills of reading, writing, calculating, and articulating, how can we possibly believe that the quality of schooling at the earliest levels doesn't make any significant difference?" (*Christopher Jencks in Perspective*, pp. 45–46.) Note the highly rhetorical, self-hypnotic effect of this characteristic bit of educationese.

8. George Levine, "Inequality," *New York Times Book Review*, November 26, 1972.

9. *Notes on Virginia*, query XIV. All of the following quotations are taken from this chapter.

10. Jencks' findings reinforce those of Ivar Berg's *Education and Jobs: The Great*

Training Robbery. See also the recent study by Bennett Harrison, *Education, Training, and the Urban Ghetto* (Johns Hopkins, 1972), p. 30: ". . . even if minority (and particularly ghetto) education is inferior in quality to the schooling received by most urban whites, the mechanism by which this contributes to nonwhite poverty and unemployment is not inadequate skills or low potential productivity, but rather the growing infatuation of private and public employers with educational credentials. The practice of 'credentialism'—the use of educational credentials as a quick and allegedly inexpensive device for screening out socially undesirable individuals—appears to be an increasingly important explanation of the correlation between completion of high school or college on the one hand, and income on the other."

(3)

How Effective Is Schooling?
A Critical Synthesis
and Review of
Research Findings

Harvey A. Averch, Stephen J. Carroll, Theodore S. Donaldson,
Herbert J. Kiesling, and John Pincus

Educational Research and Educational Policy

EACH YEAR literally thousands of educational research efforts are reported. New results are constantly being presented. The vast body of literature on educational effectiveness should provide a firm foundation for the formulation of educational policy. Thus far, it has not done so.

There are a number of reasons for the gap between educational research and educational policy. First, there are many diverse streams of educational research. In terms of traditional disciplines, research on educational effectiveness appears in economics, econometrics, political science, psychology, psychometrics, sociology, and sociometrics, as well as the discipline of education proper. Researchers have tended to follow relatively narrow, intradisciplinary paths. There have been few attempts to connect these paths; nor is there a clear map down any given path. Policy maker and researcher alike, therefore, find it very difficult to draw policy implications from these various disciplines.

Second, the sheer magnitude of the literature on educational effectiveness makes it virtually impossible to keep up-to-date on the research being conducted in any one field, let alone to keep up with what is being produced across the entire range of educational research.

Abstracted from Stephen J. Carroll, Theodore S. Donaldson, Herbert J. Kiesling, and John Pincus, *How Effective Is Schooling? A Critical Review of Research*, a comprehensive treatment of the literature published by Educational Technology Publications, Englewood Cliffs, New Jersey 07632. Copyright © 1974 The Rand Corporation. Volume Number One in the Rand Educational Policy Series.

Third, educational research has seldom been explicitly policy-oriented. A considerable volume of research has been aimed at increasing understanding of how, and under what conditions, learning takes place. But the basic research has rarely been framed in the language of decision making.

Fourth, and perhaps most important, the research is full of contradictory or inconsistent findings. The policy maker thus finds himself constantly basing his decisions on controversial and disputed research results.

This analysis is directed toward the needs of the educational policy maker. We believe that what is important for the inquiry at hand is to extract the policy-relevant findings from the research and to derive from them broadly based conclusions as to what we now know about educational effectiveness. The analysis is based upon comprehensive reviews of the many streams of educational research. We have attempted, throughout the analysis, to examine the validity and credibility of research results. In the case of each research effort reviewed we tried to discover whether the study was internally valid (did the researcher pursue proper methods for the questions he addressed?) and if it was, were the results credible in the light of accumulated knowledge (were the findings consistent with those of other studies in the area?).

The need for examination of internal validity is clear. We cannot base policy on incorrect or misleading research results. Accordingly, we must ask whether the results of any particular study were generated by a proper method of analysis.

Just as important is the issue of credibility (external validity). There is always some chance that a particular variable, or a particular set of variables, that appears to have a significant effect upon achievement is in fact unrelated to educational outcome. For this reason, educational policy cannot rely on the results of any one study. Whether studies say anything about actual educational outcomes depends, then, on results that appear consistently throughout a number of studies. If an educational resource or procedure shows up as important in a large number of studies, then we should be able to state with considerable confidence that this resource or procedure should be selected by policy makers (allowing for the relative costs of resources and procedures).

Note that an examination of credibility serves three distinct purposes: First, it provides a way of summarizing numerous disparate studies. Second, it addresses the question of what should be believed in the face of inconsistent or conflicting results. Essentially, we resolve such conflicts by "adding up" the evidence on each side of a dispute. Third, consideration of external validity enables us to deal with the avalanche of research results. No review, this one included, could possibly consider every single educational research study. But if a large number of internally valid studies yield consistent results, then one can be fairly sure that any omitted study would not have substantively changed one's conclusions.

None of the many ways of accumulating evidence from dissimilar studies to reach a conclusion as to the results of the body of research [1] is entirely satisfactory. In this analysis each research report we review can be considered as a witness presenting testimony. Our test of internal validity can be compared to cross-examination. Interstudy consistency is determined subjectively, our judgment being based upon the accumulated evidence presented by many diverse research reports. We do count the number of studies in which an independent variable is examined and calculate the proposition that finds that variable to be significant, but we do not simply weigh each study equally. Rather, we are more persuaded by studies that use larger samples or more replications, better designs, a greater number of controls for intervening variables, or more accurate measures of the variables in question. In general, then, what follows is not unquestionable "truth" but our attempt to derive meaningful conclusions from a vast and diverse body of literature.

What follows, then, is not a classical review of research, listing findings without much evaluation of the results. Rather, it is our answer to the question, What does the research tell us about educational effectiveness?

Accomplishing our objective required that this vast body of literature be organized and evaluated on the basis of some analytical structure. Our discussion of the research on educational effectiveness is organized according to five basic research approaches—that is, *according to the aspect of education that is examined in the analysis, the question being addressed, and the method deemed appropriate to answer the questions.*

Five Research Approaches

The five approaches provide a way of collecting together studies that share a similar focus and purpose and that use similar analytical techniques. We can thus identify the similarities and differences among the many streams of educational research. Individual studies or groups of similar studies are placed in perspective. Moreover, common standards of internal validity apply to studies within each approach. This simplifies the task of evaluating the results of individual research efforts. Finally, because studies in an approach tend to have a common orientation, the relationships among their results are more easily observed.

The Input-Output Approach

Much of the research produced in the input-output approach has been prominent in recent policy debates—for example, the *Equality of Educational Opportunity* survey (Coleman et al., 1966) and its various reanalyses. Research in this approach views the school as a black box containing students (Fig. 3–1). Resources are applied to the students in the box, and from this application some output flows. Output is usually defined in terms of cognitive achievement as measured by standardized achievement tests. Some studies define as outputs such variables as dropout rates or percentage of students going on to college. School resources, or inputs, generally include a broad range of factors describing teachers' characteristics (experience and verbal ability are two examples) and physical attributes of the school (the number of library books per student, age of building, class size, and the like).

Research is directed toward the question, To what extent are variations in educational outcomes due to variations in resource levels? Ideally, the research is supposed to identify the extent to which each resource contributes to educational outcomes. Policy makers should then be able to identify those resources that are most effective and restructure the current use of resources toward the more effective configurations discovered by research.

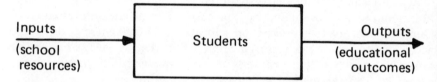

Fig. 3–1. The input-output approach.

The empirical problem is to establish the relation between input and output. In practice, statistical analysis is applied to ex post, cross-sectional data, although the desire for longitudinal data is often asserted. In other words, the analyst collects a body of data at a point in time—usually survey data—applies various statistical techniques—usually multiple regression—and tries to make statements about the effects of inputs.

The confidence we can place in research results depends upon (1) the internal validity of particular studies—the logic and design of the analysis—and (2) the external validity—the consistency of findings across studies. With respect to internal validity one asks, Were the procedures generally accepted for this approach carefully followed? And, if so, are the results consistent with the underlying model? For the input-output approach, internal validity is measured by tests of significance and goodness of fit. External validity concerns whether studies say something about the real educational world. Do they say something about the schools? Here the test is interstudy consistency. Are the resources identified as effective in one study also found to be effective in other studies? [2]

The Process Approach

The second approach—education as a process—is based on a quite different fundamental assumption about what determines educational outcomes (Fig. 3–2). Here the researcher focuses on the "inside" of the box. Resources are assumed to be predetermined or given. What matters here are the processes by which the resources are applied to the students and the response of the students to the processes. If we can correctly identify processes of education or learning, *they* will determine the quantities of resources that the schools require. The processes of concern can be those connected with teachers, students, instruction, or the interactions among them. Educational outcomes for the most part are limited measures of cognitive achievement. In a few cases noncognitive achievement is examined.

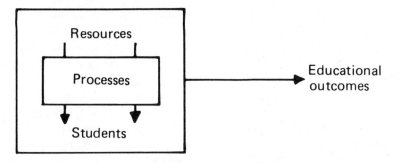

Fig. 3–2. The process approach.

In most cases, the main purpose of this approach is to extend our knowledge about educational processes. In general, there has been much less orientation toward concrete policy action among researchers here than among those who pursue the input-output approach. The policy applications have so far been secondary. To illustrate, when conducting an experiment, psychologists lay great stress on experimental control of confounding variables. Sometimes, in order to minimize the extent to which a student's previous learning experiences affect the outcome of an experiment, they deliberately examine learning tasks that are very unlike the learning tasks encountered in the classroom—memorizing lists of nonsense syllables, for example. Consequently, the results of the experiment offer little direct policy guidance.

Research here usually consists of small-scale experiments or variations of treatments, often performed in a laboratory. The problem thus becomes one of putting together the experiments or treatments that bear on the same process to see whether they are consistent. The experiments are collated through review articles varying greatly in quality. Here internal validity depends upon whether the studies have proper experimental design, whether they controlled for everything that could confound the results; external validity, again, depends upon consistency among studies. Do the same processes appear to affect academic achievement in the same way across a number of studies?

The Organizational Approach

In the organizational approach to the issue of educational effectiveness what is done in the schools is viewed as being not the result of a rational search for effective inputs or processes but a reflection of history, social demands, and organizational change and rigidities. In Fig. 3–3 we distort the shape of the "box," because its structure matters here (the school system as a whole). The inputs are the rules, the procedures, the incentives that are set up within the system. The approach is more concerned with the people in the system—teachers, administrators, appointed and elected officials—than are the previous two approaches. The measure of responsiveness to change is the ability to adapt to a changing clientele. The *assumption* is that responsive schools will deliver satisfactory academic outcomes, but not necessarily the maximum feasible outcomes.[3] Why? Because in this approach the schools have multiple objectives, not just academic outcomes; they do many things. And the schools are doing well if they get satisfactory achievement along with the other goals that have to be satisfied. The perceived crisis of the classroom is caused by an inflexible stand in the face of changing demands by students, parents, the immediate community, and the government. The purpose, then, is to understand the behavior of the whole system and describe the shape of the box and how and what happens to the people in it—not just the students, but the teachers, the administrators, and the community as a whole.

Research here primarily uses case-study methods. There are no formal tests of either internal or external validity; in fact, it is rare in these case studies to find much concern about such matters.[4] There are no statistical tests, almost by definition; interstudy consistency is hard to determine, since the point to be illustrated rarely recurs. Nevertheless, we try to apply "reasonable" criteria of our own to assess these studies.

Although the organizational approach is relatively undeveloped (as compared with the previous two approaches), we believe that it is closely related to schools' finances. The leverage of alternative financial schemes seems greater on organizational structures than it does on resources or on processes. It is hard to see how overall financial schemes could be tied to the internal use of resources or processes of school systems without creating massive problems of administration and control. It is possible that alternative financial schemes, if they can be found, could affect the shape of our educational box to make it more receptive to effective resources or processes.

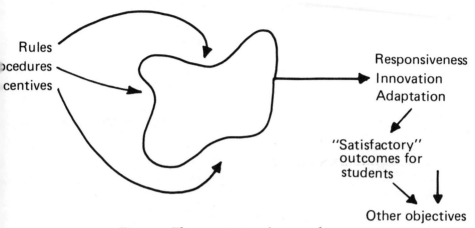

Fig. 3-3. The organizational approach.

The Evaluation Approach

Studies within the evaluation approach attempt to analyze the effectiveness of broad educational interventions that are directly related to large issues of social policy. Essentially these are analyses of programs in which treatments are devoted to "groups of children as a whole in diverse programs, taken as a whole" (Stearns, 1971a, p. 6). In such interventions the resources devoted to each child are increased substantially. *Since any number of educational inputs or processes are changed at the same time, it is difficult to tell precisely which program features are responsible, even where there is demonstrated success.* Researchers using this method tend to address the question, To what extent did a generalized intervention affect educational outcomes?

Research focuses on school systems in which there have been large-scale interventions (Fig. 3-4). The primary concern is to identify the relationship between the existence (or magnitude) of an intervention and educational outcomes. It should be noted that these analyses seldom attempt to determine why or how an intervention affected outcomes.[5] This contrasts to the other approaches in which the analyst focuses on the impact of a particular educational practice.

These studies tend to be more policy-oriented than those included in any other approach. Their general purpose or goal is to discover what "works." The implication is that if we can discover what "works," then we can replicate the intervention elsewhere.

The analytical technique used to discover whether an intervention was successful is ex post examination of the outcomes of students upon whom the intervention was focused. The evaluator typically attempts to identify a group of students who, although not themselves targets of the intervention, resemble the students who were. He then compares the outcomes of the target group of students with the outcomes of the non-target, or control, group of students. Any differences in outcomes are presumed to be reflections of the intervention's impact.

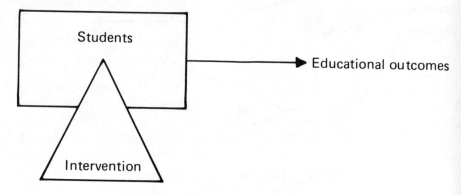

Fig. 3–4. The evaluation approach.

In evaluations, the researcher usually chooses the members of the control group after the program has begun rather than by some random process, and there is always the possibility of some systematic difference between control group members and target group members. If there is, differences in outcomes between the two groups may reflect the difference between the groups and not the impact of the evaluation. Accordingly, the question of internal validity hinges on the method by which a control group was chosen.[6]

The Experiential Approach

The experiential approach is concerned with what happens to students in schools as an end in itself. The school is viewed as an institution containing, and having an impact on, students (Fig. 3–5). It is generally (but not always) acknowledged that the impact of the school may affect educational outcomes. But this is not viewed as being the primary concern. Rather, considerable importance is placed on that impact as an outcome in itself. The primary emphasis is on the effects of school experiences on students' self-concepts and on their relation to other people and to social institutions.

The purpose of these studies is to show how the system works and its impact on those within the system. The central question addressed is, What does the school do to students? The research is conducted by "on-the-spot" observation. That is, research reports in this approach are frequently provided by participant observers in the form of descriptions of their experiences. Others were done by people outside the formal education system who were proponents of educational reform.

It is always difficult to examine the internal validity of case studies, which are often used in the experiential literature. And case studies by participant observers are usually the most difficult. The participant observer reports and interprets what he has seen, but what he has seen is in large part his own behavior and the response of others to his behavior. In fact, one of the presumed advantages of participant observations is the insight obtained by engaging directly in the activities being studied. The objectivity of the researcher becomes a major issue. Further, the majority of studies we reviewed in this approach were not conducted by professional researchers. Rather, they were provided by persons who entered the system intending to be teachers but who were so incensed at what they observed that they felt compelled to communicate their observations to others. Accordingly, their personal feelings are an important aspect of what they report.

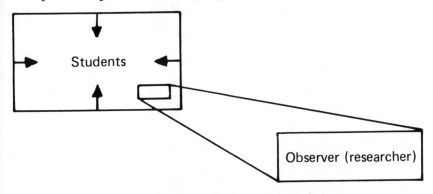

Fig. 3–5. The experiential approach.

We have attempted to examine the internal validity of these reports by asking whether they are internally consistent. (Does the author seem to interpret what he observes in a consistent manner?) We have also tried to discover whether his observations seem to be based on circumstances peculiar to his situation. (Do his observations concern his particular class, school, or system; or do his observations concern aspects of education in general?)

We have tried to derive from each work reviewed a set of propositions about the impact of the educational system on students. External validity was checked by comparing these sets of propositions to discover which seemed to be supported by a number of persons in different circumstances.

Summary and Discussion of Findings

The Input-Output Approach

This approach focuses on the relationship between the amounts of various resources that are provided to students and their educational outcomes (defined as cognitive achievement). Overall, the input-output studies provide very little evidence that school resources, in general, have a powerful impact upon student outcomes. When we examine the results across studies we find that school resources are not consistently important. The particular resources that seem to be significant in one study do not prove to be significant in other studies that include the same resources in the analysis.

Background factors, on the other hand, are always important. In study after study a student's background has a strong influence on his educational outcomes. Furthermore, the results are consistent across studies. The socioeconomic status of a student's family—his parents' income, education, and occupation—invariably prove to be significant predictors of his educational outcome.

The role of peer-group influences is more complex. There is good reason to believe that these variables are, in reality, measures of a student's background or of his school district's selection and assignment policies. On balance, there is little evidence that a student's classmates exercise a strong, independent influence on his educational outcomes.

The results from the input-output approach do not mean that school resources fail, actually or potentially, to affect student outcomes. We simply observe that so far these studies have failed to show that school resources *do* affect student outcomes. In particular, the studies do not show what would happen if the educational system received a massive increase or decrease in resources.

The Process Approach

The approach of the psychologist focuses on a very different aspect of education. Resources are taken as given or predetermined. What matters here are the processes applied to students and the interactions between teachers and students. For example, research may concentrate on the relation between teaching style and student achievement, or on the effects of grouping on achievement.

We have divided the results into two parts: those derived from studies of operating classrooms and those derived from the laboratory. For each set of results, we indicate the focus, the questions being asked, and the answers to the questions.

Looking first at the classroom studies, we find the following:

> The research on teaching approaches, teacher differences, class size, and the like shows no consistent effect on student achievement, as measured by standardized cognitive tests.

> Work on instructional methods suggests no difference among methods; none currently appears better than conventional methods. That is, in terms of differences in achievement, conventional methods appear as effective as, say, teaching by television, although the latter enables one to reach far greater numbers of students.

We consider the following results from the laboratory studies to be particularly interesting and important:

> Work on the presentation of material suggests that it is not so much the medium of instruction that is important as its sequencing and organization. There seem to be interaction effects; individual methods of presentation appear superior for some tasks and some students, but it is still hard to match student characteristics, tasks, and type of instruction.

> The work on concept attainment, retention, and learning rewards provides a number of positive findings, but the tasks in the laboratory are so unlike classroom learning that there is a difficult problem of translation. For example, the more meaningful the material, the faster it is learned and the more it is retained. But the definition of "meaningful" is a laboratory one, relating, say, to the difference between nonsense sentences or syllables and those that make sense.

> What are termed interaction effects seem to exist among various types of personality, methods of reward, ability to grasp meaningful material, and so on; but these interactions have not yet been studied in detail.

In sum, the process approach has not identified the very specific student relations involved in learning and education. There seem to be interactions between students and teachers, between students and methods, between teachers and methods, and (most complex of all) among students, teachers, and methods. The complex three-way interactions have not yet been studied carefully.

The Organizational Approach

In the work on educational organizations, schools are seen as institutions that have to satisfy multiple goals and demands from internal bureaucracies, from the community, from parents, and from students. The allocation of resources and the choice of processes in schools are seen not as the result of a rational decision-making procedure but as the outcome of history, of interactions with constituents and with government, and of simple trial and error. The question being asked is, How can we make the schools innovative, adaptive, and flexible, particularly as social demands increase and the composition of the student body changes?

Most of the work in this approach consists of case studies, and the rules for internal and external validity are weak at best. Furthermore, there have been few attempts to extract important organizational propositions from the literature. The case studies provide some evidence for the following:

> There is a positive correlation between system size and centralization.

> The larger the educational bureaucracy and the more centralization, the less innovation and adaptation there is likely to be.

> Rigidities in the schools can be overcome partly by choice of teachers and principals. However, teacher qualities that are purchased—say, experience—have little to do with innovative teaching.

> Real innovation depends on the leverage that can be exerted from outside the system—by the federal government or by citizens.

The Evaluation Approach

This approach to educational research consists of ex post analyses of comprehensive interventions in existing school systems. These studies are characterized by a macro-view of educational interventions in which treatments are devoted to groups of children in "diverse programs taken as a whole." In short, these studies ask *whether* large-scale interventions have had an effect in general, rather than what has been the effect of any particular intervention.

Virtually without exception, all the surveys of large, national compensatory education programs have shown no beneficial results on average. However, the evaluations on which the surveys report are often based upon suspect research designs.

Two or three smaller surveys show modest positive effects of compensatory education programs in the short run. And a number of quite carefully designed interventions display gains in pupil cognitive performance—again, in the short run. In particular, pupils from disadvantaged socioeconomic backgrounds tend to show greater progress in more highly structured programs. However, there is considerable evidence that many of the short-run gains from educational interventions fade away after two or three years if they are not reinforced. Also, this "fadeout" is much greater for the more highly structured programs, which are most unlike regular public school practice.

The Experiential Approach

The experiential approach is represented by the literature of educational reform. The observer, either as researcher or participant, describes the way that the experience of schooling affects the student in relation to himself, his peers, authority, and social institutions. The measure, for these writers, is not educational outcomes as indicated by standardized tests but rather the effect of the school experience on people's lives, where cognitive testing measures nothing.

Because this literature is one of social reform, it is not subject to the same tests of internal consistency as the approaches discussed above. In effect there are two elements in this literature, description and prescription.[7] The description of the schools as constituted at the present time almost invariably emphasizes a set of common themes:

Schools are authoritarian toward students.

Schools make little or no allowance for individual differences in learning styles and needs.

Schools focus on methods that stress rightness and wrongness in learning, thereby destroying independence and creativity, as well as equipping children poorly for the complexities and ambiguities of the real world.

Schools impose a certain set of social, cultural, and ethical views on their students, thereby imposing feelings of inadequacy and resentment on those who share neither those views nor the traditions they imply.

Schools as institutions are mindless in the sense that they fail, in any operationally useful way, to question either the assumption upon which they operate or the relevance of their approach to children's needs.

The prescriptions are far more varied than the descriptive research. They range from recommendations for moderate reform within the system (Silberman, 1970) to abolition of the schools (Illich, 1971). In some cases the value systems leading to the prescriptions are made explicit, in others, not. In general, however, the experiential literature agrees on the merits of educational systems that are less rigid, more responsive to individual diversity, and more decentralized than the current system.

Limitations of Available Research

Each approach is subject to substantive and methodological problems peculiar to itself. These problems were discussed earlier and will not be reviewed here. However, some research limitations appear throughout educational research and have, we feel, special importance.

First, educational outcomes are almost exclusively measured by cognitive achievement. But the educational system has many functions and many outputs. Cognitive achievement, in particular that part measured by standardized tests, is only one aspect of student learning. Higher cognitive processes (abstract reasoning, problem solving, and creativity, among others) are obviously important educational outcomes, as is noncognitive achievement. Thus, of the many and diverse kinds of student learning, almost all the educational research that examines student learning is based on a narrow range of cognitive skills. Therefore, current research cannot lead to conclusive generalizations about educational outcomes, because it cannot measure most of them well.

Second, there is virtually no examination of the cost implications of research results. By and large, educational researchers have concentrated on discovering effective educational practices. Virtually no attention has been paid to the notion of cost-effective educational practices. Research results are thus difficult to translate into policy-relevant statements.

Third, few studies maintain adequate controls over what actually goes on in the classroom as it relates to achievement. Data on classroom transactions are the only source of information on the content of the student-teacher relationship. Studies that omit transactions data can hope to identify only broad associations among variables that hold no matter what might be the nature of the relationship between student and teacher. Thus researchers' results may well be affected by circumstances unrecognized in their analyses.

Finally, the data used by researchers are, at best, crude measures of what is really happening. Concepts such as a teacher's ability to teach or a student's ability to learn are easily discussed, but objective measures of these abilities are extraordinarily elusive; and empirical analysis is based upon measurement. There is no way of knowing the extent to which inconclusive results stem from the researcher's inability to measure the variables he includes in his analysis accurately.

Conclusions and Policy Implications

With the limitations of research clearly in mind, we return to the issue of educational effectiveness. The first major implication of the research is:

Research has not identified a variant of the existing system that is consistently related to students' educational outcomes.

The term "a variant of the existing system" is used to describe the broad range of alternative educational practices that have been reviewed above. We specifically include changes in school resources, processes, organizations, and aggregate levels of funding.

We must emphasize that we are not suggesting that nothing makes a difference, or that nothing "works." Rather, we are saying that research has found nothing that *consistently* and *unambiguously* makes a difference in students' outcomes. The literature contains numerous examples of educational practices that seem to have significantly affected students' outcomes. The problem is that there are invariably other studies, similar in approach and method, that find the same educational practice to be ineffective. And we have no clear idea of why a practice that seems to be effective in one case is apparently ineffective in another.

We must also emphasize that we are not saying that school does not affect student outcomes. We have little knowledge of what student outcomes would be were students not to attend school at all. Educational research focuses on variants of the existing system and tells us nothing about where we might be without the system at all.

Furthermore, nothing we have found in the educational research literature proves that our current educational system *cannot* be substantially improved. But the research results we review above provide little reason to be sanguine. Our general conclusion, so far, is that there are few consistent, positive, policy-relevant findings. That is, the research offers little guidance to what educational practices should be implemented. This condition can arise because that is the way the world really is, or because researchers have been asking the wrong questions, or because the research methods used are not sufficiently powerful, or because the data are "bad." For whatever reason, we can only say that the educational practices examined thus far are only weakly connected to student achievement.

Finally, the educational practices for which school systems have traditionally been willing to pay a premium do not appear to make a major difference in student outcomes. Teachers' experience and teachers' advanced degrees, the two basic factors that determine salary, are not clearly related to student achievement. Reduction in class size, a favorite high-priority reform in the eyes of many school systems, seems not to be related to student outcomes. In general, the second major implication of the research (and the most important one for school finance) is:

Increasing expenditures on traditional educational practices is not likely to improve educational outcomes substantially.

The third major policy implication of the research is:

There seem to be opportunities for significant reduction or redirection of educational expenditures without deterioration in educational outcomes.

Researchers have examined many variants of the existing educational system. As we have indicated, none of these variants has been shown to improve educational outcomes consistently. A fact often overlooked is that few have been shown to lead to significantly worse outcomes either. Consequently, educational research has provided a long list of equally effective variants of the existing system. And, if these variants are not all equally expensive, then choosing the least expensive provides opportunities to redirect (or even reduce) costs without also reducing effectiveness.[8]

Educational research consists almost entirely of effectiveness studies. There are very few cost-effectiveness studies. The tremendous volume of "negative" results—negative according to the peculiar bias of educational research, which seeks only improvement on the effectiveness side —must surely contain many "positive" results in the sense of indicating less costly methods of accomplishing as much as is currently attained.

The research contains some evidence supporting a fourth major implication:

Innovation, responsiveness, and adaptation in school systems decrease with size and depend upon exogenous shocks to the system.

In other words, large systems are less likely to be innovative, responsive, or adaptive than are small systems. Further, whatever the size of the system, innovation is not apt to come from within the system. Outside pressures, from the community or from the federal government, are likely to be needed. We note, however, that relatively little research has been directed toward these issues. Hence, this finding must be viewed as tentative.

The implication of this tentative conclusion is clear. There is currently a good deal of interest in federal leverage and in the question of whether federal aid to the schools should be tied or untied. *The literature that we have examined suggests that federal influence is important in getting innovation into urban school systems,* although the hypothesis has not really been tested rigorously.

Our review of educational research supports a fifth major implication:

Educational research is seriously deficient in terms of the size, scope, and focus of research efforts and in the integration of research results.

Beyond these specific limitations, educational research has tended to be small in scale, narrow in scope, diffuse, maldistributed, and lacking in focus. By comparison with other major sectors, the amount of research activity devoted to educational problems is surprisingly small. For example, the amount of resources allocated to agricultural research and development is more than four times as large, and health research is allocated more than 13 times as much. Moreover, educational research is a relatively recent development. Quantitative research on American education goes back to the work of Joseph Meyer Rice in the 1890s;

but significant levels of activity did not begin until the late 1950s when first the National Science Foundation, then the Office of Education, began to fund a wide range of research activities. A comparison of R&D communities by institutional affiliation shows that educational research is very unlike other R&D sectors in the economy because colleges and universities perform the majority of R&D in the educational sector. The academic community tends to conduct relatively small studies on a part-time basis and to concentrate on basic research. Furthermore, educational research has tended to be almost exclusively the domain of the psychologist. Only recently has it begun to attract the attention of more than a handful of well-trained researchers in other fields.[9]

The body of educational research now available leaves much to be desired, at least by comparison with the level of understanding that has been achieved in numerous other fields. This does not reflect the quality of the contemporary educational researcher but rather the nature of the research community and its history. The typical education study is not founded on a wealth of previous knowledge and understanding nor is it directed toward the needs of the educational policy maker. There are virtually no researcher-based, problem-solving units in the typical operating agency. In 1968 there were only 1,300 man-years devoted to research, development, or innovation in the almost 20,000 state and local education agencies; most of that was devoted to testing and to gathering statistics (Levien, 1971).

Finally, the sixth major implication of our work is:

Research tentatively suggests that improvement in student outcomes, both cognitive and noncognitive, may require sweeping changes in the organization, structure, and conduct of educational experiences.

This inference follows from the first four conclusions cited above, as well as from the testimony of the experiential approach. Even the fifth conclusion, which cites the paucity of educational research, tends to reinforce this point because it implies that marginal changes in research will be inadequate to indicate clearly the directions educational improvement should take. Below we offer hypotheses that are broadly consistent with the "sweeping change" inference.

Where Do We Go from Here? The Substantive Issues

Our review of educational research found little association between various educational practices—resources, processes, organizations, and so on —and students' educational outcomes. We also inferred reasons why this seems to be so: the role of nonschool factors, interaction, and inappropriate forms of education. Although they have been recognized in the past by many educational researchers, they have not been carefully investigated to any great extent. They are *potential* explanations of why research has not revealed the expected connections between educational processes and educational outcomes.

Nonschool Factors

There is considerable evidence that nonschool factors may well be more important determinants of educational outcomes than are school factors. The research repeatedly finds high correlations between students' socioeconomic backgrounds and educational outcomes. A variety of hypotheses as to why this relationship seems so powerful have been put forward.

> At one extreme, there are some who argue that genetic differences among children are associated with their racial, cultural, or social backgrounds. According to this view there are differences among children with respect to their learning ability, and these differences are, in turn, correlated with their environments.

> Others have argued that environment is correlated with educational outcomes because much of the child's learning occurs outside of school. The child raised in an environment of poverty is seldom exposed to museums or libraries, lives in a home where few books are present, and generally is not exposed to the variety of educational experiences available to the advantaged child.

> A third and somewhat related view also argues that much of a child's learning occurs outside school. What children learn outside school, it is argued, depends upon what their environments offer to them by way of experiences. Thus the child raised in an environment of poverty learns "as much" as a child raised in a middle-class family; but precisely what he or she learns is quite different from what the middle-class child learns. However, this argument goes on, the tests or measures of educational outcomes are oriented toward the middle class and, roughly speaking, give full value to what the middle-class child has learned outside school but only partial credit to what the poor child has learned outside school.

> Still others have argued that a child's background influences his educational outcomes by affecting his attitudes. According to this view, the disadvantaged child lacks motivation or does not aspire to educational success. His parents are likely to have attained relatively low educational levels. He faces racial or class discrimination, which reduces his prospects of success (compared with the middle-class child) despite his educational attainment. The general thrust of this argument is that

the disadvantaged child is not encouraged, either directly (for example, by parental pressure) or indirectly (for example, by observation of the "payoff" of education to others like himself), to seek success in the schools.

The above are but a few of the many hypotheses as to why educational outcomes seem to be unaffected by variations in educational practices. They are not necessarily the most likely to be true, but they illustrate how a broad range of background factors may be adduced in asserting their domination of educational outcomes.

None of this means that schools do not or cannot affect outcomes, but it does imply that factors outside of the schools have a strong influence on students' educational outcomes, perhaps strong enough to "swamp" the effects of variations in educational practices. This is the important point: Are our educational problems school problems? The most profitable line of attack on these educational problems, under this hypothesis, may not be through the schools at all. But we have very little knowledge how and to what extent educational outcomes are affected by nonschool factors. We can only observe that there is considerable evidence that nonschool factors are closely associated with students' educational outcomes. The best information we have, regardless of the deficiencies we have noted, is that schools do not now have a tremendous impact on the achievement that does occur. Therefore, it is logical to infer that the whole substantive area of nonschool learning deserves much more attention than it has received from past research.

Interaction

There is some (weak) evidence that the impact of an educational practice may be conditional on other aspects of the situation.[10] Simply stated, this hypothesis argues that teacher, student, instructional method, and, perhaps, other aspects of the educational process interact with each other. Thus, a teacher who works well (is effective) with one type of student using one method may accomplish far less when working with a different type of student, even if using the same instructional method. Accordingly, the effectiveness of a teacher, or method, or whatever, may vary from one situation to another.

The important point to be made is that research has not discovered an educational practice that is consistently effective because no educational practice always "works" regardless of other aspects of the educational situation. Interaction may explain why educational research has thus far failed to identify any educational practice that is consistently effective. There may not be any *universally* effective educational practices.

Thus far, teachers (or students) are generally viewed as interchangeable within broad constraints. Educators voice concern if, say, a sixth-grade teacher is asked to teach the third grade, or if a science teacher is assigned to an English class. But if a sixth-grade teacher is teaching sixth graders, few have asked whether that teacher would be more effective if assigned to teach a different set of students. If interaction in fact exists, it may be possible to assign teachers to students so that each teacher (and student) is working with the particular type of student (and teacher) with whom he or she is particularly effective. Thus, the concept of interaction should be viewed as not only a potential explanation of our inability to identify consistently effective educational practices but also as a prospective path toward improving educational outcomes.

We must emphasize that we now know very little about interactions. There have been few attempts to examine interactions, and there is some controversy among educational psychologists as to whether interactions actually exist. Most of the evidence for the existence of interactions comes from ex post rationalization of research results. That is, some researchers, confronted with unexpected results in their analyses, have reviewed their data to "see what happened" and "discovered" that there was interaction among student, teacher, method, or whatever. The possibility that any given teacher may be more or less effective when working with one group of students than when working with another is too important to overlook and is therefore another priority field for research.

Different Forms of Education

Finally, there is a suggestion that substantial improvement in educational outcomes can be obtained only through a vastly different form of education. Those who argue this hypothesis question whether the educational system, as currently constituted in the United States, can be substantially improved. It is seen, at the extreme, as being a bureaucratic, rigid, unresponsive structure that no amount of marginal change can improve. Both the organizational approach and the experiential approach argue for this hypothesis.

In some cases, critics of the system focus on the organization of the school's basic unit, the classroom. They argue that traditional instructional practices fail to capitalize on children's natural curiosity and interest in learning. Team teaching, the use of audio-visual aids, and other instructional methods make little difference, according to these critics, so long as the child is forced to devote his attention to the teacher's choice of topics. Open schools, schools without walls, and the like, are seen as being the solution.

Other critics have found fault with the incentive structure in the schools. They argue that rewards and penalties are distributed among teachers and administrators according to implicit rules that emphasize factors unrelated to educational effectiveness. Those who share this perspective tend to argue for systems in which incentives are directly tied to educational outcomes, such as voucher systems, performance contracting, and so on.

Research tells us little about how effective these vastly different forms of education might be.[11] They are novel systems that have been only sparingly put into practice, if at all. And there is certainly a possibility that they may prove to be much less effective than the current system. Large-scale experiments or demonstrations of these vastly different forms of education should be implemented and carefully observed and evaluated.

Where Do We Go from Here? The Methodological Issues

The policy results also raise another issue: What kind of research is now possible and worth doing? To begin, we consider this issue for each approach separately; then we raise the question of what is now needed to create real policy analysis for education. First, with respect to the input-output approach, only one of the studies analyzed (Hanushek, 1970) was able to match student achievement with resources—in particular, teachers—to which the students were actually exposed. (Ordinarily, student achievement is matched to *average* school resources.) This study found that teachers make a difference (for ethnic majority students), but it was unable to identify *what qualities* of a teacher make a difference. Thus, some research should be devoted to pushing this enterprise further. But this means that more resources will have to flow into creating new data. None of the currently used and widely analyzed data sets—EEOS, Talent, Plowden—enable the investigator to match individual achievement with individual resources.

For the process approach it is important to pin down the interaction effects. This will require complex experimental designs. We also believe that it is important to work on translating promising research and development results into the operating classroom. This will mean a much closer scrutiny of the R&D experiments themselves and of the means of disseminating and evaluating results.

The organizational approach is one of the least rigorous and robust. The kinds of questions we want answered about educational organizations need to be expressed more clearly, and the sampling procedures need to be improved. A balance must be struck between the in-depth richness provided by small samples and the generalizability provided by large ones. The organizational approach had a close relation to alternative financial structures. It is hard to influence the choice of processes or resources within schools or classrooms from outside without creating massive problems of control. It may be possible to influence educational organizations through new financial schemes, but the organizational approach has as yet not identified effective methods for applying that influence.

The evaluation approach is the most policy-oriented of those considered here. Therein lies its greatest strength and also its greatest weakness. In large program evaluations, across many individual projects, the basic question to be answered is, to what extent was the program successful in general? Thus, large-scale evaluations tend to lump together individually successful and unsuccessful projects to arrive at a general conclusion about program effectiveness. This general assessment provides an estimate of what would happen if the program were implemented elsewhere, which is extremely useful to know. On the other hand, large program evaluations are seldom sufficiently detailed to explain why some projects succeeded while others failed. But this is, perhaps, the more important information. Evaluators clearly must pay much more attention to the differences between successful and unsuccessful projects within programs. If these differences can be identified and understood, the successful projects should be used as models for further within-program development.

We feel that the books and articles that make up the reform literature have provided insights rather than answers. These insights must be checked, verified, refined, and extended. We need to develop methods of analysis that will allow us to distinguish the effects of the ways in which schools are organized, the way in which a particular school is organized, and the personalities of a particular set of individuals. Thus, an elementary school teacher may tell us that the children in her school are brutalized. We have to be able to determine whether or not this situation stems from the underlying structure of our schools. Does the way in which we go about providing elementary education "build in" incentives that stimulate such treatment? Or, alternatively, does this situation come about because of a way a particular school or school district is structured? Or is this behavior a function of the types of people that happen to staff that particular school? In short, the reform literature describes the pathology of the schools. Is this pathology idiosyncratic, or applicable to a wide range of schools? Can the prescriptions of the reformers be translated into operational planning and generalized to a wide range of schools? If they can, would their prescriptions be acceptable to the clientele of the American education system—in other words, to all of us? There is, after all, substantial evidence that most Americans think the schools do pretty well now. If major increases in effectiveness require fundamental restructuring of education, then effective reform might be unacceptable to the public even if costs were thereby reduced. We believe three things are needed in educational policy analysis. *First*, it will be necessary to merge the various research approaches. If economists want to fit educational "production functions," they will have to revamp the approach completely to include in their models specific processes and organizational factors that affect students, as well as interaction effects. The failures of the input-output approach are, in fact, causing everyone to look more deeply at fundamental assumptions about education. And so the economists find themselves face to face with the psychologists and educators, being forced into a detailed analysis of what goes on in schools and classrooms. *Second*, we simply must measure education in relation to many more outcomes and dimensions (including time) than is currently being done. More resources must be devoted to designing new measures and instruments, and research will have to focus on outcomes over time. Organizationally, this implies some permanent institutional arrangement that will keep the long-run research policy relevant. *Third*, cost considerations must be brought into analyses. We are almost certainly overlooking many opportunities to redirect scarce educational resources effectively and will continue to do so until a firm base of cost-effectiveness research is built.

We have consciously avoided any explicit discussion of the aims of education for two reasons: A study of those aims was not part of our charter; furthermore, since such a study would rely ultimately on personal values, the researcher is no more competent than any other citizen to solve these issues.

Yet as James has said (1971):

We have been notably unsuccessful as a society in this century in stating our aims of education. The prospect of allowing ourselves to be pressured by narrow concerns, driven by casual circumstances—like our rather uncritical embrace of "accountability"—to set trivial goals for our educational institutions is appalling. We desperately need, for the long range, not to preoccupy ourselves with the trivial, but to shape our goals to fit our broadest perception of the needs of human life, and to challenge our model-builders to reach toward them, and to be critical of failures to reach them.

Our review here of what is known about educational effectiveness is a first short step to responding to that challenge, by identifying the limitations of our present knowledge and methods and pointing out possible paths toward improvement. The larger task set forth by James can come only from interdisciplinary efforts of an intensity, breadth, and continuity heretofore unknown, but not by that token unattainable.

NOTES

1. See, for example, Light and Smith (1971).
2. In theory, external validity could rest on acquiring new, unanalyzed data on exactly the variables considered in any given study. In practice, this would be very costly. For example, few would now advocate a replication of the Coleman survey. So the test of interstudy consistency becomes ad hoc. Do studies that address the same question with somewhat different variables and somewhat different data suggest that the same inputs are important? If so, then those who use the input-output approach say there is a case that the same kinds of resources determine the same kinds of outputs. But they can never be sure.
3. We emphasize that this is an assumption. We are aware of no empirical evidence that students' outcomes are related to the responsiveness of their school. It does, however, seem a reasonable thing to believe.
4. Although case studies flourish in educational research and elsewhere, evaluations of the methods are very difficult to find. But see Bock (1962).
5. The why or how of an intervention is often presumed in that the intervention was originally justified by a hypothesis as to why the intervention could be expected to "work." If it then does (or does not) "work" there is a tendency to assume that the hypothesis was (or was not) valid.
6. Note that we do not ask whether a study has a proper experimental design. If it had, it would have been included in the process approach.
7. The writer's triple role as observer, participant, and social critic necessarily places heavy pressure on his objectivity in describing the phenomena he observes. Nonetheless, there seems to be considerable agreement among writers with respect to description.
8. This conclusion applies only to questions of educational effectiveness as now measured. It cannot be applied to justify situations in which constant or decreasing expenditures would impair the health or safety of children and staff.
9. See Levien (1971) for a discussion of the current state of educational research.
10. See, for example, Thelen (1967).
11. But see Carpenter and Hall (1971).

REFERENCES

Adelson, J. "Personality." *Annual Review of Psychology* 20 (1969): 217–252.
Allen, D. I. "Some Effects of Advance Organizers and Level of Questions on the Learning and Retention of Written Social Studies Material." *Journal of Educational Psychology* 61 (1970): 333–339.
Allen, W. H. "Instructional Media Research: Past, Present and Future." *Audio-Visual Communications Review* 29 (1971): 5–18.
Anastasi, A. "Psychology, Psychologists, and Psychological Testing." *American Psychologist* 22 (1967): 297–306.
Anderson, James G. *Bureaucracy in Education.* Baltimore: Johns Hopkins Press, 1968.
Anderson, R. C. "Educational Psychology." *Annual Review of Psychology* 18 (1967): 103–164.

Angoff, W. H. "Scales, Norms, and Equivalent Scores." In *Educational Measurement*, edited by R. L. Thorndike, pp. 508–600. Washington, D.C.: American Council on Education, 1971.

Ashton-Warner, S. "Organic Teaching." In *Radical School Reform*, edited by B. Gross and R. Gross. New York: Simon and Schuster, 1969.

Ausubel, D. P. *The Psychology of Meaningful Verbal Learning*. New York: Grune & Stratton, 1963.

————. "An Evaluation of the Conceptual Scheme Approach to Science Curriculum Development." *Journal of Research in Scientific Teaching* 3 (1965): 255–264.

Averch, Harvey, and Kiesling, Herbert. "The Relationship of School and Environment to Student Performance: Some Simultaneous Models for the Project TALENT High Schools." Mimeographed. Santa Monica: The Rand Corporation, 1970.

Barbrack, Christopher R., and Horton, Della M. "Educational Intervention in the Home and Paraprofessional Career Development: A Second-Generation Mother Study with an Emphasis on Costs and Benefits." *DARCEE Papers and Reports* 4, no. 4 (1970).

Barth, R. S. "So You Want to Change to an Open Classroom." *Phi Delta Kappan* 53 (October 1971): 97–99.

Beller, E. Kuno. "The Evaluation of Effects of Early Educational Intervention on Intellectual and Social Development of Lower-class Disadvantaged Children." In *Critical Issues in Research Related to Disadvantaged Children*, edited by E. Grotberg. Princeton: Educational Testing Service, 1969.

Benson, Charles, et al. *State and Local Fiscal Relationships in Public Education in California*, Report of the Senate Fact Finding Committee on Revenue and Taxation, Senate of the State of California, Sacramento, March 1965.

Bereiter, C., and Engelmann, S. *Teaching Disadvantaged Children in the Preschool*. Englewood Cliffs: Prentice-Hall, 1966.

————. *Academic Preschool, Champaign, Illinois*. "It Works" series, Preschool Programs in Compensatory Education I. Washington, D.C.: Office of Education, 1969 (OE 37041).

Berg, Ivar. *Education and Jobs: The Great Training Robbery*. New York: Praeger, 1970.

Berger, Barbara. *A Longitudinal Investigation of Montessori and Traditional Prekindergarten Training with Inner City Children: A Comparative Assessment of Learning Outcomes. Three Part Study*. New York: Center for Urban Education, 1969 (ED 034 588).

Bissell, Joan S. "The Cognitive Effects of Preschool Programs for Disadvantaged Children." Ph.D. dissertation, Harvard University, 1970.

————. "Implementation of Planned Variation in Head Start: Part 1, First Year Report—Review and Summary." Mimeographed. Washington, D.C.: Department of Health, Education, and Welfare, 1971.

Bloom, B. S.; Hastings, T. J.; and Madaus, G. F. *Handbook on Formative and Summative Evaluation of Student Evaluation of Student Learning*. New York: McGraw-Hill, 1971.

Bock, E. A., ed. *Essays on the Case Method*. Inter-University Case Program. New York: International Institute of Administrative Sciences, 1962.

Bormuth, J. R. *On the Theory of Achievement Test Items*. Chicago: University of Chicago Press, 1970.

Bowles, Samuel. *Educational Production Function*. Final Report, U.S. Department of Health, Education, and Welfare, Office of Education, OEC–1–7–000451–2651, ED 037 590. Cambridge: Harvard University, February 1969.

————, and Levin, Henry M. "More on Multicollinearity and the Effectiveness of Schools." *Journal of Human Resources* 3, no. 3 (Summer 1968): 393–400.
————. "The Determinants of Scholastic Achievement—An Appraisal of Some Recent Evidence." *Journal of Human Resources* 3, no. 1 (Winter 1968): 2–24.
Brophy, J. E., and Good, T.L. "Teacher's Communication of Differential Expectations for Children's Classroom Performance." *Journal of Educational Psychology* 61 (1970): 365–374.
Brownell, W. A., and Moses, A. G. "Meaningful Versus Mechanical Learning: A Study in Grade Three Subtraction." Duke University Research Studies in Education, no. 8. Durham: Duke University Press, 1949.
Burkhead, Jesse; Fox, Thomas G.; and Holland, John W. *Input and Output in Large City High Schools.* Syracuse: Syracuse University Press, 1967.
Burton, B. B., and Goldberg, R. A. *The Effect of Response Characteristics in Multiple Life and Choice Alternatives on Learning During Programmed Instruction.* San Mateo, Calif.: American Institute for Research, 1962.
Butler, A. L. *Current Research in Early Childhood Education.* Washington, D.C.: E/K/N/E, NEA Center, 1970.
Cain, Glen, and Watts, Harold. *Problems in Making Policy Inferences from the Coleman Report.* Madison: Institute for Research on Poverty, University of Wisconsin, 1968.
Campbell, D. T., and Erlebacher, A. "How Regression Artifacts in Quasiexperimental Evaluation Can Mistakenly Make Compensatory Education Look Harmful." In *Disadvantaged Child,* vol. 3, edited by J. Hellmuth, pp. 185–211. New York: Brunner/Mazel, 1970.
Carpenter, Polly, and Hall, George R. *Case Studies in Educational Performance Contracting: Conclusions and Implications,* R-900/1-HEW. Santa Monica: The Rand Corporation, December 1971.
Center for Educational Policy Research. "Education and Inequality." Mimeographed. Cambridge: Harvard Graduate School of Education, 1971.
Chomsky, N. "Review of Verbal Behavior." *Language* 35 (1959): 26–58.
Chu, G. C., and Schramm, W. *Learning from Television.* Stanford: Institute for Communications Research, Stanford University, 1967.
Cicirelli, V. G., et al. *The Impact of Head Start: An Evaluation of the Effects of Head Start on Children's Cognitive and Affective Development.* Washington, D.C.: Office of Economic Opportunity, 1969.
Coffman, W. E. "Essay Examinations." In *Educational Measurement,* edited by R. L. Thorndike, pp. 271–302. Washington, D.C.: American Council on Education, 1971.
Cohen, D. K. "Politics and Research: Evaluation of Social Action Programs in Education." *Review of Educational Research* 40 (1970): 213–238.
Cohn, Elchanan. "Economics of Scale in Iowa High School Operations." *Journal of Human Resources* 3 (Fall 1968): 422–434.
Coleman, James S., et al. "Pupil Achievement and Motivation." In *Equality of Educational Opportunity,* chap. 3, pp. 218–333. Washington, D.C.: U.S. Department of Health, Education, and Welfare, U.S. Office of Education, OE–38001, 1966.
————. *The Evaluation of Equality of Educational Opportunity.* P–3911. Santa Monica: The Rand Corporation, August 1968.
————, and Karweit, Nancy L. *Measures of School Performance.* R–488–RC. Santa Monica: The Rand Corporation, July 1970.
Corey, S. N. "The Nature of Instruction." In *Programmed Instruction,* edited by P. C. Lang, pp. 5–27. Chicago: University of Chicago Press, 1967.
Crain, R. L. *The Politics of School Desegregation.* Chicago: Aldine, 1968.

Cronbach, L. J. "The Two Disciplines of Scientific Psychology." *American Psychology* 12 (1957): 671–684.

——. "The Logic of Experiments on Discovery." In *Learning by Discovery: A Critical Appraisal*, edited by L. S. Shulman and E. R. Keisler. Skokie, Ill.: Rand McNally, 1966.

——. *Essentials of Psychological Testing*. New York: Harper & Row, 1970.

——, and Furby, L. "How Should We Measure 'Change'—or Should We?" *Psychology Bulletin* 74 (1970): 68–80.

Cronbach, L. J., and Snow, R. E. *Final Report: Individual Differences in Learning Ability as a Function of Instructional Variables*. Stanford: Stanford University, 1969.

Dahlstrom, W. G. "Personality." *Annual Review of Psychology* 21 (1970): 1–48.

Deese, J. "Behavior and Fact." *American Psychology* 24 (1969): 515–522.

Dellas, M., and Gaier, E. L. "Identification of Creativity: The Individual." *Psychology Bulletin* 73 (1970): 55–73.

Denenberg, V. H., ed. *Education of the Infant and Young Child*. New York: Academic Press, 1970.

Dennison, George. *The Lives of Children*. New York: Random House, 1969.

DiLorenzo, Louis T. *Prekindergarten Programs for Disadvantaged Children*. New York State Education Department, Albany, Final Report to Office of Education, 1969 (ED 038 460).

Education of the Disadvantaged: An Evaluation Report on Title I Elementary and Secondary Education Act of 1965, Fiscal Year 1968. Washington, D.C.: U.S. Department of Health, Education, and Welfare, Office of Education, 1970 (HE5-237:37013-68).

Elkind, D., and Sameroff, A. "Developmental Psychology." *Annual Review of Psychology* 21 (1970): 191–238.

Engelmann, S. "The Effectiveness of Direct Instruction on IQ Performance and Achievement in Reading and Arithmetic." In *Disadvantaged Child*, vol. 3, edited by J. Hellmuth. New York: Brunner/Mazel, 1970.

Etzioni, A. "Essay Review of *Crisis in the Classroom* by C. E. Silberman." *Harvard Educational Review*, February 1971, pp. 87–96.

Featherstone, J. "The British Infant Schools." In *Radical School Reform*, edited by B. Gross and R. Gross, pp. New York: Simon and Schuster, 1969.

——. *Schools Where Children Learn*. New York: Liveright, 1971.

Ferguson, G. A. "Human Abilities." *Annual Review of Psychology* 16 (1965): 39–61.

Flavell, J. H., and Hill, J. P. "Developmental Psychology." *Annual Review of Psychology* 20 (1969): 1–56.

Fleishman, E. A., and Bartlett, C. J. "Human Abilities." *Annual Review of Psychology* 20 (1969): 349–380.

Fox, Thomas G. "School System Resource Use in Production of Interdependent Educational Outputs." Mimeographed. Denver: The Joint National Meeting, American Astronautical Society and Operations Research Society, 1969.

Friedenberg, Edgar Z. *Coming of Age in America*. New York: Random House, 1963.

Fresno, California, Preschool Program. "It Works" series, Preschool Programs in Compensatory Education I. Washington, D.C.: Office of Education, 1969, p. 109 (OE-37034).

Gagné, R. M. "The Acquisition of Knowledge." *Psychological Review* 69 (1962): 355–365.

——. "Contributions of Learning to Human Development." *Psychological Review* 75 (1968): 177–191.

——, ed. *Learning and Individual Differences*. Columbus, Ohio: Merrill, 1967.

————, and Rohwer, W. D. Jr. "Instructional Psychology." *Annual Review of Psychology* 20 (1969): 381–418.

Garrett, M., and Fodor, J. A. "Psychological Theories and Linguistic Constructs." In *Verbal Behavior and General Behavior Theory,* edited by T. R. Dixon and D. L. Horton, pp. 451–477. Englewood Cliffs: Prentice-Hall, 1968.

Getzel, J. W., and Jackson, P. W. "The Teacher's Personality and Characteristics." In *Handbook of Research on Teaching,* edited by N. L. Gage, pp. 506–582. Chicago: Rand McNally, 1963.

Gintis, H. "Education, Technology, and the Characteristics of Worker Productivity." *The American Economic Review* 61 (1971): 266–279.

Gittell, M., and Hollander, T. E. *Six Urban School Districts.* New York: Praeger, 1967.

Glaser, R., and Nitko, A. J. "Measurement in Learning and Instruction." In *Educational Measurement,* edited by R. L. Thorndike. Washington, D.C.: American Council on Education, 1970.

Glass, Gene V., et al. "Education of the Disadvantaged: An Evaluation Report on Title I, Elementary and Secondary Education Act of 1965, Fiscal Year 1969." Mimeographed. Boulder: University of Colorado, 1970.

Goodlad, J. I. "Curriculum: State of the Field." *Review of Education Research* 39 (1969): 367–375.

Goodman, Paul. *Growing Up Absurd.* New York: Vintage, 1965.

————. *The New Reformation.* New York: Random House, 1970.

Gordon, Edmund W. "Utilizing Available Information from Compensatory Education and Surveys." Final Report. Washington, D.C.: Office of Education, 1971.

Gordon, Ira. *A Parent Education Approach to Provision of Early Stimulation for the Culturally Disadvantaged.* Gainesville: University of Florida, 1967 (ED 017 339).

————. *Child Stimulation Through Parent Education.* Gainesville: Institute for the Development of Human Resources, University of Florida. Final Report to Children's Bureau, Department of Health, Education, and Welfare, 1969 (ED 033 912).

Gotkin, L. G., and McSweeney, J. F. "Learning from Teaching Machines." In *Programmed Instruction,* edited by P. C. Lang, pp. 255–283. Chicago: University of Chicago Press, 1967.

Gough, H. G., and Fink, M. B. "Scholastic Achievement Among Students of Average Ability as Predicted from the California Psychological Inventory." *Psychology in the Schools* 1 (1964): 375–380.

Gray, Susan W., and Klaus, Rupert A. "An Experimental Preschool Program for Culturally Deprived Children." *Child Development* 36, no. 4 (1965): 887–898.

————. "The Early Training Project." *Monographs of the Society for Research in Child Development* 33 (1968).

————. "The Early Training Project: A Seventh Year Report." *Child Development* 41, no. 4 (1970): 908–924.

Gross, N., and Herriott, R. E. *Staff Leadership in Public Schools.* New York: Wiley, 1965.

Gross, Ronald, and Gross, Beatrice, eds. *Radical School Reform.* New York: Simon and Schuster, 1969.

Grotelueschen, A., and Sjorgren, D. D. "Effects of Differentially Structured Introductory Material, and Learning Tasks on Learning and Transfer." *American Educational Research Journal* 2 (1968): 191–202.

Guilford, J. P. *The Nature of Human Intelligence.* New York: McGraw-Hill, 1967.

Guthrie, James W.; Kleindorfer, George B.; Levin, Henry M.; and Stout, Robert T. *Schools and Inequality*. Cambridge: M.I.T. Press, 1971.

Hanley, E. M. "Review of Research Involving Applied Behavior Analysis in the Classroom." *Review of Educational Research* 40 (1970): 597–625.

Hanushek, Eric. "The Education of Negroes and Whites." Ph.D. dissertation, Massachusetts Institute of Technology, 1968.

————. *The Value of Teachers in Teaching*. RM–6362–CC/RC. Santa Monica: The Rand Corporation, December 1970.

Harris, A. J. "The Effective Teacher of Reading." *The Reading Teacher* 23 (December 1969): 194–204, 238.

Harris, C. W., ed. *Problems in Measuring Change*. Madison: University of Wisconsin Press, 1963.

Harsh, J. Richard. "Problems of Measuring Student Gain." In *A Guide to Performance Contracting: Technical Appendix*, edited by Sue A. Haggart, G. C. Summer, and J. Richard Harsh. R–955/2–HEW. Santa Monica: The Rand Corporation, 1972.

Hartup, W. W., and Yonas, A. "Developmental Psychology." *Annual Review of Psychology* 22 (1971): 169–392.

Havighurst, R. J. *The Public Schools of Chicago*. Chicago: The Board of Education, 1964.

Hawkridge, David G.; Chalupsky, Albert B.; and Roberts, A. O. *A Study of Selected Exemplary Programs for the Education of Disadvantaged Children*. Palo Alto, Calif.: American Institutes for Research, Final Report to Office of Education, Parts I, II, 1968 (ED 023 776, ED 023 777).

Hawkridge, David; Campeau, P. L.; De Witt, K. M.; and Trickett, P. K. *A Study of Further Exemplary Programs for the Education of Disadvantaged Children*. Palo Alto, Calif.: American Institute for Research. Final Report to Office of Education, 1969 (ED 036 668).

Heckhausen, H. *The Anatomy of Achievement Motivation*. New York: Academic Press, 1967.

Hellmuth, J., ed. *Disadvantaged Child*, vol. 3. New York: Brunner/Mazel, 1970.

Henry, Jules. *Culture Against Man*. New York: Random House, 1963.

Herndon, James. *The Way It Spozed to Be*. New York: Simon and Schuster, 1968.

————. *How to Survive in Your Native Land*. New York: Simon and Schuster, 1971.

Heron, M. D. "The Nature of Scientific Enquiry as Seen by Selected Philosophers, Science Teachers, and Recent Curricular Materials." Ph.D. dissertation, University of Chicago, 1969.

Hodges, W.; Spicker, H.; and McCandless, B. "The Development and Evaluation of a Diagnostically Based Curriculum for Preschool Psychosocially Deprived Children." Washington, D.C.: Office of Education, 1966.

————. "The Development and Evaluation of a Diagnostically Based Curriculum for Preschool Psycho-socially Deprived Children." Final Report to Office of Education, Washington, D.C., 1967.

————. *Diagnostically Based Curriculum, Bloomington, Indiana*. "It Works" series, Preschool Programs in Compensatory Education. Washington, D.C.: Office of Education, 1969 (OE 37024).

Hoepfner, Ralph, ed. *CSE Elementary School Test Evaluation*. Los Angeles: Center for the Study of Evaluation, UCLA Graduate School of Education, 1970.

Holt, John. *What Do I Do on Monday?* New York: Dutton, 1970.

Holtzman, W. H. "The Changing World of Mental Measurement and Its Social Significance." *American Psychologist* 26 (1971): 546–553.

Illich, Ivan. *Deschooling Society*. New York: Harper & Row, 1971.

James, H. Thomas. Excerpt from the preliminary report to the National Academy of Education's Executive Council meeting, May 6, 1971, on the feasibility of an Academy task force to explore the reporting of performance by educational institutions.

————; Kelly, J. A.; and Garms, W. I. *Determinants of Educational Expenditures in the United States.* Washington, D.C.: Cooperative Research Project 2389, U.S. Department of Health, Education, and Welfare, Office of Education, 1966.

Jamison, D., et al. "Cost and Performance of Computer-assisted Instruction for Compensatory Education." National Bureau for Economic Research, Conference on Education as an Industry, June 1971.

Jencks, Christopher. "The Coleman Report and the Conventional Wisdom." In *On Equality of Educational Opportunity,* edited by F. Mosteller and D. P. Moynihan. New York: Vintage, 1972.

Jensen, A. R. "How Much Can We Boost IQ and Scholastic Achievement?" *Harvard Educational Review* 39 (1969).

————. "Another Look at Culture Fair Testing." In *Disadvantaged Child,* vol. 3, edited by J. Hellmuth, pp. 53–101. New York: Brunner/Mazel, 1970.

Kagan, J. "On Class Differences and Early Development." In *Education of the Infant and Young Child,* edited by V. H. Denenberg, pp. 5–24. New York: Academic Press, 1970.

Karnes, M. "Research and Development Project on Preschool Disadvantaged Children." Washington, D.C.: Office of Education, 1969a.

————. *The Ameliorative Preschool Program, Champaign, Illinois.* "It Works" series, Preschool Programs in Compensatory Education. Washington, D.C.: Office of Education, 1969b (OE 37054).

————.; Teska, J. A.; and Hodgins, A. S. "A Longitudinal Study of Disadvantaged Children Who Participated in Three Different Preschool Programs. Mimeographed. Urbana: University of Illinois, 1970.

Karraker, R. J., and Doke, L. A. "Errorless Discrimination of Alphabet Letters: Effects of Time and Method of Introducing Competing Stimuli." *Journal of Experimental Education* 38 (1970): 27–35.

Katzman, Martin T. "Distribution and Production in a Big City Elementary School System." *Yale Economic Essays* 8 (Spring 1968): 201–256.

Kiesling, Herbert J. "Measuring a Local Government Service: A Study of School Districts in New York State." *Review of Economics and Statistics* 49, no. 3 (August 1967): 356–367.

————. *The Relationship of School Inputs to Public School Performance in New York State.* P-4211. Santa Monica: The Rand Corporation, October 1969.

————. *A Study of Cost and Quality of New York School Districts.* Washington, D.C.: U.S. Department of Health, Education, and Welfare, Office of Education, 8-0264, February 1970a.

————. "A Study of Successful Compensatory Education Programs in California." Mimeographed. Santa Monica: The Rand Corporation, 1970b.

————. *Input and Output in Compensatory Education Projects in California.* R-781-CC/RC. Santa Monica: The Rand Corporation, October 1971a.

————. *Multi-variate Analysis of Schools and Educational Policy.* P-4595. Santa Monica: The Rand Corporation, March 1971b.

Klein, G. S.; Barr, H. L.; and Wolitzky, D. L. "Personality." *Annual Review of Psychology* 18 (1967): 465–560.

Klein, S. P. "The Uses and Limitations of Standardized Tests in Meeting the Demands for Accountability." *UCLA Evaluation Comment,* Center for the Study of Evaluation, 2, no. 4 (January 1971).

Kohl, H. "Can One Survive?" *The Teacher Paper*, October 1971, pp. 10–11.

Kohlberg, L. "Early Education: A Cognitive Developmental View." *Child Development* 39 (1968): 1013–1062.

Kozol, Jonathan. *Death at an Early Age.* Boston: Houghton Mifflin, 1968.

Lambie, D. J., and Weikart, D. P. "Ypsilanti Carnegie Infant Education Project." In *Disadvantaged Child*, vol. 3, edited by J. Hellmuth. New York: Brunner/Mazel, 1970.

Lange, P. C., ed. *Programmed Instruction.* 66th Yearbook of the National Society for the Study of Education, Part II. Chicago: University of Chicago Press, 1967.

Leggett, T. "The Use of Non-Professionals in Large City Systems." In *Innovation in Mass Education*, edited by D. Street, pp. 177–200. New York: Wiley-Interscience, 1969.

Lennon, R. T. "Accountability and Performance Contracting." Address to the American Educational Research Association, New York City, February 5, 1971.

Levien, Roger E. *National Institute of Education: Preliminary Plan for the Proposed Institute.* R-657-HEW. Santa Monica: The Rand Corporation, February 1971.

Levin, Henry M. *Community Control of Schools.* Washington, D.C.: Brookings, 1970a.

———. "A New Model of School Effectiveness." In *How Do Teachers Make a Difference*, pp. 55–75. Washington, D.C.: U.S. Department of Health, Education, and Welfare, Office of Education, Bureau of Educational Personnel Development (OE-58042), 1970b.

———. "Concepts of Economic Efficiency and Educational Production." NBER Conference on Education as an Industry, June 4–5, 1971.

Light, Richard J., and Smith, Paul N. "Accumulating Evidence: Procedures for Resolving Contradictions Among Different Research Studies." *Harvard Educational Review* 41 (1971): 429–471.

Los Angeles City Schools. "Evaluation ESEA Title I, 1979–1970." Technical Reports, 1970.

Macorie, Kenneth. *Up Taught.* New York: Hayden, 1970.

Maier, M., and Jacobs, P. B. "The Effects of Variations in a Self-instructional Program on Instructional Outcomes." *Psychology Reports* 18 (1966): 539–546.

Martin, Ruby, and McClure, Phyllis. *Title I of ESEA: Is It Helping Poor Children?* Washington Research Project of the Southern Center for Studies in Public Policy and the NAACP Legal Defense and Educational Fund, Inc., 1969.

Mason, W. A. "Early Deprivation in Biological Perspective." In *Education of the Infant and Young Child*, edited by V. H. Denenberg. New York: Academic Press, 1970.

Mayeske, George W., et al. *A Study of Our Nation's Schools.* Washington, D.C.: Department of Health, Education, and Welfare, 1969.

McCracken, Samuel. "Quackery in the Classroom." *Commentary*, June 1970.

Merrill, M.D. "Correction and Review on Successive Parts in Becoming a Hierarchical Task." *Journal of Educational Psychology* 56 (1965): 225–234.

———; Barton, K.; and Wood, L. E. "Specific Review in Learning a Hierarchical Imaginary Science." *Journal of Educational Psychology* 61 (1970): 102–109.

Merrill, M.D., and Stolurow, L. M. "Hierarchical Preview Versus Problem Oriented Review in Becoming an Imaginary Science." *Journal of American Educational Research* 3 (1966): 251–261.

Michelson, Stephan. "The Association of Teacher Resourceness with Children's Characteristics." In *How Do Teachers Make A Difference*, pp. 120–168. Washington, D.C.: U.S. Department of Health, Education, and Welfare, Office of Education, Bureau of Educational Personnel Development (OE-58042), 1970.

Miller, Louise B., and Dyer, Jean L. *Experimental Variation of Head Start Cur-*

ricula: A Comparison of Current Approaches. Child Development Laboratory, University of Louisville, Annual Progress Report to OEO, 1970 and 1971.

Mollenkopf, William G., and Melville, S. Donald. *A Study of Secondary School Characteristics as Related to Test Scores.* Princeton: Research Bulletin RB-56-6, Educational Testing Service, 1956.

Mosbaek, E. J., et al. "Analyses of Compensatory Education in Five School Districts: Summary." Mimeographed. Santa Barbara: TEMPO, General Electric Co., 1968.

Mosteller, Frederick, and Moynihan, Daniel P., eds. *On Equality of Educational Opportunity.* New York: Vintage, 1972.

Nitko, A. J. "A Model for Criterion-Referenced Tests Based on Use." Paper presented at the Annual Meeting of the American Educational Research Association, New York, February 4–7, 1971.

Oakland, California, Preschool Program. "It Works" series, Preschool Programs in Compensatory Education, I. Washington, D.C.: Office of Education, 1969.

Picariello, Harry. "Evaluation of Title I." Mimeographed. Washington, D.C.: American Institute for the Advancement of Science, n.d.

Piland, J. C., and Lemke, E. A. "The Effect of Ability Grouping on Concept Learning." *Journal of Educational Research* 64 (1971): 209–212.

Postman, Neil, and Weingartner, C. *Teaching as a Subversive Activity.* New York: Delacorte, 1969.

Pressey, S. J. "Teaching Machines (and Learning Theory) Crises." *Journal of Applied Psychology* 47 (1963): 1–6.

Project Head Start 1968: A Descriptive Report of Programs and Participants. Washington, D.C.: Office of Child Development, U.S. Department of Health, Education, and Welfare, 1970.

Rapp, M. L.; Carpenter, M. B.; Haggart, S. A.; Landa, S. H.; and Sumner, G. C. *Project R–3, San Jose, Calif.: Evaluation of Results and Development of a Cost Model.* R–672–SJS. Santa Monica: The Rand Corporation, March 1971.

Raymond, Richard. "Determinants of the Quality of Primary and Secondary Public Education in West Virginia." *Journal of Human Resources* 3, no. 4 (Fall 1968): 450–469.

Rist, R. C. "Student Social Class and Teacher Expectations: The Self-Fulfilling Prophecy in Ghetto Education." *Harvard Educational Review* 40 (1970): 411–451.

Rogers, David. *110 Livingston Street: Politics and Bureaucracy in the New York Schools.* New York: Random House, 1968.

Rohwer, W. D., Jr.; Ammon, M. S.; Suzuki, N.; and Levin, J. R. "Population Differences and Learning Proficiency." *Journal of Educational Psychology* 62 (1971): 1–14.

Rombert, T. A. "Current Research in Mathematics Education." *Review of Education Research* 39 (1969): 473–492.

Rosenshine, B. "Evaluation of Instruction." *Review of Educational Research* 40 (1970a): 279–300.

———. "The Stability of Teacher Effects upon Student Achievement." *Review of Educational Research* 40 (1970b): 647–662.

———, and Furst, J. "Current and Future Research on Teacher Performance Criteria." In *Research on Teacher Education: A Symposium,* edited by B. W. Smith. Englewood Cliffs: Prentice-Hall, 1971.

Rosenthal, R., and Jackson L. *Pygmalion in the Classroom: Teacher Expectation and Pupil's Intellectual Development.* New York: Holt, Rinehart and Winston, 1968.

Rusk, Bruce A. *An Evaluation of a Six Week Head Start Program Using an Academically Oriented Curriculum: Canton, 1967.* Canton, Ohio, Public Schools, 1968 (ED 026 114).

Ryder, R. G. "Birth to Maturity Revisited: A Canonical Reanalysis." *Journal of Personality and Social Psychology* 7 (1967): 168–172.

Saettler, P. *A History of Instructional Technology.* New York: McGraw-Hill, 1968.

Samuels, S. J. "Effects of Pictures on Learning to Read, Comprehension and Attitudes." *Review of Educational Research* 40 (1970): 397–407.

Sarason, I. G., and Smith, R. E. "Personality." *Annual Review of Psychology* 20 (1971): 393–446.

Schaefer, Earl S., and Aaronson, May. "Infant Education Research Project: Implementation and Implications of a Home Tutoring Program." In *The Preschool in Action: Exploring Early Childhood Programs,* edited by Ronald K. Parker, pp. 410–434. Boston: Allyn and Bacon, Inc., 1972.

Schwartz, P. A. "Prediction Instruments for Educational Outcomes." In *Educational Measurement,* edited by R. L. Thorndike, pp. 303–331. Washington, D.C.: American Council on Education, 1971.

Shulman, L. S. "Reconstruction of Educational Research." *Review of Educational Research* 40 (1970): 371–396.

————, and Keisler, E. R., eds. *Learning by Discovery: A Critical Appraisal.* Skokie, Ill.: Rand-McNally, 1966.

Silberman, C. E. *Crisis in the Classroom.* New York: Random House, 1970.

Skeels, Harold M. "Adult Status of Children with Contrasting Early Life Experiences: A Follow-up Study." *Monographs of the Society for Research in Child Development* 31, no. 3, serial no. 105. Chicago: University of Chicago Press, 1966.

Skinner, B. G. *The Technology of Teaching.* New York: Appleton-Century-Crofts, 1968.

Smith, H. A. "Curriculum Development and Instructional Materials." *Review of Educational Research* 39 (1969): 397–414.

Smith, Marshall S. "Equality of Educational Opportunity: The Basic Findings Reconsidered." In *On Equality of Educational Opportunity,* edited by F. Mosteller and D. P. Moynihan. New York: Vintage, 1972.

Snow, R. E. "Unfinished Pygmalion." *Contemporary Psychology* 14 (1969): 197–200.

————. "Mental Abilities." *The Encyclopedia of Education.* New York: Macmillan Co. and The Free Press, 1971, pp. 308–309.

Sontag, Marvin; Sella, Adina P.; and Thorndike, Robert L. "The Effect of Head Start Training on the Cognitive Growth of Disadvantaged Children." *Journal of Educational Research* 62, no. 9 (1969): 387–389.

Spicker, Howard H.; Hodges, Walter L.; and McCandless, Boyd R. "A Diagnostically Based Curriculum for Psycho-socially Deprived Preschool, Mentally Retarded Children, Interim Report." *Exceptional Children* 33 (1966): 215–220.

Sprigle, H. A. *Learning to Learn Program, Jacksonville, Florida.* "It Works" series, Preschool Programs in Compensatory Education I. Washington, D.C.: Office of Education, 1969 (OE 37056).

————, and Van der Riet, V. "The Learning to Learn Program." Mimeographed. Report presented to the Carnegie Corporation of New York, 1968.

Stake, R. E. "Objectives, Priorities, and Other Judgmental Data." *Review of Educational Research* 40 (1970): 181–212.

————. "Testing Hazards in Performance Contracting." *Phi Delta Kappan* 12 (1971): 583–589.

Stanford Research Institute. *Longitudinal Evaluation Program.* Menlo Park: Stanford Research Institute, 1971.

―――. *Implementation of Planned Variation in Head Start: Part 2, Preliminary Evaluations of Planned Variations in Head Start According to Follow Through Approaches (1969–1970).* Menlo Park: Stanford Research Institute, 1971.

Stearns, Marian Sherman. "The Effects of Preschool Programs on Children and Their Families." Mimeographed. 1971a.

―――. "Report on Preschool Programs: The Effects of Preschool Programs on Disadvantaged Children and Their Families." Final Report, Mimeographed, 1971b. Washington, D.C.: Office of Child Development (HEW), 1971.

Stephens, J. M. *The Process of Schooling.* New York: Holt, Rinehart and Winston, 1967.

Stodolsky, S. S., and Lesser, G. "Learning Patterns in the Disadvantaged." *Harvard Review of Education* 37 (1967): 546–548.

Thelen, H. A. "Programmed Materials Today: Critique and Proposal." *The Elementary School Review* 64 (1963a): 189–196.

―――. "Programmed Instruction: Insight vs. Conditioning." *Education* 83 (1963b): 416–420.

―――. *Classroom Grouping for Teachability.* New York: Wiley, 1967.

Thomas, James Alan. "Efficiency in Education: A Study of the Relationship Between Selected Inputs and Mean Test Scores in a Sample of Senior High Schools." Microfilmed. Ph.D. dissertation, Stanford University Library, 1962.

Turner, Richard L. *Differential Association of Elementary Teacher Characteristics with School System Types, Final Report.* Project 2579, U.S. Office of Education, September 1968.

―――, and Denny, D. A. "Teacher Characteristics, Teacher Behavior, and Changes in Pupil Creativity." *Elementary School Journal* 62 (1969): 265–270.

United Kingdom Ministry of Education. "Following Their Lead: Exploring the Limits of Freedom." In *Radical School Reform*, edited by B. Gross and R. Gross. New York: Simon and Schuster, 1969.

U.S. Office of Education. "Education of the Disadvantaged: An Evaluative Report on Title I, Elementary and Secondary Education Act of 1965, Fiscal Year 1968." Washington, D.C.: Office of Education, 1970.

Vandenberg, S. G. "Contributions of Twin Research to Psychology." *Psychology Bulletin* 66 (1966): 327–352.

Van der Riet, Vernon; Van der Riet, Hani; and Sprigle, Herbert. "The Effectiveness of a New Sequential Learning Program with Culturally Disadvantaged Preschool Children." *Journal of School Psychology*, 7, no. 3 (1968): 5–15.

Vernon, P. E. "Ability Factors and Environmental Influence." *American Psychology* 20 (1965): 723–733.

Wargo, M. J.; Campeau, P. L.; and Tallmadge, G. K. *Further Examination of Exemplary Programs for Educating Disadvantaged Children.* Palo Alto: American Institutes of Research, 1971.

Weikart, David P., ed. *Preschool Intervention: Preliminary Report of the Perry Preschool Project.* Ann Arbor, Mich.: Campus Publishers, 1967.

―――. *The Ypsilanti Preschool Curriculum Development Project 1968–71.* Ypsilanti, Mich.: High-Scope Educational Research Foundation, 1971a.

―――. "Early Childhood Special Education for Intellectually Subnormal and/or Culturally Different Children." Prepared for the National Leadership Institute in Early Childhood Development, Washington, D.C. Ypsilanti, Mich.: High-Scope Educational Research Foundation, October 1971b.

————, and Lambie, D. Z. "Preschool Intervention Through a Home Teaching Project." In *Disadvantaged Child*, vol. 2, edited by J. Hellmuth. New York: Brunner/Mazel, 1969.

Welch, W. W. "Curriculum Evaluation." *Review of Educational Research* 39 (1969): 429–443.

Westbury, I. "Curriculum Evaluation." *Review of Educational Research* 40 (1970): 239–260.

Westinghouse Learning Corporation. *The Impact of Head Start, an Evaluation of the Effect of Head Start on Children's Cognitive and Affective Development: Vol. I, Text and Appendices A-E.* Ohio University, Report to OEO, Clearinghouse for Federal Scientific and Technical Information, 1969.

Wiggens, J. S. "Personality Structure." *Annual Review of Psychology* 19 (1968): 293–350.

Wolff, Max, and Stein, Annie. "Head Start Six Months Later." *Phi Delta Kappan* 48 (March 1967): 349–350.

Wonnacott, R. S., and Wonnacott, T. H. *Econometrics.* New York: Wiley, 1970.

Wrightstone, J. Wayne, et al. "Evaluation of the Higher Horizons Program for Underprivileged Children." New York: New York City Board of Education, 1964.

Zimiles, Herbert. "Has Evaluation Failed Compensatory Education?" In *Disadvantaged Child*, vol. 3, edited by J. Hellmuth. New York: Brunner/Mazel, 1970.

(4)

Equalizing Education: in Whose Benefit?

Daniel P. Moynihan

A SERIES of recent state and federal court decisions, just now reaching the Supreme Court on appeal, have held that expenditure per pupil in public schools must be equal for all students in any given state, or nearly equal, or in any event not differing in amounts clearly associated with the differing per capita wealth of different school districts. The legal arguments behind these decisions have varied somewhat, but the primary thrust has been that of "equal protection of the laws," with much owing, in almost every case, to the arguments successfully presented to the California Supreme Court in the 1971 decision of *Serrano* v. *Priest*. These in turn derived in considerable measure from the 1970 study *Private Wealth and Public Education* by John E. Coons, William H. Clune, and Stephen D. Sugarman.

On first encounter, these cases conform to a familiar pattern of social reform in the present age, most notably in their use of the judicial process to bring about results that apparently cannot be obtained through the political process concerning matters theretofore deemed to be within the political realm. But these events also reveal another, more recent pattern, which has only just begun to take hold in the American polity. For the judicial actions are self-induced, or nearly so. Almost wherever one looks, government-paid lawyers are involved on behalf of the plaintiffs. There emerges an autogamous mode of government growth: big government ordering itself to become bigger.

These actions in the area of education are probably the first of a new class of cases that will now be argued in many fields. They raise important constitutional issues having to do with the extent to which the citizen is entitled as a matter of right to have the state do certain things

Reprinted with permission from *The Public Interest*, No. 29 (Fall 1972), 69–89.
Copyright © 1972, *National Affairs, Inc.*

for him. At issue too are questions of social power which the public has a right to expect will also be taken into account as these other matters go forward. The ancient query, *Cui bono?*, may be invoked: To whose benefit do these decisions redound?

What We Spend on Education

The most striking aspect of educational expenditure is how large it has become. Those who wish to argue that it is still not large enough are free to do so, and may well be right; but no one can contend that schools have been slighted in the past decade. Legislatures—in the aggregate—have levied ever-increasing amounts of money to pay for them. For the past ten years the proportion of Gross National Product expended on elementary and secondary education has risen at a rate almost half again that of the GNP itself. This education expenditure has been rising 9.7 percent annually, as against the 6.8 percent increase in GNP. The total cost of elementary and secondary education has more than doubled in the past ten years, as has expenditure per pupil. By the 1971–72 school year, current expenditure per pupil in "average daily attendance" had reached $929, and should now be near the $1,000 mark. In constant dollars this is an expenditure about three to four times as great as that during the period when the average adult reader of this article went to school. In 1971–72, some $46.8 billion was expended by public schools.

There is nothing especially notable about these rates of growth; they correspond to a general surge in public expenditure in almost every sector save defense. Writing of the ten-year period now ending, Charles L. Schultze and his colleagues at the Brookings Institution report that "in the space of 10 short years, federal civilian expenditures as a percentage of GNP almost doubled." State and local budgets, from which the great proportion of elementary and secondary school expenditure comes, rose at similar rates.

A second fact about educational expenditure is that it varies considerably by area in fairly close approximation to the wealth of the areas involved. In 1970, California, the venue of the *Serrano* decision, had the eighth highest per capita income in the nation, and the sixth highest per pupil expenditure on education. In the school year 1969–70, the average per pupil expenditure in California was $922; Mississippi spent $476. As with many of the individual school districts to which the *Serrano* class of decisions is directed, the low expenditures for education in Mississippi reflect more the low level of aggregate wealth than any manifest unwillingness to tax. In Mississippi, 4.97 percent of per capita personal income is

99

spent on elementary and secondary education, which contrasts to a national average of 4.46 percent. New York taxes at a somewhat lower rate than Mississippi, 4.92 percent of per capita income; but this produces $1,237, almost three times the per pupil expenditure figure for Mississippi. A familiar situation.

Less familiar, but central to the thrust of these decisions, is the variation in school expenditure within states. Allowing for exceptions, a simple pattern seems to be typical throughout most of the country. Suburbs spend above the average, central cities at or slightly above the average, small towns and rural areas below the average. This is a long-standing situation. State aid programs in New York, for example, begin as a deliberate effort to "equalize" expenditure between the "rich" cities and the "poor" countryside. The wealth of New York City, as George Washington Plunkitt observed, was "pie for the hayseeds," and slice it they did; but never to the point of equality.[1]

A final fact, even less familiar (or more resisted), is that after a point school expenditure does not seem to have any notable influence on school achievement. To repeat, *after* a point. A school without a roof, or without books, or without teachers would probably not be a school in which a great deal of learning went on. But once expenditure rises above a certain zone, money doesn't seem to matter that much in terms of what happens to students. This "discovery" was one of the major events in large-scale social science during the 1960s (albeit one well anticipated in small-scale work), but it is of the first importance to understand that it was not unique. Something like the same thing has been "discovered" about a whole range of public services. In the main, the finding is that the influence of these mechanistic "interventions'" (government programs) is distinct but limited, and often easily outdistanced by other influences of a more organic nature (family, peer group, and so on). Although a fair amount of recrimination has attended these "findings," they ought not to cause any great grief to competent persons. Indeed, if one is concerned with the expanding power of the state, evidence that its influence soon reaches an end with respect to many fundamental matters is, on the whole, cheering. Moreover, while the differential effects of state intervention may be small, they may be no less crucial for that reason.

Will More Money Do Any Good?

In the hope of evading the rancor that surrounds this subject in the United States, recent data from a longitudinal study of British school children may be cited. Children born in 1958 were compared in terms of family size, social class ("I" being high; "V" low), sex, and region (England, Scotland, Wales). Here are the differences (as recounted in the journal *New Society*) children absorb from the air they breathe:

The average difference in . . . test scores between, on the one hand, English boys in social class V who have four and more brothers and sisters, and on the other hand, Scottish girls in social class I who are only children, is equivalent to a gain in reading age of nearly four years.

If this is so, certain strategies come to mind. More youths might be shipped off to Scotland. A bonus might be paid for aborting fifth and sixth children. Mothers might be encouraged to have more girl babies. Income redistribution might help. Certain kinds of teaching might help. But on balance, one would not conclude from the British data that increasing educational expenditure could do much to close that gap of nearly four years.

A comparable judgment would have to be made of the American situation. There are considerable regional, class, racial, and ethnic variations in certain kinds of achievement. We would like to see them eliminated, even in the knowledge that this might nudge us yet further along toward Michael Young's dilemma. But it is simply not clear that school expenditure is the heart of the matter. In 1971, the Rand Corporation carried out for the President's Commission on School Finance a review and synthesis of research findings on the effectiveness of education. The result was thoroughly predictable, but nonetheless devastating to whatever is left of conventional wisdom in this field. Simply put, in the range of current educational practice, regarding levels of expenditure, types of teaching, and such, the researchers found that no *"variant of the existing system . . . is consistently related to students' educational outcomes."* [2] Put another way, *"research has found nothing that consistently and unambiguously makes a difference in student outcomes."* The report continues, "There is good reason to ask whether our educational problems are, in fact, school problems." And it concludes with two policy implications, each stated as gently as seemed possible:

Increasing expenditures on traditional educational practices is not likely to improve educational outcomes substantially.

There seem to be opportunities for significant redirections and in some cases reductions in educational expenditures without deterioration in educational outcomes.

A member of the President's Commission would have had to be dim indeed to fail to grasp that the Rand Corporation analysts were suggesting that with respect to school finance there is a strong possibility that we may already be spending too much.[3] This thought will offend some persons, including perhaps some who have no doubt whatever that the military is spending too much. But giving offense would seem to be the role of social science at this time. And there is worse. It is no great matter that the Scarsdale school system spends extra money and gets little extra in return. But the record of compensatory education, as reported by the Rand study, is wrenching. There is small consolation to be had in articles such as "How Regression Artifacts in Quasi-experimental Evaluation Can Mistakenly Make Compensatory Education Look Harmful," to cite from the bibliography but one effort to ease the pain of unwelcome findings. These are the facts we have to live with, and they do not at this time make any case for a general increase in educational expenditure.

Certainly, they make no case for a simple-minded mandate to impose equal expenditure on the existing system. One hastens to say that men such as John E. Coons, the prime intellectual mover behind the *Serrano* decision, have nothing of the sort in mind; and it may be that the courts are well aware of the many complexities of this subject. If so, however, the courts have not let us know this. Their decisions have been couched in the simplistic language of an unreflective and uninformed progressivism. That they mean well is not to be doubted; *but will they do good?* Or, putting that question aside, will the court orders have the effect envisioned by the court? Just possibly. That is to say, just possibly there are some genuinely learned justices on those benches who do indeed understand the probable effect of their decisions but, informed by some involute theory of judicial restraint, choose not to let the public in on the secret.

The secret is simple enough. *If school expenditures are to be equalized within states, considerable sums will have to be taken away from schools attended by the lowest-income and the highest-income students and given to schools attended by students in the middle-income range.* This assertion could be wrong; it could be refuted. But all the evidence that comes to hand suggests that this would be the overall effect of equalizing a fixed amount of school expenditure. This is so for the very simple reason stated by Chester Finn and Leslie Lenkowsky—that poor (low-income) students, generally speaking, do not live in "poor" school districts. The tendency is otherwise. Plunkitt's Hell's Kitchen was teeming with poverty and disadvantage, but New York County was the richest county in the state. For this reason the federal aid to education programs begun in the 1960s allocated funds on the basis of the income of students' families rather than the tax base of school districts.

There is little political likelihood that as a result of court decisions any large number of school districts will actually *lose* money. Politics does not work that way. Rather, the districts with low tax bases will be "equalized" up. The result, then, will be increased expenditure on schools and increased pressure on the national government to take on a larger share of the rising cost.[4]

Cui bono?

Who will benefit from this? This question is easily answered: Teachers will benefit. Any increase in school expenditure will in the first instance accrue to teachers, who receive about 68 percent of the operating expenditures of elementary and secondary schools. That these are estimable and deserving persons none should doubt, but neither should there be any illusion that they are deprived. With exceptions, they are not. In general, they are deservedly well-paid professionals. Over the past two decades teachers' pay has increased at a rate roughly twice that of wages in the private economy. The average annual salary for classroom teachers in 1970–71 was $9,210. (It has since passed $10,000.) In large cities it tended to be higher, reaching $12,186 in San Francisco. The median income of men working full time year round in 1971 was just about that of teachers—but of some 2.9 million persons employed as teachers, two million were women. In that women earn only about 59 percent of the income of men when both work full time year round, an increase in the number of teachers or an increase in teachers' pay above the general movement of wages will almost certainly increase the number of persons in higher earning brackets. Where the teacher is a married woman, family income is likely to be in the top quintile of income distribution, even the top 5 percent. Without abusing probabilities (or asserting the existence of detailed evidence), it may be said that *increasing educational expenditures will have the short-run effect of increasing income inequality.*

Now is this what the courts intend? Possibly. The Establishment is said to do such things all the time. But the far greater likelihood is that the courts simply don't know what they are doing. This is not to insist that the analysis just outlined is correct beyond a reasonable doubt. It may yet be disproved either by events or by reanalysis of the existing data; no absolute claims are made for the dependability of each of the propositions put forward here. They represent the consensus of some knowledgeable persons; not more than that. But one has no faith whatever that the courts are even aware of such possibilities, and little faith that the plaintiffs in these proceedings are aware of them either. Rather, they appear to have seized on undeniable instances in which "rich" districts contain

Daniel P. Moynihan

"rich" kids and "poor" districts, "poor" kids, and where both expenditures
and outcomes are so clearly unequal that any fair-minded person would
feel that something ought to be done. There *is* a Baldwin Park school
district in Los Angeles, *and* a Beverly Hills school district, *and* the
differences between them are probably unacceptable. *But to conceive of
this disparity as prototypical simply does not accord with the known
facts.*

What is does accord with is certain kinds of middle-class interest. There
is, first, the peripheral but discernible interest in asserting the value of
things this class values and at which it excels. This is not to be underestimated. It reflects the vigorous exercise of the middle-class citizen's
desire to decide priorities. More tangibly, however, it is also a way of
asserting the value, and increasing the value, of those services the middle
class dispenses. There is a class economic interest at stake, and that class
is pursuing its interest.

There is nothing the matter with this as such. Other groups do the
same. There is hardly a more admirable group of persons than school
teachers. Textbook manufacturers are said to be honest people also. One
hears as much of bond holders. (Not *all* the money goes to teachers'
salaries.) There are problems, however, of which one, again perhaps
peripheral, is that there is more disguising of interest in these matters
than is probably good for the integrity of public discourse. The objectives
of what lawyers call "full disclosure" are not much advanced by the
rhetoric of disinterested public service that attends what are often no
more than raids on the Treasury. We don't presume disinterestedness on
the part of persons whose interests reside in the growth and prosperity
of the private sector of the economy. Why should those whose interests
reside in the growth of the public sector be treated differently?

The Self-Aggrandizement of the Public Sector

To be sure, the public sector is better these days at making its case. The
machinery of government now routinely advances the case for more
government. We take this for granted in the military, but our instinct is to
exempt civilians, especially those in the "helping'" professions. A routine
instance comes to hand in the March–April 1972 issue of *Welfare in
Review*, which includes an article on "Undergraduate Training of AFDC
Caseworkers" (i.e., welfare workers in the Aid to Families of Dependent Children program). It begins with routine puffery:

Present-day social problems and increasing public understanding of their
complexity are adding importance to the social caseworker's role in our

society and the training he needs for his work. A master of social work degree is usually necessary for employment as a professional worker, and social work has become institutionalized.

The findings—of a survey done in New Hampshire—are set forth in the careful and competent way of this useful publication. No distinct differences were found as between caseworkers with different undergraduate majors, but one notable fact did "fall out" of the data. Asked their reasons for becoming social workers, 71 percent of this young group (median age, 28) answered "humanitarian."

Now one would wish this. It is surely a good thing for caseworkers to see themselves in this light. Or almost surely. But it tends to confuse public debate. Shoe factory workers in Manchester, almost certainly earning considerably less than social workers in the same city, are not permitted to declare that they have chosen their profession for humanitarian reasons. In any event, nobody asks them. The result is that public policy ends up taking more money away from the factory workers to give to social workers because the latter are engaged in humanitarian pursuits, while the former pursue pedestrian enterprises geared solely for profit.

The matter would seem a bit farfetched if we had not in New York City been exposed to almost a decade of incessant statements by social work professionals veritably urging more folks to get on welfare. In 1960, when, according to Nicholas Kisburg's calculation, there were 9.7 persons in private-sector wage and salary employment in New York City for every public welfare recipient, this posture might not have seemed unreasonable. But in 1971, with the ratio having declined to 2.6 to 1, a citizen might grow out of sorts, even to the point of associating such statements with the social work profession as a whole, which would be unjust. *And yet they do apply.* Not in the sense that this particular group of professional persons in the public sector actively desires to increase demand for its services, but in the sense that it does tend to benefit, as does any group of service-providers, from increased demand.

This is the second order of understanding that needs to be brought to bear on judicial decisions that mandate this or that increase in public services. There has been a lag in the general understanding of the relative status of the private and public sectors of the economy. For the longest time, and with the best of cases, liberals argued that while the private sector fattened, the public sector starved. Which of us has not thought that? How many of us have written articles, speeches, books reciting the litany of unmet needs? Who has not campaigned with, contributed to, voted for candidates pledged to redress this great imbalance? Well . . . we succeeded. There are individuals such as John Kenneth Galbraith to whom special credit is owed, but this has also been a general movement of public opinion.

Daniel P. Moynihan

If proof of our success were needed, it is best found in the continued *and accelerated* trends of civilian expenditure in recent administrations, regardless of party. Schultze et al. show this with some force, as can be seen in Table 4-1, tracing the growth in federal civilian outlays.

TABLE 4-1
Growth in Federal Civilian Outlays, Fiscal Years 1955–73

Period	Percent of Growth per Year	
	Real Outlays	Real Outlays per Capita
1955–60	7.6	5.8
1960–65	5.8	4.1
1965–70	9.1	7.9
1970–73	10.3	9.0

Source: Data adapted from Charles L. Schultze, Edward R. Fried, Alice M. Rivlin, and Nancy H. Teeters, *Setting National Priorities, The 1973 Budget* (Washington D.C.: The Brookings Institution, 1973), chap. 12.

Indeed, the only dip in this otherwise steady progression is that of the Kennedy years, brought about by a cautious administration and a hostile Congress. Otherwise the trend is steady and formidable. It is more impressive in the light of restrained military growth in the decade 1963–73, when military appropriations dropped from 53 percent of federal expenditure to 34 percent, and from 9.7 percent to 7.0 percent of GNP. Schultze, Budget Director under President Johnson, clearly had no partisan reason to call attention to these movements. They are simply unblinkable and overwhelming. That may be too strong; if they persist, they will become overwhelming.[5]

The Cycle of Denial and Diminishing Returns

Now to the irony of it all. This kind of expenditure does *not* induce a strong perception of "unmet needs" being met. Or so it would seem. Social scientists are fully capable of investigating such questions and no doubt in time some will do so. For the moment we must do with impressions, but these are quite strong. There is a generalized perception within that part of the electorate often described as "blue-collar" that they are paying for a lot more services than they are receiving. But among the service-dispensing classes, the overwhelming perception, genuine or dissembled, is that the nation has not "reordered its priorities" and must do so. Schultze et al. calculate that "Great Society" programs in the federal budget grew from $1.7 billion in FY 1963 to $35.7 in FY 1973. This has made little impression. Frequently it is simply denied. To some extent this reflects the fact that the service-dispensing classes and their political allies are overwhelmingly Democratic, and understandably wish to believe that their interests are advanced only by a Democratic administration. (How many college professors, much less college students, would know that the size of the United States Army has been cut in half in the past four years, from 1,570,000 in 1968 to some 841,000 in 1973?) But in fact that pattern has little respect for party. Johnson was damned for "slashing" programs, just as Nixon has been. As Joseph A. Schumpeter once wrote, the "technique and atmosphere of the struggle for social legislation" is no friend of truth.

A simple cycle is at work with which anyone who has worked for social legislation will be familiar. As government responds to a problem and the situation commences to change, those who initiated the response, and who benefit from it in one way or another, seek to ensure continued response by charging that the situation either has not improved, or has worsened, or has always been worse than originally asserted. For some, social legislation can have the effect of narcotic drugs on the addict: Ever-stronger doses are required, first to achieve the remembered euphoria of the early stages of addiction, and then merely to maintain the absence of distress.

It would, of course, be difficult to "prove" this last proposition. The Vietnam war almost surely "contaminated" all manner of public attitudes in the 1960s, especially among groups that press for social legislation and thereafter manage it. There is, however, a more general condition, certain to outlast the war, which does respond to attempts at verification by measurement. This is the condition of diminishing marginal utility of expenditure on various social services—and it feeds the cycle of denial and renewed demand. After a point, the charge that government efforts to solve a problem are not doing so begins to be true and can be shown to be such.

Public services follow production functions as do any other production processes. Typically, in an early stage increments of input have a high marginal utility which gradually diminishes until the exchange of input for output is no longer equal, and finally to the point where additional input is almost totally wasted as virtually no additional output results. It seems to be the case that, over a considerable range of public services, we are traversing a segment of a production function which is virtually asymptotic. (The Rand report puts it, with respect to education, that we are in a " 'flat' area.") The early and exhilarating days of large increments of output for small increments of input are long past. In these circumstances "trying harder" has no discernible effect, and a perverse equilibrium is attained, at least from the point of view of those whose pleasure or profit it is to demand more. No matter how hard the polity tries to produce "more," it never does, so that the posture of demanding more is never endangered by the prospect of fulfillment.

Education would seem to be a preeminent instance of this phenomenon. As might be expected, economists have begun to discuss the subject in such terms. In 1971, Kenneth Boulding presented a paper to the American Educational Research Association entitled, "The School Industry as a Possibly Pathological Section of the American Economy." He simply noted that more input did not seem to be producing more output. The point of optimality has long been passed. A shoe factory operating in the manner of many public school systems would have long since closed down.

The Case for Judicial Restraint

The difficulty is that public enterprises are not subject to the discipline of the market. They can be grossly inefficient, and yet go on indefinitely. Indeed, inefficiency can become a primary source of their perpetuation, for their inability to achieve declared objectives can be taken as evidence of insufficient effort and turned into a call for yet more resource allocation. The more, then, is the need for discipline—for honesty and openness and a measure of good manners—in public discussion of such matters. It is on this ground (and for my part, *only* on this ground) that the *Serrano* family of judicial decisions seems unwarranted. We have here a troubled area of public policy. Good men and women, conscientious and learned, are uncertain what to do. Is this the time for judges, some of whom come near to flaunting their indifference to research findings, to *tell* us what to do? Are laundry workers and ditch diggers and gas pumpers to be *forced* to give up more of their wages in order to pay the wages of college graduates because of some vague notion some judge picked up at law school in the 1930s? This trifles with our democracy. One fair to pleads with the judiciary to stay out of such matters. There are other areas of justice and right in which *only* they can provide remedy, and their authority in those areas ought not to be squandered by an injudicious frolic in the maze of public finance.

Three general points in favor of judicial restraint can be made. It may be that none carries any legal weight and the courts will find themselves obliged to continue on the course they have set, in which event we will have to make the best of it. But in these final hours, while the question is not yet settled, prudence suggests several powerful counterarguments.

First, if there is injustice with respect to the allocation of educational resources, a political remedy is available, and there is abundant evidence that this remedy is both availed of and effective. More and more money goes into education, and of late more and more of this is "targeted" on groups whose educational needs seem greater than most. The trend, as in the Elementary and Secondary Education Act of 1965, has been to unequal expenditure *in favor of* students with low-income backgrounds. This has not by any means been universally achieved, but it is a trend, and the courts should be concerned lest they deflect it.

Second, the courts should at least be aware of it when, in the name of equality of access to public services, they *order* measures that must result in increased inequality of private income. This is probably the result of increased educational expenditure, although an opposing argument can doubtless be made. This is not to say that such measures constitute bad public policy. Not at all. But they should at least be *voluntary* public policy, deliberately chosen and *legitimately* enacted by the elected representatives of the people. One cannot be fully at ease when government uses tax monies to employ middle-class professionals to persuade middle-class judges whose salaries are paid by tax monies to hand down orders to the effect that yet more middle-class persons should be hired and paid with yet more tax monies. This is not what the task force that drafted the Economic Opportunity Act of 1965 had in mind. Which is not to say it is for that reason wrong—and which certainly is not to question the role of poverty lawyers in so much of what they do—but they *are* part of government. A story used to be told around the State House in Albany about Al Smith's 1922 campaign for governor. He had lost out in the Harding landslide and was now running against a one-term Republican who hadn't a great deal to say but did keep harping on a bill he had signed, or refused to sign, or whatever, as a result of which he claimed the state had saved $3 million. Smith sensed that the story was catching on. He began to pursue his opponent around the state with a simple challenge: "The Governor," he would declare, "says he has saved the state $3 million. What I want to know, is where is it and who's got it." Judges can ask as much.

A third general point has to do with the overall prospects for educational expenditure: They are very good. The 1970s will see almost no increase in elementary and secondary school populations. The 1972 Manpower Report of the President projects almost no increase in the number of elementary or secondary school teachers. And yet, the economy will continue to grow, making ever-greater resources available to meet a stabilized set of needs. How can the outcome not be higher teacher salaries, higher per pupil expenditure, more equal expenditure where low-income children have been unfairly left behind, and more "extras" for low-income children who obviously need them more? Nor must we accept that these "extras" will have little or no consequences. If we are now in a "flat area" with respect to the "results" of educational expenditure, there is no reason to think we cannot break out of our present constraints into a new and much wider range of opportunity. I have been involved in public policy in these areas at the state and national level. I had something to do with the Elementary and Secondary Education Act of 1965. I had much to do with the creation of the President's Commission on School Finance in 1970. A fair number of hopes were dashed in that five-year interval, but not all hopes. To the contrary, as the subject came to be seen as more complex, it became more interesting, more attractive to talent. One did not have to know a great deal in 1970 to know what Rand Corporation researchers would find if asked to look into the state of knowledge on the effectiveness of schooling. One purpose of the Commission was to bring out this information in a politically neutral setting. There *is* such a thing as "the state of knowledge," and this, for the moment, is where we are at on this subject.

And that is the point! *The state of knowledge can change.* In the message to Congress proposing the School Finance Commission, the President also proposed the creation of a National Institute of Education to mount a sustained and powerful effort in just this direction. Congress hesitated a moment, and then overwhelmingly concurred. The case for approaching the issue in this manner is immensely persuasive, and the new Institute was enacted with strong bipartisan support. It is about to begin operations. With good luck and good management the founding of the National Institute of Education will mark a general maturing in this field and a greatly expanding federal effort extending to the whole question of school finance and the property tax. (In the recent study by the Advisory Commission on Intergovernmental Relations it was established that this is by far regarded as the worst of the general taxes levied in the nation and that there is strong support for federal intervention to reduce local property taxes.) In the meantime, the President's Commission has called for full state assumption of school costs. Are these not the signs of an active and progressive area of public policy? If so, can't the courts leave it alone? If they feel they can't, no very great harm will come. The objectives of these cases are admirable, and those who brought them have done a public service in raising the particular issue involved. But can it not be left to the normal machinery of public policy to take the hint?

The New Class

Whatever the courts decide, a political situation has been created which will be with us a long time. One hesitates to be more than allusive, thinking back to the Danish sailor in *Billy Budd* to whom long experience had taught "that bitter prudence which never interferes with aught, and never gives advice." But a larger prudence demands that the issue be raised.

The social legislation of the middle third of the century created "social space" for a new class whose privilege (or obligation) it is to dispense services to populations that are in various ways wards of the state. A generation ago, Schumpeter described how the ideology and manifestations of early capitalism had created social space for a new bourgeois class that stood upon a foundation of individual achievement in the economic field. Even then he sensed that this private sphere—the social space created for the bourgeoisie—was facing competition from a new "public sphere," which represented a different order of values and which was occupied by different persons. In *Capitalism, Socialism, and Democracy* he wrote:

This private sphere is distinct from the public sphere not only conceptually but also actually. The two are to great extent manned by different people—the history of local self-government offering the most conspicuous exception—and organized as well as run on different and often conflicting principles, productive of different and often incompatible standards.

Friction can only temporarily be absent from such an arrangement, the paradoxical nature of which would be a source of wonder to us if we were not so accustomed to it. As a matter of fact, friction was present long before it developed into antagonism in consequence of the wars of conquest waged upon the bourgeois domain with ever increasing success by the men of the public sphere.

These "wars of conquest" do not cease. The advent of new champions is always hailed no matter what their subsequent fate. By 1972 the *New York Times* could refer to Mayor Lindsay's newest budget as a "bloated $10 billion monster," but these were hardly the terms in which he was first welcomed on the scene, and that budget, having got to $10 billion, is not going to recede. It now amounts to an expenditure of $625 per year for every man, woman, and child in the city. The money does not *go* to every man, woman, and child, but it goes to enough of them so that he who challenges the expenditure risks devastating retorts about "human needs" and may expect no allies save such as will add to his discredit.

It was not always so. Interestingly, the labor movement was for the longest time (and in many ways still is) profoundly skeptical of eleemosynary initiatives undertaken with tax money. In a 1916 editorial in the *American Federationist,* Samuel Gompers wrote, "There is a very close connection between *employment* as experts and the enthusiasm for human welfare." Gompers' view was tolerant enough. His own movement was devoted to improving the circumstances of its members, and he saw the "experts" as doing no' more than this for their own people. What he objected to was the "experts" contention that they were doing something for the workers. Trade unionism among public employees has necessarily moderated the force of this view—not long ago an important spokesman for teachers asked that the expenditure on education as a percentage of GNP be almost doubled—but the skepticism remains.

Here and there in other parts of the liberal spectrum a similar anxiety is to be encountered. Caution about "big government" can derive from more than opposition to heavy taxes. Among those who retain some of the qualities of an earlier liberalism there is a discernible concern over the "ever increasing success by the men of the public sphere." The aggression is unmistakable, and seemingly irresistible, not least because the self-interest of the new class is merged with a manifestly sincere view of the public interest. This view, that the general good is served by advancing the interests of the public sphere, is apparently the dominant social view of the time, and is terribly difficult to argue against with any success.

An example from yet another area of education may help to clarify this point. It happens that I negotiated the phrasing of the 1964 Democratic platform plank which constituted agreement by the Roman Catholic hierarchy of the United States that it would support legislation for federal aid to education, an initiative it had successfully blocked for many years. In the understanding of the Bishops—or at least in my understanding—the platform plank represented a commitment that parochial schools would share federal aid with public schools on some approximate principle of equal treatment. The plank was adopted, the support was forthcoming, the legislation was passed, and the parochial schools got—nothing. Or near to nothing. Certainly they were not dealt with as they had reason to think they would be. They have not publicly complained. (Nor has anyone ever raised the 1964 "understandings" with me.) But they were nonetheless "used." Their mistake (and mine, too, as I look back) probably was in seeing the issue in terms of past prejudice against Catholic institutions. (Everyone was being very civilized in 1964. After all, did not the British government give aid to Catholic schools as to any other?) But this was not, I now think, the issue. The issue was that Catholic schools were not in the public sphere.

The 1972 Democratic party calls for equalization of school expenditure, in the *Serrano* manner. One has greater confidence that this commitment *will* be carried out, in large part with federal funds, and at federal initiative. These probabilities are symbolic of a new political situation: *Education has entered national politics.* Those of us who worked for this to happen may yet live to regret it. There was wisdom in keeping educational politics nonpartisan—as are most school board elections—and diffused. Bringing it into partisan politics at the national level makes for much ugliness. The increasingly corporate nature of the American social structure means that fierce, organized pressures will be brought to bear to raise expenditure, and that these will be supported by a civic culture that sees increased expenditure as a general public good. Anyone who on any grounds opposes such an increase opposes the interest of a class, and the preconceptions of the culture. There are energetic representatives of such interests, like Albert Shanker of the United Federation of Teachers, men and women who fight for their members, fight well, and fight clean. But the temptation to debase political language is considerable. The opponent of greater school expenditure readily becomes the enemy of children. This aspect of the changed political situation makes for a second somewhat ironical conclusion.

Strategies for National Education Policy

The increasing political influence of the public sphere will make for increasing political instability unless public services become more effective. At long last we are going to have to take public services and public administration seriously. It is not a question of efficiency but of perceived efficacy. With the fortunes of the individual declared more and more to depend on what he receives from the public sphere, the areas in which government must successfully perform are greatly expanded, while the margins of tolerance contract. A familiar prediction. But today the condition has actually come about, and it must now be attended to. A final example from education will suggest the options seemingly open to us.

Three general strategies could be pursued as a national education policy. The first would be to leave well enough alone, even to cut back on expenditures, where they are high, to the point an economist might identify as the optimal use of resources. There is a rational case for this, and a good psychological one also. As a nation we have been generous and conscientious about education. Schools have at least processed successive cohorts of newcomers which have gone on to spectacular intellectual success. In one section of the nation one part of the population was for the longest time deliberately kept apart in segregated school systems, and there seems no question that a heavy price was paid. This calls for recompense. Such efforts can and should be made even if "things-as-they-are" is on balance accepted. (As far as *schools* go an entirely fortuitous but still spectacular compensatory event has already occurred. The pattern of ethnic succession in the cities of the North and West has been such that to a strikingly uniform degree Southern migrants have moved into previously Jewish neighborhoods. This means that one of our most educationally deprived populations is now heavily concentrated in schools which a generation earlier produced the intellectual, cultural, professional, and to a degree, economic elite of the world's most powerful nation. If it's "good" schools we're looking for, surely these begin to approximate them.) But of course this first strategy will not be adopted. It violates the principle of autogamous growth. Politicians who espouse any such approach will be effectively driven from public life.

A second strategy would be to continue increasing educational effort in the existing mode in the expectation of getting a yet better educational "product." This means pushing more and more resources along that "flat" area in the curve, or perhaps more accurately, jamming evermore resources into the ever-tightening angle of an asymptotic production function. Save where there are grossly unacceptable inequalities of resources (a condition that could be remedied under the first strategy), this strategy will bring about almost no changes in the standard measurements by which the existing educational system assesses results. For this reason, each new increment of resources will be demanded and justified by increasingly threatening rhetoric. Distrust and suspicion will mount.

This second strategy is the one we are now following, and it is inherently unstable. For one thing, as the public sphere expands in the announced quest for greater equality, the almost certain outcome is greater inequality deriving from the transfer of income from lower to higher social levels. This, along with the inability of services to deliver on promises beyond a certain point, leads to corruption. The public sphere begins to lie about outcomes, as by falsifying test scores—a resort so far only tentatively employed— or by manipulating outcomes through familiar devices such as social quotas.

As this is rather a dim prospect, the case becomes stronger for a third general strategy, which is to launch a serious and sustained effort to discover effective ways to achieve the goals the public has come to expect. A decade ago this would have seemed a bland enough statement. We know it not to be. To achieve what we would wish in education, for example, is likely to require a quality of brute genius which may or may not come along. But it *could* happen; a *new* curve could be discovered. A whole new set of parameters could come into being. The education process that emerges is likely to be quite different from the schooling process we now know. A great many interests would have to be set aside to achieve such a new condition, but in the end the public interest would be served. Government has got into the business of promising more than it knows how to deliver; as there is little likelihood of cutting back on the promises, the success of the society turns on its ability to improve its performance. It is probably not a good thing to have got into this situation, but the social dynamics of an industrial society everywhere seem to lead in this direction, and to do so with special vehemence in the United States.

How Should the Court Proceed?

For the moment, the issue before the nation is not the general one of a national educational policy, nor the wide implications of the continued and self-induced expansion of the public sphere, but simply whether the courts shall order equal educational expenditure as a matter of constitutional right. One uses the phrase "before the nation" because whatever the courts order, government at large will have to put the orders into effect, and this follow-through will in turn be shaped by public opinion.

It is not unreasonable to ask the courts to know what they are ordering. The question easily divides into two parts: First, ought there to be equal educational expenditure across school districts and—let us get it over with—across states? Second, ought there to be greater educational expenditure?

One can readily imagine that the courts, pursuing general notions of equality, might find for equal expenditure. It is difficult to see how anyone would be harmed by this. An argument could be made that present arrangements make for a certain amount of diversity and local option, with the result that parents who "care" about education can "buy" more of it by moving into selected school districts. But this argument can be countered by the equally reasonable assertion that not all parents have such options, and further that the society ought to minimize the "return" from racial and class differentiation. Equal expenditure would probably "hurt" a fair number of poor children who live in high-expenditure central city school districts, but there is no evidence that it would hurt them much, and in any event it is late in the day to think of such matters.

When the courts, or rather the Court, makes its ruling on the matter of equal expenditure, it should in all conscience acknowledge that it is getting close to the question of whether the Fourteenth Amendment permits parents to send children to private schools, where per pupil expenditure is considerably higher than in public institutions. There is an inevitable statist quality to these decisions which must be hostile to de-

Daniel P. Moynihan

vices for evading state control. Just as important, the Court might touch on the question of whether it is constitutional for Catholic children to be sent to schools where fragmentary but persistent evidence suggests that they are educated for a fraction of the cost of education in the public schools. (They emerge just as well, or badly, schooled, which suggests something.) But in any event, the Court surely can rule for equal expenditure without doing any great injury or injustice to anyone.

On the other hand, one cannot readily imagine that the courts would knowingly order greater inequality of income distribution in the nation by mandating—or setting in motion forces that will almost surely lead to—markedly greater educational expenditure. The *Serrano* plaintiffs have not desired this. Coons and his associates have specifically argued for a formula that would permit variation in expenditure but not linked to variation in school district wealth. But one fears for the fate of any such subtlety. The issue is already discussed almost solely in the old terms of equal expenditure. In practice, this means greater expenditure.

Educational expenditure is growing, and will continue to grow, but this is the result of political choice, not court order. For the courts to order it is to risk scandal. The scandal may be simply stated. It is that of middle-aged and elderly men imposing social nostrums which recent social science has seriously questioned, if not demolished, and doing so slothfully, without having mastered the not always simple modes of analysis by which social scientists have developed the new evidence. The legal encounters so far (if impressions may be permitted) have been rather one-sided. The state education departments, or whatever, have been represented by the kind of counsel that represents state education departments. The plaintiffs have had razor-sharp men on their side. But at the substantive level, neither the judges nor the plaintiffs have shown any taste for facts. To the contrary, they have shown considerable reluctance to stir from their *confort intellectuel,* the cozy verities of 30-year-old liberalism. It won't do. It would mean taking money from the pockets of people who need it considerably more than those into whose pockets it will be put. This is a rebuttable assertion, of course, but the courts should insist that it be rebutted before ordering anything of the sort. In the meantime there is a simple, equitable solution to the dilemma posed by the desire to bring about equality without adding to inequality. If the *Serrano* cases are to be upheld, the decision should be accompanied by an order that total expenditure not be increased as a result. That is to say, the present amount and proportion of funds expended for education should be divided up equally, raising some districts, lowering others. If overall expenditure is thereafter to be increased, it should be done through the political process, which has shown itself rather inclined in that direction. Only in this manner shall we avoid another miserable encounter between the courts and the political system of the democracy.

NOTES

1. I write these lines in a one-room schoolhouse in upstate New York which was not closed until the year I matriculated in a veritable palace of a high school newly opened in East Harlem under the patronage of Vito Marcantonio and Fiorello LaGuardia.

2. Harvey A. Averch et al., *How Effective Is Schooling? A Critical Review and Synthesis of Research Findings* (Santa Monica: The Rand Corporation, January 1972), pp. xii, xiii. (All italics theirs.)

3. Item: In 1966 Congress directed a nation-wide program of driver education, at just that moment when it became unmistakable that no case could be made that driver training has any significant favorable effect on driver performance. Vast sums have been expended since and will be expended hence. See my *Report of the Secretary's Advisory Committee on Traffic Safety* (U.S. Dept. of HEW, 1968); also, Harry H. Harman et al., *Evaluation of Driver Education and Training Programs* (Princeton, N.J.: Educational Testing Service, 1969).

4. In a report issued June 13, 1972, the Pennsylvania Department of Education estimated that to bring per capita expenditure throughout that state up to 80 percent of the expenditure in the highest district—a reasonable upward/downward settlement—would cost $1,052,263,235, an increase of approximately 35 percent over the 1970–71 expenditure on elementary and secondary education in the state as a whole.

5. In the summer of 1972, word began to come out of Washington that an "obscure" provision of a 1967 statute providing 75 percent of federal financing of "social services" for the poor was turning into a fiscal hemorrhage. The provision lay latent for several years until discovered, according to reliable reports, by an HEW official who reported it to his home state. In 1969, HEW paid out $354 million under the "program." By 1972, state applications reached $4.8 billion. In March 1972, Maryland budgeted $22.9 million in federal aid to its social services. By June the sum had risen to $417 million. Mississippi asked for an amount roughly two-thirds its entire state budget. The uses to which such funds are put are presumably so varied at this point that no firm generalization should be made, but it would be fair to expect that a great deal of the money ended up with the middle-class professionals who dispense the "social services" specified by the legislation. A point to note is that, if spent on income transfers, $4.8 billion would eliminate about half the poverty in the land. This is only a little less than the sum required for the Nixon Administration's Family Assistance Plan, proposed in 1969, and 1972 still to be acted on by Congress. $4.8 billion in "social services" will do little to eliminate poverty, but the dynamic of national politics at this time inserts the "social services" provision and prevents even a vote on the Family Assistance Plan. It may come as no surprise to learn that the social services professions have systematically opposed any guaranteed income plan that had any chance of passage by the Congress.

II

What
Determines
Income?

INTRODUCTION

THE BEST WAY to study the effect of education on economic success is to look at the more general question of the determination of income. *Inequality* and many other studies applied the methods of path analysis to sample surveys in an attempt to answer the larger questions. The surveys gathered either longitudinal or retrospective information on family background, ability and education, and current economic status. Models of the process of status determination were constructed with the variables, and regression analyses were used to provide a numerical expression for the strength of the relationships among the variables.

Much of the critical reaction to *Inequality* focused on the technical details of the data analysis: on the choice of control variables, on measurement error, on assumptions of linearity. This sort of criticism, while often correct, is essentially trivial: The errors it identifies are small and it accepts the basic methodology. We do not include any of the technical criticisms in this volume, nor do we present studies of income determination which use path or regression analysis on individual data.

Policy questions of what to do about income inequality cannot, in fact, be answered by exclusive reliance on the kind of analysis reported in *Inequality*. Policy analysis wants to know what would happen if things were changed: what would happen to income under a different educational system, stricter affirmative action requirements, or new employment patterns. Regression analysis of data describing existing relationships can give only very limited guidance to policy makers.

The regression coefficient of income on education predicts what would happen to income if the distribution of income changed and if everything else remained the same. And that of course is the rub. Only over a rather small range of changes in education or any other variable is everything else likely to remain the same. Big changes are certainly capable of altering the relationships as well as altering the levels of particular variables. Moreover, many proposed policies are specifically directed

121

toward altering the relationships and making structural changes in the labor market or the society.

Predictions about the effects of structural changes depend on understanding how the existing structure works and on comparing the workings of different social and economic systems. Weisbrod fully explores the structure of the human capital approach and pays particular attention to what economists call "externalities," that is, the way in which investments in human capital produce benefits to society beyond those the individual receives. The Mincer article summarizes, in completely nontechnical language, the conclusions of the human capital school of economics. These economists think of education as an investment which increases people's productivity and thus increases their contribution to the economic system, consequently increasing the economic rewards they receive. Mincer discusses the rate of return to education, and outlines some of the problems with using rate of return calculations to make predictions about the future.

The other two articles in this part are less traditional attempts to understand or compare structures. Schultz looks at changes in the income distribution over time, in an attempt to understand the changing structure of the American economic system. Historical comparisons, like cross-cultural comparisons, view economic events through a broader perspective than cross-sectional studies can employ. Examining the relationship of education and income over time is a way of testing whether the relationships observed at a given point in time also hold true when both education and the economy are changing.

Thurow's article proposes a way of looking at the relationship between education and earnings which is capable of reconciling the time series and cross-sectional data. Time series data shows no trend toward economic equality accompanying increased educational equality, while cross-sectional data reveals a relatively strong relationship. Thurow suggests that this apparent contradiction reflects the fact that education serves as a ranking mechanism used to sort people into jobs, rather than directly increasing their economic productivity. Jobs and their associated wages are structured by the economic system. People are then sorted into jobs by education, the most educated to the best jobs, the medium educated to the middle-status jobs, the poorly educated to the worst jobs. Education, in this view, is a currency subject to inflation, a notion which suggests that future research on the issues could profit from more historical and international comparisons.

(5)

Education and
Investment in
Human Capital

Burton A. Weisbrod [1]

AS technological developments have altered production techniques, types of mechanical equipment, and varieties of outputs, society has begun to recognize that economic progress involves not only changes in machinery but also in men—not only expenditures on equipment but also on people. Investment in people makes it possible to take advantage of technical progress as well as to continue that progress. Improvements in health make investment in education more rewarding by extending life expectancy. Investment in education expands and extends knowledge, leading to advances which raise productivity and improve health. With investment in human capital and nonhuman capital both contributing to economic growth and welfare and in what is probably an interdependent manner, more attention should be paid to the adequacy of the level of expenditures on people.

The principal forms of direct investment in the productivity and well-being of people are: health, learning (both in school and on the job), and location (migration). Formal education and health constitute two large components of public and private spending in the United States. Private expenditures alone for hospital and physician services were over $18 billion in 1959, having risen from $8.6 billion in 1950.[2] Public education expenditures rose to $19.3 billion in 1960 from $7.3 billion at the turn of the decade.[3] Priced at cost, gross investment in education in the United

Reprinted from the *Journal of Political Economy*, vol. 70, no. 5, pt. 2, supplement, October 1962, with permission of the author and publisher. © 1962, University of Chicago Press.

Burton A. Weisbrod

States has risen from 9 percent of gross physical investment in 1900 to 34 percent in 1956.[4]

Investment in future productivity is occurring increasingly outside the private market and in intangible forms. Our traditional conception of investment as a private market phenomenon and only as tangible plant, machinery, and equipment must give way to a broader concept which allows not only for government investment but also for intangible investment in the quality of human capital.

Most economic analysis of return from education has focused on the contribution of education to earning capacity (and, presumably, to production capacity). While this has been valuable, it is only part of the picture, and perhaps not even a large part. Even aside from market imperfections, which create inequalities between wage rates and marginal productivity, earnings are an incomplete measure of the productivity of education to the extent that production occurs outside the market. In addition, emphasis on incremental earnings attributable to education disregards external effects. Schooling benefits many persons other than the student. It benefits the student's future children, who will receive informal education in the home; and it benefits neighbors, who may be affected favorably by the social values developed in children by the schools and even by the quietness of the neighborhood while the schools are in session. Schooling benefits employers seeking a trained labor force; and it benefits the society at large by developing the basis for an informed electorate. Compulsory school attendance and public (rather than private) support for education in the United States both suggest that external economies from either the production or consumption of education are believed to be important.[5]

From the vantage point of one interested in Pareto optimal resource allocation, it is essential to consider all benefits from some action (as well as all costs). Whether the benefits (or costs) involve explicit financial payments, or whether they are internal to, or external from, a particular decision maker is irrelevant.

In the private sector of the economy, private benefits from goods and services are reflected in consumer demand; assuming economic rationality, competition, and the absence of external effects, private producers will meet the demand in a socially optimum manner. But when goods and services either have significant external effects or are indivisible (in the sense that consumption by one person does not reduce consumption opportunities for others—as, for example, national defense), the private market is inadequate. If the public sector attempts to provide the service, and if consumer sovereignty is to reign, the extent of consumer demand must be judged. Thus arises the need for benefit-cost analysis.

Within the benefit-cost framework this paper focuses principal atten-

124

tion on the ways by which a society benefits from formal education, discussing much more briefly some of the ways by which it incurs costs in providing education. It is worth emphasizing that analyzing benefits (or costs) does not preclude specifying which people reap the returns (or incur the costs). We shall attempt to identify the benefits of education by recognizing the beneficiaries of the education process.

In the discussion which follows, a "benefit" of education will refer to anything that pushes outward the utility possibility function for the society. Included would be: (1) anything which increases production possibilities, such as increased labor productivity; (2) anything which reduces costs and thereby makes resources available for more productive uses, such as increased employment opportunities, which may release resources from law enforcement by cutting crime rates; and (3) anything which increases welfare possibilities directly, such as development of public-spiritedness or social consciousness of one's neighbor. Anything which merely alters relative prices without affecting total utility opportunities for the group under consideration will not be deemed a social benefit (or loss). For example, if expanded education reduces the numbers of household servants, so that the wage rates of those remaining rise, this rise would not constitute either a benefit or loss from education but rather a financial transfer. Without making interpersonal utility comparisons we cannot say more. Of course, the increased productivity of those with the additional education is a benefit of type 1.

In addition to an analysis of the forms of education benefits and the nature of the beneficiaries, I shall investigate opportunities for quantifying these returns and some implications of the benefits analysis for the financing of education.[6] I shall consider benefits which the individual receives in the form of market opportunities—including additional earnings resulting from increased productivity and benefits which the individual receives in ways other than earnings. I shall also consider benefits which the individual does not capture but which accrue to other persons. Benefits from elementary, secondary, and higher education will receive attention.

In this section we examine those benefits of education (or returns from education) which are realized directly by the student. One form of such benefits is the "financial return" accompanying additional education. A second form is the "financial option" return. Previously unconsidered, this benefit involves the value of the opportunity to obtain still further education. Third are the nonmonetary "opportunity options," involving the broadened individual employment choices which education permits; fourth are the opportunities for "hedging" against the vicissitudes of technological change. And fifth are the nonmarket benefits.

Burton A. Weisbrod

Direct Financial Return

Census Bureau data relating level of earnings to level of educational attainment show an unmistakable positive correlation. A number of investigators have estimated the percentage return from investment in education by attributing these observed earnings differentials to education.[7] Some have attempted to adjust for or, at least, to recognize factors other than education which affect earnings and which are positively correlated with level of education. These include intelligence, ambition, informal education in the home, number of hours worked, family wealth, and social mobility. One factor which I believe has not been considered is that a positive correlation of educational attainment with family wealth suggests that those with more education may live longer and consequently tend to receive greater lifetime incomes, education aside, although it is true that longer life is not synonymous with longer working life. We are led to the presumption that, in general, persons who have obtained more education would have greater earnings than persons with less education, even without the additional schooling.[8] At the same time, at least one study has attempted to isolate some of the noneducation variables affecting earnings, with the finding that median salaries rose with additional amounts of post–high school education, even after adjustments were made for: (1) level of high school class rank; (2) intelligence test scores; and (3) father's occupation.[9] Apparently at least part of the additional earnings of the more educated population are the results of their education.

Although earning differentials attributable to education may be of considerable significance to the recipients, the social significance depends upon the relationship between earnings and marginal productivities. However, we know that market imperfections may make earnings a poor measure of one's contribution to output and that in a growing economy cross section age-earnings data will understate future earnings. Mary Jean Bowman has suggested that older workers may receive more than their marginal productivity because status and seniority rules may maintain income although their productivity is falling.[10] But even assuming that earnings equal current marginal productivity, estimation of lifetime productivity from cross section earnings data tends to understate future productivity of today's young men; this is true because in a growing society each new cohort of people into the labor force comes with better education and knowledge. These two examples suggest that the observed current earnings of men are less than fully satisfactory as reflections of future marginal productivity. Much work remains before we can feel confident of our ability to measure adequately the productivity return to education. Perhaps more serious, because apparently it has not been recognized, is a methodological limitation to previous estimates of the financial return to education.

Financial Option Return

Given our interest in resource allocation, we should like to know what financial return from additional education a person can expect. I suggested above that earnings differentials associated with education-attainment differentials would have to be adjusted for differences in ability, ambition, and other variables before we could isolate the education effects; and that an adjustment for systematic differences between earnings and productivity would also be required. Let us assume that these adjustments have been made and that we have computed the present values of expected future earnings of an average person with J and with K years of education, *ceteris paribus;* it is my contention that this would be an erroneously low estimate of the gross return which may be expected from the additional education. The value of the additional education may be thought of as having two components: *a*) the additional earnings resulting from completion of a given level of education (properly discounted to the present, of course), and *b*) the value of the "option" to obtain still further education and the rewards accompanying it. It is *b* which I wish to elaborate upon here.

In formula (1) below, the first term represents the rate of return over cost for education unit *j*, as computed in the usual manner; it is the difference between the present value of expected future earnings of a person who has attained, but not exceeded, level *j*, and the present value of expected future earnings of a person without education *j*, as a percentage of the additional cost of obtaining *j*. This is the rate of return as computed heretofore.

Subsequent terms in the formula measure the option value of completing *j* and should be understood as follows: each of the R^* are rates of return on incremental education a, computed in the manner described in the paragraph above. $\bar{R}$ is the opportunity cost of expenditure on education in terms of the percentage return obtainable from the next best investment opportunity, so that $R^*_\alpha - \bar{R}$ indicates any "supernormal" percentage return. C_a = the marginal social cost of obtaining the incremental education a (where each cost ratio, C_a/C_j, is a weighting factor, permitting the percentage returns on the costs of various levels of education to be added), and P_a is the probability that a person who has attained level *j* will go on to various higher levels.

Burton A. Weisbrod

$$R_j = R_i^* + (R_k^* - \bar{R}) \frac{C_k}{C_j} \cdot P_k$$

$$+ (R_l^* = \bar{R}) \frac{C_l}{C_j} \cdot P_l + \ldots$$

$$+ (R_z^* - \bar{R}) \frac{C_z}{C_j} \cdot P_z = R_j^*$$

$$+ \sum_{\alpha=k}^{z} (R_\alpha^* - \bar{R}) \frac{C_\alpha}{C_j} \cdot P_\alpha$$

(1)

Thus, for example, a decision to obtain a high school education involves not only the likelihood of obtaining the additional earnings typically realized by the high school graduate but also involves the value of the opportunity to pursue a college education.[11] The value of the option to obtain additional education will tend to be greater the more elementary the education. For the "highest" level of formal education, the value of the option is clearly zero,[12] except insofar as the education provides the option to pursue independent work.

The option-value approach attributes to investment in one level of schooling a portion of the additional return over cost which can be obtained from further education—specifically, that portion which is in excess of the opportunity cost rate of return. Although part of the return from college education is indeed attributed to high school education, there is no double-counting involved. In fact, the procedure is the same as that involved in the valuation of any asset, where the decision to retain or discard it may be made at various times in the life of the asset. Consider the following case: A machine is offered for sale. The seller, anxious to make the sale, offers an inducement to the buyer in the form of a discount on the purchase of a replacement machine when the present one wears out. Analyzing the prospective buyer's current decision, we see that he is being offered a combination of: (1) a machine now; and (2) a discount (or option) "ticket" for possible future use. Both may have value, and both should be considered by the prospective buyer.

Let us assume that the machine has been purchased and used, and the owner is now deciding whether he should buy a replacement. Needless to say, the rate of return expected from the prospective machine will be a function of its cost net of the discount. The profit-maximizing buyer will compare the rate of return on the net cost and compare it with the opportunity cost of capital. Thus, in a real sense, the discount ticket has entered into two decisions: to buy the original machine and to buy the replacement. But this is not equivalent to any erroneous double-counting.

The machine discount ticket analogy also makes clear the point that the value of the option (or discount) cannot be negative. If a greater rate of return (or discount) is available elsewhere, the value of the option merely becomes zero, as long as it need not be used. Thus, as long as a high school graduate need not go on to college the value of the option to go on cannot be negative. It is formally conceivable, however, that a positive option value of elementary school education could consist of a negative value for the high school component and a larger, positive value for the college component.

Formula (1) indicates that the value of the option to pursue additional schooling depends upon: (1) the probability of its being exercised; and (2) the expected value if exercised. Without further information, factor 1 may be estimated by the proportion of persons completing a particular level of education who go on to a higher level. The expected value of the option if exercised, factor 2, is any excess of the return on that increment of education over the return obtainable on the best comparable alternative investment, where the latter may be assumed to equal, say, 5 percent. Actually, the "excess" returns should be discounted back to the decision date from the time the higher education level would begin, but to illustrate the point simply I shall disregard this, at least to begin with.

According to some recent estimates reported elsewhere, the return to the individual on total high school costs (including foregone earnings) for white urban males in 1939 [13] was approximately 14 percent and the return on college costs for those who graduated was estimated at 9 percent.[14] We might assume the return to be somewhat lower—say, 8 percent—for those who did not complete their college training.[15] Then with approximately 44 percent of high school male graduates beginning college and 24 percent graduating,[16] the a priori expected return on a social investment in high school education in 1939 was, substituting in equation (1) above, 17.4 percent, as shown in equation (2).

To reiterate, the first term, 14, is the estimated percentage return to high school education. In subsequent terms, the first element is an estimate of the return in excess of alternatives, obtainable on additional education; the second element is the total cost of the additional education as a proportion of the cost of high school education;[17] the third element is the proportion of high school graduates who obtain the additional education. If the returns to college education were discounted back four years to the date at which high school education was initiated, at a 5 percent discount rate the expected return to high school education would drop to $14 + 2.1 + 0.7 = 16.8$, instead of 17.4 percent.

In the example above it was assumed that a decision to complete high school would be realized with certainty. Other assumptions could be fitted easily into the framework. And if knowledge existed regarding the prospective high school student's college plans, then average probabilities of his continuation should not be used.

If the option value of education has been overlooked by parents as it has been by economists there would be a tendency toward underinvestment in education. If time horizons are short so that, for example, a prospective high school student and his parents sometimes fail to consider that a few years later the child may wish he could be going on to college, there will be a systematic downward bias to the valuation of education by individuals. Even disregarding graduate education, the option value of high school education increased the rate of return of high school costs from 14 to 17 percent, considering only the "monetary" returns. For grade school education, recognition of the value of the option to obtain additional education increases the expected 1939 return even more substantially above the previous estimate of 35 percent,[18] see equation (3).

High School Graduates	College Graduates	Some College (Assumed = 2 years)

$$14 \quad + (9-5)(2.70)(.24) + (8-5)(1.35)(.20)$$

$$(2)$$

$$= 14 + 2.6 + 0.8 = 17.4 \text{ percent}$$

Grade School Graduates	High School Graduates	College Graduates	Some College (Assumed = 2 years)

$$35 \quad + (14-5)(2.3)(.67) + (9-5)(6.3)(.16) + (8-5)(3.1)(.13)$$

$$(3)$$

$$= 35 + 13.9 + 3.8 + 1.2 = 53.9 \text{ percent}$$

The option turns out to be quite valuable indeed, increasing the return on elementary education from 35 to 54 percent. It could be argued in this case that whether the return is 35 percent or 54 percent [19] is relatively immaterial for policy purposes, both being considerably greater than available alternatives. However, given the state of our confidence in the previously computed rates of return, it is comforting to see the estimates moved further from the decision-making margin. Of course, in addition to these returns, assuming they are attributable solely to education, are the nonmarket returns to education, including the direct consumption value of learning and the opportunity to lead the "full life."

Nonfinancial Options

The words "option" and "opportunity" have appeared in the discussion above a number of times. Indeed, it seems that in many respects the value of education is a function of the additional options which became available to a person having it—job options, income-leisure-security options, additional schooling options, on-the-job learning options, way-of-life options.

Recognizing the existence of such options suggests a possible means of estimating the monetary equivalent value of nonmonetary returns from education. Thus, the college graduate who chooses to go to graduate school and then enter academic life may be assumed to obtain a total (not merely monetary) return on his graduate education costs at least equal to what he could have obtained from a comparable alternative investment. In general, added education permits widened job choices, and to some extent people with more education will choose employment which provides nonmonetary rewards (for example, greater security) at the expense of monetary rewards. To the extent that this is correct and that knowledge of alternatives exists, previous estimates of the individual returns to education, utilizing incremental earnings figures for people with two different levels of education, have had a downward bias. If monetary returns from, say, graduate education turn out to be less than comparable alternative returns, the difference would be a minimum measure of nonmonetary returns, though not necessarily of the employment-associated return alone.

"Hedging" Option

There is another respect in which education provides a person with options: the increased ability to adjust to changing job opportunities. With a rapid pace of technological change, adaptability (which may be a noteworthy output of additional education) becomes important. Education may be viewed as a type of private (and social) hedge against technological displacement of skills. New technology often requires new skills and knowledge; [20] and those persons having more education are likely to be in a position to adjust more easily than those with less education, and to reap the returns from education which the new technology has made possible. This line of reasoning suggests that a more general academic curriculum is desirable since it permits greater flexibility than a curriculum which requires earlier specialization.

Insofar as the return resulting from greater flexibility is realized in the form of earnings, it will be reflected directly in the estimated monetary value of education. The hedging option has additional value, however, to the extent that people have a preference for greater security and stability of earnings.

The hypothesis that added schooling develops added labor force flexibility and thereby facilitates adjustments to changing skill requirements suggests the following implication: the greater the level of an individual's formal education attainment, the more he can benefit from additional on-the-job training, and, therefore, the more on-the-job training he will obtain. Jacob Mincer's data support this view;[21] through time, investment in learning on the job is increasingly being concentrated on persons with education beyond elementary school. He estimates that in all three years, 1939, 1949, and 1958, on-the-job training costs per person were positively correlated with the level of education. Moreover, a trend is observable—in 1939, on-the-job training costs per person with elementary education were 38 percent of costs per college-educated person; in 1949 they were 30 percent; and by 1958, 28 percent. Over the 20-year period, training costs per capita for elementary-educated persons actually declined (in constant dollars), while they climbed 13 percent for college-trained persons.

Nonmarket Returns

So far we have discussed the return to education which is realized by the individual in terms of his employment conditions. But some of the value of education to the individual accrues in other forms. For example, the fruits of literacy—an output of elementary education—include, in addition to consumption aspects, the implicit value of its nonmarket use. To illustrate: When a person prepares his own income tax return he performs a service made possible by his literacy. Were this service provided through the market, it would be priced and included in national income.[22]

Assume that roughly 50 million of the 60 million personal income tax returns filed per year are prepared by the taxpayer himself. At a value of $5.00 per return, a low estimate of an average charge by an accountant for preparing a not-too-complex return, we arrive at an annual market value of the tax return services performed by taxpayers for themselves of $250 million. Relative to Schultz's estimate of total elementary school costs of $7.8 billion in 1956,[23] this suggests a current-year return of 3.2 percent of the current investment in literacy! And this is only one, obviously minor, form of return from literacy which the individual enjoys.

This attempt to place a value on a particular use of literacy is subject to at least the following criticism: Were it not for the widespread literacy in this country we would probably not have the present type of income tax system operating, and, therefore, we would adjust to illiteracy in a less costly way than having others (say, accountants) prepare tens of millions of returns. The adjustment might involve government tax assessments or a resort to another type of tax such as one on expenditures. This suggests that the literacy value estimate above is on the high side, in terms of the alternative tax collection cost in the absence of literacy.

I have attempted a very rough estimate of the alternative cost of collecting an alternative form of tax—a sales tax—which would not require such a literate population, in order to compare it with the collection cost of the income tax.[24] The assumption is that a principal reason for the relative tax collection efficiency of the income tax is the work performed by the taxpayer in preparing his own return. For the year 1940, the all-states average cost of collecting state personal income taxes was $1.50 per $100 collected, while the comparable figure for the general sales taxes of states was $2.00 per $100 collected. In the same year, collection costs per $100 of federal personal income tax were estimated at $1.68,[25] while there was, of course, no federal sales tax.[26]

In the absence of a superior alternative I have assumed that, as was true for the state tax collection costs presented above, a federal sales tax would cost one-third more to collect than the federal personal income tax. Assuming the 1960 Internal Revenue Service estimate of collection costs, of approximately 40 cents per $100, to apply to the personal income tax, then a one-third increase in the cost of collecting $50 billion (1959 individual income tax receipts) would involve an additional $66 million—approximately 0.8 percent of elementary-school costs.[27]

In this section we consider the benefits of education which are external to the student. If all the benefits of education accrued to the student, then, assuming utility-maximizing behavior and access to capital markets, there would be little reason for public concern about the adequacy of education expenditures—unless publicly supported education were an efficient way of altering the personal distribution of income in a desired way.

Income redistribution effects aside, it seems clear that access to the capital market is imperfect and also that a child, even at high school or college age, is in a poor position to make sensible long-run decisions regarding the amount or type of education, though advice from teachers, counselors, and parents may improve the decision. But these imperfections hardly appear to justify the massive public expenditures in support of education—more than $19 billion in 1960, including capital outlays.[28] We are led to the position that, to understand why education is of public concern as well as to project demand for education and determine whether expanded education is warranted on allocative-efficiency grounds, we should pay more attention to identifying and quantifying external benefits of education.[29] This section of the paper suggests a framework for analyzing these benefits and considers opportunities for measurement.

As economists, our interest in external benefits is typically related to the question of whether all benefits (as well as costs) of some action are taken into account by the decision maker. The issue is whether the benefits are or are not captured by the decision maker, since the assumption of profit maximization has the implication that benefits will be recognized by the decision maker if, but only if, he is able to obtain them. Insofar as parents and children make joint decisions on purchases of education, with none of them being a very expert, experienced buyer, those benefits which are less apparent and indirect are likely to be overlooked. Parents thinking of their children may even neglect the less direct benefits to themselves, discussed below. Moreover, benefits to non-family members are probably not considered at all.

In principle, the recipients of external benefits from some activity (for example, education) should be willing to subsidize the activity and, indeed, should seek to subsidize it. The voting mechanism and taxation provide the means for subsidization. Analysis of voting behavior may shed some light on the question whether external benefits are recognized and have an effect on decisions. But regardless whether or not subsidies are actually paid by "outsiders," we need to identify and measure the magnitudes of external benefits to determine the rate of return on resources devoted to education.

Persons receiving external benefits from a student's education may be divided into three broad groups, though the same people may be in more than one: (1) residence-related beneficiaries—those who benefit by virtue of some relationship between their place of residence and that of the subject; (2) employment-related beneficiaries—those who benefit by virtue of some employment relationship with the subject; (3) society in general.

Residence-Related Beneficiaries

Current family of the subject. While the purpose of schooling is obviously education, the manner in which it is provided may result in incidental, and even accidental, by-products; in the case of elementary education, such a by-product is child care. Schools make it possible for mothers who would otherwise be supervising their youngsters to do other things. For those mothers who choose to work, we have an estimate of the productivity of the child-care services—their earnings. This rests on the assumption that the mothers would not work if a sitter had to be hired but do work when the child is in school. If mothers would make other child-care arrangements in the absence of schools, then a better measure of value than earnings obtained would be the cost of hiring a baby-sitter or making some alternative custodial arrangement.

In March 1956 there were 3.5 million working mothers in the United States with children six to eleven years of age.[30] Assuming that as few as one million of these mothers would not work except for the schools (the others being willing to let their children stay with hired persons or simply care for themselves), and assuming $2,000 as the earnings of each mother during the school year, the value of the child-care services of elementary school may be estimated as roughly $2 billion per year.[31] Estimating total resource costs (excluding capital outlays but including implicit interest and depreciation) of public and private elementary schools in 1956 at $7.8 billion,[32] we reach the startling conclusion that elementary school support provided a return of 25 percent of cost in the by-product form of child-care services, alone.[33] This disregards the value of these services to mothers who do not choose to work; since the value is certainly greater than zero, the total value of the child-care is even more than 25 percent of cost.

The increased production from working mothers tends to offset the foregone production from students in school. Various writers have emphasized students' foregone earnings as a cost of education, and have debated its magnitude,[34] but have not considered the fact that some mothers' earnings are made possible by the fact that children forego earnings to remain in school.

Future family of the subject. When the student reaches adulthood and becomes a parent, the children will benefit from his or her education by virtue of the informal education which the children receive in the home. The presence and relevance of such education is recognized, but to my knowledge no attempts to estimate its value have been made. If scores on achievement tests could be related to educational attainments of parents, adjusting for variation in students' ability, we might obtain some information about the extent of education in the home. This might be translated into equivalent years in school, to which a value, perhaps average cost, could be attributed.

If we think of the investment-consumption distinction as involving whether or not benefits accrue in the "present" (consumption) or in the "future" (investment), then education has an investment component in the form of these intergeneration benefits.[35] If we generalize the conception of investment to include not only intertemporal benefits,[36] but also interpersonal benefits, then the child-care role of schools, discussed above, represents an investment in the productivity of mothers. Similarly, other interpersonal benefits examined below will constitute investment aspects of educational expenditures.

Neighbors. As we consider more extended groups, beginning with the individual receiving the education and then his family (present and future), we come to his neighbors. Education affects them at least in the following ways: by inculcating acceptable social values and behavior norms in the community children and by providing children with alternatives to unsupervised activities which may have antisocial consequences. The second is essentially of short-period significance—during the time the child is of school age. The first effect is clearly of long-period consequence, following the student as he grows, and as he moves. As the student achieves adulthood, and as he migrates, the social values developed in part through his education continue to affect his "neighbors." [37]

The hypothesis that education does affect neighbors might be tested by studying voting behavior on school issues among nonparents. We might expect that their voting would be influenced by the extent to which students emigrate after completion of school, so that any potential external benefits or costs to neighbors would be realized by persons in other communities. Perhaps some notion of the magnitude of external, neighborhood benefits—at least to the extent they are recognized —could be obtained in this manner.

Taxpayers. Related to the effects of education on neighbors are the effects on those who pay (directly or indirectly) for the consequences of the lack of education. For example, insofar as lack of education leads to employment difficulties and crime, law-enforcement costs will tend to be high. Thus may education provide social benefits by reducing the need for incurring these "avoidance costs," to the advantage of taxpayers.

Education also benefits taxpayers in other communities. The migration of poorly educated persons having behavioral patterns and educational attainments differing from those prevailing in the new areas may necessitate additional effort and expense to permit the in-migrant children to adjust to the new school conditions.[38] Thus, people in areas of in-migration have a stake in the education of children in the areas of out-migration. People who are or may be in the same fiscal unit with an individual have a financial stake in his education.

Employment-Related Beneficiaries

The education of one worker may have favorable external effects on the productivity of others. Where production involves the cooperative effort of workers, flexibility and adaptability of one worker will redound to the advantage of others. Productivity of each member of the group influences the productivity of each other member. In such a case, each worker has a financial interest in the education of his fellow workers. Again, the relevance of this interdependence for the present context rests on the assumption that education develops the properties of flexibility and adaptability. Further analysis is required to determine the extent to which the assumption is valid, and if it is, to estimate its significance.

Employers may also have a financial interest in the schooling and training of their employees. Much of education improves the quality of the labor force and thereby bestows some benefits to employers of the workers insofar as market imperfections or the "specific" [39] nature of the education result in failure of the employer to pay the marginal revenue product of a worker.

Society in General

Some of the benefits from education are enjoyed by individuals and groups that are reasonably identifiable, as we have seen. But some of the benefits are distributed broadly either spatially or temporarily, so that the nature of individual beneficiaries is obscure. These shall be considered under the heading, "Society in General," which thus becomes somewhat of a residual category of benefits.

Literacy is not only of value to the individual possessing it and to employers but also is of value to others. Without widespread literacy the significance of books, newspapers, and similar media for the transmission of information would dwindle; and it seems fair to say that the communication of information is of vital importance to the maintenance of competition and, indeed, to the existence of a market economy, as well as to the maintenance of political democracy.

Along the same lines it should be noted that the substantial role played by checking deposits in our economy requires, among other things, generalized literacy and competence with arithmetic operations. It is not necessary to argue the issue of cause versus effect, but only to recognize the essentiality of literacy—a principal output of elementary education—to the present state of our economic development. Nor does saying this deny the possibility that other factors were also indispensable to growth.

Equality of opportunity seems to be a frequently expressed social goal. Education plays a prominent role in discussions of this goal, since the financial and other obstacles to education confronted by some people are important barriers to its achievement.[40] If equality of opportunity is a social goal, then education pays social returns over and above the private returns to the recipients of the education.

Although the long-term effect of education on future earnings is surely the most powerful income distribution consequence of education,[41] there are also some short-term effects. These occur through the provision by schools of things traditionally considered to be private consumer goods and services—including subsidized lunch programs, musical instrument lessons, and driver training courses.

Earlier we distinguished between the output of education in the form of the student's training and the output of the system or means by which the training was accomplished—the latter being illustrated by custodial or child-care services. The same distinction may be made with respect to higher education, the point being that the training of students is not the only output of schools; a joint product is the research activity of college and university faculties, from which society reaps benefits. It is undoubtedly true that were it not for the higher education system the volume of basic research would be smaller. A question exists regarding the extent to which the value of the research is reflected in salaries and, thereby, in private returns. The relation of education to research and of research to social returns deserves more attention from economists.[42]

Training of persons in particular kinds of skills may result in important external benefits if there are bottlenecks to economic development. In the context of underdeveloped economies, one writer, while particularly noting the political significance of primary and higher education, and the prestige significance of the latter, argues: "Secondary education is essential to the training of 'medium' personnel (elementary teachers, monitors, officials, middle classes). The shortage of such people is today a real obstacle to economic development." [43] But without perfect capital markets and appropriate subsidization programs, these socially valuable people may be unable to capture for themselves the full value of their contribution. Therefore, their earnings would understate the full benefits of their education.

In the preceding pages I have asked: "Who receive the benefits from education?" In addition, I have considered some of the limited possibilities for quantifying certain of the benefits. As plans are developed for future research I urge that more attention be directed to the spatial and temporal dimensions of these benefits.

While much work remains, we might summarize our findings. We have noted that some of the benefits of education are realized at the time the education is being received (that is, in the "short" run); others, after the formal education has been completed (that is, in the "long" run). Benefits to mothers, in terms of the child-care role of schools, and benefits to neighbors, in keeping children "off the streets" are realized while the education is being obtained. Any benefits associated with subsequent employment of the student as well as benefits to the student's future children are realized later.

We have found, further, that benefits from education occur not only at various times but also in various places. The benefits of education do not necessarily accrue to people in the area or in the school district which financed the child's education. In particular, some of the benefits depend upon the individual's place of residence, which may change. Location of many residence-related benefits as well as employment-related benefits will be determined partly by population migration, though this is not generally true of benefits to family members and to society as a whole. While it is not necessarily true that total benefits will depend upon one's location, the point is that the particular beneficiaries will be a function of the location of the individual. Thus, the process of migration is a process of spatial shifting of some of the external effects of education.

Some interesting questions are raised simply by the recognition that external benefits of education exist, and that they are not all in broad, amorphous form; that is, that to some extent these benefits accrue to particular, rather well-defined, groups. Thus, to the extent that the education system at the elementary level is producing child-care services as an output, benefit-principle taxation would suggest that families of the children might pay for these benefits.[44] In general, a desire to use this taxation principle would imply attempts to identify various groups of education beneficiaries and to assess taxes in recognition of the distribution of benefits.[45]

It seems to me that there is a legitimate question concerning the justice of requiring broad, public support for education insofar as the benefits are narrow and private, except as an income-redistributive device. For example, to the extent that there is really no educational sacrifice involved in having children attend split-shift classes, so that the real motive for the abolition of split shifts is to make life more comfortable for mothers who have all of their children in school at the same time, then a question of equity arises: Should nonparents be expected to share the costs associated with the provision of these child-care services for parents? The answer may not be an unequivocal "no," but the question deserves further consideration. Except for lack of information, or a disavowal of benefit-principle taxation, there is little rationale for failure of our education-tax system to recognize the existence of particular groups of beneficiaries.

Burton A. Weisbrod

There is another strong reason in addition to the alleged justice of benefit-principle taxation for identifying benefits and beneficiaries. To the extent that the distribution of tax burdens for the support of education differs substantially from the distribution of education benefits, it is likely that education will be either undersupported or oversupported from an allocative-efficiency standpoint, given the existing preference structure and distribution of income and wealth.[46]

Both with respect to equity and to efficiency in education finance, the increasing phenomenon of migration needs to be recognized. Insofar as some of the benefits of education depend upon the location of the individual and insofar as this location is a variable over his lifetime, some of the benefits from education accrue to people who have played no part at all in the financing of this particular person's education. This would seem to be especially pertinent with respect to areas of substantial net in- or out-migration. Areas experiencing net in-migration might be expected, on benefit-principle grounds, to subsidize areas of net out-migration, particularly if highly productive people are involved. Subsidy in the opposite direction might be justified insofar as the in-migrants to an area are relatively unproductive compared to its out-migrants. Needless to say, there are good and powerful arguments in favor of keeping all the financing of education at a local level. However, a thorough analysis of the issue would seem to require recognition of the points raised here.

The analytic approach to benefit identification employed in this paper is one of many alternatives; it does appear to have the advantage of focusing on the time and the location of education benefits, and these are relevant to the study both of efficiency in the allocation of resources between education and other ends and of equity in the financing of education.

It is clear that even with much additional effort we shall be unable to measure all the relevant benefits of education. At the same time the following four points are worth noting, and they summarize the views expressed in this paper: (1) identification of benefits is the logical step prior to measurement and, therefore, recognizing the forms of benefits represents some progress; (2) determination of what it is we are trying to measure will make it easier to develop useful quantification methods; (3) some reasonable measures of some education benefits are possible; (4) even partial measurement may disclose benefits sufficiently sizable to indicate a profitable investment, so that consideration of the nonmeasured benefits would, a fortiori, support the expenditure decision.

In any event, and however difficult the measurement task is, it remains true that education expenditure decisions will be made, and they will be made on the basis of whatever information is available.

Appendix: Costs of Education

The objective here is to consider briefly, at the conceptual level, some of the issues involved in estimating costs of education. There is no doubt that a complete picture of the cost of education would include all foregone opportunities, whether or not reflected by actual expenditures. Thus, the attempt to measure foregone production by looking at foregone earnings of students in school is fully appropriate. There is, of course, the difficult question of how to estimate the foregone earnings—in particular, whether they may be estimated by looking at the earnings of people of comparable age and sex who were not in school.

One of the issues is whether those in school are not, in general, more able and ambitious, so that their opportunity cost of schooling exceeds the earnings by their "dropout" counterparts. Another involves the effect on earnings (actually, on the value of marginal productivity) of a large influx to the labor market, such as would occur if all college, or all high school, students entered the labor force.

But it seems to me that this latter issue is beside the point. Studies involving cost and benefits of education are surely not directed to the question whether there should or should not be education. Rather the issue is the profitability or productivity of reasonably small increments or decrements to education. The issue is whether fewer or more people should be encouraged to go further in school. Only marginal changes are being contemplated.

Still on the subject of estimating foregone production among students by estimating foregone earnings, there is the additional question of the validity of using earnings of employed people when there is a question whether resources released from the schools would or would not find employment. Thus, the view is not uncommon that measuring foregone earnings of students by the earnings of presently employed people is satisfactory only if there is little unemployment.[47] This question arises frequently, especially when public investment is being considered. Thus, it inevitably arises when the economic efficiency of public health expenditures is being discussed; would the additional labor resources made available by an improvement in public health be able to find employment? And with regard to education, would labor resources released from schools be able to find employment?

It seems to me to be analytically unwise to mix study of the allocative efficiency of additional expenditures on education with study of the efficiency of monetary and fiscal policy in maintaining full employment. I would like to urge that in looking at the question of whether to invest more in education, we consider what students could earn and produce,

Burton A. Weisbrod

not what they might actually earn or produce, as affected by unemployment. The efficiency of educational expenditures in dealing with unemployment is a quite different question from the efficiency of education as an allocation problem. Although there might be short-run transitional unemployment associated with some movement of students into the labor force, the basic issue of investment in people through education is of the long run.[48]

The alternative production foregone because of education also involves the government services used by educational institutions. Since many of these services are rendered without charge to the schools, they are generally, and mistakenly, omitted from discussion of costs. Recognition by R. C. Blitz of the relevance of these services to estimation of education costs is a valid and important point.[49] However, estimating the social cost of these services as equal to the value of the property and sales taxes which the schools would have paid had they not been exempt is conceptually inappropriate (albeit perhaps pragmatically reasonable). To the extent that the services rendered to schools by governments are "pure public services," the actual marginal cost of providing these services to the school is zero. The essence of "pure" public services is that everyone may enjoy them in common, and the consumption by one person does not subtract from the amount available to others. For example, it is not at all clear how much additional police or fire services will be required in a community by virtue of the fact that there is a school within its limits.

At the same time, services performed by governments are never entirely of a "pure public service" nature—particularly in the long run (for example, public libraries, which are frequently used by students)—so the marginal cost of providing them to a school will, in general, exceed zero. But the marginal cost is likely to be below average cost and, therefore, to be below the estimated foregone property and sales taxes, which are related to average costs of providing public services.

Since social costs represent alternatives foregone, it is certainly not correct to include among the costs of education costs which would have been incurred anyway; therefore, all the food, shelter, and clothing costs of students while they are at school should not be considered a cost of education.[50] At the same time, if any of these maintenance costs are higher for students than they would be were the children not in school, then these additional costs are justifiably charged against the education process. If additional clothing, laundry, and transportation costs are incurred by virtue of a person being a student, these incremental costs are quite relevant to the issue of the productivity of investment in education. Such cost may be particularly high for college students living away from home, though they may not equal zero for college students living at home, or for elementary or high school students.

142

NOTES

1. The research reported herein was in part supported through the Cooperative Research Program of the Office of Education, United States Department of Health, Education, and Welfare. I would also like to acknowledge the helpful comments by Theodore W. Schultz, Richard Goode, W. Lee Hansen, Elbert Segelhorst, William Swift, and Donald Yett on earlier versions of this paper.

2. United States Department of Health, Education, and Welfare, *Health, Education and Welfare Trends, 1961* (Washington, D.C.: Government Printing Office, 1961), p. 23.

3. *Ibid.*, p. 53.

4. T. W. Schultz, "Capital Formation by Education," *Journal of Political Economy*, December 1960, p. 583.

5. Similarly, but perhaps more clearly, compulsory smallpox vaccination together with public provision of vaccine reflects external economies of "consumption" of the vaccine.

6. While I shall refer throughout this paper to the research of others I should like to mention particularly the excellent survey recently completed by Alice M. Rivlin; see her "Research in the Economics of Higher Education: Progress and Problems," in *Economics of Higher Education*, ed. Selma J. Mushkin (Washington, D.C.: United States Department of Health, Education, and Welfare [forthcoming]).

7. On the relation between educational attainment and earnings see G. Becker, "Underinvestment in College Education?" *American Economic Review, Proceedings*, May 1960, pp. 346–354; H. S. Houthakker, "Education and Income," *Review of Economics and Statistics*, February 1959, pp. 24–28; H. P. Miller, "Annual and Lifetime Income in Relation to Education," *American Economic Review*, December 1960, pp. 962–986; E. F. Renshaw, "Estimating the Returns to Education," *Review of Economics and Statistics*, August 1960, pp. 318–324.

8. See D. S. Bridgman, "Problems in Estimating the Monetary Value of College Education," *Review of Economics and Statistics, Supplement*, August 1960, p. 181.

9. Dael Wolfle, "Economics and Educational Values," *Review of Economics and Statistics, Supplement*, August 1960, pp. 178–179. See also his *America's Resources of Specialized Talent* (New York: Harper & Bros., 1954); and Wolfle and Joseph G. Smith, "The Occupational Value of Education for Superior High School Graduates," *Journal of Higher Education*, 1956, pp. 201–213.

10. "Human Capital: Concepts and Measures," in Mushkin, *Higher Education*.

11. Research by Jacob Mincer suggests that additional schooling also provides opportunities to obtain additional on-the-job training (see his "On-the-Job Training: Costs, Returns, and Some Implications," *Journal of Political Economy* 70, no. 5, pt. 2, Supplement, October 1962, Table 1). The value of this opportunity should be included in the financial option approach developed here.

12. Thus, for estimating the return from college or graduate education, omission of the value of the option may not be quantitatively significant. At the same time, since the return from higher education as previously estimated seems to be close to the return on business investments, recognition of the value of the option might tip the balance.

13. T. W. Schultz, "Education and Economic Growth," *Social Forces Influencing American Education* (Chicago: National Society for the Study of Education, 1961), chap. iii, referring to G. S. Becker's work. H. H. Villard has seriously disagreed with these estimates. See his "Discussion" of Becker's "Underinvestment in College Education?" in *American Economic Review, Proceedings*, May 1960, pp. 375–378. See also

W. L. Hansen, "Rate of Return on Human versus Non-human Investment" (draft paper, October 1960).

14. Schultz, "Economic Growth," p. 78.

15. While this paper deals with education benefits, quantitative comparison of benefits with costs are made to help assess the relative magnitudes of benefits. In doing this I do not intend to imply complete satisfaction with the cost estimates. The appendix of this paper presents some of the issues involved in defining and measuring social costs.

16. Computed from 1960 data for males of ages 25–29, in United States Bureau of the Census, Current Population Reports: Population Characteristics, Projections of Educational Attainments in the United States, 1960–1980 (hereinafter cited as Educational Attainments) (Series P-20, No. 91 [January 12, 1959, p. 8, Table 2]).

17. Computed from data in Schultz, "Economic Growth," p. 79.

18. Again disregarding the discounting. The 35 percent estimate is from Schultz, "Economic Growth," p. 81. Relative costs were estimated from the same source (p. 79), except that Schultz's elementary school cost figure was doubled, since it applied to only four years of school. The proportions of children continuing on to higher education were estimated from Educational Attainments, p. 8.

In this paper I do not discuss any option value for college education; however, there may be a positive option value related to opportunities for graduate study and additional on-the-job training.

19. Previous estimates of rates of return represented a discounting of costs and returns back to the beginning of that particular level of schooling; since our time bench mark is the beginning of grade school, the values of the high school and college options should be discounted back to the beginning of grade school. Doing so, at a discount rate of 5 percent, reduces the 54 percent return to $35 + 9.5 + 2.1 + 0.7 = 47.3$. The return would almost certainly be larger if persons obtaining only some high school education were considered.

20. This view seems to be shared by H. Coombs, who states that "there will be many unpredictable shifts in the proportions needed of specific categories of . . . manpower. Thus, it will be important . . . to enlarge the total supply of high ability manpower available for all purposes" ("Some Economic Aspects of Educational Development," in Some Economic Aspects of Educational Development in Europe, International Association of Universities [Paris: International Universities Bureau, 1961], p. 78).

21. Mincer, "On-the-Job Training," Tables 1 and 2. But F. F. Renshaw predicts that the principal educational requirements of the 1960s, with respect to the labor force, will be directed toward trade schools and apprenticeship programs ("Investment in Human Capital" [unpublished manuscript, 1960], p. 13).

22. It could be argued that the service (like many others in national income and product) is not a final output, but a cost item (cost of tax collection), and thus should not be included in estimates of production; but since it is often difficult to distinguish clearly outputs from inputs in our national accounts, and since our national income and product accounts principally measure effort expended, it would be interesting to make some estimate of the market value equivalent of the services performed by a person in preparing his own income tax return.

Inclusion of the value of this nonmarket production as an educational benefit presupposes that this represents a net increase in the value of the individual's total nonmarket activities and that the opportunity cost of performing additional nonmarket production is essentially zero.

Richard Goode has suggested that, although the failure to consider nonmarket production leads to understatement of the return to education, "nevertheless, there seems to be little danger that this omission will lead to an undervaluation of educational benefits in comparing time periods, countries, and population groups with different amounts of formal education." He presents "the hypothesis that the greater the amount of formal education the greater the proportion of goods and services acquired through the market. If this is true, estimates based on money earnings or national income statistics may exaggerate the contribution of education to real income differentials or growth."

23. Schultz, "Economic Growth," p. 64, Table 5.

24. This disregards the different distributive effects of the two forms of tax.

25. James W. Martain, "Costs of Tax Administration: Statistics of Public Expenses," *Bulletin of the National Tax Assoication*, February 1944, pp. 132–147, as cited in Charles A. Benson, *The Economics of Public Education* (Boston: Houghton-Mifflin, 1961), p. 145.

26. Estimation of collection costs is subject to the common difficulty of the allocation of joint costs; furthermore, we really know little about scale economies in tax collection, or about the difference in degree of enforcement of state and federal taxes, so that it is dangerous to apply state cost figures to the federal level.

27. Actually we should note that a number of years of education is required to develop "literate" people but also that, once developed, they presumably retain the knowledge. Were we to take into account the number of tax returns an average person may be expected to file during his lifetime, a higher rate of return would appear.

28. HEW, *Health, Education and Welfare Trends, 1961*, pp. 52, 53.

29. It is true, however, that economies of scale (with respect to the number of students) would also be a sufficient explanation for the public interest in education.

30. United States Bureau of the Census, *Marital and Family Status of Workers: 1956* (Series P-50, No. 73 [April 1957]), p. 11, Table 3.

31. For those mothers who would be willing to hire baby-sitters, obtainable for, perhaps, $1,000 per year, the value of the school child-care services is this alternative cost of $1,000, instead of $2,000. Of the 3.5 million working mothers with children six to eleven years old, approximately 1.5 million also had children 12 to 17. Some of the older children could conceivably care for the younger ones; but even considering the remaining 2 million, the assumption that one-half would not work except for the care provided by schools seems plausible and even conservative.

32. Schultz, "Economic Growth," p. 85.

33. If working mothers employ housekeepers as substitutes and if they incur other additional costs in working (for example, transportation and additional clothes), these added costs should be deducted from the gross returns.

34. See Appendix.

35. Schultz has also recognized this point: "The education of women . . . reduces the subsequent effective costs of education because of the critical role that mothers play in motivating their children to obtain an education and to perform well while they are attending school. Thus, if we could get at the factors underlying the perpetuation of education, it is likely that we would discover that the education of many persons not in the labor force contributes heavily to the effective perpetuation of the stock of education. To the extent that this is true, some part of the education not in the labor force contributes to this investment process" ("Economic Growth," pp. 74–75).

36. Tax implications of the existence of intertemporal education returns have been discussed by R. Goode, "Educational Expenditures and Income Tax," in Mushkin, *Higher Education*.

37. One writer points out: "Education has effects on the caliber of voluntary

community activities: choral groups, drama, clubs, local art shows, etc." (Benson, *Economics of Public Education,* p. 349).

38. See, for example, C. F. Schmid, V. A. Miller, and B. Abu-Laban, "Impact of Recent Negro Migration on Seattle Schools," *International Population Conference Papers* (Vienna: Union International pour l'Étude Scientifique de la Population, 1959), pp. 674–683.

39. As the term is used by Gary S. Becker "specific" training is that which raises the marginal productivity of the worker in one firm more than it raises his productivity in other firms. By contrast, "general" training raises marginal productivity equally in many firms. Since, under competitive conditions, wage rates are determined by workers' marginal productivities in other firms, a worker with "specific" training would be expected to receive a wage less than his actual marginal revenue productivity but more than his alternative productivity.

40. Even if it were true that educating everyone would widen the personal distribution of earnings compared with what it would be with less education, it would not follow that additional education for some people would worsen their relative or absolute economic position.

41. The relation between education and income distribution has been studied by J. Mincer ("Investment in Human Capital and Personal Income Distribution," *Journal of Political Economy,* August 1958, pp. 281–302) and L. Soltow ("The Distribution of Income Related to Changes in the Distributions of Education, Age and Occupation," *Review of Economics and Statistics,* November 1960, pp. 450–453).

42. For an interesting study of returns from research see Z. Griliches, "Research Costs and Social Returns: Hybrid Corn and Related Innovations," *Journal of Political Economy,* October 1958, pp. 419–431.

43. Michael Debeauvals, "Economic Problems of Education in the Underdeveloped Countries," in International Association of Universities, *Some Economic Aspects,* pp. 116–117.

44. This point came out in a discussion with Julius Margolis.

45. This is not to argue that the benefit principle, in contrast to the ability-to-pay or some other principle, should necessarily prevail.

46. However, an objective of education may be to change the distribution.

47. See, for example, Rivlin, "Research," p. 12.

48. Mary Jean Bowman shares this view: "Such validity, if any, as may attach to it [the view that marginal social opportunity costs of education are zero when unemployment is serious] is in any case limited to short-term marginal valuations, whereas we are interested in long-term averages and aggregates. When long-term aggregate human capital formation is the focus, social opportunity costs are not zero even with chronic unemployment" ("Human Capital: Concepts and Measures," in Mushkin, *Higher Education*).

49. "The Nation's Education Outlay," in Mushkin, *Higher Education.*

50. See discussion by Rivlin, "Research," pp. 11–12, correctly criticizing the study by Harold F. Clark and Ruth E. Sobokov for including them.

(6)

Long-Term Change in Personal Income Distribution: Theoretical Approaches, Evidence, and Explanations

T. Paul Schultz

IT IS a commonly accepted fact that inequality in personal incomes in the United States diminished up to and during World War II, but that this long-term trend was not sustained during the last 25 years. Given the unavoidable differences of opinion that attach to the meaning and measurement of income inequality, even this most generally observed fact is not free of controversy. The purpose of this paper is to bring discussion to a sharper focus on certain specific facts and their alternative interpretations. Advancement in the empirical study of the distribution of personal income awaits agreement on the most significant dimensions of the phenomenon. These attributes depend on the questions asked, and ultimately on the specification of models that promise to answer them.

In the first section, I present the logic for adopting one conceptual and statistical approach in measuring and analyzing income inequality. In the second section, I assemble empirical evidence on income inequality from 1939 to 1970. But to interpret the evidence and illuminate the

Rand P–4767, reprinted with permission of the author, © 1972.

forces responsible for secular trends will require a brief survey of recent contributions to the human capital literature. In traditional form, I conclude by stressing the need for new directions for research.

Measurement and Meaning of Income Inequality

One traditional objective of studies of income distribution is to discover a single or modest number of parameters that efficiently summarize size distributions of personal income. This search has produced numerous papers over the years extolling the merits of particular functional forms as approximations for the frequency distribution of incomes. I think it is fair to say, nonetheless, that there has emerged no single "best fit," in large part because for alternative purposes data are arrayed by different recipient units and income is measured differently.

In the choice of a measure of income inequality, reliance on a normative or positive conceptual framework has greater attraction than simply curve fitting. There are two reasons to be interested in income inequality: First, social welfare is thought to depend on both the level and personal distribution of income; second, economic analysis may usefully describe some of the systematic factors affecting income inequality. These two approaches to income inequality are concerned with different problems, attempting in the first instance to assign a social cost to disparities in personal income and in the second instance to attribute these disparities to various causes. Measurement of inequality as implied by one approach need not be suitable to the other, although overlap would prove convenient.

From a normative view, Dalton observed in 1930 that "the economist is primarily interested, not in the distribution of income as such, but in the effect of the distribution of income upon the distribution and total amount of economic welfare, which may be derived from income" (p. 348). This linkage between income and welfare implies the specification of a social utility function and embodies obvious value judgments. In a recent paper Atkinson (1970) notes the parallel between the ranking of distributions of outcomes in decision making under uncertainty and the ranking of income distributions by a generally prescribed social utility function. Thus, following Atkinson's formulation, the degree of "inequality-aversion" one professes alters one's preferred ordering of observed distributions of personal income. For a general class of socially utility functions proposed by Atkinson, a single parameter, ϵ, reflects social sensitivity to income transfers at different relative income levels.[1] Most conventional measures of inequality do not imply, by this standard, a uniform degree of inequality aversion with the exception of the variance of the logarithms of income for which $\epsilon = 2$.[2] Since the log variance of income attaches equal importance to equal *relative* differences in income, it attributes greater weight to equal transfers to the poor than to the rich. Given the general concern expressed over conditions of the poor, the choice of $\epsilon = 2$ or perhaps more would not appear to misrepresent society's egalitarian preferences.[3]

The second and more attractive basis for arriving at a definition of income inequality is to adopt a measure that conforms to the requirements of an analytical model that promises to describe the distribution and identify the causes of income inequality. The most thoroughly elaborated approach to the economic determination of income inequality is that associated with the works of Becker, Mincer, and Chiswick.[4] Using the concept of human capital as the principal systematic determinant of differences in labor earnings, a number of propositions are deduced about cohort age profiles and inequality of earnings by schooling and on-the-job experience. The measure of income inequality that is useful for the human capital approach is the variance of the logarithms of income.[5] Thus, the log variance has the convenient attraction as a single parameter of income inequality both because of the consistent and plausible nature of the social welfare function it implies and because it conforms to the dependent variable determined by the human capital model of earnings inequality.

Concept of Income and Income Recipient Unit

Having indicated why I shall adopt a particular measure of income inequality, there still remains the task of defining the recipient unit and the concept of income consistent with normative and positive concepts of economics. It is difficult to interpret inequality of income among household units from a normative point of view because the composition of household units varies across social groups at one point in time and in a group over time, and this variation is not independent of the underlying distribution of resources among persons.

Schemes are often proposed to cope with these normative problems of noncomparability and horizontal equity—for instance, a couple with five children and retired parents in the household has greater consumption needs than a childless couple.[6] But standardization of data neglects the margin of choice that is likely to influence the composition of household units. How individuals choose to arrange themselves into household units, how they divide their time among labor market, home production, and leisure activities, and how many children couples seek—each of these decisions influences measured inequality of income among them. Each decision is also likely to be influenced by the economic endowments of individuals as well as by other social and economic conditions.[7]

Unfortunately these well-known problems cannot be resolved now except by avoiding altogether the household unit as a basis for inequality comparisons; subsequent analysis therefore concentrates on the distribution of income among individual persons. Numerous problems still exist in the study of income data for persons, but at least they are more manageable in principle, even if in practice they are severe for the study of secondary workers. Nonetheless, the study of household units requires the formulation of wholly new analytical concepts.

The time frame for comparisons of income inequality would logically be the individual's life cycle. Not only is the alleged link between equality and equity forged in terms of the distribution of lifetime (or even intergenerational) opportunities, the human capital framework also emphasizes the role of individual investment decisions as a determinant of different age-earnings profiles. Both approaches to the analysis of income inequality call for cohort time series information, but in lieu of these more appropriate data, empirical analysis has in fact almost always relied on contemporaneous cross-sectional data, interpreting differences among age groups, adjusted perhaps for neutral secular trends in productivity, as evidence on the behavior of income inequality over the life cycle. This jump from cross-sectional data to time series inferences deserves far more study than it has received.

Approaches to income inequality diverge, however, in defining a working concept of income. Nonhuman wealth is undoubtedly a most important source of "inequitable" differences in personal lifetime opportunities, leading the normative analyst to prefer the broadest possible concept of labor and capital income including, if possible, capital gains and inheritances. From a positive point of view, human capital theory has implications primarily for the returns to labor as augmented by human capital, calling for a concept of "income" no broader than labor earnings of perhaps only wages and salaries.[8] Another related class of problems is concealed from view by necessary reliance on measures of pretax money income that neglect income taxes, income in kind,[9] and nonpecuniary benefits associated with different investment, occupational, and migration choices made by individuals over their lifetime.

Variation in Time Worked

A final difficulty for interpreting income inequality is the variation in the amount of time that individuals work in the labor market. This variation in hours worked can be attributed to both supply and demand factors, but integrated analysis has not clearly differentiated their respective roles: (1) individuals can invest time to enhance future productivity, given their abilities, cost of investable funds, and time and risk preferences; (2) individuals allocate remaining time among market production, nonmarket, and consumption (leisure) activities, given their preferences for market and nonmarket goods; and (3) individuals may not find employment for the wage they expect to receive and therefore go unemployed.[10]

Earnings are observed in the market gross of returns on past human capital investments and net of current time invested in further training. Therefore, the profile of potential (full-time) earnings and life cycle human capital investments cannot be derived uniquely for an individual from his observed age profile of earnings. The existence of depreciation and obsolescence of human capital complicates further the underdetermined character of the human capital model. Strong assumptions arc required to constrain the life cycle investment process to draw inferences about its nature from available data. Ben-Porath (1967, 1969) and more generally Rosen (1970, 1971, 1972) derive life cycle investment behavior from attractive optimizing models, but the value of their models as a framework for empirical analysis is yet to be clearly demonstrated. Mincer's (1970a, 1971b) formulation of this problem, although arbitrary in assuming a linear or exponential rate of decline of time equivalent postschooling investment (see also T. Johnson, 1970), has, on the contrary, shown its ability to distinguish between important sources of earnings inequality. A novel implication of Mincer's formulation is the notion of an *overtaking period*, seven to ten years after on-the-job training commences, when the log variance of cohort earnings can be interpreted as a measure of in lifetime earnings opportunities. The lack of a satisfactory empirical approximation for postschooling investments for women and secondary workers *currently* limits the appliation of Mincer's model to supply considerations underlying earnings inequality among prime-age men. Promising approaches to preschool investments and ultimately childhood nutrition (Selowsky and Taylor, 1971) should also be accommodated within the evolving generalized household human capital framework.

The second source of variation in time worked in the labor force is the allocation of "uninvested" time between market and nonmarket activities. Empirical study of this behavioral process is as yet crude for want of satisfactory measures of nonmarket productivity. Since only a measure of the pecuniary product of time allocated to the labor market is observed, inequality of earnings opportunities can only be expressed per unit time worked. Although wage rate comparisons are one response to this problem, another is to restrict analysis to annual earnings of those fully employed, i.e., according to the current Census Bureau definition; persons working 35 and more hours per week or 50 to 52 weeks a year. To the extent that time worked is positively correlated among individuals with wage rates, earnings inequality among the fully employed will be less than total income inequality.

The third source of variation in overtime in the supply of labor to the market, unemployment, is generally attributed to demand factors. If our central concern is with secular change in income inequality, there is reason to limit our analysis to periods in the business cycle when labor markets are equally tight. But with data for 1939 and the post-war period, no comparisons are possible between 1939 and any postwar year, for postwar levels of unemployment have fortunately not reached 1939's 17.2 percent of the civilian labor force. The incidence and duration of unemployment may also differ by age, education, and possibly experience classes, and thus a part of the association between annual earnings and education can be attributed to the partial correlation between hours worked and education, and thus incorporated into the supply model (Becker, 1964; Oi, 1962; Bowman and Anderson, 1966; Mincer, 1971).[11]

From this review of the literature, it is clear the concept of income that both normative and positive analysts seek is a measure of inequality in lifetime income opportunities. The human capital model interprets differences in earnings among schooling groups as due to life cycle investment decisions modified by the correlation among preschooling, schooling, and postschooling investments, capital market imperfections and time and risk preferences (Friedman, 1958). Inequality within schooling groups is then viewed as an approximation of measurement error (i.e., unobserved variations in postschooling investment and quality of schooling) plus the underlying variance and covariance of individual ability and opportunity (Becker, 1967; Mincer, 1970b).

But this model by itself does not take account of the second and third sources of variation in the time worked by individuals. Except as human capital is linked to cyclical variation in education-specific unemployment, unemployment does not yet fit comfortably within the human capital model of income distribution. Nor is this theory applicable to measured inequality among secondary workers whose life cycle attachment to the labor force is sporadic. This model is then most clearly applicable to earning inequality among fully employed male workers. Data for this group across age groups and over time are used in the next section to determine the extent of change in income inequality in the United States.

Some Empirical Evidence: Facts

Estimates of average income and the variance of the logarithms of income are reported in Tables 6–1 and 6–2 *for all persons with income* by sex and age. These annual estimates—for the years 1947 through

TABLE 6–1

Estimates of Average Annual U.S. Personal Incomes by Sex and Age: 1947–1970
(for persons 14 years and over with income in current dollars)

Sex/Age	1947	1948	1949	1950	1951	1952	1953	1954	1955	1956	1957	1958	1959	1960	1961	1962	1963	1964	1965	1966	1967	1968	1969	1970
Male	2563	2692	2604	2894	3200	3356	3515	3539	3711	3975	4040	4177	4451	4627	4894	4956	5163	5378	5593	5709	6449	6925	7508	7956
14–19	706	660	569	607	699	724	744	679	604	640	607	579	635	628	609	635	646	753	867	919	1075	1097	1143	1225
20–24	1652	1911	1815	1972	2327	2311	2296	2290	2436	2657	2618	2647	2792	2809	2952	2967	2935	3150	3467	3729	3868	4020	4254	4497
25–34	2658	2868	2831	3059	3454	3681	3879	3767	3979	4395	4567	4663	4926	5127	5342	5357	5726	6062	6267	6889	7285	7840	8568	8917
35–44	3211	3357	3200	3604	3983	4093	4407	4406	4606	5107	5196	5853	5606	6179	6365	6644	6856	7218	7521	8168	8696	9387	10225	10792
45–54	3213	3204	3185	3539	3728	4072	4246	4377	4688	4925	5097	5211	5606	5903	6201	6394	6647	6903	7431	8000	8599	9094	10046	10776
55–64	2711	2858	2695	2993	3279	3442	3701	3732	3993	4149	4184	4495	4988	5011	5517	5571	5801	5867	6147	6789	7258	7978	8617	9153
65 +	1695	1642	1751	1805	1869	2094	2092	2118	2238	2292	2210	2251	2512	2674	2899	2878	3003	3262	3107	3259	3614	3954	4271	4476
Female	1258	1266	1256	1300	1416	1493	1587	1581	1609	1631	1707	1735	1820	1847	1946	2008	2041	2183	2382	2414	2686	2831	3008	3230
14–19	637	654	609	591	650	808	619	716	614	660	645	603	573	598	574	699	579	592	892	765	971	905	927	940
20–24	1233	1346	1308	1370	1428	1541	1602	1662	1626	1719	1782	1779	1829	1944	1891	1906	2039	2169	2562	2386	2550	2708	2874	3038
25–34	1327	1445	1429	1472	1653	1712	1856	1794	1781	1853	1981	1932	2045	2120	2275	2171	2273	2404	2641	2750	3118	3237	3419	3747
35–44	1469	1483	1321	1513	1686	1786	1818	1837	1844	2035	2126	2136	2159	2292	2543	2442	2495	2687	2851	2959	3308	3439	3708	3999
45–54	1494	1534	1466	1532	1598	1815	1971	1903	2055	2076	2136	2224	2377	2403	2582	2656	2769	2857	3113	3212	3578	3739	4086	4815
55–64	1271	1202	1384	1333	1473	1659	1597	1712	1849	1852	1882	2003	2096	2048	2177	2460	2510	2583	2796	2888	3139	3386	3709	3837
65 +	984	809	721	779	793	964	1027	1043	986	998	1049	1050	1172	1180	1210	1297	1331	1531	1504	1616	1749	1975	2123	2275
Both Sexes	2148	2225	2158	2350	2574	2696	2809	2823	2925	3082	3147	3198	3451	3526	3705	3769	3876	4047	4247	4518	4834	5103	5613	5849

Source: Derived from Current Population Reports, Consumer Income, Series P–60, Bureau of the Census.

TABLE 6–2

Estimates of the Variance of the Logarithms of U.S. Personal Income by Sex and Age: 1947–1970
(among persons 14 years and over with income)

Sex/Age	1947	1948	1949	1950	1951	1952	1953	1954	1955	1956	1957	1958	1959	1960	1961	1962	1963	1964	1965	1966	1967	1968	1969	1970
Male	.6675	.6867	.7536	.7754	.7295	.7251	.8350	.8534	.8798	.9042	.9272	.9636	.9751	1.022	1.069	1.034	1.062	1.076	1.092	1.047	1.116	1.128	1.163	1.187
14–19	.8184	.7334	.9579	.6760	.9051	.7484	1.145	1.052	.9795	1.092	1.052	1.223	1.099	1.055	1.123	1.146	1.039	.8567	.9476	.8754	1.013	.9771	.9560	1.038
20–24	.4082	.3861	.4495	.5136	.4690	.4398	.5664	.5289	.5291	.5884	.6044	.6498	.6428	.6887	.7547	.7425	.8065	.7829	.7802	.7534	.8023	.7754	.7605	.8226
25–34	.3515	.3548	.3791	.3783	.3108	.3117	.3908	.4449	.4444	.3963	.4197	.4447	.4422	.4276	.4943	.4482	.4407	.4258	.4258	.3906	.3866	.3891	.4179	.4578
35–44	.4938	.4448	.5378	.4709	.4099	.4257	.4668	.5400	.4659	.4908	.5184	.4891	.4779	.5542	.5583	.5513	.4903	.4947	.5408	.4558	.4588	.4543	.4687	.4807
45–54	.5407	.5852	.6804	.6425	.5496	.5306	.6105	.7018	.6938	.6923	.6968	.7269	.6917	.7190	.7457	.6782	.6372	.6240	.6398	.5730	.5457	.5672	.5722	.5854
55–64	.6242	.7132	.8309	.7941	.7600	.6843	.7272	.8103	.8004	.8285	.7950	.8173	.8999	.8619	.8383	.8460	.8741	.8318	.8240	.7923	.7660	.7424	.7392	.7676
65+	.9647	.8398	.9568	.9961	.9427	.8392	.8762	.8964	.8450	.7881	.7252	.6896	.7328	.7109	.7642	.6488	.6509	.7270	.6318	.6568	.6872	.6598	.6087	.6408
Female	.6702	.6811	.7203	.7755	.7986	.8248	.8470	.8484	.9066	.9259	.9523	.9057	1.006	1.003	1.050	1.035	1.052	1.072	1.095	1.077	1.136	1.108	1.126	1.169
14–19	.8146	.8198	.8952	.6400	.6971	.8832	1.204	.7596	.6482	1.006	.8485	.8648	1.207	1.227	1.250	.9886	1.270	1.263	1.287	.8997	1.087	.9954	.9641	1.036
20–24	.4661	.5085	.5146	.5554	.5560	.6424	.6554	.6233	.6977	.7332	.6836	.8255	.8344	.8582	.9091	.8817	.8709	.8961	.9586	.9814	.9732	.9292	.8822	.9310
25–34	.5292	.5980	.6460	.6879	.6686	.7914	.7895	.7775	.8213	.9203	.9060	.9745	.9971	1.003	1.045	1.008	1.048	1.047	1.055	1.056	1.110	1.099	1.118	1.189
35–44	.6084	.6244	.6864	.7381	.7370	.7801	.7389	.7953	.8875	.9913	.9142	.9226	.9633	.9689	1.030	1.016	1.008	1.045	1.010	1.004	1.017	1.025	1.103	1.079
45–54	.7085	.6936	.7460	.4306	.7682	.7777	.8594	.8176	.8509	.9034	.8925	.9132	.9514	.9634	1.000	.9843	1.055	.9628	.9655	.9599	.9688	.9536	1.005	1.041
55–64	.7738	.7288	.7768	.8070	.8249	.8546	.7771	.8835	.9339	.9403	.9421	1.056	.9830	.9594	1.020	1.063	1.058	1.043	1.048	1.023	1.023	1.030	1.074	1.095
65+	.9857	.5198	.4901	.5556	.5590	.6254	.6597	.6429	.5516	.7506	.7709	.6775	.5342	.5246	.5078	.5137	.5211	.5935	.5163	.5672	.6288	.5988	.6002	.5912
Both Sexes	.7852	.8114	.8708	.9369	.9298	.9338	1.006	1.017	1.081	1.129	1.146	1.184	1.257	1.251	1.300	1.267	1.297	1.302	1.304	1.324	1.353	1.338	1.388	1.406

Source: Derived from *Current Population Reports, Consumer Income,* Series P–60, Bureau of the Census.

1970—are based on published tabulations from the March Current Population Survey. (See Rand P-4671-data application for method of estimation of log variance from published group data.)

Overall Inequality

According to Table 6–2, income inequality, as measured by the log variance, has apparently increased substantially among both men and women since World War II. However, as I will show shortly, secular trends in labor force commitments of women and men confound in these data the underlying trends in inequality of wages or earnings opportunities. Among men 25 to 64 years of age, who are likely to have been full-time participants in the labor force throughout this period, income inequality has increased much less sharply. The variance of the logs of income among all males over 14 with income increased 78 percent over this 23-year period; inequality increased only 17 percent among men 25 to 64. Some of this increase, moreover, can be attributed to changes over time in the age composition.[12]

TABLE 6–3

Log Variance of Incomes by Time Worked, Sex, and Race in 1939 and 1969

1939 Wages and Salaries	All Persons in Labor Force	Persons With Wages and Salaries [a]	Worked 12 Months in 1939 [a]
Males	2.206	.7852	.4708
White	[b]	.7377	.4155
Nonwhite	[b]	.6221	.4383
Females	1.443	.7905	.4616
White	[b]	.7730	.3504
Nonwhite	[b]	.5970	.4062

1969 Income [c]	All Persons With Income	Worked Last Year	Work at Full-Time Job	Worked 50–52 Weeks at Full-Time Job
Males	1.282	1.265	.7566	.4205
Whites	1.271	1.253	.7338	.4118
Negroes	1.144	1.137	.7377	.3386
Females	1.280	1.308	.8286	.3207
Whites	1.283	1.269	.8135	.3058
Negroes	1.206	1.204	.8784	.3854

[a] Excluding emergency workers.
[b] Not tabulated in 1940 Census Publications.
[c] Income data by time worked are available annually from the CPS after 1956. From 1956 to 1970 the log variance of income increased among all workers by 30 to 50 percent but evidenced no trend among the fully employed males and females.

155

T. Paul Schultz

A large fraction of income inequality in a cross section is related to differences in the time persons work, as shown in Table 6–3 for 1939 and 1969. The log variance of wage and salary income in 1939 is four times as large among all men in the labor force as it is among those who worked a full 12 months. In 1969 all men with income exhibit income inequality three times as large as those with a full-time job for 50 to 52 weeks.

For either positive or normative analyses of income inequality, it is clearly important to understand why persons in a cross section work different amounts of time in the labor force. Changes in the distribution of income or earnings opportunities over time may be obscured by changes in the time persons work, due to cyclical unemployment, extended schooling, women's participation, and timing of retirement. Time series analysis, therefore, might better focus on incomes of persons by age,

TABLE 6–4

Earnings of Full-Time Workers: 1939 and 1967 by Sex and Age

Sex and Age	1939 Wages and Salaries of Full-Time Workers		1967 Income of Civilians Working Year-Round Full-Time	
	Average	Log Variance	Average	Log Variance
Males	1,590	.4656	8,357	.4427
14–19	512	.4671	2,863	.9313
20–24	913	.3410	5,353	.4235
25–34	1,405	.3318	7,811	.2802
35–44	1,824	.3829	9,249	.3463
45–54	1,953	.4257	9,246	.3973
55–64	1,849	.5019	8,375	.5130
65 +	1,639	.6677	7,332	.7753
Females	884	.4612	4,632	.4049
14–19	489	.4718	3,299	.7767
20–24	727	.3188	4,056	.3656
25–34	917	.3706	4,731	.3287
35–44	1,012	.4917	4,708	.3799
45–54	1,008	.5664	4,893	.3735
55–64	930	.6343	4,766	.4096
65 +	797	.7894	4,721	.6975
Both Sexes	1,410	.5299	7,623	.4658

Source: Derived from *16th Census of The United States: 1940, Population: The Labor Force; Wage and Salary Income in 1939*, table 6a, p. 106; *Current Population Reports, Consumer Income*, Series P-60, no. 64, Bureau of the Census (October 6, 1969), table 19, p. 52.

sex, and where possible race, who are fully employed in the labor force.[13] For at least men between the ages of 25 and 64, the difference between aggregate income inequality and income inequality among the fully employed can be attributed largely to the incidence of unemployment.

Inequality among the Fully Employed

Inequality by age in wage and salary income in 1939 is contrasted with inequality in earnings in 1967 in Table 6–4.[14] Over this 28-year period inequality among fully employed workers increased among men and women less than 25 years old, but was otherwise relatively constant for men and decreased among women in each older age group. If the differences in Census and CPS concepts can be neglected, these data support several major conclusions:

1. Inequality among fully employed men 25 to 64 exhibited remarkable stability.

TABLE 6–5

*Income of Men: Working Year-Round Full-Time
in 1967 by Age and Schooling*

Years of Schooling	25 and Over	25–34	35–44	45–54	55–64	65 and Over
			Average Income			
1–7	5,188	4,814	5,221	5,385	5,277	4,772
8	6,589	5,747	6,503	7,011	6,672	6,232
9–11	7,306	6,411	7,516	7,807	7,440	7,348
12	8,490	7,602	8,747	9,311	8,777	7,612
13–15	9,911	8,407	10,408	11,012	10,681	9,176
16 +	13,342	10,445	14,228	15,233	15,366	13,642
All	8,656	7,811	9,249	9,246	8,376	7,332
			Variance of Log Income			
1–7	.4190	.3853	.3051	.4097	.4984	.5072
8	.3637	.2562	.3308	.3202	.3657	.7449
9–11	.3255	.3023	.2477	.2865	.4022	.8040
12	.2728	.1980	.2627	.2766	.4084	.6879
13–15	.2809	.1993	.1968	.3528	.4638	.7260
16 +	.3625	.2452	.3420	.3814	.4638	.9727
All	.3974	.2802	.3463	.3973	.5130	.7753

Source: Current Population Reports, Consumer Income, Series P-60, no. 64, Bureau of the Census (October 4, 1969), table 20, pp. 53–56.

2. Most of the reduction in earnings inequality in the United States between 1939 and the present can be attributed to the postwar reduction in unemployment.

3. Changes in employment among women over the age of 25 with income account fully for the apparent postwar increase in income inequality for women shown in Table 6–2.

4. The increase in inequality among young men and women less than age 25, noted in Table 6–2, is not caused solely by individual variation in time employed, but may be linked to increasing variation in postschooling investment behavior.

Although I have been unable to construct a time series on earnings of fully employed workers by schooling, age, and sex, Tables 6–5 and 6–6 summarize evidence for 1967.[15] Several regularities in these cross-sectional data are of interest and may parallel cohort time series, were they available. Full-time income inequality *does not* monotonically increase with age *within* schooling groups as predicted by most simple

TABLE 6–6
Income of Women: Working Year-Round Full Time in 1967 by Age and Schooling

Years of Schooling	25 and Over	25–34	35–44	45–54	55–64	65 and Over
			Average Income			
1–7	3,073	2,951	2,871	2,865	3,069	4,094[a]
8	3,651	3,274	3,583	3,838	3,674	3,489
9–11	3,980	3,913	3,903	4,047	4,119	n.a.
12	4,698	4,558	4,624	4,850	4,785	4,988
13–15	5,614	5,234	5,683	5,888	5,594	n.a.
16 +	7,303	6,316	7,384	7,953	7,654	n.a.
All	4,799	4,731	4,708	4,893	4,766	4,721
			Variance of Log Income			
1–7	.4826	.4554	.4575	.3825	.4354	.9188[a]
8	.3890	.4316	.3765	.3549	.3723	.5170
9–11	.3566	.3645	.3022	.3538	.3587	n.a.
12	.2783	.2370	.3171	.2632	.2992	.3631
13–15	.3271	.3380	.3184	.3127	.2442	n.a.
16 +	.2868	.2551	.2793	.2672	.2852	n.a.
All	.3911	.3287	.3800	.3735	.4096	.6975

Source: *Current Population Reports, Consumer Income,* Series P–60, no. 64, Bureau of the Census (October 4, 1969), table 20, pp. 53–56.
[a] Uncommon concentration of CPS sample in next to highest income bracket. Probably sampling variability.

stochastic models of income distribution; inequality among men is lowest in either the 35–44 or 25–34 age group, while there is no regular age pattern among women. Inequality does not increase systematically with levels of education. Income inequality among women within schooling groups appears to decline systematically with increased schooling. The most frequently noted cross-sectional characteristics of income inequality by age and education are therefore primarily associated with variation in time worked by these groups, and are much less important in explaining inequality among full-time workers. These findings suggest to me that the more salient differences in earnings inequality may not have their origin in supply factors as is typically assumed by the human capital approach. Rather, variation in time worked, which may be largely demand-determined, appears to be an important source of measured inequality.[16]

Women's average full-time earnings by age have changed in shape from 1939 to 1967, as shown in Table 6–4. In the earlier period they were similar to men's, increasing sharply to age 35–44; in 1967 they are virtually flat from age 25 to 64. Even within schooling groups, as estimated in Table 6–6, average income records only a modest increase with age for women with 12 or more years of schooling.

Income Disparities by Race and Sex

Aside from differences in earnings by age and schooling, for which numerous explanations have been offered, interest also attaches to differences in the *level* of earnings between the races and sexes as a reflection

TABLE 6–7

Ratio of Nonwhite to White and Female to Male Incomes,
1939–1969

1939 Wages and Salaries	Nonwhite/White		Women/Men	
	Women	Men	Nonwhite	White
All Persons with Some				
Wages and Salaries	.40	.42	.56	.59
Worked 12 months	.40	.43	.54	.58
1969 Income				
With Some Income	.80	.58	.56	.40
Worked Full-Time				
50–52 Weeks	.81	.63	.71	.55

Source: *16th Census of the United States: 1940, Population: The Labor Force; Wage and Salary Income in 1939,* Tables 5–5a, pp. 75–88; *Current Population Reports, Consumer Income,* Series P–60, no. 75, Bureau of the Census (December 14, 1970), tables 54, pp. 124–125.

TABLE 6-8

Ratio of Women's Average Earnings to Men's: 1967, Year-Round
Full-Time Workers by Age and Schooling

Years of Schooling	25 and Over	25–34	35–44	45–54	55–64	65 and Over
1–7	.592	.613	.550	.532	.582	.858
8	.554	.570	.551	.547	.551	.560
9–11	.545	.610	.519	.518	.554	n. a.
12	.553	.600	.529	.521	.545	.655
13–15	.566	.623	.546	.535	.524	n. a.
16 +	.547	.605	.518	.522	.498	n. a.
All	.554	.606	.509	.529	.569	.644
1939 Wages and Salaries All Persons with Wages and Salaries (not on relief)	.561	.653	.555	.516	.503	.486

Source: Tables 6–4, 6–5, 6–6.
n.a. = not available.

of current and past discrimination in education, training, and job opportunities. Table 6–7 indicates that the ratio of nonwhite to white full-time earnings have increased for men from .43 in 1939 to .63 in 1969, and from .40 to .81 for women. The nonwhite woman has advanced not only with respect to her white counterpart, but also relative to the nonwhite man. The same cannot be said for the white woman; the relative gap between earnings of white women and men has not changed appreciably from 1939 to 1969.

The frequently noted tendency for the earnings status of the black male to deteriorate relative to the white male as his educational attainment increases is not as evident in the relative earnings status of women to men by schooling (Table 6–8). Only in the age group 55 to 64 does women's relative earnings status decline monotonically with increased schooling. The low level of earnings and the flatness of age-earnings profiles (in the cross section) of women is often explained in terms of their sporadic attachment to the labor force. Home production and child bearing interrupt a woman's accumulation of labor force experience and may impose a higher rate of depreciation on her stock of market-specific skills than is the case with men. This hypothesis could account for the difference in earnings age profiles of the sexes, but it also implies that women would earn relatively more (per unit time) than men at younger ages when men presumably forego much of their potential earnings to purchase job options that transmit valuable experiences (Rosen, 1971). In fact, the relative earnings status of women is only 10 percent greater in the youngest age group than for all ages together (Table 6–8).[17] Until a much broader and better economic explanation of earnings differences by sex is proposed and found valid, the claims of substantial discrimination in employment opportunities ring true.[18]

The Tenuous Link between Cross Sections and Time Series

Finally, the relationship between cross-sectional age average-income profiles can be briefly examined. Time series and cross-sectional evi-

TABLE 6–9

Average Percentage Change in Mean Real Income and Variance of Log Income: 1947–1970[a]

	Mean Real Income		Variance of Log Income	
	Men	Women	Men	Women
A. Between Age Groups (24) (Cross Section) [b]				
25–34/35–44	18.	6.2	21.	0.1
35–44/45–54	−2.5	5.4	30.	−1.9
45–54/55–64	−14.	−11.	25.	9.2
B. Within Birth Cohorts (14) (Times Series) [c]				
25–34/35–44	69.	34.	30.	31.
35–44/45–54	37.	38.	34.	22.
45–54/55–64	18.	16.	28.	32.
C. Within Age Groups (14) (Time Series of Cross Sections) [d]				
25–34	38.	22.	12.	35.
35–44	42.	28.	4.3	26.
45–54	41.	31.	1.4	25.
55–64	42.	35.	5.2	19.

[a] All conceivable pairwise comparisons from Tables 6–1 and 6–2 (the number of which is reported in parentheses) are expressed as a percentage change from the base year, and the arithmetic average of these values is reported here. Since the consumer price index increased approximately 25 percent per decade between 1947 and 1970, this amount was subtracted from time series calculations of change in mean incomes.
[b] Cross-sectional comparisons are between adjacent ten-year age groups in the same year; for instance, between the income of men 25 to 34 and men 35 to 44 in every possible year, 1947 through 1970.
[c] Time series comparisons are between a ten-year cohort's income in a base year and ten years later; for instance, between the income of men 25 to 34 in 1947, etc., and men 35 to 44 in 1957, etc., minus the 25 percent adjustment for inflation of income levels.
[d] Time series of cross sections are comparisons between specific ten-year age groups ten years apart; for instance, between the income of men 25 to 34 in 1947, etc., and men 25 to 34 in 1957, etc., minus the 25 percent adjustment for inflation of income levels.

dence implicit in Tables 6–1 and 6–2 is summarized in Table 6–9. *Cross-sectional* income levels peak for men at age 35–44 and for women at age 45–54, whereas *time series* age profiles for both sexes increase to the retirement ages 55–64. Secular growth in labor productivity is usually assumed to account for this divergence between cross-sectional and time series evidence, and this growth factor is conveniently assumed to benefit all ages (and schooling) groups by an equal percentage amount. Becker (1964, p. 74) assumed a 1.25 percent annual secular growth in male earnings; estimates for the postwar period implied by Table 6–9 suggest a 3 to 5 percent annual growth in male productivity (i.e., subtract from birth cohort time series increase the age group cross-sectional increase to obtain implicit adjustment factor per decade).[19] Since the difference between time series and cross-sectional profiles is greater for younger men, the age-neutrality assumption may be questioned. For women there is no assurance that the birth cohort increase is unaffected by compositional changes, but the evidence suggests a 2 to 4 percent secular growth in labor productivity, favoring women less than 50 years of age.

Income inequality or log variance of incomes increases for men between 20 and 35 percent per decade both in the cross section and time series, although the time series changes are slightly larger. Within age groups, which was interpreted before as evidence on long-term trends, income inequality increased less than 5 percent per decade between the ages 35 and 64, but about 12 percent among the youngest age group.[20] Among women inequality changed relatively little by age in cross sections, but increased in time series at about the same rate as for men. Within age groups the large increase in measured inequality for women, as noted before, is due to changing participation patterns and is not an adequate reflection of long-term change in the inequality of earnings opportunities of women. In general, cross-sectional evidence on income differences among men between and within age groups appears to be a relatively satisfactory basis for drawing conclusions about income differences experienced by birth cohorts, but the same cannot be said for the study of income differences among women or between men and women.

Long-Term Trends and Their Explanation

Although cyclical behavior of income inequality has been plausibly linked to aggregate indices of demand, such as growth in real output, inflation, and unemployment (Schultz, 1968, 1969; Metcalf, 1969; McCall,

1971), economic explanations of secular change in income inequality are less satisfactory (Kuznets, 1963; Soltow, 1965, 1968; Weisskoff, 1970). The lack of sufficiently long, appropriately defined time series may account in part for this unsatisfactory state, but the absence of a theory of the size distribution of personal incomes has been the main source of analytical difficulty.

To my way of thinking, the most promising theoretical start is the human capital earnings distribution model, but its current shortcomings are nonetheless still very severe. In a recent paper, Chiswick and Mincer (1972) have applied this model to predict and extrapolate U.S. time series for male income inequality. Although the predictions of their model are statistically significantly associated with the observed series for the log variance of annual incomes of men, much of their "success," so it seems to me, is a function of their inclusion of a variable for the "variance of annual weeks worked." One may want to include in a reduced-form type model this sensitive indicator of unemployment and slack in aggregate demand, but the predictive power of the resulting model cannot then be interpreted as confirmation of the human capital framework which is formulated mainly in terms of labor supply variables. The theoretically designated variables in the Chiswick-Mincer model—the level and dispersion of schooling, the level and dispersion of age (a proxy for labor force experience), and intercorrelation terms—tend to cancel each other out over longer periods, such as between 1939 and 1970. The earlier cited evidence that age-specific earnings inequality among fully employed men did not change substantially during this period may be viewed as tenuous support for their model.[21]

Alternatively, one may entertain the null hypothesis that widely noted and explained patterns of income inequality, such as the tendency for inequality to increase with age, education, and the passage of time (during the postwar period), do not persist when the analysis focuses only on fully employed persons. Although it seems reasonable to presume that much of the variation in time worked by persons over their life cycle is a function of human capital investment decisions and evolving personal comparative advantage within the family in market and nonmarket production, the much simplified human capital model does not as yet cope adequately with the complexity of the process underlying observed time allocation and annual income inequality. The large differences across groups and over time within groups in the allocation of time to market activities should be accounted for largely within the human capital model and not observed as an ad hoc explanatory variable. This is obviously true across age, sex, and marital status groups, and over time the additional importance of demand factors must be taken into account. Until this broader set of decisions is treated as jointly determined and the role of exogenous demand variables is firmly

T. Paul Schultz

identified, models of earnings distribution based on schooling and age still remain seriously incomplete.

After decades of confidence in the egalitarian redistributive influence of the U.S. economy (Burns, 1954), a reappraisal of our progress toward equalizing economic opportunities may be warranted. Apparently most, if not all, of the reduction since 1939 in the inequality of annual earnings among men and women in the United States can be attributed to the reduction in postwar unemployment and the improved management of aggregate demand. Of course, changes in the share and personal distribution of unearned income may also have played an equalizing role over the long run (Kuznets, 1953; Lampman, 1962), but the magnitude of this development cannot be directly assessed from the data available to me. Variation in annual earnings inequality arises from the interaction of supply and demand factors that affect both the personal allocation of time to market activity and wage rates as influenced by life cycle human capital investments. An integrated explanation of this process does not now exist, but the conceptual and econometric framework for such an explanation is beginning to emerge.

NOTES

1. Assuming that the measure of social welfare derived from the personal distribution of income is invariant to proportionate changes in all incomes (the real value of mean income also enters social welfare), Atkinson proposes a class of social utility functions defined as

$$U(y) = A + B \frac{y^{1-\epsilon}}{1-\epsilon}, \quad \epsilon \neq 1$$

and

$$U(y) = \log_e (y), \quad \epsilon = 1$$

where y is individual income, $U(y)$ is the social utility produced by this income, A and B are shift and scale parameters, and ϵ a measure of inequality aversion. In discrete form this function is shown by Atkinson to imply an index of inequality, I, which is useful for ranking distributions:

$$I = 1 - \left\{ \sum_i \frac{(y_i)^{1-\epsilon}}{\mu} f(y_i) \right\}^{1/(1-\epsilon)}$$

where μ is the mean income and $\epsilon \geq 0$ to insure concavity. For $\epsilon = 0$, income are simply summed, with no regard to how they are distributed, whereas for $\epsilon = 1$, transfers from the rich to middle class are weighted equally with those from middle class to poor. Most conventional measures of inequality, such as the Gini coefficient or coefficient of variation, rank distributions approximately as though $\epsilon = 1$. The index of inequality has the attractive property of being the share of income that would be required to yield the current level of social welfare if income were distributed equally.

2. Theil uses a measure of inequality which is similar if the distribution is log normal, $T = \sigma^2/2$ where σ^2 is the variable of the logarithms of the variate, e.g., income.

3. If some sources of inequality are required as incentives to sustain an efficient allocation of resources, society must arrive at a trade-off between (growth in) income level and inequality to obtain a static (dynamic) optimum (see H. Johnson, 1972). Thus, perfect equality is an infrequent social goal, because it probably implies socially undesired levels and patterns of resource accumulation and allocation, respectively.

4. See Becker (1964, 1967); Becker and Chiswick (1966); Chiswick (1968, 1971); Chiswick and Mincer (1972); and Mincer (1958, 1962, 1970a, 1970b, 1971).

5. If labor earnings for the ith individual, Y_i, are equal to man's innate earnings potential, Y_o, and a return, r_i, on the cost of his training, C_i, then

$$Y_i = Y_o + r_i C_i$$

and where training is measured in time-equivalents (years) as S_i, the earnings function becomes

$$Y_i = Y_o \left(1 + r_i\right) S_i$$

Taking logarithms of both sides gives the approximation where r_i is small of

$$\log y_i \cong \log Y_o - r_i S_i$$

If Y_o, S_i, and r_i are uncorrelated, the log variance of earning is expressed as

$$\sigma^2 \log y_i = \sigma^2 \log y_o + \bar{r}^2 \, \sigma^2 \, s_i + \bar{S}^2 \, \sigma^2 \, r_i + \sigma^2 \, s_i \, \sigma^2 \, r_i$$

The log variance of earnings is expected to be positively related to the variance in training and returns on training, to the level of training and the rate of return, and the covariance of the two. Intercorrelations between the rate of return on human capital (ability) and the amount of training (opportunity) modify the model's predictions as to how the level of training (schooling) will influence the log variance of earnings (Becker, 1967). See also Mincer (1970a, 1970b) for elaboration of framework to include postschooling investments in training.

6. See Friedman (1952) for the original approach to problem, and for a recent elaboration of this scheme see Seneca and Taussig (1971).

7. The classic example of this problem is noted by Goldsmith (1958), Kuznets (1953, 1962), and Brady (1965), among others, in comparing inequality before and after World War II. The "undoubling" of composite families after the war created the impression of relatively increased inequality among families, because the newly "visible" old and young household units were disproportionately at a relatively low income level.

8. Inequality, as measured by the log variance, is often of similar magnitude when based on these different current concepts of income. In 1969, for instance, among all men with some of the specified income, the log variance of total income was 1.163, and wages and salaries 1.205; average incomes are also nearly identical

in this year. But, of course, this does not imply that the same explanation of inequality should hold for different concepts of income.

9. Income in kind referred in the past largely to home-produced food and fuel and such barter arrangements as employers saw fit to use, whereas today probably the bulk of these transfers occur under the postwar incentives of tax shelter such as business expense accounts and employee fringe benefits and options. Their magnitude and distribution are unknown, but I hazard to guess that their personal distribution is positively correlated with money income, and hence increases real income inequality.

10. Minimum wage legislation (Kosters and Welch, 1970) and income maintenance programs (Greenberg and Kosters, 1970) may permanently preclude some wage offers and increase some wage expectations, respectively, adding to the persisting level of frictional unemployment.

11. Mincer (1970b) has estimated this partial correlation between weeks worked and education from the 1960 Census 1/1,000 sample.

12. Holding age weights (number of individuals with income in a particular ten year age group) constant, and allowing only the relative size distribution of incomes in each group to vary, the increase in inequality with 1947 population weights is 15 percent from 1947 to 1970 for males 25 to 64.

13. The tautness of the labor market influences not only the proportion of the civilian labor force fully employed, it is also likely to affect the inequality (structure) of earnings among those fully employed (Schultz, 1968, 1969). Thus changes in income inequality among the fully employed from 1939 to 1967 may tend to overstate secular trends between two years of equal unemployment. In 1967 unemployment was less than one-fourth the level recorded in 1939: 3.8 versus 17.2 percent of the civilian labor force.

14. 1967 income data are also available and are consistent with all relationships noted for earnings (Table 6–4).

15. The small size of the cells in three-way tabulations of the Current Population Survey from which my estimates were derived imply that sampling variability is a serious shortcoming of these estimates.

16. Demand-determined factors include both those operating through market employment opportunities and, particularly for secondary workers, those factors that influence nonmarket productivities. Mincer (1970b) is justified in maintaining that the higher incidence and greater cyclical variability of unemployment among less schooled groups is another incentive to obtain more schooling. Also, the more schooled person may have a stronger pecuniary incentive to avoid unemployment (and postpone retirement, and so on) because of the greater opportunity cost it entails for him relative to the less schooled. These may be viewed as supply factors influencing the time persons work, but their importance apart from demand factors is moot.

17. It is also more difficult to invoke the "quality" of schooling argument used to account for part of racial earnings differences (Welch, 1967; Wohlstetter and Coleman, 1970) when analyzing sex earnings differences. The quality or cost of schooling is probably quite similar for men and women, but their different courses of study may have quite different pecuniary value to the market activities in which they later engage. Hence, the consumption and investment components of education may differ by sex.

18. Differences in the occupational mix of men and women would certainly "account" for a significant share of the earnings differences shown in Table 6–8. But this fact doesn't explain why more women than men tend to be found in lower-paying occupations. Are women inclined to choose jobs where earnings are

low and training limited (i.e., supply-determined), or are employers inclined to choose women for such jobs (i.e., demand-determined)? I have not seen any adequate analysis to answer this important question.

19. Becker's (1964, p. 76) calculated rate of return on native white male college education was 14.5 percent for 1949, assuming that the secular rate of growth in earnings was 1.25 percent. A growth factor of at least 4 percent, as implied here for men of all schooling groups, would have increased by one-fifth his estimated rate of return.

20. This growth in inequality among the younger age groups is undoubtedly due in part to the increase in the variance of schooling and postschooling investments within this age group. With reference to Table 6–4, the sharp increase in inequality among men 20–24 between 1939 and 1967 must be largely a function of the increase in the proportion of this group attending school from 7 to 32 percent, respectively.

21. Chiswick and Mincer include in their regression equation the predicted inequality (based on supply and demand factors) and also a time trend in linear and quadratic form. The statistical significance of the two trends in time suggests that systematic changes in inequality have occurred over the postwar period and should be accounted for by theoretically more appropriate variables than time and time squared.

REFERENCES

Atkinson, Anthony B. "On the Measurement of Inequality." *Journal of Economic Theory* 2, no. 3 (1970): 244–263.

Aitchison, J., and Brown, J. A. C. *The Lognormal Distribution* (Cambridge Dept. of Applied Economic Monographs Service). New York: Cambridge University Press, 1957.

Becker, Gary S. *Human Capital: A Theoretical and Empirical Analysis.* New York: National Bureau of Economic Research, 1964.

———. "A Theory of the Allocation of Time." *Economic Journal* 75 (September 1965).

———. *Human Capital and the Personal Distribution of Income: An Analytical Approach.* Ann Arbor: University of Michigan Press, 1967.

———, and Chiswick, Barry R. "Education and the Distribution of Earnings." *American Economic Review* 56, no. 2 (1966): 358–368.

Ben-Porath, Yoram. "The Production of Human Capital and the Life Cycle of Earnings." *Journal of Political Economy* 75, no. 4 (1967): 352–365.

———. "The Production of Human Capital Over Time." In *Education, Income and Human Capital*, edited by W. L. Hansen. New York: National Bureau of Economic Research, 1969.

Bowman, Mary Jean, and Anderson, C. A. "Distributional Effects of Educational Programs." In *Income Distribution Analysis*. Raleigh, N.C.: Agricultural Policy Institute, N.C. State University, 1966.

Brady, D. S. *Age and Income Distribution.* Washington, D.C.: Social Security Administration, Research Report No. 8, 1965.
Burns, Arthur F. *The Frontiers of Economic Knowledge.* New York: National Bureau of Economic Research, 1954.
Chiswick, Barry R. "The Average Level of Schooling and the Intra-Regional Inequality of Income: A Clarification." *American Economic Review* 58, no. 3 (1968): 495–500.
———. "Earnings Inequality and Economic Development." *Quarterly Journal of Economics* 85, no. 1 (1971).
———, and Mincer, Jacob. "Time Series Changes in Personal Income Inequality in the U.S. from 1939, with Projections to 1985." *Journal of Political Economy.* May/June 1972, supplement.
Dalton, Hugh. "The Measurement of the Inequality of Incomes." *Quarterly Journal of Economics* 30 (1930): 348–361.
Davidon, W. "Variable Metric Method for Minimization." AEC Res. Dev. Rept. ANL-5990 (Ref.), 1959.
Fletcher, R., and Powell, M. "A Rapidly Convergent Descent Method for Minimization." *Computer Journal* 6 (1963): 163–168.
Friedman, Milton. "A Method of Comparing Incomes of Families Differing in Composition." New York: National Bureau of Economic Research, *Studies in Income and Wealth* 15, 1952.
———. "Choice, Chance and the Personal Distribution of Income." *Journal of Political Economy* 61, no. 4 (1958).
Goldsmith, Selma F. "Size Distribution of Personal Income." *Survey of Current Business,* April 1958.
Greenberg, David H., and Kosters, Marvin. *Income Guarantees and the Working Poor: The Effects of Income Maintenance Programs on the Hours of Work of Male Family Heads.* Santa Monica: The Rand Corporation, R-579, December 1970.
Johnson, Harry G. "The Alternatives Before Us." *Journal of Political Economy,* May/June 1972, supplement.
Johnson, Thomas. "Returns from Investment in Human Capital." *American Economic Review* 60, no. 4 (1970): 546–560.
Kosters, Marvin, and Welch, Finis. *The Effects of Minimum Wages on the Distribution of Changes in Aggregate Employment.* Santa Monica: The Rand Corporation, 1970.
Kuznets, Simon. *Shares of Upper Income Groups in Income and Savings.* New York: National Bureau of Economic Research, 1953.
———. "Income Distribution and Changes in Consumption." In *The Changing American Population,* edited by H. S. Simpson. Report of the Arden House Conference. New York: Institute of Life Insurance, 1962.
———. "Quantitative Aspects of the Economic Growth of Nations: VIII, Distribution of Income by Size." *Economic Development and Cultural Change* 11, no. 2 (1963): p. II.
Lampman, Robert J. *The Share of Top Wealth Holders on National Wealth, 1922–1956.* Princeton: National Bureau of Economic Research, 1962.
Lydall, Harold. *The Structure of Earnings.* New York: Oxford University Press, 1968.
McCall, John J. "Miscellaneous Measures of Income Distribution." Mimeographed. October 1971.
Metcalf, Charles E. "The Size Distribution of Personal Income During the Business Cycle." Part I. *American Economic Review* 59, no. 4 (1969): 657–668.
Mincer, Jacob. "Investment in Human Capital and Personal Income Distribution." *Journal of Political Economy* 66, no. 4 (1958).

————. "On the Job Training: Costs, Returns and Some Implications." *Journal of Political Economy* 70, no. 5 (1962), pt. 2.

————. "The Distribution of Labor Incomes: A Survey." *Journal of Economic Literature* 8, no. 1 (1970a): 1–26.

————. *Schooling, Experience, and Earnings* (Studies in Human Behavior and Institutions, No. 2) National Bureau of Economic Research, 1974 (Dist. by Columbia University Press, N.Y.).

————. "Education, Experience and the Distribution of Earnings and of Employment." Mimeographed. Available from Department of Economics, Columbia University.

Oi, W. Y. "Labor as a Quasi Fixed Factor." *Journal of Political Economy* 70, no. 6 (1962): 538–555.

Rosen, Sherwin. "Knowledge, Obsolescence and Income." Mimeographed. National Bureau of Economic Research, November 1970.

————. "Learning and Experience in the Labor Market." *Journal of Human Resources* 7, no. 3 (summer 1972): 326–342.

————. "Learning by Experience as Joint Production." *Quarterly Journal of Economics* 86, no. 3 (August 1972): 366–382.

Schultz, T. Paul. "Secular Equalization and Cyclical Behavior of Income Distribution." *Review of Economic Statistics* 50, no. 2 (1968): 259–267.

————. "Secular Trends and Cyclical Behavior of Income Distribution in the United States, 1944–1965." In *Six Papers on the Size Distribution of Wealth and Income*, edited by L. Soltow. New York: National Bureau of Economic Research, 1969.

Selowsky, Marcelo, and Taylor, Lance. "The Economics of Malnourished Children: A Study of Disinvestment in Human Capital." Mimeographed. 1971.

Seneca, Joseph P., and Taussig, Michael K. "Family Equivalence Scales and Personal Income Tax Exemptions for Children." *Review of Economic Statistics* 53, no. 3 (1971): 253–262.

Soltow, Lee. *Toward Income Equality in Norway.* Madison: University of Wisconsin Press, 1965.

————. "Long Run Changes in British Income Inequality." *Economic Historical Review* 21, no. 1 (1968): 17–29.

Stewart, G., III. "A Modification of Davidon's Minimization Method to Accept Difference Approximations of Derivatives." *Journal of the Association of Computing Machinery* 14, no. 1 (1967): 72–83.

Theil, Henri. *Economics and Information Theory.* New York: 1967.

U.S. Bureau of the Census. *Current Population Reports, Consumer Income.* Series P-60, No. 4–80, Washington, D.C.

————. *16th Census of the United States: 1940, Population, The Labor Force, Wage and Salary Income in 1939.* Washington, D.C.: U.S. Government Printing Office, 1943.

Weisskoff, Richard. "Income Distribution and Economic Growth in Puerto Rico, Argentina and Mexico. *Review of Income and Wealth* 16, no. 4 (1970).

Welch, Finis. "Labor-Market Discrimination: An Interpretation of Income Differences in the Rural South." *Journal of Political Economy* 75, no. 3 (1967): 225–240.

————. "Education in Production." *Journal of Political Economy* 78, no. 1 (1970): 35–39.

————. "The NBER Approach to Human Resource Problems." Mimeographed. New York: National Bureau of Economic Research, March 1971.

Wohlstetter, Albert, and Coleman, S. B. *Race Differences in Income.* Santa Monica: The Rand Corporation, 1970.

Education and
Economic Equality

Lester C. Thurow

HOWEVER MUCH they may differ on other matters, the left, the center, and the right all affirm the central importance of education as a means of solving our social problems, especially poverty. To be sure, they see the education system in starkly contrasting terms. The left argues that the inferior education of the poor and of the minorities reflects a discriminatory effort to prevent them from competing with better-educated groups, to force them into menial, low-income jobs. The right argues that the poor are poor because they have failed to work hard and get the education which is open to them. Moderates usually subscribe to some mixture of these arguments: The poor are poor because they have gotten bad educations, partly as a result of inadequately funded and therefore inferior school systems, but partly also as a result of sociological factors (e.g., disrupted families) that prevent poor children from absorbing the education that is available. Yet despite these differences, people at all points of the political spectrum agree that, if they were running the country, education policy would be the cornerstone of their effort to improve the condition of the poor and the minorities: If the poor or the minorities were better educated, they could get better jobs and higher income. This idea has had a profound influence on public policy in the last decade.

This acceptance of the efficacy of education is itself derived from a belief in the standard economic theory of the labor market. According to this theory, the labor market exists to match labor demand with labor supply. At any given time, the pattern of matching and mismatching gives off various signals: Businesses are "told" to raise wages or redesign

Reprinted with permission from *The Public Interest*, No. 28 (summer 1972), pp. 61–81. Copyright © 1972, *National Affairs, Inc.*

jobs in skill-shortage sectors, or to lower wages in skill-surplus sectors; individuals are "told" to acquire skills in high-wage sectors and are discouraged from seeking skills and jobs in sectors where wages are low and skills are in surplus. Each skill market is "cleared," in the short run, by increases or reductions in wages, and by a combination of wage changes, skill changes, and production-technique changes over the long run. The result, according to the theory, is that each person in the labor market is paid at the level of his marginal productivity. If he adds $3,000 to total economic output, he is paid $3,000; if he adds $8,000, he is paid $8,000.

This theory posits *wage competition* as the driving force of the labor market. It assumes that people come into the labor market with a definite, preexisting set of skills (or lack of skills), and that they then compete against one another on the basis of wages. According to this theory, education is crucial because it creates the skills which people bring into the market. This implies that any increase in the educational level of low-income workers will have three powerful—and beneficial— effects. First, an educational program that transforms a low-skill person into a high-skill person raises his productivity and therefore his earnings. Second, it reduces the total supply of low-skill workers, which leads in turn to an increase in *their* wages. Third, it increases the supply of high-skill workers, and this lowers their wages. The net result is that total output rises (because of the increase in productivity among formerly uneducated workers), the distribution of earnings becomes more equal, and each individual is still rewarded according to merit. What could be more ideal?

Empirical studies seemingly have confirmed this theory. The economic literature on "human capital" is full of articles that estimate the economic rate of return for different levels of education; while the results differ slightly depending on the data and methods used, most studies find a rate of return on higher education slightly above 10 percent per year for white males. This rate of return, as it happens, is approximately the same as that of investments in "physical capital" (e.g., new machines). From these findings, two conclusions seem to follow. First, educational investment produces just as much additional output as physical investments in plant and capital; and second, education is a powerful tool for altering the distribution of income in society. Such calculations are in common use in discussions of public education policy, and they form a major justification for heavy public investment in education.

Yet, despite this seeming confirmation, there is reason to doubt the validity of this view of the labor market and the importance of the economic role it assigns to education. As we shall see, a large body of evidence indicates that the American labor market is characterized less by wage competition than by *job competition*. That is to say, instead of people looking for jobs, there are jobs looking for people—for "suitable" people. In a labor market based on job competition, the function of education is not to confer skill and therefore increased productivity and higher wages on the worker; it is rather to certify his "trainability" and to confer upon him a certain status by virtue of this certification. Jobs and higher incomes are then distributed on the basis of this certified status. To the extent that job competition rather than wage competition prevails in the American economy, our longstanding beliefs about both the economic benefits of education and the efficacy of education as a social policy which makes for greater equality may have to be altered.

Defects of the "Wage Competition" Theory

While it is possible to raise a number of theoretical objections against the "human capital" calculations which seem to confirm the wage competition theory, it is more instructive to see if in our actual postwar experience, existing educational programs have had the effects that the wage competition theory would predict. In fact, there are a number of important discrepancies. The first arises from the fact that, in the real world, the distributions of education and IQ are more equal than the distribution of income, as Figure 7-1 indicates. The usual explanation for this disparity is that income is disproportionately affected by the *combination* of education and intelligence. This would explain the wider *dispersion* of income than of education or intelligence—but it cannot explain the markedly different *shapes* of the distributions. Clearly, other factors are at work.

A second discrepancy is revealed by the fact that, while the distribution of education has moved in the direction of greater equality over the postwar period, the distribution of income has not. In 1950 the bottom fifth of the white male population had 8.6 percent of the total number of years of education, while the top fifth had 31.1 percent (see Table 7-1). By 1970 the share of the bottom fifth had risen to 10.7 percent and that of the top fifth had dropped to 29.3 percent. According to the wage competition theory, this should have led to a more equal distribution of earnings, whereas in fact the distribution of income among white males has become more *un*equal, as Table 7-2 indicates. From 1949 to 1969 the share of total income going to the lowest fifth has dropped from 3.2 percent to 2.6 percent while the share

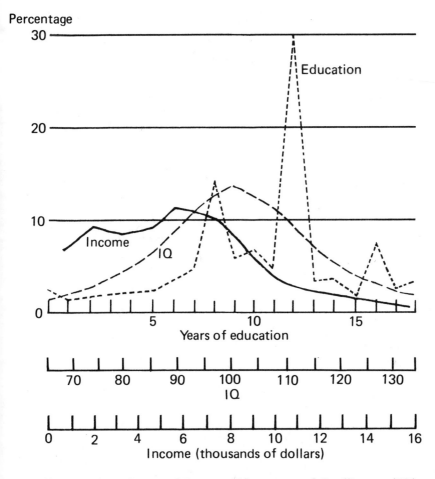

Fig. 7-1. Distribution of Income, Education, and Intelligence (IQ) of Males 25 Years of Age and Over in 1965.

Sources: Income data from U.S. Bureau of the Census, *Current Population Reports,* Series P–60, no. 51, "Income in 1965 of Families and Persons in the United States" (1967), p. 34; education data estimated from U.S. Bureau of the Census, *Statistical Abstract of the United States: 1967,* p. 113; IQ data from David Wechsler, *Wechsler Adult Intelligence Scale Manual* (Psychological Corp., 1955), p. 20.

going to the highest fifth rose from 44.8 percent to 46.3 percent. Empirically, education has not been having the equalizing impact that the rate-of-return calculations would have led one to expect.

Black/white income gaps reveal the same discrepancies. From 1952 to 1968 the mean education of black male workers rose from 67 percent to 87 percent of that of white male workers—yet median wage and salary incomes rose only from 58 percent to 66 percent. Most of this increase, moreover, can be traced to black emigration from the South,

TABLE 7–1
Distribution of Education Among Adult White Males

	Percentage Share of Years of Educational Attainment	
	1950	1970
Lowest Fifth	8.6	10.7
Second Fifth	16.4	16.4
Middle Fifth	19.0	21.3
Fourth Fifth	24.9	22.3
Highest Fifth	31.1	29.3

TABLE 7–2
Distribution of Income Among Adult White Males

	Percentage Shares of Total Money Income	
	1949	1969
Lowest Fifth	3.2	2.6
Second Fifth	10.9	9.4
Middle Fifth	17.5	16.7
Fourth Fifth	23.7	25.0
Highest Fifth	44.8	46.3

with its lower relative incomes for blacks. As a result, education does not seem to have equalized black and white incomes in the manner that the rate-of-return calculations would indicate.

Similarly, a more rapid rate of growth of education should have led to a more rapid growth of the economy. In the early 1950s the college-educated labor force was growing at a rate of 3 percent per year. In the late 1960s it was growing at a 6 percent rate. Yet there does not seem to be any evidence that the rate of growth of productivity of the economy as a whole has accelerated correspondingly. If anything, the opposite has happened. Productivity today may be increasing more slowly than its historic rate of growth of 2.9 percent per year.

Moreover, the entire theory assumes a labor market where wage competition is the most important short-run method for equilibrating the supplies and demands for different types of labor. Yet the real world reveals very sluggish wage adjustments in most sectors of the economy. Not only is there considerable variance in wages for different individuals with the same skills; there is also little tendency for the existence of unemployment to lower wages. There may be many unemployed airline pilots or engineers today, but their joblessness does not lead to lower wages for those lucky enough to remain employed. In fact, wage competition simply is not the all-pervasive force that economic theory supposes it to be.

Perhaps the most devastating problem with the simple wage competition view is that it cannot explain the existence of unemployment. When the demand for labor falls, wages are supposed to fall until enough jobs have been generated to keep everyone fully employed at the new lower wages. Yet the real world is full of unemployed workers whose presence does not seem to have led to falling wages for those who are employed.

The absence of wage competition is also indicated by employers' lack of interest in relative wage differentials when designing new plants. In the several cases investigated by Piore and Doeringer, plant designers typically did not take account of (or even know) the relative prices of different types of labor when designing new plants. They could not economize on expensive skills since they did not know which skills were expensive and which cheap. They simply used an average wage rate in making their calculations.

Now there are plausible *ad hoc* explanations for all of these aberrant observations—but the necessity for so many *ad hoc* explanations is itself suspicious. Our experience with large investments in higher education entitles us to have doubts about the value of education as a means of altering the distribution of income. In the postwar years, this experience has not been encouraging. Large investments have been made. What little has happened to the postwar distribution of adult white male incomes has been contrary to expectation. Before further investments are made for such purposes, we should first get clear on why past investments have not had the expected and desired results.

The "Job Competition" Model

Governmental education and training policies have not had the predicted impact because they have ignored the "job competition" elements in the labor market. In a labor market based on job competition, an individual's income is determined by: a) his relative position in the labor queue, and b) the distribution of job opportunities in the economy. Wages are based on the characteristics of the job, and workers get the best (highest-income) jobs. According to this model, labor skills do not exist in the labor market; on the contrary, most actual job skills are acquired informally through on-the-job training *after* a worker finds an entry job and a position on the associated promotional ladder.

As a matter of fact, such a training process is clearly observable in the American economy. A survey of how American workers acquired their actual job skills found that only 40 percent were using skills that they had acquired in formal training programs or in specialized education—and, of these, most reported that some of the skills they were currently using had been acquired through informal on-the-job training. The remaining 60 percent acquired all of their job skills through such informal on-the-job training. More than two-thirds of the college graduates reported that they had acquired job skills through such informal processes. When asked to list the form of training that had been most helpful in acquiring their current job skills, only 12 percent listed formal training and specialized education.

Thus the labor market is primarily a market, not for matching the demands for and supplies of different job skills, but for matching trainable individuals with training ladders. *Because most skills are acquired on the job, it is the demand for job skills which creates the supply of job skills.* The operative problem in a job competition economy is to pick and train workers to generate the desired productivity with the least investment in training costs. For new workers and for entry-level jobs, it is the "background characteristics" of the workers that form the basis of selection. Those workers whose backgrounds promise the lowest training costs will be hired. For workers with previous job experience, existing job skills (including skills like reliability and punctuality) are relevant to the selection process to the extent that they might lead to lower training costs.

In such a system, depending as it does on informal on-the-job transmission of knowledge and skills, the absence of direct wage competition and the restriction of any job competition to entry-level jobs are absolutely necessary. If workers feel that they are training a potential wage or job competitor every time they show another worker how to do their job, they have every incentive to stop giving such informal training. Each man, under the circumstances, would try to build his own little monopoly by hoarding skills and information and by resisting any technical improvements that would reduce the number of job opportunities in his occupation. But in a training system where no one is trained unless a job is available (which is what on-the-job training means), where strong seniority provisions exist, and where there is no danger of some competitor bidding down your wages, employees can freely transmit information to new workers and more readily accept new techniques. If anyone is made redundant by such techniques, it will be a clearly defined minority —new workers.

In a labor market governed by job competition, employers rank workers on a continuum from the best potential worker (trainee) to the worst potential worker (trainee) on the basis of estimated potential training costs. (Such costs certainly include the costs of inculcating norms of industrial discipline and good work habits.) But because employers rarely have direct and unambiguous evidence of the specific training costs for specific workers, they end up ranking workers according to their background characteristics—e.g., age, sex, educational attainment, previous skills, and performance on psychological tests. Each of these is used as an indirect measure of the costs necessary to produce some standard of work performance.

Entirely subjective and arbitrary elements may also affect the labor queue. If employers discriminate against blacks, blacks will find themselves lower in the labor market queue than their training costs would warrant. To some extent, the smaller the actual differences in training costs, the more such subjective preferences can determine the final ordering. If every individual had identical training costs, blacks could be placed at the bottom of the labor queue with no loss in efficiency.

The national labor queue depends upon the distribution of these background characteristics and upon employers' ranking of different background characteristics. While no two workers may be exactly alike, the costs of discovering small differences are so large that individuals are ranked on a finite number of background characteristics. This means that there are a finite number of rankings in the labor queue and that many individuals have identical rankings.

Jobs and their corresponding training ladders are distributed to individuals in order of their rank, working from those at the top of the queue down to those at the bottom. The best jobs go to the best workers and the worst jobs to the worst workers. Given a need for untrained labor, some workers at the bottom of the queue will receive little or no training on their jobs. In periods of labor scarcity, training will extend farther and farther down the queue as employers are forced to train more costly workers to fill job vacancies. In periods of labor surplus, it is those at the bottom of the labor queue who will be unemployed.

To the extent that education and formal training are an important background characteristic used for screening individuals, alterations in the distribution of education can have an important impact on the shape of the labor queue. This queue can be skinnier at the top, at the bottom, or in the middle. The relevant empirical question is the weight that is attached to education in screening, relative to the weight that is attached to other factors. Although this obviously differs from job to job, educational screening tests are in fact ubiquitous. But although education can affect the shape of the labor queue, this does not necessarily mean that it can change the actual distribution of income. This is a function, not only of the labor queue, but also of the distribution of job opportunities. An equal group of laborers (with respect to potential training costs) might be distributed across a relatively unequal distribution of job opportunities. After receiving the resultant on-the-job training, the initially equal workers would have unequal productivities since they would now have unequal skills. As a result, the distribution of incomes is determined by the distribution of job opportunities and not by the distribution of the labor queue, which only determines the order of access—and the distribution of access—to job opportunities.

The Distribution of Job Opportunities

The shape of the job distribution (and hence of the income distribution) across which individual laborers will be spread is governed by three sets of factors: (1) the character of technical progress, which generates certain kinds of jobs in certain proportions; (2) the sociology of wage determination—trade unions, traditions of wage differentials, and so on; and (3) the distribution of training costs between employees and employers, which will influence the wage that is associated with each job. The interaction among these factors is exceedingly complicated—and little studied.[1] The outcome of such studies would tell us with some assurance where exactly the American economy is to be located on a continuum between a wage competition economy and a job competition economy. Let me point out, however, that observed changes over the postwar period are in accordance with a job competition model.

If, at the beginning of the postwar period, an observer had been told that the composition of the adult white male labor force was going to change from 47 percent with a grade school education, 38 percent with a high school education, and 15 percent with a college education, to 20 percent with a grade school education, 51 percent with a high school education, and 28 percent with a college education (the actual 1949 to 1969 changes), expectations about the distribution of income would have been very different depending upon whether the observer subscribed to a job competition model or a wage competition model. Assuming there were no offsetting changes on the demand side of the market, the observer subscribing to a wage competition model of the economy would have predicted a substantial equalization of earnings. But the observer subscribing to the job competition model would have predicted something quite different. He would have expected an equalization of income within the most preferred group (college-educated workers), a rise in its incomes relative to other groups, and a decrease relative to the national average. He would have reasoned as follows: As the most preferred group expanded, it would filter down the job distribution into lower-paying jobs. This would lead to a fall in wages relative to the national average. As it moved into a denser portion of the national job (income) distribution, it would, however, experience within-group equalization of income. By taking what had previously been the best high school jobs, college incomes would rise relative to high school incomes.

Such a prediction would have been correct. The proportion of college incomes going to the poorest 25 percent of white male college-educated workers rose from 6.3 to 9.0 percent from 1949 to 1969, while the proportion going to the richest 25 percent fell from 53.9 percent to 46.0 percent. While the median income of college-educated workers was rising from 198 percent to 254 percent of the median for grade school–educated workers and from 124 percent to 137 percent of the median for high school–educated workers, it was falling from 148 percent to 144 percent of the national median.

As the least preferred group (those with a grade school education) contracted in size, a job competition observer would have expected it to be moving out of the denser regions of the income distribution and becoming more and more concentrated on the lower tail of the income distribution. Given the shape of the lower tail of the American income distribition, such a movement would have led to falling relative incomes and increasing income equality. In fact, the incomes of grade school laborers have fallen from 50 percent to 39 percent of college incomes and from 63 percent to 54 percent of high school incomes. The income going to the poorest 25 percent of all grade school laborers has risen from 2.9 percent to 6.6 percent of the group's total, and the income going to the richest 25 percent has fallen from 53.5 percent to 49.4 percent.

Predictions of the position of the middle group (the high school–educated) would have depended upon an analysis of the relative densities of the income distribution at its margin with the college-educated and the grade school–educated. Since the American income distribution is denser on the margin with the grade school–educated than on the margin with the college-educated, an expansion in the size of the middle group should have led to more within-group equality, an income rise relative to the grade school–educated, and an income fall relative to the college-educated. In fact, the proportion of income going to the poorest 25 percent of all the high school–educated has risen from 8.2 percent to 10.2 percent, while the proportion going to the highest 25 percent has fallen from 46.0 percent to 41.6 percent. High school incomes have risen relative to grade school incomes (from 160 percent to 185 percent) and fallen relative to college incomes (from 81 percent to 73 percent).

An alternative method for viewing the same changes is to look at the probability each of these educational groups has of holding a job at

TABLE 7-3
Normalized Probabilities (Adult White Males) [a]

	Percent of Total Males in Each Job Class, in 1950 and 1970, by Educational Attainment (Divided by Percent of Total Males with that Educational Attainment that Year)					
Quality of Jobs (Determined By Income of Total Males with Income, 25 Yrs. and Older)	Elementary		High School		College	
	(1950)	(1970)	(1950)	(1970)	(1950)	(1970)
10% Best Jobs—1950: $5,239.3 and up / 1970: $15,000 and up	.436	.1714	1.066	.648	2.715	2.549
2nd Best 10%—1950: $4,028.84–$5,239.2 / 1970: $12,506.26–$14,999	.599	.3535	1.337	1.130	1.523	1.468
3rd 10%—1950: $3,519.7–$4,028.83 / 1970: $10,012.9–$12,506.25	.772	.3535	1.354	1.130	.940	1.468
4th 10%—1950: $3,025.2–$3,519.6 / 1970: $8,752–$10,012.8	.776	.621	1.354	1.248	.927	.960
5th 10%—1950: $2,553.6–$3,025.1 / 1970: $7,573.9–$8,751	.952	.692	1.221	1.251	.649	.881
6th 10%—1950: $2,101–$2,553.5 / 1970: $6,449.6–$7,573.8	1.079	.871	1.069	1.238	.5695	.704
7th 10%—1950: $1,530–$2,100 / 1970: $5,148.3–$6,449.5	1.193	1.128	.910	1.148	.5629	.586
8th 10%—1950: $706–$1,529 / 1970: $3,576.6–$5,148.2	1.328	1.564	.708	.933	.5827	.500
9th 10%—1950: $270.6–$705 / 1970: $2,008.2–$3,576.5	1.500	1.960	.527	.712	.4304	.468
10% Worst Jobs—1950: $0–$270.5 / 1970: $0–$2008.1	1.458	2.303	.564	.552	.4768	.3818

[a] Figures for: 1950—money income in 1949, population in 1950; 1970—money income in 1969, population in 1970.

different levels in the American job hierarchy. The increasing economic segregation based on education can be seen in Table 7–3, where each cell has been adjusted for changes in the proportions of those with college, high school, and grade school educations. (The table is constructed so that each cell would have the number 1.000 if incomes were randomly drawn with respect to education.) In 1949 a college graduate was six times as likely to hold a job in the top tenth of jobs as a grade school graduate, but by 1969 he was 15 times as likely to hold a job in the top tenth. Conversely, the probability of a grade school graduate holding a job in the lowest tenth has risen from three to six times that of a college graduate. Similarly, probabilities of holding the best job have risen for college graduates relative to high school graduates (from 2.5 to 4 times those of high school graduates), while there has been a rise in relative probabilities of holding the worst jobs for high school graduates (from 1.2 to 1.5 times those of college graduates). Extrapolation of these trends for another 20 years would lead to a world where income was almost perfectly segregated according to education.

Although the job competition model seems to "postcast" accurately what happened to the American distribution of income in the postwar period, postcasting is not a definitive test, and there are other possible explanations for what happened in the postwar period. One explanation would be that increasing technical progress has simply made education more necessary for acquiring income-producing skills. Training costs differentials have risen, and this could explain the increasing economic segregation based on education. Another explanation would be that higher education has become more meritocratic in the postwar period (i.e., it is becoming more perfectly correlated with other income-producing factors), which would create the appearance of more economic segregation based on education. Still another explanation would be that the American economy has become more of a "credential society," in which education is used as a cheap (or defensible) screening device even though it is not very closely related to training costs.

Economic Implications

While education has many noneconomic benefits, its strictly economic benefits may be of three types: First, education directly increases the productivity of a country's labor force and indirectly increases the productivity of its physical capital. The result is more output and a higher real living standard. Second, by altering the distribution of individual productivities, education can lead to changes in the distribution of earned income between rich and poor. It can help the poor to catch up with the rich. Third, education can lead to economic mobility. Black earnings may catch up with white earnings, and the children of low-productivity parents need not themselves be low-productivity individuals. It is important to recognize, however, that each of these three impacts is merely possible. They may or may not occur. Whether they do or do not is an empirical question.

Even on the wage competition view of the labor market, education can be expanded to the point where it no longer increases a country's productivity. Nevertheless, large observed earnings differentials between the high school–educated and the college-educated (after standardization for other factors such as IQ) have been taken as evidence to substantiate the fact that there are actual gains to be made. But if there is a substantial element of job competition in the economy, education's impact on individual productivity cannot be determined simply with rate-of-return calculations based on normalized income differentials. The exact impact on productivity of an alteration in the distribution of education depends upon a set of factors beyond the scope of this essay, but large observed income differentials could persist after the productivity impact of education was exhausted. An increasing supply of the college-educated would lead them to accept jobs farther down the job opportunities distribution. In the process, they would take the best high school jobs and thus bring down average high school incomes. This would preserve the observed wage differential between college and high school labor, but the differential would not indicate potential productivity gains or opportunities to equalize incomes between rich and poor.

There is, then, a need to be much more agnostic about the productivity impacts of education than public rhetoric would indicate to be our present inclination. In the wage competition view of education, additional education for someone with more education than I can never hurt my prospects. If anything, it must raise my potential earnings. From the job competition point of view, however, education may become a defensive necessity. As the supply of educated labor increases, individuals find that they must improve their educational level simply to defend their current income positions. If they don't, others will, and they will find their current job no longer open to them. Education becomes a good investment, not because it would raise people's incomes above what they would have been if no one had increased his education, but rather because it raises their income above what it will be if others acquire an education and they do not. *In effect, education becomes a defensive expenditure necessary to protect one's "market share."* The larger the class of educated labor and the more rapidly it grows, the more such defensive expenditures become imperative. Interestingly, many students currently object to the defensive aspects of acquiring a college education.

This complaint makes no sense from a wage competition point of view, but it makes good sense from a job competition point of view. While the current public policy emphasis on on-the-job training programs seems to fit in with the job competition view of the world, on-the-job training programs can have an impact only if they really lead to the training of a different class of workers than would ordinarily have been trained through the job market. Unfortunately, many government training programs have simply led to the training of the groups that would have been trained in any case; the only operative difference is that government foots the training bills.

Based on a wage competition view of the labor market, government programs to equalize incomes and to raise the productivity of low-income individuals have been almost entirely devoted to changing the labor characteristics that an individual brings into the labor market. This is done in spite of the fact that individual labor characteristics typically do not explain more than half of the observed income differences between black and white, rich and poor, or male and female. Thus the emphasis has been entirely on changing the supplies of different types of workers rather than the demands for different types of workers.

In addition to being uncalled for by economic theory, this emphasis on altering labor supplies is at variance with our own history. To find a period of increasing income equality it is necessary to go back to the Great Depression and World War II. From 1929 to 1941 the share of total income going to the bottom 40 percent of the population rose from 12.5 percent to 13.6 percent, while the share of income going to the top 5 percent fell from 30.0 percent to 24.0 percent and the share of income going to the top 20 percent fell from 54.4 percent to 48.8 percent. From 1941 to 1947 the share going to the bottom 40 percent rose to 16.0 percent, while the share going to the top 5 percent fell to 20.9 percent and the share going to the top 20 percent fell to 46.0 percent. In both cases alterations in the demand side, rather than the supply side, of the market seem to have provided the mechanism for equalizing incomes.

In the Great Depression an economic collapse was the mechanism for changes. Individual fortunes were lost, firms collapsed, and a wage structure emerged that was noticeably more equal than before the collapse. While interesting, the deliberate collapsing of an economy in order to equalize the distribution of income is not a policy that commends itself.

The World War II period is more interesting from this vantage point. As a result of an overwhelming consensus that the economic burdens of the war should be shared equally, the federal government undertook two major actions. First, it instituted a very progressive income tax (more progressive than the current federal income tax) that converted a regressive tax system into a mildly progressive tax system. Second, it used a combination of wage controls and labor controls to equalize market wages. This was accompanied by a conscious policy of restructuring jobs to reduce skill requirements and to make use of the existing skills of the labor force. To some extent, old skill differences were simply cloaked with a new set of relative wages and, to some extent, skill differentials were actually collapsed. Together the two factors led to an equalization of market incomes that was not dissipated after the war ended.

To some extent the wage policies of World War II were a deliberate—and successful—attempt to change the sociology of what constitutes "fair" wage differentials. As a result of the war, our judgments as to what constituted fair differentials changed, and this was reflected in wage patterns. As a consequence of the widespread consensus that wage differentials should be reduced, it was possible to make a deliberate attempt to reduce wage differentials. After they had been embedded in the labor market for a number of years, these new differentials came to be regarded as the "just" differentials and stuck after the egalitarian pressures of World War II disappeared.

From this experience, I would suggest that any time a consensus emerges on the need for more equality, it can be at least partly achieved by making a frontal attack on wage differentials. Elaborate educational programs are not necessary. Without such a consensus, I would suggest, massive educational investments are apt to be wasted. They simply will not bring about the desired equalization.

In addition to a frontal attack on wage differentials, programs to alter the demands for different types of employees would include research and development efforts to alter the skill-mix generated by technical progress; guaranteed government jobs; fiscal and monetary policies designed to create labor shortages; public wage scales designed to pressure low-wage employers; and incentives to encourage private employers to compress their wage differentials. If quick results are desired, quotas must seriously be considered since they are the only technique for quickly altering the types of laborers demanded.

In any case, I would argue that our reliance on education as the ultimate public policy for curing all problems, economic and social, is unwarranted at best and in all probability ineffective.

NOTE

1. Further discussion of this matter may be found in Lester C. Thurow, "The American Distribution of Income: A Structural Problem," Committee Print, U.S. Congress Joint Economic Committee, 1972.

(8)

Youth, Education, and Work

Jacob Mincer

FULL-TIME WORK rather than full-time education was the major activity of teenage youth throughout history, until recently. Very few Americans finished high school a century ago; today the proportion is near 75 percent. Urbanization reduces the involvement of youth in a wide variety of work activities which are experienced in farm households. Even the acquisition of specific occupational work experience is progressively postponed as the period of schooling lengthens.

At the same time, the economic functions of the household are reduced by economic growth, and its membership continues to decline, from the extended to the nuclear family and from large to small nuclear units. The family "work force" employed in household tasks diminishes even more rapidly than its membership as productivity growth induces shifts of labor from nonmarket to market activities.

Compared to the large farm households in which farm and household work and the learning of related skills were combined, the contemporary urban setting reveals a separation of family, school education, and work. Children are segregated in environments of peers in classrooms, and in homes, where the few siblings are of similar age, and where fathers and, increasingly, mothers are absent most of the day. The factory, office, or store into which father and mother disappear for much of the day become increasingly remote as work experience of children is progressively delayed by lengthened schooling.

These trends are being noted with growing apprehension by many observers, especially by psychologists and sociologists among the social scientists. The apprehension is succinctly expressed by Coleman: "Due to

Reprinted with permission from the *National Bureau for Economic Research* (#11), January 1973. © 1973, *National Bureau for Economic Research*.

changes in the institutions of family, school, and workplace, young people are shielded from responsibility, held in dependent status, and kept away from productive work—all of which makes their transition into adulthood a difficult and troublesome process." [1] Undoubtedly, apprehension has been intensified in recent years by highly visible and often destructive manifestations of youthful discontent, particularly in schools and campuses, and to some extent also by an apparent high level of youth unemployment.

If the lengthening of schooling and the associated delay in work experience are the sociological villains of the piece, in what light do they appear from an economic point of view? Has schooling become excessive and unduly long? What are the economic bases and interpretations of some of the trends in family, school, and working life? Though economics cannot provide a complete insight into, and even less a basic solution for, a complex societal problem, it can contribute to both by adding a perspective to those of the psychologists, sociologists, and educators.

In my attempt to do this, I first indicate the essentials of the economic analysis of education as an investment in human capital and its relevance to the questions posed about reasons and consequences of educational trends. Developments in the family represent much too large a subject and are touched only briefly. Developments in the youth labor market receive somewhat closer attention.

Education as Investment in Human Capital

Education is viewed by economists as an investment in human capital. It is an investment because it involves current costs and yields returns distributed over many periods. The capital embodied in man is accumulated knowledge and skill, both social and technical. This investment produces future satisfactions including augmented earning power.

The costs and returns of education might be evaluated from the vantage point of individuals (students), their families (parents), or society at large. Since the incidence of perceived costs and benefits is different for each of these parties, some of the attitudes and some of the behavioral responses are also different. Since actual investments depend on effective access to financing, economists distinguish between private and public investment decisions in education, and tend to ignore the distinction between the family and the dependent child (student), the family being viewed as a collective decision maker—whether or not the decisions represent a wholehearted consensus or an uneasy compromise. The latter distinction is not unimportant, either to the continuity or to the effectiveness of investment, but it has not, as yet, received sufficient analytical attention.

The costs and returns are monetary and nonmonetary, direct and indirect. The major elements of costs are schooling expenditures (tuition in the private account, total school costs in the public calculation) and foregone earnings of students. The returns are the incremental real incomes obtained in consequence of the investment by the individual and by society. The largely unobservable or difficult-to-evaluate components are: effects of education on nonmarket ("consumption") productivities, and so-called external effects. The latter occur when some benefits accrue to or some costs are borne by people other than the investors. Therefore, social returns (or costs) may be greater or smaller than the sum of private returns (or costs). The difference between the social and private sums is the value (positive or negative) of the externality.

Given the concepts of costs and returns to educational investments, economists ask the following basic questions:

1. Are activities which produce education efficiently organized?
2. Are too few or too many resources allocated to these activities?

Economists have made no significant attempts to grapple with the first question. There is a tendency to equate education with school education, and the inquiry into the study of efficiency of schools as firms which produce education is relegated by economists to "educationists," just as the study of the organization and efficiency within business firms is left to engineers and "management scientists." The central concept which serves to provide answers to the second question is the (marginal) rate of return to the investment. This rate is the rate of discount (interest) which equates the discounted sum of costs to the discounted sum of returns at the time the (incremental) decision is made. The optimal amount of a particular investment is one at which the marginal rate of return is the same as in alternative activities. A dollar transferred from an investment activity with a lower rate of return earns more elsewhere, so total income is increased.

Externalities and Public Policy

If there are beneficial external effects of education and they outweigh the excess of social over private costs, the social rate of return exceeds the private rate. If so, and if the latter is not clearly lower in education than elsewhere, there is no educational overinvestment from a social point of view.

What are examples of such externalities? It is often suggested that they include, among others, informed and responsible citizenship, communication skills, lawful behavior, and standards of health. The existence of such externalities is invoked to justify public efforts to stimulate minimal educational investments by all families. Such efforts can take many forms. It is not clear, for example, that the best policy implied by the existence of externalities is a publicly owned school system rather than direct subsidies to students. The absence of competition among schools and the vast bureaucratic machinery in public school systems is likely to foster and perpetuate inefficiencies.

Another question is the extent of minimal education implied by externalities, hence the extent of government support that is required. It is not clear that positive externalities can be attributed to mass, universal education beyond that of a general and elementary kind.

There are, of course, other reasons for public intervention, some of which also represent a response to a somewhat different kind of externality. This is the concern with the distribution rather than with the total volume of educational investments. Helping children of poor or of unloving parents to acquire a minimal degree of earning power is an objective for which schooling is viewed as an instrument. Private charity is not a dependable alternative, since it carries externalities as well: charity of givers is likely to reduce the giving of others, though it may induce the giving of some. Since poverty is viewed as a relative concept, the amount of minimal universal government-supported education has been progressively lengthening as average education (and income) have increased. It is not obvious, however, how long the span of such minimal education should be at any given time. Nor is it obvious that a legislated minimal age of compulsory and "free" schooling—it is not free, because of foregone earnings—is the best policy for a redistribution of wealth. An example of an alternative might be to provide a money-equivalent of the desired increment in wealth for each child to be used for education or training at any time and possibly for some other purposes as well. This would reduce losses in foregone earnings and wasted opportunities for investment alternatives other than formal schooling.

Nonmarket Productivity Effects

If education positively affects not only earnings but also productivity in nonmarket (household, consumption) activities, the rate of return estimated from earnings data may be understated. The most important illustration is the education of girls. Since women—on average—spend less than half as much time as men do in earning activities, it might seem that provision of equal amounts of schooling to them is wasteful, unless the nonmarket, or consumption effects are strong. The fact that more educated women tend to spend more of their time in the labor market, at the same levels of husbands' income, is consistent with the hypothesis that education increases their earnings in the market more than their productivity in the home. This finding is reversed, however, when small children are present: more educated mothers curtail their work in the labor market to a greater extent than the less educated. Whether this phenomenon represents a productivity effect of mother's education in raising children is an open question which is important and researchable.

If better-educated mothers produce greater human capital in children and a better quality of family life, apart from contributing to family money income, the provision of equal amounts of schooling to both sexes need not be questioned on economic grounds. Indeed, it is rarely questioned as a matter of public policy.

Though the real benefits to the family from educating men and women may be equal, their content is generally not the same. The relative importance of market earnings of men and of nonmarket production of women reflects a division of labor within families. Of course, the degree of specialization in family roles is not fixed across cultures or over time, though their sex linkage appears to be universal. The question for educational policy is whether it provides the appropriate preparation for the future family and occupational life of boys and girls, given the current division of labor in the family and the expected pace of change in it. The educational system tends to overlook this question, implicitly ascribing similar career expectations to both sexes, while parental models of behavior tend to impart expectations of differential roles which are likely to err in the opposite direction. A better understanding of the functions of the family, of the division of labor within it, and of forces producing changes, would contribute to more realistic aspirations and preparations for the expected or desired mix of market and nonmarket activities.

As long as the family will remain a viable institution, it will continue to imply a division of labor and a complementarity in the activities of its members. The nature of the family and its production function are subjects largely outside the economist's province at this stage of our knowledge. However, secular changes in the division of labor within the family as between market and nonmarket activities have been affected by known economic forces. Economic growth due to growing productivity in industry has meant that the same amount of time spent in the labor market purchases increasingly larger volumes of goods and services than can be produced at home. This induces shifts from work in households to work in the labor market.

Since child bearing and child rearing are time-intensive activities, fewer children are born in successive cohorts, as mother's value of time rises in the labor market, and the demand for outside institutions such as schools to take over the child care functions increases. At the same time, partly as a result of growing demands in the labor market, growing family income, and partly as a substitute of quality for reduced quantity of children, larger amounts (and longer periods) of education are demanded by families for each of their children.

Evidently, powerful economic forces are, at least in part, responsible for the increasingly prolonged separation of adults and of age-graded children in the dissimilar environments of home, school, and workplace. These forces are the forces of economic growth, spurred by the growth of science and technology and producing growth in real incomes. If there is a need to ameliorate some of their consequences, it is not a call to stop economic growth.

Is There a Problem?

When we look at the massive trends in schooling in this century and in the past decades and years we wonder whether we have not been overschooling our children. Certainly, there are signals of distress coming from the young and from many concerned parents and educators.

Yet, if we view schooling as an investment process, there is no evidence that the profitability of that investment has declined as numbers of students have grown. The private rate of return to schooling has remained roughly constant around a respectable 10 percent figure (with deviations depending on data and analysis) in the past three decades. This figure, as usually calculated, necessarily omits externalities and consumption effects, so it is probably understated. Evidently, during most of this period demand for educated labor has been rising in step with its supply.

It appears that in the past few years this happy conjuncture has given way to a surplus of supply in the markets for highly educated labor, particularly in the sciences. Rates of return calculations do not immediately capture these changes, since relatively long streams of earning experience (at least a decade) are required for the calculation. Even if we imprudently ignore these latest, and hopefully transitory developments, we must keep in mind that the calculated rate of return is an average over the student population, which conceals a wide dispersion. This means that for, say, 20–30 percent of students at any level, the additional schooling has been a waste at least in terms of earnings. Assuming no change in the fraction of failures, and assuming that the distribution of results is reflected in attitudes even before graduation, the distress is more strongly felt and expressed today than in the past, because the student population is older, therefore more articulate, more educated, therefore suffering a greater loss from overschooling, and much more numerous, therefore more visible.

It should also be noted that when the overall schooling level was lower, the inability to obtain further education was the source of distress of many people. Only the privileged few continued schooling for prolonged periods. The locus of unhappiness was diffuse, outside of school. When few do not go on to higher levels of schooling, it is the reluctant or "captive" student that is unhappy, and the distress is strongly concentrated in schools.

Labor Market Developments

The high and stable rate of return to schooling in the past decades is not safely extrapolated into the future. To begin with, the greatest expansion of high school completion and post–high school enrollment took place in the past 25 years, in a period of seemingly insatiably growing demand for educated labor, and in a period demographically favorable to the young in the labor market: young people aged 16–24 constituted a declining proportion of the total labor force until quite recently. Most recently job opportunities and starting relative wages of college graduates have begun to decline in some fields. It will not be clear for some time whether this phenomenon is of longer-run significance beyond the recent sectoral and business cycle decline in demand.

One disturbing index of conditions in the more general youth labor market throughout the 1960s has been the rather high unemployment rate, which has actually risen in the past decade both absolutely and relative to the unemployment rate of the adult population. The fact that the unemployment rate of young people is higher than that of adults is not surprising. Entry into the labor force and job shopping during the early years of work experience are reflected in high unemployment counts. This is certainly true of the 16–19 age group and somewhat less so of the 20–24 group.

There are several additional factors which contribute to the size and

Jacob Mincer

growth of the unemployment rate in the young population groups. First, the number of students working seasonally (in the summer) and otherwise part time has increased greatly. The large turnover—between work and school—is associated with unemployment. As the proportion of students and of student job searchers grows, this component of unemployment increases in importance. Indeed, about 75 percent of the unemployment observed in the 16–19 group is associated with entry and re-entry into the labor force. Second, the young people in these age groups who left school have progressively shorter work experience, since the successive cohorts graduate later. Higher unemployment is typical of less experienced workers, so growing unemployment is the statistical reflection of diminishing experience in (fixed) young age groups.

None of these factors represent obvious distress. A worsening of employment conditions should be reflected in the duration of unemployment. But the duration of youth unemployment is short (most of it is less than six weeks), and has not increased together with the rate (except in recessions). However, some of the effects of unemployment may not show up in duration to the extent that lack of success results in dropping out of the labor force back to school or to other activities not in the labor market.

One factor which adversely affects the condition of young inexperienced workers in the labor market is the upward trend in minimum wages. Most 16–19-year-olds are employed at or below minimum hourly rates. Each successive hike in the minimum wage, relative to the general wage level, and the progressive expansion of coverage reduces employer demand for inexperienced, initially low-productivity workers.

The particularly bad effect of minimum wage hikes is that they limit the opportunities for training or learning on the job. Apprentices and informal learners must accept initially low-paying jobs—their lower wages reflect not only lower productivity but also the costs of training which the firms provide, formally or informally. The minimum wage blocks this route to advancement and forces a detour via more school learning, at best.

Not all of those prevented from job experience at young ages stay longer at school. According to empirical analysis of minimum wage effects, the labor force participation rate of nonstudents has also been adversely affected. What happens to the double dropouts (out of school and work) may be guessed, but is not well documented.

The increasing tendency of by-passing relatively unskilled work experience via schooling is, of course, strengthened by the growth of public subsidies to universal schooling at progressively higher levels. The minimum wage hikes (and draft policies in the recent past) are additional factors producing a growing number of reluctant students. To some extent the growth of a (largely seasonal) and part-time student labor force represents an attempt to overcome the growing confinement of youth to schooling and the growing postponement of economic and personal independence.

In Conclusion

If a social problem exists, its universality is probably overstated by the tendency of observers to focus on the more visible segments of the population. The analysis available to economists does not suggest any obvious persistent economic malfunctions in the growth of schooling. The rate of return to schooling appears to be reassuring thus far, though the average certainly conceals distributional problems, and the most recent developments are not clearly reflected. The review of youth labor market conditions does reveal some symptoms of distress, though the size and trend in the unemployment figures tend to convey an exaggerated picture of it.

One large area of ignorance makes the economic analysis far from complete: This is the question of efficiency of the educational production function, the effects of its "industrial," curricular, and pedagogical organization. The observed rate of return does not tell us whether activities which produce education could not be more efficiently organized. Economists are only now beginning to take an interest in studying the educational production function. Much of the interest, however, centers on the production function within schools, yet education is a much broader concept than schooling.

Once *educational* purposes or functions are defined, the place and nature of *schooling* as one of several (alternative and/or coexisting) institutions can be envisaged, in the light of changes in technology and in society.

Broadly speaking, education of the young involves transmission of knowledge, socialization, identification and encouragement of talent, preparation for work, and orientation toward future personal, household, and public responsibilities. It seems obvious that much, perhaps most of these purposes cannot be achieved in the traditional classroom. Group or individual learning should depend on function and on available technology. Acquisition of social skills, and participatory activities such as sports, arts, and recreation require social, though not necessarily age-segregated environments. The same is true of the acquisition of information about and experience in a variety of work activities. The management of households, of health, of family finances are matters of social and individual learning. At the same time, the acquisition of intellectual knowl-

193

edge through reading, listening to lectures, and writing can be pursued individually, without fixed schedules, and at the student's own pace. Certainly, present-day technology should make the best teaching and teaching aids available to all students. Of course, provision must be made for feedbacks in form of discussions, testing, and guidance.

The institutional settings need to be envisaged and experimented with. It is not a matter of reversing trends and of somehow bringing the workplace to school and family, or any two of these institutions to the third. The progressively shrinking family, the increasingly abstract occupations, and the existing schooling which at best prepares for further schooling cannot simply be conjoined and revitalized for the education of the young. The new institutions will have to provide direction and guidance for all the functions, whose loci may well be diffused according to needs and technology, while providing maximum autonomy and variety for individual growth paths.

NOTE

1. James S. Coleman, "How Do the Young Become Adults?" Report 130, Center for Social Organization of Schools, Johns Hopkins University, May 1972.

III

Equality, Equity, and Equal Opportunity

INTRODUCTION

LTHOUGH the Declaration of Independence stated that "all men are created equal," Americans have never agreed on the importance of equality in various spheres of activity or on the appropriate formulation of the concept. Thomas Jefferson's words have never been interpreted as advocating complete equality of income, wealth, or social position. But the framers of the Constitution incorporated into the document their revulsion at the trappings of aristocracy, and the ideal of America as a classless society persisted in the face of ample evidence that such was not the reality. Public concern about poverty—inequality at the bottom rather than the top—waxes and wanes as a recurring theme in American politics.

The question of how much and what kind of equality is the proper goal of public policy is controversial, crucial, and unresolved. *Inequality,* offering a relatively weak utilitarian justification, made the assumption that economic equality, or at least more economic equality, was good in itself. That assumption may express many people's values, but it is by no means accepted by everyone. Indeed, the whole notion of inequality as well as the strategies for increasing or decreasing it need examination and clarification.

The articles in this part regard the notions of equality and equal opportunity from a variety of perspectives. They are both historical and analytical. Two, by Coleman and Weiskopf, look at the historical development of concern about equality and equal opportunity, examining shifts and movements in political thinking. In the process of historical examination, they clarify the meanings which have been attached to the concepts and focus attention on current usages as a product of historical development. The other two are more purely analytical. The articles by Rawls and by Nozick start with a theory of justice, an image of the just society, and attempt to derive specific principles and institutions which would embody well-formulated ideas of distributive justice in a functioning economic system. The articles taken together illustrate various facets of the continuing debate over equality and distributive justice.

Most Americans, according to available survey and interview data, do not value economic equality per se. Instead, they hold that economic inequalities are necessary incentives for achieving a prosperous and interesting society. What is important is that people have equal chances to succeed, that no one is prevented from using all his or her talents and energies to rise as high in the economic hierarchy as he or she can and desires.

Coleman's article examines this concept of equality of opportunity as it has been formulated throughout American history. He traces the development of the concept to its logically inevitable definition as equality of results, the notion used in the Coleman report. His historical discussion illuminates many of the confusions in the popular use of the term.

Weisskopf examines the notion of equality of opportunity as a special case of a general historical process of legitimizing and delegitimizing economic inequalities. He argues that inequalities must be justified and legitimated by prevailing social values. When a legitimating theory is challenged, as the labor theory of value was, and as the "Horatio Alger" myth was questioned in the 1930s, pressures arise to reduce inequalities. Weisskopf sees "meritocracy" justifications being challenged now, and predicts a new demand for reduction of inequalities which cannot be justified.

The selection from Rawls' *A Theory of Justice* sketches a notion of distributive justice which may provide a new standard for examining social and economic inequalities. His analysis includes but is not limited to equality of opportunity. Rawls, arguing from a contractarian framework, provides criteria for evaluating the extent to which various kinds of inequality are consistent with social justice. The core of his argument is the difference principle, which states that social and economic inequalities are justified only if they are attached to positions open to all, and if they work to the benefit of the least advantaged members of the society. Rawls' work is powerful and influential both substantively and methodologically. It is already being cited by economists as well as philosophers, and will no doubt be a force to be reckoned with for some time to come.

Nozick presents a quite different theory of distributive justice, one which is probably more similar than that of Rawls to the intuitions of Americans, and certainly one which must be considered when the task is incremental societal change rather than beginning anew. Nozick argues that a distribution is just if it results from fair rules for the ownership and transfer of property. It is a more purely procedural theory than Rawls' and evaluates a different sort of information. The two perspectives may or may not be compatible; certainly they will both help in clarifying what is meant by equality and fairness.

(9)

The Concept
of Equality of
Educational Opportunity

James A. Coleman

THE CONCEPT of "equality of educational opportunity" as held by members of society has had a varied past. It has changed radically in recent years, and is likely to undergo further change in the future. This lack of stability in the concept leads to several questions. What has it meant in the past, what does it mean now, and what will it mean in the future? Whose obligation is it to provide such equality? Is the concept a fundamentally sound one, or does it have inherent contradictions or conflicts with social organization? But first of all, and above all, what is and has been meant in society by the idea of equality of educational opportunity?

To answer this question, it is necessary to consider how the child's position in society has been conceived in different historical periods. In preindustrial Europe, the child's horizons were largely limited by his family. His station in life was likely to be the same as his father's. If his father was a serf, he would likely live his own life as a serf; if his father was a shoemaker, he would likely become a shoemaker. But even this immobility was not the crux of the matter; he was a part of the family production enterprise and would likely remain within this enterprise throughout his life. The extended family, as the basic unit of social organization, had complete authority over the child, and complete responsibility for him. This responsibility ordinarily did not end when the child became an adult because he remained a part of the same economic unit

Reprinted with permission from the *Harvard Educational Review*, 38: winter, 1968, pp. 7–22. Copyright © 1968 by President and Fellows of Harvard College.

James A. Coleman

and carried on this tradition of responsibility into the next generation. Despite some mobility out of the family, the general pattern was family continuity through a patriarchal kinship system.

There are two elements of critical importance here. First, the family carried responsibility for its members' welfare from cradle to grave. It was a "welfare society," with each extended family serving as a welfare organization for its own members. Thus it was to the family's interest to see that its members became productive. Conversely, a family took relatively small interest in whether someone in *another* family became productive or not—merely because the mobility of productive labor between family economic units was relatively low. If the son of a neighbor was allowed to become a ne'er-do-well, it had little real effect on families other than his own.

The second important element is that the family, as a unit of economic production, provided an appropriate context in which the child could learn the things he needed to know. The craftsman's shop or the farmer's fields were appropriate training grounds for sons, and the household was an appropriate training ground for daughters.

In this kind of society, the concept of equality of educational opportunity had no relevance at all. The child and adult were embedded within the extended family, and the child's education or training was merely whatever seemed necessary to maintain the family's productivity. The fixed stations in life which most families occupied precluded any idea of "opportunity" and, even less, equality of opportunity.

With the industrial revolution, changes occurred in both the family's function as a self-perpetuating economic unit and as a training ground. As economic organizations developed outside the household, children began to be occupationally mobile outside their families. As families lost their economic production activities, they also began to lose their welfare functions, and the poor or ill or incapacitated became more nearly a community responsibility. Thus the training which a child received came to be of interest to all in the community, either as his potential employers or as his potential economic supports if he became dependent. During this stage of development in eighteenth-century England, for instance, communities had laws preventing immigration from another community because of the potential economic burden of immigrants.

Further, as men came to employ their own labor outside the family in the new factories, their families became less useful as economic training grounds for their children. These changes paved the way for public education. Families needed a context within which their children could learn some general skills which would be useful for gaining work outside the family; and men of influence in the community began to be interested in the potential productivity of other men's children.

It was in the early nineteenth century that public education began to appear in Europe and America. Before that time, private education had grown with the expansion of the mercantile class. This class had both the need and resources to have its children educated outside the home, either for professional occupations or for occupations in the developing world of commerce. But the idea of general educational opportunity for all children arise only in the nineteenth century.

The emergence of public, tax-supported education was not solely a function of the stage of industrial development. It was also a function of the class structure in the society. In the United States, without a strong traditional class structure, universal education in publicly supported free schools became widespread in the early nineteenth century; in England, the "voluntary schools," run and organized by churches with some instances of state support, were not supplemented by a state-supported system until the Education Act of 1870. Even more, the character of educational opportunity reflected the class structure. In the United States, the public schools quickly became the common school, attended by representatives of all classes; these schools provided a common educational experience for most American children—excluding only those upper-class children in private schools, those poor who went to no schools, and Indians and Southern Negroes who were without schools. In England, however, the class system directly manifested itself through the schools. The state-supported, or "board schools" as they were called, became the schools of the laboring lower classes with a sharply different curriculum from those voluntary schools which served the middle and upper classes. The division was so sharp that two government departments, the Education Department and the Science and Art Department, administered external examinations, the first for the products of the board schools, and the second for the products of the voluntary schools as they progressed into secondary education. It was only the latter curricula and examinations that provided admission to higher education.

What is most striking is the duration of influence of such a dual structure. Even today in England, a century later (and in different forms in most European countries), there exists a dual structure of public secondary education with only one of the branches providing the curriculum for college admission. In England, this branch includes the remaining voluntary schools which, though retaining their individual identities, have become part of the state-supported system.

This comparison of England and the United States shows clearly the impact of the class structure in society upon the concept of educational opportunity in that society. In nineteenth-century England, the idea of *equality* of educational opportunity was hardly considered; the system was designed to provide *differentiated* educational opportunity appropriate to one's station in life. In the United States as well, the absence of educational opportunity for Negroes in the South arose from the caste and feudal structure of the largely rural society. The idea of differentiated educational opportunity, implicit in the Education Act of 1870 in England, seems to derive from dual needs: the needs arising from industrialization for a basic education for the labor force, and the interests of parents in having one's own child receive a good education. The middle classes could meet both these needs by providing a free system for the children of laboring classes, and a tuition system (which soon came to be supplemented by state grants) for their own. The long survival of this differentiated system depended not only on the historical fact that the voluntary schools existed before a public system came into existence but on the fact that it allows both of these needs to be met: the community's collective need for a trained labor force, and the middle-class individual's interest in a better education for his own child. It served a third need as well: that of maintaining the existing social order—a system of stratification that was a step removed from a feudal system of fixed estates, but designed to prevent a wholesale challenge by the children of the working class to the positions held for children of the middle classes.

The similarity of this system to that which existed in the South to provide differential opportunity to Negroes and whites is striking, just as is the similarity of class structures in the second half of nineteenth-century England to the white-Negro caste structure of the southern United States in the first half of the twentieth century.

In the United States, nearly from the beginning, the concept of educational opportunity had a special meaning which focused on equality. This meaning included the following elements:

1. Providing a *free* education up to a given level which constituted the principal entry point to the labor force.
2. Providing a *common curriculum* for all children, regardless of background.
3. Partly by design and partly because of low population density, providing that children from diverse backgrounds attend the *same school.*
4. Providing equality within a given *locality,* since local taxes provided the source of support for schools.

This conception of equality of opportunity is still held by many persons; but there are some assumptions in it which are not obvious. First, it implicitly assumes that the existence of free schools eliminates economic sources of inequality of opportunity. Free schools, however, do not mean that the costs of a child's education become reduced to zero for families at all economic levels. When free education was introduced, many families could not afford to allow the child to attend school beyond an early age. His labor was necessary to the family—whether in rural or urban areas. Even after the passage of child labor laws, this remained true on the farm. These economic sources of inequality of opportunity have become small indeed (up through secondary education); but at one time they were a major source of inequality. In some countries they remain so; and certainly for higher education they remain so.

Apart from the economic needs of the family, problems inherent in the social structure raised even more fundamental questions about equality of educational opportunity. Continued school attendance prevented a boy from being trained in his father's trade. Thus, in taking advantage of "equal educational opportunity," the son of a craftsman or small tradesman would lose the opportunity to enter those occupations he would most likely fill. The family inheritance of occupation at all social levels was still strong enough, and the age of entry into the labor force was still early enough, that secondary education interfered with opportunity for working-class children; while it opened up opportunities at higher social levels, it closed them at lower ones.

Since residue of this social structure remains in present American society, the dilemma cannot be totally ignored. The idea of a common educational experience implies that this experience has only the effect of widening the range of opportunity, never the effect of excluding opportunities. But clearly this is never precisely true so long as this experience prevents a child from pursuing certain occupational paths. This question still arises with the differentiated secondary curriculum: an academic program in high school has the effect not only of keeping open the opportunities which arise through continued education, but also of closing off opportunities which a vocational program keeps open.

A second assumption implied by this concept of equality of opportunity is that opportunity lies in *exposure* to a given curriculum. The amount of opportunity is then measured in terms of the level of curriculum to which the child is exposed. The higher the curriculum made available to a given set of children, the greater their opportunity.

The most interesting point about this assumption is the relatively passive role of the school and community, relative to the child's role. The school's obligation is to "provide an opportunity" by being available, within easy geographic access of the child, free of cost (beyond the value of the child's time), and with a curriculum that would not exclude him from higher education. The obligation to "use the opportunity" is on the child or the family, so that his role is defined as the active one: the responsibility for achievement rests with him. Despite the fact that the school's role was the relatively passive one and the child's or family's role the active one, the use of this social service soon came to be no longer a choice of the parent or child, but that of the state. Since compulsory attendance laws appeared in the nineteenth century, the age of required attendance has been periodically moved upward.

This concept of equality of educational opportunity is one that has been implicit in most educational practice throughout most of the period of public education in the nineteenth and twentieth centuries. However, there have been several challenges to it; serious questions have been raised by new conditions in public education. The first of these in the United States was a challenge to assumption two, the common curriculum. This challenge first occurred in the early years of the twentieth century with the expansion of secondary education. Until the report of the committee to the National Education Association, issued in 1918, the standard curriculum in secondary schools was primarily a classical one appropriate for college entrance. The greater influx of non-college-bound adolescents into the high school made it necessary that this curriculum be changed into one more appropriate to the new majority. This is not to say that the curriculum changed immediately in the schools, nor that all schools changed equally, but rather that the seven "cardinal principles" of the N.E.A. report became a powerful influence in the movement toward a less academically rigid curriculum. The introduction of the new nonclassical curriculum was seldom if ever couched in terms of a conflict between those for whom high school was college preparation, and those for whom it was terminal education; nevertheless, that was the case. The "inequality" was seen as the use of a curriculum that served a minority and was not designed to fit the needs of the majority; and the shift of curriculum was intended to fit the curriculum to the needs of the new majority in the schools.

In many schools, this shift took the form of *diversifying* the curriculum, rather than supplanting one by another; the college-preparatory curriculum remained though watered down. Thus the kind of equality of opportunity that emerged from the newly designed secondary school curriculum was radically different from the elementary school concept that had emerged earlier. The idea inherent in the new secondary school curriculum appears to have been to take as given the diverse occupational paths into which adolescents will go after secondary school, and to say (implicitly): there is greater equality of educational opportunity for a boy who is not going to attend college if he has a specially-designed curriculum than if he must take a curriculum designed for college entrance.

There is only one difficulty with this definition: it takes as *given* what should be problematic—that a given boy is going into a given postsecondary occupational or educational path. It is one thing to take as given that approximately 70 percent of an entering high school freshman class will not attend college; but to assign a *particular child* to a curriculum designed for that 70 percent closes off for that child the opportunity to attend college. Yet to assign all children to a curriculum designed for the 30 percent who will attend college creates inequality for those who, at the end of high school, fall among the 70 percent who do not attend college. This is a true dilemma, and one which no educational system has fully solved. It is more general than the college/noncollege dichotomy, for there is a wide variety of different paths that adolescents take on the completion of secondary school. In England, for example, a student planning to attend a university must specialize in the arts or the sciences in the later years of secondary school. Similar specialization occurs in the German gymnasium; and this is wholly within the group planning to attend university. Even greater specialization can be found among noncollege curricula, especially in the vocational, technical, and commercial high schools.

The distinguishing characteristic of this concept of equality of educational opportunity is that it accepts as given the child's expected future. While the concept discussed earlier left the child's future wholly open, this concept of differentiated curricula uses the expected future to match child and curriculum. It should be noted that the first and simpler concept is easier to apply in elementary schools where fundamental tools of reading and arithmetic are being learned by all children; it is only in secondary school that the problem of diverse futures arises. It should also be noted that the dilemma is directly due to the social structure itself: if there were a virtual absence of social mobility, with everyone occupying a fixed estate in life, then such curricula that take the future as given would provide equality of opportunity relative to that structure. It is only because of the high degree of occupational mobility between generations—that is, the greater degree of equality of *occupational* opportunity—that the dilemma arises.

The first stage in the evolution of the concept of equality of educational opportunity was the notion that all children must be exposed to the same curriculum in the same school. A second stage in the evolution of the concept assumed that different children would have different occupational futures and that equality of opportunity required providing different curricula for each type of student. The third and fourth stages in this evolution came as a result of challenges from opposing directions to the basic idea of equality of educational opportunity. The third stage can be seen at least as far back as 1896 when the Supreme Court upheld the southern states' notion of "separate but equal" facilities. This stage ended in 1954 when the Supreme Court ruled that legal separation by race inherently constitutes inequality of opportunity. By adopting the "separate but equal" doctrine, the southern states rejected assumption three of the original concept, the assumption that equality depended on the opportunity to attend the same school. This rejection was, however, consistent with the overall logic of the original concept, since attendance at the same school was an inherent part of that logic. The underlying idea was that opportunity resided in exposure to a curriculum; the community's responsibility was to provide that exposure, the child's to take advantage of it.

It was the pervasiveness of this underlying idea which created the difficulty for the Supreme Court. For it was evident that even when identical facilities and identical teacher salaries existed for racially separate schools, "equality of educational opportunity" in some sense did not exist. This had also long been evident to Englishmen as well, in a different context, for with the simultaneous existence of the "common school" and the "voluntary school," no one was under the illusion that full equality of educational opportunity existed. But the source of this inequality remained an unarticulated feeling. In the decision of the Supreme Court, this unarticulated feeling began to take more precise form. The essence of it was that the *effects* of such separate schools were, or were likely to be, different. Thus a concept of equality of opportunity which focused on *effects* of schooling began to take form. The actual decision of the Court was in fact a confusion of two unrelated premises: this new concept, which looked at results of schooling, and the legal premise that the use of race as a basis for school assignment violates fundamental freedoms. But what is important for the evolution of the concept of equality of opportunity is that a new and different assumption was introduced, the assumption that equality of opportunity depends in some fashion upon effects of schooling. I believe the decision would have been more soundly based had it not depended on the effects of schooling, but only on the violation of freedom; but by introducing the question of effects of schooling, the Court brought into the open the implicit goals of equality of educational opportunity—that is, goals having to do with the *results* of school—to which the original concept was somewhat awkwardly directed.

That these goals were in fact behind the concept can be verified by a simple mental experiment. Suppose the early schools had operated for only one hour a week and had been attended by children of all social classes. This would have met the explicit assumptions of the early concept of equality of opportunity since the school is free, with a common curriculum, and attended by all children in the locality. But it obviously would not have been accepted, even at that time, as providing equality of opportunity, because its effects would have been so minimal. The additional educational resources provided by middle- and upper-class families, whether in the home, by tutoring, or in private supplementary schools, would have created severe inequalities in results.

Thus the dependence of the concept upon results or effects of schooling, which had remained hidden until 1954, came partially into the open with the Supreme Court decision. Yet this was not the end, for it created more problems than it solved. It might allow one to assess gross inequalities, such as that created by dual school systems in the South, or by a system like that in the mental experiment I just described. But it allows nothing beyond that. Even more confounding, because the decision did not use effects of schooling as a criterion of inequality but only as justification for a criterion of racial integration, integration itself emerged as the basis for still a new concept of equality of educational opportunity. Thus the idea of effects of schooling as an element in the concept was introduced but immediately overshadowed by another, the criterion of racial integration.

The next stage in the evolution of this concept was, in my judgment, the Office of Education Survey of Equality of Educational Opportunity. This survey was carried out under a mandate in the Civil Rights Act of 1964 to the Commissioner of Education to assess the "lack of equality of educational opportunity" among racial and other groups in the United States. The evolution of this concept, and the conceptual disarray which this evolution had created, made the very definition of the task exceedingly difficult. The original concept could be examined by determining the degree to which all children in a locality had access to the same schools and the same curriculum, free of charge. The existence of diverse secondary curricula appropriate to different futures could be assessed relatively easily. But the very assignment of a child to a specific curriculum implies acceptance of the concept of equality which takes futures as given. And the introduction of the new interpretations, equality as measured by results of schooling and equality defined by racial integration, confounded the issue even further.

As a consequence, in planning the survey it was obvious that no single concept of equality of educational opportunity existed and that the survey must give information relevant to a variety of concepts. The basis on which this was done can be seen by reproducing a portion of an internal memorandum that determined the design of the survey:

The point of second importance in design [second to the point of discovering the intent of Congress, which was taken to be that the survey was not for the purpose of locating willful discrimination, but to determine educational inequality without regard to intention of those in authority] follows from the first and concerns the definition of inequality. One type of inequality may be defined in terms of differences of the community's input to the school, such as per-pupil expenditure, school plants, libraries, quality of teachers, and other similar quantities.

A second type of inequality may be defined in terms of racial composition of the school, following the Supreme Court's decision that segregated schooling is inherently unequal. By the former definition, the question of inequality through segregation is excluded, while by the latter, there is inequality of education within a school system so long as the schools within the system have different racial composition.

A third type of inequality would include various intangible characteristics of the school as well as the factors directly traceable to the community inputs to the school. These intangibles are such things as teacher morale, teachers' expectations of students, level of interest of the student body in learning, or others. Any of these factors may affect the impact of the school upon a given student within it. Yet such a definition gives no suggestion of where to stop, or just how relevant these factors might be for school quality.

Consequently, a fourth type of inequality may be defined in terms of consequences of the school for individuals with equal backgrounds and abilities. In this definition, equality of educational opportunity is equality of results, given the same individual input. With such a definition, inequality might come about from differences in the school inputs and/or racial composition and/or from more intangible things as described above.

Such a definition obviously would require that two steps be taken in the determination of inequality. First, it is necessary to determine the effect of these various factors upon educational results (conceiving of results quite broadly, including not only achievement but attitudes toward learning, self-image, and perhaps other variables). This provides various measures of the school's quality in terms of its effect upon its students. Second, it is necessary to take these measures of quality, once determined, and determine the differential exposure of Negroes (or other groups) and whites to schools of high and low quality.

A fifth type of inequality may be defined in terms of consequences of the school for individuals of unequal backgrounds and abilities. In this definition, equality of educational opportunity is equality of results given *different* individual inputs. The most striking examples of inequality here would be children from households in which a language other than English, such as Spanish or Navaho, is spoken. Other examples would be low-achieving children from homes in which there is poverty of verbal expression or an absence of experiences which lead to conceptual facility.

Such a definition taken in the extreme would imply that educational equality is reached only when the results of schooling (achievement and attitudes) are the same for racial and religious minorities as for the dominant group.

The basis for the design of the survey is indicated by another segment of this memorandum:

Thus, the study will focus its principal effort on the fourth definition, but will also provide information relevant to all five possible definitions. This insures the pluralism which is obviously necessary with respect to a definition of inequality. The major justification for this focus is that the results of this approach can best be translated into policy which will improve education's effects. The results of the first two approaches (tangible inputs to the school, and segregation) can certainly be translated into policy, but there is no good evidence that these policies will improve education's effects; and while policies to implement the fifth would certainly improve education's effects, it seems hardly possible that the study could provide information that would direct such policies.

Altogether, it has become evident that it is not our role to define what constitutes equality for policy-making purposes. Such a definition will be an outcome of the interplay of a variety of interests, and will certainly differ from time to time as these interests differ. It should be our role to cast light on the state of inequality defined in the variety of ways which appear reasonable at this time.

The survey, then, was conceived as a pluralistic instrument, given the variety of concepts of equality of opportunity in education. Yet I suggest that despite the avowed intention of not adjudicating between these different ideas, the survey has brought a new stage in the evolution of the concept. For the definitions of equality which the survey was designed to serve split sharply into two groups. The first three definitions concerned input resources: first, those brought to the school by the actions of the school administration (facilities, curriculum, teachers); second, those brought to the school by the other students, in the educational backgrounds which their presence contributed to the school; and third, the intangible characteristics such as "morale" that result from the interaction of all these factors. The fourth and fifth definitions were concerned with the effects of schooling. Thus the five definitions were divided into three concerned with inputs to school and two concerned with effects of schooling. When the report emerged, it did not give five different measures of equality, one for each of these definitions; but it did focus sharply on this dichotomy, giving in Chapter Two information on inequalities of input relevant to definitions one and two, and in Chapter Three information on inequalities of results relevant to definitions four and five, and also in Chapter Three information on the relation of input to results again relevant to definitions four and five.

Although not central to our discussion here, it is interesting to note that this examination of the relation of school inputs to effects on achievement showed that those input characteristics of schools that are most alike for Negroes and whites have least effect on their achievement. The magnitudes of differences between schools attended by Negroes and those attended by whites were as follows: least, facilities and curriculum; next, teacher quality; and greatest, educational backgrounds of fellow students. The order of importance of these inputs on the achievement of Negro students is precisely the same: facilities and curriculum least, teacher quality next, and backgrounds of fellow students, most.

By making the dichotomy between inputs and results explicit, and by focusing attention not only on inputs but on results, the report brought into the open what had been underlying all the concepts of equality of educational opportunity but had remained largely hidden: that the concept implied *effective* equality of opportunity, that is, equality in those elements that are effective for learning. The reason this had remained half-hidden, obscured by definitions that involve inputs is, I suspect, because educational research has been until recently unprepared to demonstrate what elements are effective. The controversy that has surrounded the report indicates that measurements of effects is still subject to sharp disagreement; but the crucial point is that *effects* of inputs have come to constitute the basis for assessment of school quality (and thus equality of opportunity) in place of using certain inputs by definition as measures of quality (e.g., small classes are better than large, higher-paid teachers are better than lower-paid ones, by definition).

It would be fortunate indeed if the matter could be left to rest there—if merely by using effects of school rather than inputs as the basis for the concept, the problem were solved. But that is not the case at all. The conflict between definitions four and five given above shows this. The conflict can be illustrated by resorting again to the mental experiment discussed earlier—providing a standard education of one hour per week, under identical conditions, for all children. By definition four, controlling all background differences of the children, results for Negroes and whites would be equal, and thus by this definition equality of opportunity would exist. But because such minimal schooling would have minimal effect, those children from educationally strong families would enjoy educational opportunity far surpassing that of others. And because such educationally strong backgrounds are found more often among whites than among Negroes, there would be very large overall Negro-white achievement differences—and thus inequality of opportunity by definition five.

It is clear from this hypothetical experiment that the problem of what constitutes equality of opportunity is not solved. The problem will become even clearer by showing graphs with some of the results of the Office of Education Survey. The highest line in Figure 9-1 shows the achievement in verbal skills by whites in the urban Northeast at grades 1, 3, 6, 9, and 12. The second line shows the achievement at each of these grades by whites in the rural Southeast. The third shows the achievement of Negroes in the urban Northeast. The fourth shows the achievement of Negroes in the rural Southeast.

When compared to the whites in the urban Northeast, each of the other three groups shows a different pattern. The comparison with whites in the rural South shows the two groups beginning near the same point

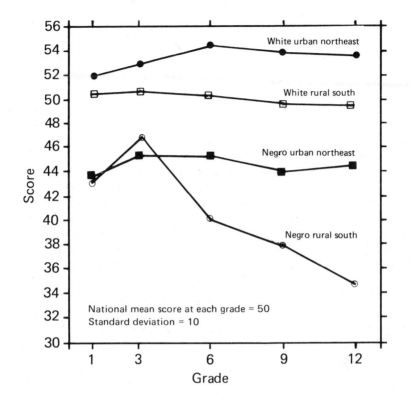

Fig. 9–1. Patterns of Achievement in verbal skills at various grade levels by race and region.

in the first grade, and diverging over the years of school. The comparison with Negroes in the urban Northeast shows the two groups beginning farther apart at the first grade and remaining about the same distance apart. The comparison with Negroes in the rural South shows the two groups beginning far apart and moving much farther apart over the years of school.

Which of these, if any, shows equality of educational opportunity between regional and racial groups? Which shows greatest inequality of opportunity? I think the second question is easier to answer than the first. The last comparison showing both initial difference and the greatest increase in difference over grades 1 through 12 appears to be the best candidate for the greatest inequality. The first comparison, with whites in the rural South, also seems to show inequality of opportunity, because of the increasing difference over the 12 years. But what about the second comparison, with an approximately constant difference between Negroes and whites in the urban Northeast? Is this equality of opportunity? I suggest not. It means, in effect, only that the period of school has left the average Negro at about the same level of achievement relative to whites as he began—in this case, achieving higher than about 15 percent of the whites, lower than about 85 percent of the whites. It may well be that in the absence of school those lines of achievement would have diverged due to differences in home environments; or perhaps they would have remained an equal distance apart, as they are in this graph (though at lower levels of achievement for both groups, in the absence of school). If it were the former, we could say that school, by keeping the lines parallel, has been a force toward the equalization of opportunity. But in the absence of such knowledge, we cannot say even that.

What would full equality of educational opportunity look like in such graphs? One might persuasively argue that it should show a convergence, so that even though two population groups begin school with different levels of skills on the average, the average of the group that begins lower moves up to coincide with that of the group that begins higher. Parenthetically, I should note that this does *not* imply that all students' achievement comes to be identical, but only that the *averages* for two population groups that begin at different levels come to be identical. The diversity of individual scores could be as great as, or greater than, the diversity at grade 1.

Yet there are serious questions about this definition of equality of opportunity. It implies that over the period of school there are no other influences, such as the family environment, which affect achievement over the 12 years of school, even though these influences may differ greatly for the two population groups. Concretely, it implies that white family environments, predominantly middle class, and Negro family environments, predominantly lower class, will produce no effects on achievement that would keep these averages apart. Such an assumption seems highly unrealistic, especially in view of the general importance of family background for achievement.

However, if such possibilities are acknowledged, then how far can they go before there is inequality of educational opportunity? Constant difference over school? Increasing differences? The unanswerability of such questions begins to give a sense of a new stage in the evolution of the concept of equality of educational opportunity. These questions concern the *relative intensity* of two sets of influences: those which are alike for the two groups, principally in school, and those which are different, principally in the home or neighborhood. If the school's influences are not only alike for the two groups, but very strong relative to the divergent influences, then the two groups will move together. If school influences are very weak, then the two groups will move apart. Or more generally, the relative intensity of the convergent school influences and the divergent out-of-school influences determines the effectiveness of the educational system in providing equality of educational opportunity. In this perspective, complete equality of opportunity can be reached only if all the divergent out-of-school influences vanish, a condition that would arise only in the advent of boarding schools; given the existing divergent influences, equality of opportunity can only be approached and never fully reached. The concept becomes one of degree of proximity to equality of opportunity. This proximity is determined, then, not merely by the *equality* of educational inputs, but by the *intensity* of the school's influences relative to the external divergent influences. That is, equality of output is not so much determined by equality of the resource inputs, but by the power of these resources in bringing about achievement.

Here, then, is where the concept of equality of educational opportunity presently stands. We have observed an evolution which might have been anticipated a century and a half ago when the first such concepts arose, yet one which is very different from the concept as it first developed. This difference is sharpened if we examine a further implication of the current concept as I have described it. In describing the original concept, I indicated that the role of the community and the educational institution was relatively passive; they were expected to provide a set of free public resources. The responsibility for profitable use of those resources lay with the child and his family. But the evolution of the concept has reversed these roles. The implication of the most recent concept, as I have described it, is that the responsibility to create achievement lies with the educational institution, not the child. The difference in achievement at grade 12 between the average Negro and the average white is, in effect, the degree of inequality of opportunity, and the reduction of that inequality is a responsibility of the school. This shift in responsibility follows logically from the change in the concept of equality of educational opportunity from school resource inputs to effects of schooling. When that change occurred, as it has in the past few years, the school's responsibility shifted from increasing and distributing equally *its* "quality" to increasing the quality of its *students'* achievements. This is a notable shift, and one which should have strong consequences for the practice of education in future years.

(10)

The Dialectics
of Equality

Walter A. Weisskopf

ABSTRACT: Equality and inequality are discussed from the philosophical and sociopsychological, rather than from the economic, point of view. Social inequalities are bearable only if they are felt to be legitimate and justifiable in terms of the predominant hierarchy of values. Movements for equality are caused by doubts about the legitimacy of existing inequalities. Modern individualism, libertarianism, and equalitarianism were a rebellion against the existing order. In premodern times, inequalities were justified by ascription and were derived from inherent characteristics, such as birth and caste. Industrial society justified inequalities by achievement of economic success. This orientation is reflected in the labor theory of value, as well as in marginalist value theory. In the American creed, equalitarianism was combined with the acceptance of inequalities through the principle of equality of opportunity which justifies inequalities by the assumption of an equal start for everyone. Under the impact of the great depression and of the organizational revolution, economic achievement was replaced by intellectual merit, knowledge, and academic credentials as justification for inequalities. Under the impact of growing doubts about this kind of achievement, a new equalitarian trend is under way, supported by the antigrowth and the environmental protection movements, as well as by the tradition of protection for the underprivileged which was always an intrinsic part of the market economy.

Economics developed during a period in which segmentalization became the rule in the social sciences. The fragmented approach makes it

Reprinted with permission from the *Annals of the American Academy of Social and Political Science*, September 1973. © 1973 American Academy of Social and Political Science.

214

difficult for economists to deal with the philosophical, psychological, social, political, and economic dimensions of equality and inequality. Yet, the noneconomic aspects should be discussed if the purely economic aspects of income inequality are to be understood. The very question of the economic effects of equality or inequality of incomes entails value judgments and transcends, therefore, the realm of economics as it is usually considered. An integrative approach must start with the recognition that equality and inequality are related in dialectical interdependence: They are like two sides of the same coin; they give meaning to each other; one would be senseless without the other.

The Dialectics of Participation-Individualization

The equality-inequality dichotomy is one of the many antinomies which beset the human condition. It is related to the antinomy of individualization and participation; this is an existential antinomy, a category of human existence. Man participates in his world, in his environment. He is a part of a whole, a member of a larger entity. This participation is one of the existential roots of the experience of equality. It is the root of the experience of the "I am one with the world," of the "I am thou," and of the unity of all creation. It underlies ideas such as "we are all children of God" and "we are all members of the brotherhood of man."

At the same time, man has the experience of individualization, separateness, and distinctness—being one self, and not the other. This is the root of the experience of the I versus the Other, of existing as a person different from other beings and persons. This is the existential source of incomparability and inequality and the idea of the uniqueness of personality—I am I; nothing and no one is, nor can be, like me.

The Social Dialectics of Equality

The antinomy of participation and individualization is reflected in man's social existence. Again, one finds centripetal and centrifugal tendencies. On the one hand, men have an innate propensity for solidarity, community, and integration and, on the other hand, for separation, distinction, and differentiation. Solidarity and community are the basis for the experience of equality. As a member of a family, group, tribe, clan, or nation, I am equal to other members; such membership forms a common link which generates the feeling of equality with other members. Each member of a group has common traits with other members. The very concept of society implies an element of equality, consisting in group membership, if nothing else—for example, the concept that "we are all Americans." This element of equality through group membership is enhanced by the inclusion-exclusion principle. A group includes insiders and excludes outsiders; the equality of the insiders is underscored by the inequality, inferiority, of the outsiders.

The centrifugal force in society is related to individualization. In his own life history, and in the history of societies, the individual tends to emancipate himself from the primordial ties with the mother, the parents, the family, the peer group, the home town, and even the nation. Self-consciousness leads to a split between individual and group which tends to counteract the experiences of belonging and equality. Insofar as the individual becomes psychologically separated from the community, the common denominator on which equality rests is destroyed. Equality requires comparability; when the individual becomes aware of his separateness and uniqueness, there is no basis for either comparison or equality.

The Historical Dialectics of Equality and Inequality

The conflict between equality and inequality is ineluctable in human existence. However, historical conditions determine when and how this conflict becomes conscious. Under certain historical conditions, there is little awareness of inequalities and, therefore, little desire for equality; under other conditions, existing inequalities are experienced as an intolerable burden and strong equalitarian movements develop. In Western history, such a situation arose in the eighteenth century; during this era, it was assumed that society generates unfreedom and inequalities of power, status, and wealth and, thus, destroys the individual's natural state of freedom and equality. This intellectual scheme was developed in the eighteenth century, but had its roots in the thought of the Sophists, the Stoa, and Roman law. According to this pattern—clearest in the thought of Locke and Rousseau—the individual surrendered his natural freedom and equality to the state for the sake of economic cooperation and physical safety. This constitutes the famous social contract, which assumes that the accomplishment of common purposes necessitates the voluntary surrender of primary, natural equality and freedom to social inequalities. This ideological scheme underlies most modern thinking about equality and inequality.

The scheme, however, is not borne out by history. Individualism, with its claim to freedom and equality, is a late historical phenomenon. In all cultures, man is originally part of a group, integrated into a community, linked with others and hardly aware of his individual existence. His ties with the group are supported by religious belief, value systems, and institutions which are part of an uncritically and unconsciously accepted natural order. The individual becomes aware of himself as a separate entity only when the stable structure of beliefs, values, and institutions begins to disintegrate. Then, consciousness awakens and existing institutions are examined by reason. This process may confirm prevailing beliefs, values, and institutions. But, sooner or later, it leads to a critique of the existing order and to alienation from it.[1]

This is the point where individualism, libertarianism, and equalitarianism emerge. Individualistic and equalitarian thought owes its origin to an intellectual rebellion against the existing order; thus, they began as phenomena of social disintegration and change. Individualism implies a fundamental doubt in the legitimacy and justice of the prevailing social hierarchy. All societies, with the exception of a few small esoteric groups, require some hierarchy of organizational structure with superiority, subordination, and a structure of authority, command, and obedience. Society, but not community, is synonymous with some unfreedom, inequality, suppression, and restriction of individuals. Originally, these restrictions were not experienced as oppressive, because they were presumed to be rooted in divine, or natural, order. When reason is applied to this order, the hierarchy requires rational legitimation and justification; it must appear to conform to principles of justice. In premodern times, such justification was based on ascription: Differentials of power, status, and wealth were derived from inherent characteristics such as ancestry, birth, or caste; people were privileged or underprivileged because of what they were and not for what they accomplished. During the last 400 years, modern Western industrial society replaced ascription by achievement: differences were justified by the degree to which different individuals attained social goals and values. Ascriptive aristocracy was replaced by a meritocracy wherein merit consisted of achieving that which society valued most.

It is misleading both to identify inequalities based on achievement with meritocracy and to maintain that inequalities based on ascription have nothing to do with merit. The courtiers in ancient Egypt, the citizens of the Greek Polis, the Senate and the people of Rome, the feudal lords—all groups whose status rested on ascription—considered themselves as the better, more worthy, and superior ones and, thus, deserving their privileges because of their inherent merits. In a way, social hierarchies based on ascription are also meritocracies; they rest on the conviction that the existing inequalities are legitimate and just. After all, the Greek word *aristocracy* means the rule of the best. The difference between ascriptive and achievement-oriented meritocracy lies in the yardstick for merit: in the case of ascription, it is being and belonging to a group; in the case of achievement, it is doing and performing. Hierarchies based on ascription are also more rigid, whereas those based on achievement allow upward, and downward, mobility; one can never change what one is, but one can change one's social position by achievement and performance.

Achievement replacing ascription as the legitimizing principle went hand in hand with a class struggle. The bourgeoisie, in its struggle with the aristocracy in England and with *l'ancien regime* in France, attacked the traditional ascriptive inequalities through their demand for liberty and equality. The ideal of equality had the sociohistorical function of attacking the existing inequalities, but it led, in turn, to new inequalities based on achievement.

Equality and Inequality in Economics

The new inequalities are reflected in the history of capitalism and economic thought. The ideas presented by Max Weber, in the *Protestant Ethic and the Spirit of Capitalism,* show the transition from the principle of ascription to the one of achievement. The belief in predestination through the inscrutable counsel of the Lord is ascriptive; one is chosen regardless of one's merit. However, every Calvinist and Puritan tried to prove his salvation by his economic success, achieved by practicing economic virtues: systematic, methodic, unrelenting pursuit of gain combined with intensive impulse control through hard work, thrift, frugality, and avoidance of spontaneous enjoyment. Achievement of economic success gradually replaced ascriptive salvation; economic performance became the source of individual worth.

It is important to understand that this transition from an ascriptive to an achievement-oriented society took place hand in hand with the emergence of capitalism; thus, the way for a meritocratic mobile society was opened 200 years ago. Meritocracy is not an invention of postindustrial society.[2] The achievement orientation of capitalism was, and is, supposed to be meritocratic. Merit consists of living up to the work ethic and therefore reaping the reward of one's performance. A change in the basis of merit distinguishes the postindustrial meritocracy of the mid-twentieth century from the bourgeois meritocracy of the nineteenth; the economic virtues have been replaced by the intelligence quotient (IQ) and by educational credentials.

The work and success ethos performed two historical functions: (1) it destroyed the basis for ascriptive inequalities of the old order; (2) it also provided a justification for the new inequalities of wealth and income in the new order of the market economy. The labor theory of value in economic thought reflects this justification.

The pure labor theory of value, as formulated by Adam Smith and Ricardo, justified the inequalities of income. This theory is essentially meritocratic: in an economy of independent producers—without wage labor and without private property of land—prices would reflect differences in effort, measured by labor-time used in production; thus, those who work longer and harder would sell a higher-priced product and receive a higher reward. The classics used this theory to justify the existing price system—therefore, Ricardo's desperate, although unsuccessful, attempts to eliminate profits as a determinant of price and his theory of rent which interpreted land income as an effect, rather than a cause, of price.[3] Profit and rent are not earned through labor; therefore, they do not fit into the moral philosophy of the labor value theory. Ricardo thus tried to prove that they were not causal for price differentials. If that were true, such differentials would be caused only by differences in labor-time used in the production of goods; such differentials would be morally justified according to the labor theory of value: more work leads to higher prices and incomes.

Marx used the same theory to castigate the price system. In contrast to Ricardo, he acknowledged the influence of profits on prices. But to Marx, the surplus value—profit—is an unearned increment which the capitalist did not earn by his own labor. Therefore, a profit economy leads to inequalities which are unfair by the standards of the labor theory of value. The union movement and the modern women's liberation movement use the same theory—as in the slogan "equal pay for equal work"—to attain equality. Equality is based on merit and is quite compatible with inequalities of unequal pay for unequal work.

The labor theory of value was later replaced by marginalist value theories. Originally, they also contained the seeds of moral justification of differentials in prices and incomes. When economists state that in a competitive market system everyone's wage, or income, will be equal to one's marginal value product, they actually state: "to each according to his productive contribution." This is a meritocratic justification of economic inequalities.

In the twentieth century, economic thought has become evermore value-neutral and value-empty. Few economists today would openly try to justify wage and income differentials by their proportionality to productive contribution. Their apologetics for the existing income distribution would rest on functional grounds: inequalities are necessary as incentives for increasing the supply of scarce resources. However, the idea that higher income and wealth are deserved and caused by personal virtues and higher contributions has been absorbed by popular feeling and vulgar economic philosophizing. Social Darwinism is still very much alive; those who have succeeded in the competitive struggle regard themselves as the fittest and as better than others. This attitude underlies the Nixon administration's attack on the welfare state. The economy is viewed as a meritocracy of the rich; they supposedly deserve their exalted status.

Equality of Opportunity

The existing inequalities, however, had to be made compatible with the equalitarian, individualistic, and libertarian tradition of the American creed. The combination between egalitarianism and justification of inequalities was achieved by the idea of equality of opportunity. It contains an element of equalitarianism—everybody is supposed to begin at the same starting line—but the inequalities that emerge in the competitive struggle are accepted. The idea of equality of opportunity makes possible the representation of the resulting unequal income distribution as just: because of initial equality, the resulting inequalities are supposedly based on merit.[4]

The idea of equality of opportunity can serve its purpose to justify existing inequalities only if one believes everyone has an equal start and accepts the resulting inequalities as meritorious. Both beliefs are open to grave doubts. There are obvious flaws in the assumption of an equal start; differences in environment, background, education, and genes distribute the chances very unevenly, indeed. But the main source of discontent is the conviction, ever growing in the twentieth century, that the privileges of higher income and wealth are not deserved—that the present form of the free enterprise system is not a meritocracy. Corporate concentration and market power made the inequalities in economic opportunities more visible. The events of the Great Depression of the 1930s made it obvious that hardly anybody is master of his economic fate and that economic success and failure have little to do with individual merit. Under these circumstances, the Horatio Alger myth and the idea that the higher income receivers are the fittest appeared to be ludicrous. These ideas were supposed to justify economic inequalities, but the underprivileged and the intelligentsia began to reject them. People feel that high incomes are not based on just desert. As long as there was an unspoken, implicit, often unconscious consensus about the justice of income differentials, equalitarianism remained marginal, remedial, and ameliorative. When this consensus evaporated, the inequalities lost their psychological base. They can then be maintained only by the power structure of the existing institutions.

Meritocracy

A more recent source of discontent with the principle of equal opportunity is found in the changing character of the meritocracy. This term is not usually applied to the merits of the rich and successful, but to what Galbraith calls the "technostructure" and the "education-scientific estate." [5] Previously, merit was based on the virtues of the work ethic and of the adventurous, successful entrepreneur. Since World War II—in what is fashionably called the postindustrial society—merit and differentials in status and power are attributed to the knowledge of the highly educated and trained experts with academic credentials who are supposed to have become the real decision makers and power structure in business, government, and even politics. Under present conditions, this further restricts the equal start necessary for real equality of opportunity; higher education and expertise are to many even less accessible than economic success. Equalitarianism, once directed against the rich, is now directed against the status of those with credentials of higher education and expert knowledge.

Trying to justify the existing hierarchy of status and power as an intellectual meritocracy—as does the literary crowd writing in *The Public Interest* [6]—is even less effective than the justification of income differentials on the basis of the work ethic and entrepreneurial success.

First, the trend toward a meritocracy of the intellectual elite has aggravated inequalities in the economy. It has reinforced the dual economy: minority groups have been shut off from the mainstream of the economy; they do not even benefit from expansion and prosperity, because of their lack of background and education. More and more, the better jobs require educational credentials of achievement which these minorities are unable to acquire. Without the certificates they are not needed by the economy. Therefore, they cannot improve their situation by organizing and withholding their services—by strikes. They are not exploited—needed, but underpaid—but discriminated against—discarded, not in demand. This aggravates their unequal status because the system does not provide any legitimate remedies: they are in the minority, therefore, they have little political power; they do not have an equal start, therefore, they have little upward mobility. A meritocracy based on IQ and academic credentials condemns these groups to social inferiority.

However, the resentment against the intellectual elite is not confined to the disadvantaged minorities. The resentment is also caused by doubts about the value and meaning of intellectual, white-collar work. Recent interviews of blue-collar workers in the Boston area have thrown some light on this attitude.[7] After 20 years as a meat cutter, a blue-collar worker—who had been forced to quit high school—became a white-collar bank clerk; however, he harbors an innate disrespect for educated white-collar work: "These jobs are not real work where you make something—it's just pushing papers." He feels a "revulsion against the work of educated people in the bank, and a feeling that manual labor has more dignity." Children of blue-collar workers, with more education than their parents, "feel that they have more opportunity open to them than their manual-laboring parents. At the same time they see their parents' work as intrinsically more interesting and worthwhile. . . ." These men see "knowledge through formal education as giving a man the tools for achieving freedom. . . . As things actually stand, however, certified knowledge does not mean dignity . . . it is the reverse, it is sham."

In part, this attitude is a heritage of the industrial society in which production of goods was the main economic activity. It is an attitude reminiscent of the Marxist glorification of the manual worker as the only real productive factor. However, this traditional belief in the superior dignity of manual work has become amalgamated with a more recent distrust in expertise, intelligence quotients, academic credentials, and the achievements of the intelligentsia in general. The growing resentment of Middle America against the "best and the brightest"' seems to bear this out. The issue of postindustrial society is not merely intellectual meritocracy versus equality, as sociologist Daniel Bell maintains, but the growing doubts about the merits of the meritocracy.

Considering the kind of world the experts in science, technology, and business have helped to create, these doubts are not without justification. Yet, the source of these doubts lies deeper. They are—consciously or unconsciously—connected with the basic problem of postindustrial society: the longing both for a ground for legitimizing equality and inequality and for the fusion of order and freedom.[8] The postindustrial meritocratic, intellectual elite owes its high status to its mastery of a restrictive intellectuality of a cognitive, analytical, measuring, and technical nature. They use instrumental rationality which can choose means, but can say nothing about ends. This rationality has destroyed a deeper philosophical kind of reason which could deal with ends, goals, purposes, and ultimate meanings.[9]

The merits of the meritocracy are based on a rationality which makes it impossible to establish standards for any merits whatsoever. Their high IQs and their academic credentials enable them to serve the existing order, but not to justify it, nor to replace it by one that can be accepted as legitimate by its citizenry. The hunger for such legitimacy, called by Irving Kristol the dominant political fact in the world of today, cannot be satisfied by the instrumental, technical intellect of the experts. Therefore, their merits are not accepted by the community.

Thus, today's egalitarian resentment of the underprivileged against the privileged is based less on need than on a loss of the belief in the justice, legitimation, and justification of existing inequalities. The traditional approach that the starving masses resent the abundance of the rich has become, with some notable exceptions, obsolete in our relatively affluent society. The main cause of egalitarian trends is the disintegration of the belief that the privileges of higher income, wealth, and education are based on just desert and merit.

The Tradition of Social Protection

There is, however, another source of egalitarianism which is related to poverty. It does not originate with the poor, the disadvantaged, and the underprivileged, but with society as a whole—or better, with the privileged groups. This is the tradition of charity and compassion and the idea that society has to take care of those who cannot take care of themselves.

In the Middle Ages, the poor were almost exclusively the impotent poor who were not able to support themselves. They were the object of charity which was, and is, a method of practicing a Christian virtue and of assuaging guilt feelings of the privileged. In the free market system, the impotent poor were joined by the able-bodied poor and the unemployed. Various measures were used to force them into employment but they were also made the beneficiaries of charity and compassion through some measure of relief—for example, the allowance system of Speenhamland, 1795. Aside from trying to solve socioeconomic problems of poverty, this constituted an enlargement of the group to which charity and compassion was extended from the physically, to the economically, helpless. The reason for this extension was, and is, the guilt feelings of the haves toward the have-nots. This is probably one of the strongest roots of egalitarian welfare measures and of the orientation of social responsibility. Not only does the resentment of the underprivileged, but also the guilt feelings of the haves, grow when income

223

differentials are felt to be illegitimate; the less they feel that their privileges are deserved, the more they feel obligated to ameliorate the situation of the poor and underprivileged—for example, as in the 1930s in the United States. It was much less the case early in the nineteenth century, when wealth was equated with morality, and poverty with immorality. Thus, demands for a more equal distribution of income originate not merely with those who want more, but also with those who feel badly about having more.

However, there is more to this trend than the guilt feelings of the privileged. The free market system required, almost from its beginnings, a protection of society from the system's detrimental effects. As Karl Polanyi has pointed out, the free market tended to destroy man and his environment by treating labor and land as commodities.[10] When they are used or not used according to the vagaries of the market, human beings and their natural habitat may be injured or destroyed. A countervailing force—which Karl Polanyi calls social protectionism—was required, including all types of social legislation and welfare measures. Social protectionism forms a necessary counterweight against the free market. Without it, the free market would lose its infrastructure, the supporting framework of a viable society.

Social protectionism, nourished by the Christian tradition of charity and compassion toward the underprivileged, rests squarely on the principle of ascription: we help the disadvantaged not for what they do or achieve, but for what they are—namely, human beings in need. The ascriptive principle has never been completely abandoned as the meritocrats maintain. It has been applied as a countervailing force, as a balance against the ravages wrought by the inequalities of the market economy. Significantly, social protectionism was often supported by nonbourgeois, conservative groups, such as the Tories in England and Bismarck and the Junkers in Germany, and by a growing civil service bureaucracy.

Conclusions

Where does this kaleidoscopic and dialectical picture leave us today? The antinomic forces pulling toward greater economic equality, on the one hand, and the countertendencies pushing back the equalitarian trend to protect the existing order, on the other hand, are still at work. If the equality-inequality dichotomy is an existential antinomy, the struggle will not cease, whatever the structure of our society and economy. However, the two forces are never in a static equilibrium; there are always trends in one or the other direction. Surface appearances to the contrary, the pendulum will probably swing in a direction of greater equality based on ascription and away from income differentials based on either financial or educational achievement. One of the reasons is that economic growth, at least in the developed countries, may become less and less desirable and possible. Growing affluence makes an increase in the standards of living, in terms of more and more income and wealth, less attractive. This, in turn, may weaken the resistance against measures toward a more equal income distribution, such as a guaranteed minimum income. The economies of the developed countries may turn toward an improvement of the quality of life, which would imply a weakening of the acquisitive ethos. Time and energy— the really scarce resources—may be increasingly devoted to the production of psychic income in the form of playful, artistic, and contemplative pursuits to satisfy the higher needs, and to games, circuses, fishing, and loafing to satisfy lower needs.

The likelihood of such a development is greatly enhanced by the dangers predicted by the ecologists. If population growth, exhaustion of basic resources, pollution, and the problems of waste absorption should actually set absolute limits to economic growth, the basic economic orientation of the present economic systems will have to change. Mankind, especially in the West, will have to turn to a life style which consumes less resources and leads to less waste than the present system. Thus, production and income, in the traditional sense, will lose their importance and a more equal distribution of income will be more acceptable merely because there will be fewer uses for money income. The basic values of life may change; market values will have to be replaced by noneconomic values. People will have to pursue goals which will cost more time and energy, but less resources, and will not generate detrimental by-products. Friendship, love, enjoyment of nature, contemplation, mere loafing, and so forth, will have to become more important than income and purchasing power.

This does not mean an end to inequality, but it will be based on different grounds than income and wealth. Inequalities may be based on noneconomic—such as aesthetic, spiritual, and communal—standards. These differences may be based on achievements outside the economic dimension. In the economic field, we may return to the principle of ascription. Income will have to be separated from production of traditional goods and services; meaningful activity will have to be defined as more than the earning of income; and a guaranteed minimum to everyone, with strict regulation of what can be produced and bought without ecological dangers, will have to be instituted. The realm of "goods" will have to be restricted and the realm of "bads" greatly increased. If all this sounds utopian, it is; however, without utopia, there can be no vision and no survival.

The problem of equality is ultimately a philosophical, and not an economic, question. Differences of status, wealth, power, natural endowment, and social functions are unavoidable in any society. When people talk about equality and human dignity, they really want acceptance —I shy away from the word love, but that is what it is—in spite of all differences. They want to be accepted and loved as they are, even in spite of what they are. This love and acceptance—Christian theology calls it agape—is not primarily a creation of any social system; it is needed to soften the nonegalitarian harshness of society. This is the real meaning of the longing for a classless society and for a plurality of values. It is expressed beautifully in the brilliant social science fiction of Michael Young:

The classless society would be one which both possessed and acted upon plural values. Were we to evaluate people, not only according to their intelligence and their education, their occupation, and their power, but according to their kindliness and their courage, their imagination and sensitivity, their sympathy and generosity, there could be no classes. Who would be able to say that the scientist was superior to the porter with admirable qualities as a father, the civil servant with unusual skill at gaining prizes superior to the lorrydriver with unusual skill at growing roses? The classless society, in which individual differences were actively encouraged as well as passively tolerated, in which full meaning was at last given to the dignity of man. Every human being would then have equal opportunity, not to rise up in the world in the light of any mathematical measure, but to develop his own special capacities for leading a rich life.[11]

This is, of course, a fable. But where, today, would a description of the ideal be found if not in a fable?

NOTES

1. Walter A. Weisskopf, *Alienation and Economics* (New York: E. P. Dutton, 1971), pp. 33 ff.
2. This seems to be the position of Daniel Bell, "Meritocracy and Equality," *Public Interest* 29 (Fall 1972): 29 ff.
3. Walter A. Weisskopf, *The Psychology of Economics* (Chicago: University of Chicago Press, 1955), pp. 51 ff.

THE DIALECTICS OF EQUALITY

4. For a critique of the principle of equality of opportunity, see J. H. Schaar, "Equality of Opportunity and Beyond," in *Equality*, ed. J. R. Pennock and J. W. Chapman (New York: Atherton Press, 1967), pp. 228 ff.

5. John K. Galbraith, *The New Industrial State* (Boston: Houghton Mifflin, 1967), chaps. 8, 25.

6. *The Public Interest* 29 (Fall 1972), issue on equality.

7. R. Sennett and J. Cobb, *The Hidden Injuries of Class* (New York: Alfred A. Knopf, 1972), pp. 21ff., from which the following quotations are taken.

8. I. Kristol, "Capitalism, Socialism and Nihilism," *The Public Interest* 31 (Spring 1973): 15.

9. Weisskopf, *Alienation and Economics*, pp. 37 ff.

10. K. Polanyi, *The Great Transformation* (New York: Farrar & Rinehart, 1944), pt. II.

11. M. Young, *The Rise of Meritocracy 1870–2033* (New York: Penguin Books, 1958), p. 169.

(11)

A Theory
of Justice

John Rawls

Two Principles of Justice

I SHALL now state in a provisional form the two principles of justice that I believe would be chosen in the original position.* In this section I wish to make only the most general comments, and therefore the first formulation of these principles is tentative. As we go on I shall run through several formulations and approximate step by step the final statement. I believe that doing this allows the exposition to proceed in a natural way.

The first statement of the two principles reads as follows:

First: each person is to have an equal right to the most extensive basic liberty compatible with a similar liberty for others.

Second: social and economic inequalities are to be arranged so that they are both: a) reasonably expected to be to everyone's advantage; and b) attached to positions and offices open to all.

There are two ambiguous phrases in the second principle, namely "everyone's advantage" and "equally open to all." Determining their sense more exactly will lead to a second formulation of the principle (under the heading "Democratic Equality and the Difference Principle").

By way of general comment, these principles primarily apply to the basic structure of society. They are to govern the assignment of rights

---

* Rawls' "original position of equality" corresponds to the state of nature in the traditional theory of the social contract.—*Ed.*

Reprinted by permission of the publishers from *A Theory of Justice*, by John Rawls, Cambridge, Mass.: The Belknapp Press of Harvard University Press; Oxford: The Clarendon Press, © 1971 by the President and Fellows of Harvard College, pp. 60–80, 83–90.

and duties and to regulate the distribution of social and economic advantages. As their formulation suggests, these principles presuppose that the social structure can be divided into two more or less distinct parts, the first principle applying to the one, the second to the other. They distinguish between those aspects of the social system that define and secure the equal liberties of citizenship and those that specify and establish social and economic inequalities. The basic liberties of citizens are, roughly speaking, political liberty (the right to vote and to be eligible for public office) together with freedom of speech and assembly; liberty of conscience and freedom of thought; freedom of the person along with the right to hold (personal) property; and freedom from arbitrary arrest and seizure as defined by the concept of the rule of law. These liberties are all required to be equal by the first principle, since citizens of a just society are to have the same basic rights.

The second principle applies, in the first approximation, to the distribution of income and wealth and to the design of organizations that make use of differences in authority and responsibility, or chains of command. While the distribution of wealth and income need not be equal, it must be to everyone's advantage, and at the same time, positions of authority and offices of command must be accessible to all. One applies the second principle by holding positions open, and then, subject to this constraint, arranges social and economic inequalities so that everyone benefits.

These principles are to be arranged in a serial order with the first principle prior to the second. This ordering means that a departure from the institutions of equal liberty required by the first principle cannot be justified, or compensated for, by greater social and economic advantages. The distribution of wealth and income, and the hierarchies of authority, must be consistent with both the liberties of equal citizenship and equality of opportunity.

It is clear that these principles are rather specific in their content, and their acceptance rests on certain assumptions that I must eventually try to explain and justify. A theory of justice depends upon a theory of society in ways that will become evident as we proceed. For the present, it should be observed that the two principles (and this holds for all formulations) are a special case of a more general conception of justice that can be expressed as follows:

All social values—liberty and opportunity, income and wealth, and the bases of self-respect—are to be distributed equally unless an unequal distribution of any, or all, of these values is to everyone's advantage.

Injustice, then, is simply inequalities that are not to the benefit of all. Of course, this conception is extremely vague and requires interpretation.

As a first step, suppose that the basic structure of society distributes certain primary goods, that is, things that every rational man is presumed to want. These goods normally have a use whatever a person's rational plan of life. For simplicity, assume that the chief primary goods at the disposition of society are rights and liberties, powers and opportunities, income and wealth. These are the social primary goods. Other primary goods such as health and vigor, intelligence and imagination, are natural goods; although their possession is influenced by the basic structure, they are not so directly under its control. Imagine, then, a hypothetical initial arrangement in which all the social primary goods are equally distributed: everyone has similar rights and duties, and income and wealth are evenly shared. This state of affairs provides a bench mark for judging improvements. If certain inequalities of wealth and organizational powers would make everyone better off than in this hypothetical starting situation, then they accord with the general conception.

Now it is possible, at least theoretically, that by giving up some of their fundamental liberties men are sufficiently compensated by the resulting social and economic gains. The general conception of justice imposes no restrictions on what sort of inequalities are permissible; it only requires that everyone's position be improved. We need not suppose anything so drastic as consenting to a condition of slavery. Imagine instead that men forego certain political rights when the economic returns are significant and their capacity to influence the course of policy by the exercise of these rights would be marginal in any case. It is this kind of exchange which the two principles as stated rule out; being arranged in serial order they do not permit exchanges between basic liberties and economic and social gains. The serial ordering of principles expresses an underlying preference among primary social goods. When this preference is rational so likewise is the choice of these principles in this order.

In developing justice as fairness I shall, for the most part, leave aside the general conception of justice and examine instead the special case of the two principles in serial order. The advantage of this procedure is that from the first the matter of priorities is recognized and an effort made to find principles to deal with it. One is led to attend throughout to the conditions under which the acknowledgment of the absolute weight of liberty with respect to social and economic advantages, as defined by the lexical order of the two principles, would be reasonable. Offhand, this ranking appears extreme and too special a case to be of much interest; but there is more justification for it than would appear at first sight. Furthermore, the distinction between fundamental rights and liberties and economic and social benefits marks a difference among primary social goods that one should try to exploit. It suggests an important division in the social system. Of course, the distinctions drawn and the ordering proposed are bound to be at best only approximations. There are surely circumstances in which they fail. But it is essential to depict clearly the main lines of a reasonable conception of justice; and under many conditions anyway, the two principles in serial order may serve well enough. When necessary we can fall back on the more general conception.

The fact that the two principles apply to institutions has certain consequences. Several points illustrate this. First of all, the rights and liberties referred to by these principles are those which are defined by the public rules of the basic structure. Whether men are free is determined by the rights and duties established by the major institutions of society. Liberty is a certain pattern of social forms. The first principle simply requires that certain sorts of rules, those defining basic liberties, apply to everyone equally, and that they allow the most extensive liberty compatible with a like liberty for all. The only reason for circumscribing the rights defining liberty and making men's freedom less extensive than it might otherwise be is that these equal rights as institutionally defined would interfere with one another.

Another thing to bear in mind is that when principles mention persons, or require that everyone gain from an inequality, the reference is to representative persons holding the various social positions, or offices, or whatever, established by the basic structure. Thus in applying the second principle I assume that it is possible to assign an expectation of well-being to representative individuals holding these positions. This expectation indicates their life prospects as viewed from their social station. In general, the expectations of representative persons depend upon the distribution of rights and duties throughout the basic structure. When this changes, expectations change. I assume, then, that expectations are connected: by raising the prospects of the representative man in one position we presumably increase or decrease the prospects of representative men in other positions. Since it applies to institutional forms, the second principle (or rather the first part of it) refers to the expectations of representative individuals. As I shall discuss below, neither principle applies to distributions of particular goods to particular individuals who may be identified by their proper names. The situation in which someone is considering how to allocate certain commodities to needy persons who are known to him is not within the scope of the principles. They are meant to regulate basic institutional arrangements. We must not assume that there is much similarity from the standpoint of justice between an administrative allotment of goods to specific persons and the appropriate design of society. Our common sense intuitions for the former may be a poor guide to the latter.

Now the second principle insists that each person benefit from permissible inequalities in the basic structure. This means that it must be reasonable for each relevant representative man defined by this structure, when he views it as a going concern, to prefer his prospects with the inequality to his prospects without it. One is not allowed to justify differences in income or organizational powers on the ground that the disadvantages of those in one position are outweighed by the greater advantages of those in another. Much less can infringements of liberty be counterbalanced in this way. Applied to the basic structure, the principle of utility would have us maximize the sum of expectations of representative men (weighted by the number of persons they represent, on the classical view); and this would permit us to compensate for the losses of some by the gains of others. Instead, the two principles require that everyone benefit from economic and social inequalities. It is obvious, however, that there are indefinitely many ways in which all may be advantaged when the initial arrangement of equality is taken as a bench mark. How then are we to choose among these possibilities? The principles must be specified so that they yield a determinate conclusion. I now turn to this problem.

Interpretations of the Second Principle

I have already mentioned that since the phrases "everyone's advantage" and "equally open to all" are ambiguous, both parts of the second principle have two natural senses. Because these senses are independent of one another, the principle has four possible meanings. Assuming that the first principle of equal liberty has the same sense throughout, we then have four interpretations of the two principles. These are indicated in the table below.

	"Everyone's advantage"	
"Equally open"	Principle of efficiency	Difference principle
Equality as careers open to talents	System of Natural Liberty	Natural Aristocracy
Equality as equality of fair opportunity	Liberal Equality	Democratic Equality

I shall sketch in turn these three interpretations: the system of natural liberty, liberal equality, and democratic equality. In some respects this sequence is the more intuitive one, but the sequence via the interpretation of natural aristocracy is not without interest and I shall comment on it briefly. In working out justice as fairness, we must decide which interpretation is to be preferred. I shall adopt that of democratic equality, explaining what this notion means.

The first interpretation (in either sequence) I shall refer to as the system of natural liberty. In this rendering the first part of the second principle is understood as the principle of efficiency adjusted so as to apply to institutions or, in this case, to the basic structure of society; and the second part is understood as an open social system in which, to use the traditional phrase, careers are open to talents. I assume in all interpretations that the first principle of equal liberty is satisfied and that the economy is roughly a free market system, although the means of production may or may not be privately owned. The system of natural liberty asserts, then, that a basic structure satisfying the principle of efficiency and in which positions are open to those able and willing to strive for them will lead to a just distribution. Assigning rights and duties in this way is thought to give a scheme which allocates wealth and income, authority and responsibility, in a fair way, whatever this allocation turns out to be. The doctrine includes an important element of pure procedural justice which is carried over to the other interpretations.

At this point it is necessary to make a brief digression to explain the principle of efficiency. This principle is simply that of Pareto optimality (as economists refer to it) formulated so as to apply to the basic structure.[1] I shall always use the term "efficiency" instead because this is literally correct, and the term "optimality" suggests that the concept is much broader than it is in fact.[2] To be sure, this principle was not originally intended to apply to institutions but to particular configurations of the economic system, for example, to distributions of goods among consumers or to modes of production. The principle holds that a configuration is efficient whenever it is impossible to change it so as to make some persons (at least one) better off without at the same time making other persons (at least one) worse off. Thus a distribution of a stock of commodities among certain individuals is efficient if there exists no redistribution of these goods that improves the circumstances of at least one of these individuals without another being disadvantaged. The organization of production is efficient if there is no way to alter inputs so as to produce more of some commodity without producing less of another. For if we could produce more of one good without having to give up some of another, the larger stock of goods could be used to better the circumstances of some persons without making that of others any worse. These applications of the principle show that it is, indeed, a principle of efficiency. A distribution of goods or a scheme of production is inefficient when there are ways of doing still better for some individuals without doing any worse for others. I shall assume that the parties in the original position accept this principle to judge the efficiency of economic and social arrangements. (See the accompanying discussion of the principle of efficiency.)

The Principle of Efficiency

Assume that there is a fixed stock of commodities to be distributed between two persons, x_1 and x_2. Let the line AB represent the points such that given x_1's gain at the corresponding level, there is no way to distribute the commodities so as to make x_2 better off than the point indicated by the curve. Consider the point $D = (a,b)$. Then holding x_1 at the level a, the best that can be done for x_2 is the level b. In Figure 11-1 the point O, the origin, represents the position before any commodities are distributed. The points on the line AB are the efficient points. Each point on AB can be seen to satisfy Pareto's criterion: there is no redistribution that makes either person better off without making the other worse off. This is conveyed by the fact that the line AB slopes downward to the right. Since there is but a fixed stock of items, it is supposed that as one person gains the other loses. (Of course, this assumption is dropped in the case of the basic structure which is a system of cooperation producing a sum of positive advantages.) Normally the region OAB is taken to be a convex set. This means that given any pair of points in the set, the points on the straight line joining these two points are also in the set. Circles, ellipses, squares, triangles, and so on, are convex sets.

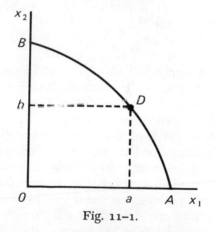

Fig. 11-1.

It is clear that there are many efficient points, in fact, all the points on the line AB. The principle of efficiency does not by itself select one particular distribution of commodities as the efficient one. To select among the efficient distributions some other principle, a principle of justice, say, is necessary.

Of two points, if one is northeast of the other, this point is superior by the principle of efficiency. Points to the northwest or southwest cannot be compared. The ordering defined by the principle of efficiency is but a partial one. Thus in Figure 11–2 while C is superior to E, and D is superior to F, none of the points on the line AB are either superior or inferior to one another. The class of efficient points cannot be ranked. Even the extreme points A and B at which one of the parties has everything are efficient, just as other points on AB.

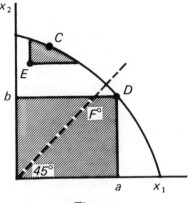

Fig. 11–2.

Observe that we cannot say that any point on the line AB is superior to *all* points in the interior of OAB. Each point on AB is superior only to those points in the interior southwest of it. Thus the point D is superior to all points inside the rectangle indicated by the dotted lines joining D to the points a and b. The point D is not superior to the point E. These points cannot be ordered. The point C, however, is superior to E and so are all the points on the line AB belonging to the small shaded triangular region that has the point E as a corner.

On the other hand, if one takes the 45° line as indicating the locus of equal distribution (this assumes an interpersonal cardinal interpretation of the axes, something not supposed in the preceding remarks), and if one counts this as an additional basis of decision, then all things considered, the point D may be preferable to both C and E. It is much closer to this line. One may even decide that an interior point such as F is to be preferred to C, which is an efficient point. Actually, in justice as fairness the principles of justice are prior to considerations of efficiency and therefore, roughly speaking, the interior points that represent just distributions will generally be preferred to efficient points which represent unjust distributions. Of course, Figure 11–2 depicts a very simple situation and cannot be applied to the basic structure.

There are, however, many configurations which are efficient. For example, the distributions in which one person receives the entire stock of commodities is efficient, since there is no rearrangement that will make

235

some better off and none worse off. The person who holds the whole stock must lose out. But of course not every distribution is efficient, as might be suggested by the efficiency of such disparities. As long as a distribution leaves some persons willing to swap goods with others, it cannot be efficient; for the willingness to trade shows that there is a rearrangement which improves the situation of some without hurting that of anyone else. Indeed, an efficient distribution is one in which it is not possible to find further profitable exchanges. In that sense, the allocation of goods in which one man has everything is efficient because the others have nothing to give him in return. The principle of efficiency allows then that there are many efficient configurations. Each efficient arrangement is better than some other arrangements, but none of the efficient arrangements is better than another.

Now the principle of efficiency can be applied to the basic structure by reference to the expectations of representative men.[3] Thus we can say that an arrangement of rights and duties in the basic structure is efficient if and only if it is impossible to change the rules, to redefine the scheme of rights and duties, so as to raise the expectations of any representative man (at least one) without at the same time lowering the expectations of some (at least one) other representative man. Of course, these alterations must be consistent with the other principles. That is, in changing the basic structure we are not permitted to violate the principle of equal liberty or the requirement of open positions. What can be altered is the distribution of income and wealth and the way in which organizational powers, and various other forms of authority, regulate cooperative activities. Consistent with the constraints of liberty and accessibility, the allocation of these primary goods may be adjusted to modify the expectations of representative individuals. An arrangement of the basic structure is efficient when there is no way to change this distribution so as to raise the prospects of some without lowering the prospects of others.

There are, I shall assume, many efficient arrangements of the basic structure. Each of these specifies a particular division of advantages from social cooperation. The problem is to choose between them, to find a conception of justice that singles out one of these efficient distributions as also just. If we succeed in this, we shall have gone beyond mere efficiency yet in a way compatible with it. Now it is natural to try out the idea that as long as the social system is efficient there is no reason to be concerned with distribution. All efficient arrangements are in this case declared equally just. Of course, this suggestion would be outlandish for the allocation of particular goods to known individuals. No one would suppose that it is a matter of indifference from the standpoint of justice whether any one of a number of men happens to have everything. But the suggestion seems equally unreasonable for the basic structure. Thus it may be that under certain conditions serfdom cannot be significantly reformed without lowering the expectations of some representative man, say that of landowners, in which case serfdom is efficient. Yet it may also happen under the same conditions that a system of free labor cannot be changed without lowering the expectations of some representative man, say that of free laborers, so this arrangement is likewise efficient. More generally, whenever a society is relevantly divided into a number of classes, it is possible, let us suppose, to maximize with respect to each one of its representative men at a time. These maxima give at least this many efficient positions, for none of them can be departed from to raise the expectations of any one representative man without lowering those of another, namely, the representative man with respect to whom the maximum is defined. Thus each of these extremes is efficient but they surely cannot be all just, and equally so. These remarks simply parallel for social systems the situation in distributing particular goods to given individuals where the distributions in which a single person has everything is efficient.

Now these reflections show only what we knew all along, that is, that the principle of efficiency cannot serve alone as a conception of justice.[4] Therefore it must be supplemented in some way. Now in the system of natural liberty the principle of efficiency is constrained by certain background institutions; when these constraints are satisfied, any resulting efficient distribution is accepted as just. The system of natural liberty selects an efficient distribution roughly as follows. Let us suppose that we know from economic theory that under the standard assumptions defining a competitive market economy, income and wealth will be distributed in an efficient way, and that the particular efficient distribution which results in any period of time is determined by the initial distribution of assets, that is, by the initial distribution of income and wealth, and of natural talents and abilities. With each initial distribution, a definite efficient outcome is arrived at. Thus it turns out that if we are to accept the outcome as just, and not merely as efficient, we must accept the basis upon which over time the initial distribution of assets is determined.

In the system of natural liberty the initial distribution is regulated by the arrangements implicit in the conception of careers open to talents (as earlier defined). These arrangements presuppose a background of equal liberty (as specified by the first principle) and a free market economy. They require a formal equality of opportunity in that all have at least the same legal rights of access to all advantaged social positions. But since there is no effort to preserve an equality, or similarity, of social conditions, except insofar as this is necessary to preserve the requisite background institutions, the initial distribution of assets for any period of time is strongly influenced by natural and social contingencies. The existing distribution of income and wealth, say, is the cumulative effect of prior distributions of natural assets—that is, natural talents and abilities—as these have been developed or left unrealized, and their use favored or disfavored over time by social circumstances and such chance contingencies as accident and good fortune. Intuitively, the most obvious injustice of the system of natural liberty is that it permits distributive shares to be improperly influenced by these factors so arbitrary from a moral point of view.

The liberal interpretation, as I shall refer to it, tries to correct for this by adding to the requirement of careers open to talents the further condition of the principle of fair equality of opportunity. The thought here is that positions are to be not only open in a formal sense, but that all should have a fair chance to attain them. Offhand it is not clear what is meant, but we might say that those with similar abilities and skills should have similar life chances. More specifically, assuming that there is a distribution of natural assets, those who are at the same level of talent and ability, and have the same willingness to use them, should have the same prospects of success regardless of their initial place in the social system, that is, irrespective of the income class into which they are born. In all sectors of society there should be roughly equal prospects of culture and achievement for everyone similarly motivated and endowed. The expectations of those with the same abilities and aspirations should not be affected by their social class.[5]

The liberal interpretation of the two principles seeks, then, to mitigate the influence of social contingencies and natural fortune on distributive shares. To accomplish this end it is necessary to impose further basic structural conditions on the social system. Free market arrangements must be set within a framework of political and legal institutions which regulates the overall trends of economic events and preserves the social conditions necessary for fair equality of opportunity. The elements of this framework are familiar enough, though it may be worthwhile to recall the importance of preventing excessive accumulations of property and wealth and of maintaining equal opportunities of education for all. Chances to acquire cultural knowledge and skills should not depend upon one's class position, and so the school system, whether public or private, should be designed to even out class barriers.

While the liberal conception seems clearly preferable to the system of natural liberty, intuitively it still appears defective. For one thing, even if it works to perfection in eliminating the influence of social contingencies, it still permits the distribution of wealth and income to be determined by the natural distribution of abilities and talents. Within the limits allowed by the background arrangements, distributive shares are decided by the outcome of the natural lottery; and this outcome is arbitrary from a moral perspective. There is no more reason to permit the distribution of income and wealth to be settled by the distribution of natural assets than by historical and social fortune. Furthermore, the principle of fair opportunity can be only imperfectly carried out, at least as long as the institution of the family exists. The extent to which natural capacities develop and reach fruition is affected by all kinds of social conditions and class attitudes. Even the willingness to make an effort, to try, and so to be deserving in the ordinary sense is itself dependent upon happy family and social circumstances. It is impossible in practice to secure equal chances of achievement and culture for those similarly endowed, and therefore we may want to adopt a principle which recognizes this fact and also mitigates the arbitrary effects of the natural lottery itself. That the liberal conception fails to do this encourages one to look for another interpretation of the two principles of justice.

Before turning to the conception of democratic equality, we should note that of natural aristocracy. On this view no attempt is made to regulate social contingencies beyond what is required by formal equality of opportunity, but the advantages of persons with greater natural endowments are to be limited to those that further the good of the poorer sectors of society. The aristocratic ideal is applied to a system that is open, at least from a legal point of view, and the better situation of those favored by it is regarded as just only when less would be had by those below, if less were given to those above.[6] In this way the idea of *noblesse oblige* is carried over to the conception of natural aristocracy.

Now both the liberal conception and that of natural aristocracy are unstable. For once we are troubled by the influence of either social contingencies or natural chance on the determination of distributive shares, we are bound, on reflection, to be bothered by the influence of the other. From a moral standpoint the two seem equally arbitrary. So however we move away from the system of natural liberty, we cannot be satisfied short of the democratic conception. This conception I have yet to explain. And, moreover, none of the preceding remarks are an argument for this conception, since in a contract theory all arguments, strictly speaking, are to be made in terms of what it would be rational to choose in the original position. But I am concerned here to prepare the way for the favored interpretation of the two principles so that these criteria, especially the second one, will not strike the reader as too eccentric or bizarre. I have tried to show that once we try to find a rendering of them which treats everyone equally as a moral person, and which does not weight men's share in the benefits and burdens of social cooperation according to their social fortune or their luck in the natural lottery, it is clear that the democratic interpretation is the best choice among the four alternatives. With these comments as a preface, I now turn to this conception.

Democratic Equality and the Difference Principle

The democratic interpretation, as the table suggests, is arrived at by combining the principle of fair equality of opportunity with the difference principle. This principle removes the indeterminateness of the principle of efficiency by singling out a particular position from which the social and economic inequalities of the basic structure are to be judged. Assuming the framework of institutions required by equal liberty and fair equality of opportunity, the higher expectations of those better situated are just if and only if they work as part of a scheme which improves the expectations of the least advantaged members of society. The intuitive idea is that the social order is not to establish and secure the more attractive prospects of those better off unless doing so is to the advantage of those less fortunate. (See the discussion of the difference principle that follows.)

The Difference Principle

Assume that indifference curves now represent distributions that are judged equally just. Then the difference principle is a strongly egalitarian conception in the sense that unless there is a distribution that makes both persons better off (limiting ourselves to the two-person case for simplicity), an equal distribution is to be preferred. The indifference curves take the form depicted in Figure 11–3. These curves are actually made up of vertical and straight lines that intersect at right angles at the 45° line (again supposing an interpersonal and cardinal interpretation of the axes). No matter how much either person's situation is improved, there is no gain from the standpoint of the difference principle unless the other gains also.

Suppose that x_1 is the most favored representative man in the basic structure. As his expectations are increased so are the prospects of x_2, the least advantaged

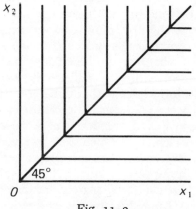

Fig. 11–3.

man. In Figure 11–4 let the curve OP represent the contribution to x_2's expectations made by the greater expectations of x_1. The point O, the origin, represents the hypothetical state in which all social primary goods are distributed equally. Now the OP curve is always below the $45°$ line, since x_1 is always better off. Thus the only relevant parts of the indifference curves are those below this line, and for this reason the upper left-hand part of Figure 11–4 is not drawn in. Clearly the difference principle is perfectly satisfied only when the OP curve is just tangent to the highest indifference curve that it touches. In Figure 11–4 this is at the point a.

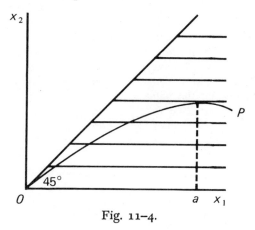

Fig. 11–4.

Note that the contribution curve, the curve OP, supposes that the social cooperation defined by the structure is mutually advantageous. Is is no longer a matter of shuffling about a fixed stock of goods. Also, nothing is lost if an accurate interpersonal comparison of benefits is impossible. It suffices that the least favored person can be identified and his rational preference determined.

A view less egalitarian than the difference principle, and perhaps more plausible at first sight, is one in which the indifference lines for just distributions (or for all things considered) are smooth curves convex to the origin,

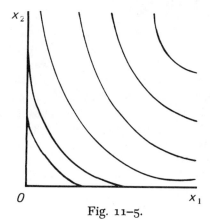

Fig. 11–5.

as in Figure 11–5. The indifference curves for social welfare functions are often depicted in this fashion. This shape of the curves expresses the fact that as either person gains relative to the other, further benefits to him become less valuable from a social point of view.

A classical utilitarian, on the other hand, is indifferent as to how a constant sum of benefits is distributed. He appeals to equality only to break ties. If there are but two persons, then assuming an interpersonal cardinal interpretation of the axes, the utilitarian's indifference lines for distribution are straight lines perpendicular to the $45°$ line. Since, however, x_1 and x_2 are representative men, the gains to them have to be weighted by the number of persons they each represent. Since presumably x_2 represents rather more persons than x_1, the indifference lines become more horizontal, as seen in Figure 11–6. The ratio of the number of advantaged to the number of disadvantaged defines the slope of these straight lines. Drawing the same contribution curve OP as before, we see that the best distribution from a utilitarian point of view is reached at the point which is beyond the point b where the OP curve reaches its maximum. Since the difference principle selects the point b and b is always to the left of a, utilitarianism allows, other things equal, larger inequalities.

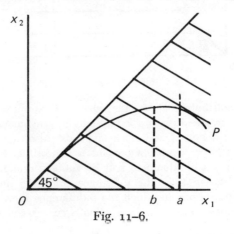

Fig. 11–6.

To illustrate the difference principle, consider the distribution of income among social classes. Let us suppose that the various income groups correlate with representative individuals by reference to whose expectations we can judge the distribution. Now those starting out as members of the entrepreneurial class in a property-owning democracy, say, have a better prospect than those who begin in the class of unskilled laborers. It seems likely that this will be true even when the social injustices which now exist are removed. What, then, can possibly justify this kind of initial inequality in life prospects? According to the difference principle, it is justifiable only if the difference in expectation is to the advantage of the representative man who is worse off, in this case the representative unskilled worker. The inequality in expectation is permissible only if lowering it would make the working class even more worse off. Supposedly, given the rider in the second principle concerning open positions, and the principle of liberty generally, the greater expectations allowed to entrepreneurs encourage them to do things which raise the long-term prospects of laboring class. Their better prospects act as incentives so that the economic process is more efficient, innovation proceeds at a faster pace, and so on. Eventually the resulting material benefits spread throughout the system and to the least advantaged. I shall not consider how far these things are true. The point is that something of this kind must be argued if these inequalities are to be just by the difference principle.

I shall now make a few remarks about this principle. First of all, in applying it, one should distinguish between two cases. The first case is that in which the expectations of the least advantaged are indeed maximized (subject, of course, to the mentioned constraints). No changes in the expectations of those better off can improve the situation of those worst off. The best arrangement obtains, what I shall call a perfectly just scheme. The second case is that in which the expectations of all those better off at least contribute to the welfare of the more unfortunate. That is, if their expectations were decreased, the prospects of the least advantaged would likewise fall. Yet the maximum is not yet achieved. Even higher expectations for the more advantaged would raise the expectations of those in the lowest position. Such a scheme is, I shall say, just throughout, but not the best just arrangement. A scheme is unjust when the higher expectations, one or more of them, are excessive. If these expectations were decreased, the situation of the least favored would be improved. How unjust an arrangement is depends on how excessive the higher expectations are and to what extent they depend upon the violation of the other principles of justice, for example, fair equality of opportunity; but I shall not attempt to measure in any exact way the degrees of injustice. The point to note here is that while the difference principle is, strictly speaking, a maximizing principle, there is a significant distinction between the cases that fall short of the best arrangement. A society should try to avoid the region where the marginal contributions of those better off are negative, since, other things equal, this seems a greater fault than falling short of the best scheme when these contributions are positive. The even larger difference between rich and poor makes the latter even worse off, and this violates the principle of mutual advantage as well as democratic equality.

A further point is this. We saw that the system of natural liberty and the liberal conception attempt to go beyond the principle of efficiency by moderating its scope of operation, by constraining it by certain background institutions and leaving the rest to pure procedural justice. The democratic conception holds that while pure procedural justice may be invoked to some extent at least, the way previous interpretations do this still leaves too much to social and natural contingency. But it should be noted that the difference principle is compatible with the principle of efficiency. For when the former is fully satisfied, it is indeed impossible to make any one representative man better off without making another worse off, namely, the least advantaged representative man whose expectations we are to maximize. Thus justice is defined so that it is consistent with efficiency, at least when the two principles are perfectly fulfilled. Of course, if the basic structure is unjust, these principles will authorize changes that may lower the expectations of some of those better off; and therefore the democratic conception is not consistent with the principle of efficiency if this principle is taken to mean that only changes which improve everyone's prospects are allowed. Justice is prior to efficiency and requires some changes that are not efficient in this sense. Consistency obtains only in the sense that a perfectly just scheme is also efficient.

Next, we may consider a certain complication regarding the meaning of the difference principle. It has been taken for granted that if the principle is satisfied, everyone is benefited. One obvious sense in which this is so is that each man's position is improved with respect to the initial arrangement of equality. But it is clear that nothing depends upon being able to identify this initial arrangement; indeed, how well off men are in this situation plays no essential role in applying the difference principle. We simply maximize the expectations of the least favored position subject to the required constraints. As long as doing this is an improvement for everyone, as we assume it is, the estimated gains from the situation of hypothetical equality are irrelevant, if not largely impossible to ascertain anyway. There may be, however, a further sense in which everyone is advantaged when the difference principle is satisfied, at least if we make certain natural assumptions. Let us suppose that inequalities in expectations are chain-connected: that is, if an advantage has the effect of raising the expectations of the lowest position, it raises the expectations of all positions in between. For example, if the greater expectations for entrepreneurs benefit the unskilled worker, they also benefit the semiskilled. Notice that chain connection says nothing about the case in which the least advantaged do not gain, so that it does not mean that all effects move together. Assume further that expectations are close-knit: that is, it is impossible to raise or lower the expectation of any representative man without raising or lowering the expectation of every other representative man, especially that of the least advantaged. There is no loose-jointedness, so to speak, in the way expectations hang together. Now with these assumptions there is a sense in which everyone benefits when the difference principle is satisfied, for the representative man who is better off in any two-way comparison gains by the advantages offered him, and the man who is worse off gains from the contributions which these inequalities make. Of course, these conditions may not hold. But in this case those who are better off should not have a veto over the benefits available for the least favored. We are still to maximize the expectations of those most disadvantaged.

Fair Equality of Opportunity and Pure Procedural Justice

I should now like to comment upon the second part of the second principle, henceforth to be understood as the liberal principle of fair equality of opportunity. It must not then be confused with the notion of careers open to talents; nor must one forget that since it is tied in with the difference principle its consequences are quite distinct from the liberal interpretation of the two principles taken together. In particular, this principle is not subject to the objection that it leads to a meritocratic society. Here I wish to consider a few other points, especially its relation to the idea of pure procedural justice.

First, though, I should note that the reasons for requiring open positions are not solely, or even primarily, those of efficiency. I have not maintained that offices must be open if in fact everyone is to benefit from an arrangement. For it may be possible to improve everyone's situation by assigning certain powers and benefits to positions despite the fact that certain groups are excluded from them. Although access is restricted, perhaps these offices can still attract superior talent and encourage better performance. But the principle of open positions forbids this. It expresses the conviction that if some places were not open on a basis fair to all, those kept out would be right in feeling unjustly treated even though they benefited from the greater efforts of those who were allowed to hold them. They would be justified in their complaint not only because they were excluded from certain external rewards of office such as wealth and privilege, but because they were debarred from experiencing the realization of self which comes from a skillful and devoted exercise of social duties. They would be deprived of one of the main forms of human good.

Now I have said that the basic structure is the primary subject of justice. This means, as we have seen, that the first distributive problem is the assignment of fundamental rights and duties and the regulation of social and economic inequalities and of the legitimate expectations founded on these. Of course, any ethical theory recognizes the importance of the basic structure as a subject of justice, but not all theories regard its importance in the same way. In justice as fairness society is interpreted as a cooperative venture for mutual advantage. The basic structure is a public system of rules defining a scheme of activities that leads men to act together so as to produce a greater sum of benefits and assigns to each certain recognized claims to a share in the proceeds. What a person does depends upon what the public rules say he will be entitled to, and what a person is entitled to depends on what he does. The distribution which results is arrived at by honoring the claims determined by what persons undertake to do in the light of these legitimate expectations.

These considerations suggest the idea of treating the question of distributive shares as a matter of pure procedural justice.[7] The intuitive idea is to design the social system so that the outcome is just whatever it happens to be, at least so long as it is within a certain range. The notion of pure procedural justice is best understood by a comparison with perfect and imperfect procedural justice. To illustrate the former, consider the simplest case of fair division. A number of men are to divide a cake: assuming that the fair division is an equal one, which procedure, if any, will give this outcome? Technicalities aside, the obvious solution is to have one man divide the cake and get the last piece, the others being allowed their pick before him. He will divide the cake equally, since in this way he assures for himself the largest share possible. This example illustrates the two characteristic features of perfect procedural justice. First, there is an independent criterion for what is a fair division, a criterion defined separately from and prior to the procedure which is to be followed. And second, it is possible to devise a procedure that is sure to give the desired outcome. Of course, certain assumptions are made here, such as that the man selected can divide the cake equally, wants as large a piece as he can get, and so on. But we can ignore these details. The essential thing is that there is an independent standard for deciding which outcome is just and a procedure guaranteed to lead to it. Pretty clearly, perfect procedural justice is rare, if not impossible, in cases of much practical interest.

Imperfect procedural justice is exemplified by a criminal trial. The desired outcome is that the defendant should be declared guilty if and only if he has committed the offense with which he is charged. The trial procedure is framed to search for and to establish the truth in this regard. But it seems impossible to design the legal rules so that they always lead to the correct result. The theory of trials examines which procedures and rules of evidence, and the like, are best calculated to advance this purpose consistent with the other ends of the law. Different arrangements for hearing cases may reasonably be expected in different circumstances to yield the right results, not always but at least most of the time. A trial, then, is an instance of imperfect procedural justice. Even though the law is carefully followed, and the proceedings fairly and properly conducted, it may reach the wrong outcome. An innocent man may be found guilty, a guilty man may be set free. In such cases we speak of a miscarriage of justice: the injustice springs from no human fault but from a fortuitous combination of circumstances which defeats the purpose of the legal rules. The characteristic mark of imperfect procedural justice is that while there is an independent criterion for the correct outcome, there is no feasible procedure which is sure to lead to it.

By contrast, pure procedural justice obtains when there is no independent criterion for the right result: instead, there is a correct or fair procedure such that the outcome is likewise correct or fair, whatever it is, provided that the procedure has been properly followed. This situation is illustrated by gambling. If a number of persons engage in a series of fair bets, the distribution of cash after the last bet is fair, or at least not unfair, whatever this distribution is. I assume here that fair bets are those having a zero expectation of gain, that the bets are made voluntarily, that no one cheats, and so on. The betting procedure is fair and freely entered into under conditions that are fair. Thus the background circumstances define a fair procedure. Now any distribution of cash summing to the initial stock held by all individuals could result from a series of fair bets. In this sense all of these particular distributions are equally fair. A distinctive feature of pure procedural justice is that the procedure for determining the just result must actually be carried out; for in these cases there is no independent criterion by reference to which a definite outcome can be known to be just. Clearly we cannot say that a particular state of affairs is just because it could have been reached by following a fair procedure. This would permit far too much and would lead to absurdly unjust consequences. It would allow one to say that almost any distribution of goods is just, or fair, since it could have come about as a result of fair gambles. What makes the final outcome of betting fair, or not unfair, is that it is the one which has arisen after a series of fair gambles. A fair procedure translates its fairness to the outcome only when it is actually carried out.

In order, therefore, to apply the notion of pure procedural justice to distributive shares it is necessary to set up and to administer impartially a just system of institutions. Only against the background of a just basic structure, including a just political constitution and a just arrangement of economic and social institutions, can one say that the requisite just procedure exists. The intuitive idea of a basic structure that has the necessary features is familiar. Suppose that law and government act effectively to keep markets competitive, resources fully employed, property and wealth (especially if private ownership of the means of production is allowed) widely distributed by the appropriate forms of taxation, or whatever, and to guarantee a reasonable social minimum. Assume also that there is fair equality of opportunity underwritten by education for all; and that the other equal liberties are secured. Then it would appear that the resulting distribution of income and the pattern of expectations will tend to satisfy the difference principle. In this complex of institutions, which we think of as establishing social justice in the modern state, the advantages of the better situated improve the condition of the least favored. Or when they do not, they can be adjusted to do so, for example, by setting the social minimum at the appropriate level. As these institutions presently exist they are riddled with grave injustices. But there presumably are ways of running them compatible with their basic design and intention so that the difference principle is satisfied consistent with the demands of liberty and fair equality of opportunity. It is this fact which underlies our assurance that these arrangements can be made just.

It is evident that the role of the principle of fair opportunity is to insure that the system of cooperation is one of pure procedural justice. Unless it is satisfied, distributive justice could not be left to take care of itself, even within a restricted range. Now the great practical advantage of pure procedural justice is that it is no longer necessary in meeting the demands of justice to keep track of the endless variety of circumstances and the changing relative positions of particular persons. One avoids the problem of defining principles to cope with the enormous complexities which would arise if such details were relevant. It is a mistake to focus attention on the varying relative positions of individuals and to require that every change, considered as a single transaction viewed in isolation, be in itself just. It is the arrangement of the basic structure which is to be judged, and judged from a general point of view. Unless we are prepared to criticize it from the standpoint of a relevant representative man in some particular position, we have no complaint against it. Thus the acceptance of the two principles constitutes an understanding to discard as irrelevant as a matter of social justice much of the information and many of the complications of everyday life.

In pure procedural justice, then, distributions of advantages are not appraised in the first instance by confronting a stock of benefits available with given desires and needs of known individuals. The allotment of the items produced takes place in accordance with the public system of rules, and this system determines what is produced, how much is produced, and by what means. It also determines legitimate claims the honoring of which yields the resulting distribution. Thus in this kind of procedural justice the correctness of the distribution is founded on the justice of the scheme of cooperation from which it arises and on answering the claims of individuals engaged in it. A distribution cannot be judged in isolation from the system of which it is the outcome or from what individuals have done in good faith in the light of established expectations. If it is asked in the abstract whether one distribution of a given stock of things to definite individuals with known desires and preferences is better than another, then there is simply no answer to this question. The conception of the two principles does not interpret the primary problem of distributive justice as one of allocative justice.

By contrast the allocative conception of justice seems naturally to apply when a given collection of goods is to be divided among definite individuals with known desires and needs. The goods to be allotted are not produced by these individuals, nor do these individuals stand in any existing cooperative relations. Since there are no prior claims on the things to be distributed, it is natural to share them out according to desires and needs, or even to maximize the net balance of satisfaction. Justice becomes a kind of efficiency, unless equality is preferred. Suitably generalized, the allocative conception leads to the classical utilitarian view. For as we have seen, this doctrine assimilates justice to the benevolence of the impartial spectator and the latter in turn to the most efficient design of institutions to promote the greatest balance of satisfaction. As I observed earlier, on this conception society is thought of as so many separate individuals each defining a separate line along which rights and duties are to be assigned and scarce means of satisfaction allocated in accordance with rules so as to give the most complete fulfillment of desire. I shall put aside consideration of the other aspects of this notion until later. The point to note here is that utilitarianism does not interpret the basic structure as a scheme of pure procedural justice. For the utilitarian has, in principle anyway, an independent standard for judging all distributions, namely, whether they produce the greatest net balance of satisfaction. In this theory, institutions are more or less imperfect arrangements for bringing about this end. Thus given existing desires and preferences, and the natural continuations into the future which they allow, the statesman's aim is to set up those social schemes that will best approximate an already specified goal. Since these arrangements are subject to the unavoidable constraints and hindrances of everyday life, the basic structure is a case of imperfect procedural justice.

For the time being I shall suppose that the two parts of the second principle are lexically ordered. Thus, we have one lexical ordering within another. But when necessary, this ordering can be modified in the light of the general conception of justice. The advantage of the special conception is that it has a definite shape and suggests certain questions for investigation, for example, under what conditions if any would the lexical ordering be chosen? Our inquiry is given a particular direction and is no longer confined to generalities. Of course, this conception of distributive shares is obviously a great simplification. It is designed to characterize in a clear way a basic structure that makes use of the idea of pure procedural justice. But all the same we should attempt to find simple concepts that can be assembled to give a reasonable conception of justice. The notions of the basic structure, of the veil of ignorance, of a lexical order, of the least favored position, as well as of pure procedural justice are all examples of this. By themselves none of these could be expected to work, but properly put together they may serve well enough. It is too much to suppose that there exists for all or even most moral problems a reasonable solution. Perhaps only a few can be satisfactorily answered. In any case social wisdom consists in framing institutions so that intractable difficulties do not often arise and in accepting the need for clear and simple principles.

NOTES

1. There are expositions of this principle in most any work on price theory or social choice. A perspicuous account is found in T. C. Koopmans, *Three Essays on the State of Economic Science* (New York: McGraw-Hill, 1957), pp. 41–66. See also A. K. Sen, *Collective Choice and Social Welfare* (San Francisco: Holden-Day Inc., 1970), pp. 21 f. These works contain everything (and more) that is required for our purposes; and the latter takes up the relevant philosophical questions. The principle of efficiency was introduced by Vilfredo Pareto in his *Manuel d'économie politique* (Paris, 1909), chap. 6, §53, and the appendix, §89. A translation of the relevant passages can be found in A. N. Page, *Utility Theory: A Book of Readings* (New York: Wiley, 1968), pp. 38 f. The related concept of indifference curves goes back to F. Y. Edgeworth, *Mathematical Psychics* (London, 1888), pp. 20–29; also in Page, pp. 160–167.

2. On this point see Koopmans, *Three Essays*, p. 49. Koopmans remarks that a term like "allocative efficiency" would have been a more accurate name.

3. For the application of the Pareto criterion to systems of public rules, see J. M. Buchanan, "The Relevance of Pareto Optimality," *Journal of Conflict Resolution* 6 (1962), as well as his book with Gordon Tullock, *The Calculus of Consent* (Ann Arbor: University of Michigan Press, 1962). In applying this and other principles to institutions I follow one of the points of "Two Concepts of Rules," *Philosophical Review* 64 (1955). Doing this has the advantage, among other things, of constraining the employment of principles by publicity effects.

4. This fact is generally recognized in welfare economics, as when it is said that efficiency is to be balanced against equity. See, for example, Tibor Scitovsky, *Welfare*

and Competition (London: Allen and Unwin, 1952), pp 60–69 and I. M. D. Little, A Critique of Welfare Economics, 2nd ed. (Oxford: The Clarendon Press, 1957), chap. 6, esp. pp. 112–116. See Sen's remarks on the limitations of the principle of efficiency, Collective Choice, pp. 22, 24–26, 83–86.

5. This definition follows Sidgwick's suggestion in The Methods of Ethics, 7th ed. (New York: Dover Publications, 1907), p. 285n. See also R. H. Tawney, Equality (London: Allen and Unwin, 1931), chap. 2, sec. ii; and B. A. O. Williams, "The Idea of Equality," in Philosophy, Politics, and Society, ed. Peter Laslett and W. G. Runciman (Oxford: Basil Blackwell, 1962), pp. 125 f.

6. This formulation of the aristocratic ideal is derived from Santayana's account of aristocracy in chap. 4 of Reason and Society (New York:. Scribner, 1905), pp. 109 f. He says, for example, "An aristocratic regimen can only be justified by radiating benefit and by proving that were less given to those above, less would be attained by those beneath them." I am indebted to Robert Rodes for pointing out to me that natural aristocracy is a possible interpretation of the two principles of justice and that an ideal feudal system might also try to fulfill the difference principle.

7. For a general discussion of procedural justice, see Brian Barry, Political Argument (London: Routledge and Kegan Paul, 1965), chap. 6. On the problem of fair division, see R. D. Luce and Howard Raiffa, Games and Decisions (New York: Wiley, 1957), pp. 363–368; and Hugo Steinhaus, "The Problem of Fair Division," Econometrica 16 (1948).

(12)

Distributive Justice

Robert Nozick

THE TERM "distributive justice" is not a neutral one. Hearing the term "distribution," most people presume that some thing or mechanism uses some principle or criterion to give out a supply of things. Into this process of distributing shares some error may have crept. So it is an open question, at least, whether redistribution should take place; whether we should do again what has already been done once, though poorly. However, we are not in the position of children who have been given portions of pie by someone who now makes last-minute adjustments to rectify careless cutting. There is no central distribution, no person or group entitled to control all the resources, (jointly) deciding how they are to be doled out. What each person gets, he gets from others who give to him in exchange for something, or as a gift. In a free society, diverse persons control different resources, and new holdings arise out of the voluntary exchanges and actions of persons. There is no more a distributing or distribution of shares than there is a distributing of mates in a society in which persons choose whom they shall marry. The total result is the product of many individual decisions which the different individuals involved are entitled to make. Some uses of the term "distribution," it is true, do not imply a previous distributing appropriately judged by some criterion (e.g., "probability distribution"); nevertheless, despite the title of this essay, it would be best to use a terminology that clearly is neutral. We shall speak of people's holdings; a principle of justice in holdings describes (part of) what justice tells us (requires) about holdings. I shall state first what I take to be the correct view about justice in holdings, and then turn to the discussion of alternative views.[1]

The Entitlement Theory

The subject of justice in holdings consists of three major topics. The first is the *original acquisition of holdings,* the appropriation of unheld things. This includes the issues of how unheld things may come to be held, the process(es) by which unheld things may come to be held, the things that may come to be held by these processes, the extent of what comes to be held by a particular process, and so on. We shall refer to the complicated truth about this topic, which we shall not formulate here, as the principle of justice in acquisition. The second topic concerns the *transfer of holdings* from one person to another. By what processes may a person transfer holdings to another? How may a person acquire a holding from another who holds it? Under this topic come general descriptions of voluntary exchange, and gift, and (on the other hand) fraud, as well as reference to particular conventional details fixed upon a given society. The complicated truth about this subject (with placeholders for conventional details) we shall call the principle of justice in transfer. (And we shall suppose it also includes principles governing how a person may divest himself of a holding, passing it into an unheld state.)

If the world were wholly just, the following inductive definition would exhaustively cover the subject of justice in holdings.

1. A person who acquires a holding in accordance with the principle of justice in acquisition is entitled to that holding.
2. A person who acquires a holding in accordance with the principle of justice in transfer, from someone else entitled to the holding, is entitled to the holding.
3. No one is entitled to a holding except by (repeated) applications of 1 and 2.

The complete principle of distributive justice would say simply that a distribution is just if everyone is entitled to the holdings he possesses under the distribution.

A distribution is just if it arises from another (just) distribution by legitimate means. The legitimate means of moving from one distribution to another are specified by the principle of justice in transfer. The legitimate first "moves" are specified by the principle of justice in acquisition.[2] Whatever arises from a just situation by just steps is itself just. The means of change specified by the principle of justice in transfer, preserve justice. As correct rules of inference are truth preserving, and any conclusion deduced via repeated application of such rules from only true premises is itself true, so the means of transition from one situation to another specified by the principle of justice in transfer are justice preserving, and any situation actually arising from repeated transitions in accordance with the principle from a just situation is itself just. The parallel between justice-preserving transformations and truth-preserving transformations illuminates where it fails as well as where it holds. That a conclusion could have been deduced by truth-preserving means from premises that are true suffices to show its truth. That a situation *could* have arisen via justice-preserving means from a just situation does *not* suffice to show its justice. The fact that a thief's victims voluntarily *could* have presented him with gifts does not entitle the thief to his ill-gotten gains. Justice in holdings is historical; it depends upon what actually has happened. We shall return to this point below.

Not all actual situations are generated in accordance with the two principles of justice in holdings: the principle of justice in acquisition and the principle of justice in transfer. Some people steal from others, or defraud them, or enslave them, seizing their product and preventing them from living as they choose, or forcibly exclude others from competing in exchanges. None of these are permissible modes of transition from one situation to another. And some persons acquire holdings by means not sanctioned by the principle of justice in acquisition. The existence of past injustice (previous violations of the first two principles of justice in holdings) raises the third major topic under justice in holdings: the rectification of injustice in holdings. If past injustice has shaped present holdings in various ways, some identifiable and some not, what now, if anything, ought to be done to rectify these injustices? What obligations are the performers of injustice under to their victims? What obligations do the beneficiaries of injustice have to those whose position is worse than it would have been had the injustice not been done? Or than it would have been had compensation been paid promptly? How, if at all, do things change if the beneficiaries and those made worse off are not the direct parties in the act of injustice, but, for example, their descendants? Is an injustice done to someone whose holding was itself based upon an unrectified injustice? How far back must one go in wiping clean the historical slate of injustices? What may victims of injustice permissibly do in order to rectify the injustices being done to them, including the many injustices done by persons acting through their government? I do not know of a thorough or theoretically sophisticated treatment of such issues. Idealizing greatly, let us suppose theoretical investigation will produce a principle of rectification. This principle uses historical information about previous situations and injustices done in them (as defined by the first two principles of justice, and rights against interference), and information about the actual course of events that flowed from these injustices, up until the present, and it yields a description (or descriptions) of holdings in the society. The principle of rectification presumably will make use of (its best estimate of) subjunctive information about what would have occurred (or a probability distribution over what might have occurred, using the expected value) if the injustice had not taken place. If the actual description of holdings turns out not to be one of the descriptions yielded by the principle, then one of the descriptions yielded must be realized.[3]

The general outlines of the theory of justice in holdings are that the holdings of a person are just if he is entitled to them by the principles of justice in acquisition and transfer, or by the principle of rectification of injustice (as specified by the first two principles). If each person's holdings are just then the total set (distribution) of holdings is just. To turn these general outlines into a specific theory we would have to specify the details of each of the three principles of justice in holdings: the principle of acquisition of holdings, the principle of transfer of holdings, and the principle of rectification of violations of the first two principles. I shall not attempt that task here.

Historical Principles and End-Result Principles

The general outlines of the entitlement theory illuminate the nature and defects of other conceptions of distributive justice. The entitlement theory of justice in distribution is *historical;* whether a distribution is just depends upon how it came about. In contrast, *current time-slice principles* of justice hold that the justice of a distribution is determined by how things are distributed (who has what) as judged by some *structural* principle(s) of just distribution. A utilitarian who judges between any two distributions by seeing which has the greater sum of utility and, if these tie, who applies some fixed equality criterion to choose the more equal distribution, would hold a current time-slice principle of justice, as would someone who had a fixed schedule of trade-offs between the sum of happiness and equality. All that needs to be looked at, in judging the justice of a distribution, according to a current time-slice principle, is who ends up with what; in comparing any two distributions one need look only at the matrix presenting the distributions. No further information need be fed into a principle of justice. It is a consequence of such principles of justice that any two structurally identical distributions are equally just. (Two distributions are structurally identical if they present the same profile, but [perhaps] have different persons occupying the particular slots. My having ten and your having five, and my having five and your having ten are structurally identical distributions.) Welfare economics is the theory of current time-slice principles of justice. The subject is conceived as operating on matrices representing only current information about distribution. This, as well as some of the usual conditions (e.g., the choice of distribution is invariant under relabeling of columns), guarantees that welfare economics will be a current time-slice theory, with all of its inadequacies.

Most persons do not accept current time-slice principles as constituting the whole story about distributive shares. They think it relevant in assessing the justice of a situation to consider not only the distribution it embodies, but also how that distribution came about. If some persons are in prison for murder or war crimes, we do not say that to assess the justice of the distribution in the society we must look only at what this person has, and that person has, and that person has . . . , at the current time. We think it relevant to ask whether someone did something so that he *deserved* to be punished, deserved to have a lower share. Most will agree to the relevance of further information with regard to punishments and penalties. Consider also desired things. One traditional socialist view is that workers are entitled to the product and full fruits of their labor; they have earned it; a distribution is unjust if it does not give the workers what they are entitled to. Such entitlements are based upon some past history. No socialist holding this view would find it comforting to be told that because the actual distribution A happens to coincide structurally with the one he desires D, A therefore is no less just than D; it differs only in that the "parasitic" owners of capital receive under A what the workers are entitled to under D, and the workers receive under A what the owners are entitled to (under D), namely very little. Rightly in my view, this socialist holds onto the notions of earning, producing, entitlement, desert, and so on, and he rejects (current time-slice) principles that look only to the structure of the resulting set of holdings. (The set of holdings resulting from what? Isn't it implausible that how holdings are produced and come to exist has no effect at all on who should hold what?) His mistake lies in his view of what entitlements arise out of what sorts of productive processes.

We construe the position we discuss too narrowly by speaking of *current* time-slice principles. Nothing is changed if structural principles operate upon a time sequence of current time-slice profiles and, for example, give someone more now to counterbalance the less he has had earlier. A utilitarian or an egalitarian or any mixture of the two over time will inherit the difficulties of his more myopic comrades. He is not helped by the fact that *some* of the information others consider relevant in assessing a distribution is reflected, unrecoverably, in past matrices. Henceforth, we shall refer to such unhistorical principles of distributive justice, including the current time-slice principles, as *end-result principles* or *end-state principles*.

In contrast to end-result principles of justice, *historical principles* of justice hold that past circumstances or actions of people can create differential entitlements or differential deserts to things. An injustice can be worked by moving from one distribution to another structurally identical one, for the second, in profile the same, may violate people's entitlements or deserts; it may not fit the actual history.

Patterning

The entitlement principles of justice in holdings that we have sketched are historical principles of justice. To understand their precise character better, we shall distinguish them from another subclass of the historical principles. Consider, as an example, the principle of distribution according to moral merit. This principle requires total distributive shares to vary directly with moral merit; no person should have a greater share than anyone whose moral merit is greater. (If moral merit could be not merely ordered but measured on an interval or ratio scale, stronger principles could be formulated.) Or consider the principle that results by substituting "usefulness to society" for "moral merit" in the previous principle. Or instead of "distribute according to moral merit," or "distribute according to usefulness to society," we might consider "distribute according to the weighted sum of moral merit, usefulness to society, and need," with the weights of the different dimensions equal. Let us call a principle of distribution *patterned* if it specifies that a distribution is to vary along with some natural dimension, weighted sum of natural dimensions, or lexicographic ordering of natural dimensions. And let us say a distribution is patterned if it accords with some patterned principle. (I speak of natural dimensions, admittedly without a general criterion for them, because for any set of holdings some artificial dimensions can be gimmicked up to vary along with the distribution of the set.) The principle of distribution in accordance with moral merit is a patterned historical principle, which specifies a patterned distribution. "Distribute according to IQ" is a patterned principle that looks to information not contained in distributional matrices. It is not historical, however, in that it does not look to any past actions creating differential entitlements to evaluate a distribution; it requires only distributional matrices whose columns are labeled by IQ scores. The distribution in a society, however, may be composed of such simple patterned distributions, without itself being simply patterned. Different sectors may operate different patterns, or some combination of patterns may operate in different proportions across a society. A distribution composed in this manner, from a small number of patterned distributions, we also shall term patterned. And we extend the use of "pattern" to include the overall designs put forth by combinations of end-state principles.

Almost every suggested principle of distributive justice is patterned: to each according to his moral merit, or needs, or marginal product, or how hard he tries, or the weighted sum of the foregoing, and so on. The principle of entitlement we have sketched is *not* patterned.[4] There is no one natural dimension or weighted sum or combination of (a small number of) natural dimensions that yields the distributions generated in accordance with the principle of entitlement. The set of holdings that results when some persons receive their marginal products, others win at gambling, others receive a share of their mate's income, others receive gifts from foundations, others receive interest on loans, others receive gifts from admirers, others receive returns on investment, others make for themselves much of what they have, others find things, and so on, will not be patterned. Heavy strands of patterns will run through it; significant portions of the variance in holdings will be accounted for by pattern variables. If most people most of the time choose to transfer some of their entitlements to others only in exchange for something from them, then a large part of what many people hold will vary with what they held that others wanted. More details are provided by the theory of marginal productivity. But gifts to relatives, charitable donations, bequests to children, and the like, are not best conceived, in the first instance, in this manner. Ignoring the strands of pattern, let us suppose for the moment that a distribution actually gotten by the operation of the principle of entitlement is random with respect to any pattern. Though the resulting set of holdings will be unpatterned, it will not be incomprehensible, for it can be seen as arising from the operation of a small number of principles. These principles specify how an initial distribution may arise (the principle of acquisition of holdings) and how distributions may be transformed into others (the principle of transfers of holdings). The process whereby the set of holdings is generated will be intelligible, though the set of holdings itself that results from this process will be unpatterned.

The writings of F. A. Hayek focus less than others' upon what patterning distributive justice requires. Hayek argues that we cannot know enough about each person's situation to distribute to each according to his moral merit (but would justice demand we do so if we did have this knowledge?); and he goes on to say: "Our objection is against all attempts to impress upon society a deliberately chosen pattern of distribution, whether it be an order of equality or of inequality." [5] However, Hayek concludes that in a free society there will be distribution in accordance with value rather than (moral) merit; that is, in accordance with the perceived value of a person's actions and services to others. Despite his rejection of a patterned conception of distributive justice, Hayek himself suggests a pattern he thinks justifiable—distribution in accordance with the (perceived) benefits given to others—and so leaves room for the complaint that a free society does not realize exactly this pattern. Stating this patterned strand of a free capitalist society more precisely, we get: "To each according to how much he benefits others who have the resources for benefiting those who benefit them." This will seem arbitrary unless some acceptable initial set of holdings is specified, or unless it is held that the operation of the system over time washes out any significant effects from the initial set of holdings. As an example of the latter, if almost anyone would have bought a car from Henry Ford, the supposition that it was an arbitrary matter who held the money then (and so bought) would not place Henry Ford's earnings under a cloud. In any event, *his* coming to hold it is not arbitrary. Distribution according to benefits to others *is* a major patterned strand in a free capitalist society, as Hayek correctly points out, but it is only a strand and does *not* constitute the whole pattern of a system of entitlements (viz., inheritance, gifts for arbitrary reasons, charity, and so on) or a standard one should insist a society fit. Will people tolerate for long a system yielding distributions that (they believe) are unpatterned? [6] No doubt people will not long accept a distribution they believe is *unjust*. People want their society to be and to look just. But must the look of justice reside in a resulting pattern rather than in the underlying generating principles? We are in no position to conclude the inhabitants of a society embodying an entitlement conception of justice in holdings will find it unacceptable. Still, it must be granted that were people's reasons for transferring some of their holdings to others always irrational or arbitrary, we would find this disturbing. (Suppose people always determined what holdings they would transfer, and to whom, by using a random device.) We feel more comfortable upholding the justice of an entitlement system if most of the transfers under it are done for reasons. This does not mean necessarily that all deserve what holdings they receive. It means only that there is a purpose or point to someone's transferring a holding to one person rather than to another; that usually we can see what the transferrer thinks he's gaining, what cause he thinks he's serving, what goals he thinks he's helping to achieve, and so on. Since often in a capitalist society people transfer holdings to others in accordance with how much they perceive these others benefiting them, the fabric constituted by the individual transactions and transfers is largely reasonable and intelligible. (Gifts to loved ones, bequests to children, charity to the needy also are nonarbitrary components of the fabric.) In stressing the large strand of distribution in accordance with benefit to others, Hayek shows the point of many transfers, and so shows that the system of transfer of entitlements is not just spinning its gears aimlessly. The system of entitlement is defensible when constituted by the individual aims of individual transactions. No overarching aim is needed, no distributional pattern is required.

To think that the task of a theory of distributive justice is to fill in the blank in "to each according to his ———," is to be predisposed to search for a pattern; and the separate treatment of "from each according to his —————," treats production and distribution as two separate and independent issues. On an entitlement view these are *not* two separate questions. Whoever makes something, having bought or contracted for all other held resources used in the process (transferring some of his holdings for these cooperating factors), is entitled to it. The situation is *not* one of something's getting made, and there being an open question of who is to get it. Things come into the world already attached to people having entitlements over them. From the point of view of the historical entitlement conception of justice in holdings, those who start afresh to complete "to each according to his —————," treat objects as if they appeared from nowhere, out of nothing. A complete theory of justice might cover this limit case as well; here perhaps is a use for the usual conceptions of distributive justice.

So entrenched are maxims of the usual form that perhaps we should present the entitlement conception as a competitor. Ignoring acquisition and rectification, we might say:

From each according to what he chooses to do, to each according to what he makes for himself (perhaps with the contracted-for aid of others) and what others choose to do for him and choose to give him of what they've been given previously (under this maxim) and haven't yet expended or transferred.

This, the discerning reader will have noticed, has its defects as a slogan. So as a summary (and not as a maxim with any independent meaning) and great simplification we have:

From each as they choose, to each as they are chosen.

How Liberty Upsets Patterns

It is not clear how those holding alternative conceptions of distributive justice can reject the entitlement conception of justice in holdings. For suppose a distribution favored by one of these nonentitlement conceptions is realized. Let us suppose it is your favorite one and call this distribution D_1; perhaps everyone has an equal share, perhaps shares vary in accordance with some dimension you treasure. Now suppose that Wilt Chamberlain is greatly in demand by basketball teams, being a great gate-attraction. (Also suppose contracts run only for a year, with players being free agents.) He signs the following sort of contract with a team: In each home game, 25 cents from the price of each ticket of admission goes to him. (We ignore the question of whether he is "gouging" the owners, letting them look out for themselves.) The season starts, the people cheerfully attend his team's games; they buy their tickets, each time dropping a separate 25 cents of their admission price into a special box with Chamberlain's name on it. They are excited about seeing him play; it is worth the total admission price to them. Let us suppose that in one season one million persons attend his home games, and Wilt Chamberlain winds up with $250,000, a much larger sum than the average income and larger even than anyone else has. Is he entitled to this income? Is this new distribution D_1 unjust? If so, why? There is *no* question about whether each of the people was entitled to the control over the resources they held, in D_1, because that was the distribution (your favorite) that (for the purposes of argument) we assumed was acceptable. Each of these persons *chose* to give 25 cents of their money to Chamberlain. They could have spent it on going to the movies, or on candy bars, or on copies of *Dissent* magazine, or of *Monthly Review*. But they all, at least one million of them, converged on giving it to Wilt Chamberlain in exchange for watching him play basketball. If D_1 was a just distribution, and people voluntarily moved from it to D_2, transferring parts of their shares they were given under D_1 (what was it for if not to do something with?), isn't D_2 also just? If the people were entitled to dispose of the resources to which they were entitled (under D_1), didn't this include their being entitled to give it to, or exchange it with, Wilt Chamberlain? Can anyone else complain on grounds of justice? Each other person already has his legitimate share under D_1. Under D_1 there is nothing that anyone has that anyone else has a claim of justice against. After someone transfers something to Wilt Chamberlain, third parties *still* have their legitimate shares; *their* shares are not changed. By what process could such a transfer among two persons give rise to a legitimate claim of distributive justice on a portion of what was transferred, by a third party who had no claim of justice on any holding of the others *before* the transfer? [8] To cut off objections irrelevant here, we might imagine the exchanges occurring in a socialist society, after hours. After playing whatever basketball he does in his daily work, or doing whatever other daily work he does, Wilt Chamberlain decides to put in *overtime* to earn additional money. (First his work quota is set; he works time over that.) Or imagine it is a skilled juggler people like to see, who puts on shows after hours.

Why might some people work overtime in a society in which it is assumed their needs are satisfied? Perhaps because they care about things other than needs. I like to write in books that I read, and to have easy access to books for browsing at odd hours. It would be very pleasant and convenient to have the resources of Widener Library in my back yard. No society, I assume, will provide such resources close to each person who would like them as part of his regular allotment (under D_1). Thus, persons either must do without some extra things that they want, or be allowed to do something extra to get (some of) these things. On what basis could the inequalities that would eventuate be forbidden? Notice also that small factories would spring up in a socialist society, unless forbidden. I melt down some of my personal possessions (under D_1) and build a machine out of the material. I offer you, and others, a philosophy lecture once a week in exchange for your cranking the handle on my machine, whose products I exchange for yet other things, and so on. (The raw materials used by the machine are given to me by others who possess them under D_1, in exchange for hearing lectures.) Each person might participate to gain things over and above their allotment under D_1. Some persons even might want to leave their jobs in socialist industry, and work full time in this private sector. I say something more about these issues elsewhere. Here I wish merely to note how private property, even in means of production, would occur in a socialist society that did not forbid people to use as they wished some of the resources they are given under the socialist distribution D_1. The socialist society would have to forbid capitalist acts between consenting adults.[9]

The general point illustrated by the Wilt Chamberlain example and the example of the entrepreneur in a socialist society is that no end-state principle or distributional pattern principle of justice can be continuously realized without continuous interference into people's lives. Any favored pattern would be transformed into one unfavored by the principle, by people choosing to act in various ways; e.g., by people exchanging goods and services with other people, or giving things to other people, things the transferrers are entitled to under the favored distributional pattern. To maintain a pattern one must either continuously interfere to stop people from transferring resources as they wish to, or continually (or periodically) interfere to take from some persons resources that others for some reason chose to transfer to them. (But if some time limit is to be set on how long people may keep resources others voluntarily transfer to them, why let them keep these resources for *any* period of time? Why not have immediate confiscation?) It might be objected that all persons voluntarily will choose to refrain from actions which would upset the pattern. This presupposes unrealistically: a) that all will most want to maintain the pattern (are those who don't to be "reeducated" or forced to undergo "self-criticism"?); b) that each can gather enough information about his own actions and the ongoing activities of others to discover which of his actions will upset the pattern; and c) that diverse and far-flung persons can coordinate their actions to dovetail into the pattern. Compare the manner in which the market is neutral among persons' desires, as it reflects and transmits widely scattered information via prices, and coordinates persons' activities.

It puts things perhaps a bit too strongly to say that every patterned (or end-state) principle is liable to be thwarted by the voluntary actions of the individual parties transferring some of their shares they receive under the principle. For perhaps some *very* weak patterns are not so thwarted.[10] Any distributional pattern with any egalitarian component is overturnable by the voluntary actions of individual persons over time, as is every patterned condition with sufficient content so as actually to have been proposed as presenting the central core of distributive justice. Still, given the possibility that some weak conditions or patterns may not be unstable in this way, it would be better to formulate an explicit description of the kind of (interesting and contentful) patterns under discussion, and to prove a theorem about their instability. Since the weaker the patterning, the more likely it is that the entitlement system itself satisfies it, a plausible conjecture is that any patterning either is unstable or is satisfied by the entitlement system.

Sen's Argument

Our conclusions are reinforced by considering a recent general argument of Amartya K. Sen.[11] Suppose individual rights are interpreted as the right to choose which of two alternatives is to be more highly ranked in a social ordering of the alternatives. Add the weak condition that if one alternative unanimously is preferred to another then it is ranked higher by the social ordering. If there are two different individuals each with individual rights, interpreted as above, over different pairs of alternatives (having no members in common), then for some possible preference rankings of the alternatives by the individuals, there is no linear social ordering. For suppose that person I has the right to decide among (X,Y) and person II has the right to decide among (Z,W); and suppose their individual preferences are as follows (and that there are no other individuals). Person I prefers W to X to Y to Z, and person II perfers Y to Z to W to X. By the unanimity condition, in the social ordering W is preferred to X (since each individual perfers it to X), and Y is preferred to Z (since each individual perfers it to Z). Also in the social ordering, X is preferred to Y, by person I's right of choice between these two alternatives. Combining these three binary rankings, we get W preferred to X preferred to Y preferred to Z, in the social ordering. However, by person II's right of choice, Z must be preferred to W in the social ordering. There is no transitive social ordering satisfying all these conditions, and the social ordering, therefore, is nonlinear. Thus far, Sen.

The trouble stems from treating an individual's right to choose among alternatives as the right to determine the relative ordering of these alternatives within a social ordering. The system is no better that has individuals rank *pairs* of alternatives, and separately rank the individual alternatives; their ranking of pairs feeds into some method of amalgamating

Robert Nozick

preferences to yield a social ordering of pairs; and the choice among the alternatives in the highest ranked pair in the social ordering is made by the individual with the right to decide between this pair. This system also has the result that an alternative may be selected although *everyone* prefers some other alternative; e.g., 1 selects X over Y, where (X,Y) somehow is the highest ranked *pair* in the social ordering of pairs, although everyone, including 1, perfers W to X. (But the choice person 1 was given was only between X and Y.)

A more appropriate view of individual rights is as follows. Individual rights are copossible; each person may exercise his rights as he chooses. The exercise of these rights fixes some features of the world. Within the constraints of these fixed features, a choice may be made by a social choice mechanism based upon a social ordering, if there are any choices left to make! Rights do not determine a social ordering but instead set the constraints within which a social choice is to be made, by excluding certain alternatives, fixing others, and so on. (If I have a right to choose to live in New York or in Massachusetts, and I choose Massachusetts, then alternatives involving my living in New York are not appropriate objects to be entered in a social ordering.) Even if all possible alternatives are ordered first, apart from anyone's rights, the situation is not changed: for then the highest ranked alternative *that is not excluded by anyone's exercise of his rights* is instituted. Rights do not determine the position of an alternative or the relative position of two alternatives in a social ordering; they *operate upon* a social ordering to constrain the choice it can yield.

If entitlements to holdings are rights to dispose of them, then social choice must take place *within* the constraints of how people choose to exercise these rights. If any patterning is legitimate, it falls within the domain of social choice, and hence is constrained by people's rights. *How else can one cope with Sen's results?* The alternative of first having a social ranking with rights exercised within *its* constraints, is no alternative at all. Why not just select the top ranked alternative and forget about rights? If that top ranked alternative itself leaves some room for individual choice (and here is where "rights" of choice is supposed to enter in), there must be something to stop these choices from transforming it into another alternative. Thus Sen's argument leads us again to the result that patterning requires continuous interference with individuals' actions and choices.[12]

Redistribution and Property Rights

Apparently patterned principles allow people to choose to expend upon themselves, but not upon others, those resources they are entitled to (or rather, receive) under some favored distributional pattern D_1. For if each of several persons chooses to expend some of his D_1 resources upon one other person, then that other person will receive more than his D_1 share, disturbing the favored distributional pattern. Maintaining a distributional pattern is individualism with a vengeance! Patterned distributional principles do not give people what entitlement principles do, only better distributed. For they do not give the right to choose what to do with what one has; they do not give the right to choose to pursue an end involving (intrinsically, or as a means) the enhancement of another's position. To such views, families are disturbing; for within a family occur transfers that upset the favored distributional pattern. Either families themselves become units to which distribution takes place, the column occupiers (on what rationale?), or loving behavior is forbidden. We should note in passing the ambivalent position of radicals toward the family. Its loving relationships are seen as a model to be emulated and extended across the whole society, while it is denounced as a suffocating institution to be broken, and condemned as a focus of parochial concerns that interfere with achieving radical goals. Need we say that it is not appropriate to enforce across the wider society the relationships of love and care appropriate within a family, relationships which are voluntarily undertaken? [13] Incidentally, love is an interesting instance of another relationship that is historical, in that (like justice) it depends upon what actually occurred. An adult may come to love another because of the other's characteristics; but it is the other person, and not the characteristics, that is loved. The love is not transferable to someone else with the same characteristics, even to one who "scores" higher for these characteristics. And the love endures through changes of the characteristics that gave rise to it. One loves the particular person one actually encountered. Why love is historical, attaching to persons in this way and not to characteristics, is an interesting and puzzling question.

Proponents of patterned principles of distributive justice focus upon criteria for determining who is to receive holdings; they consider the reasons for which someone should have something, and also the total picture of holdings. Whether or not it is better to give than to receive, proponents of patterned principles ignore giving altogether. In considering the distribution of goods, income, and so on, their theories are theories of recipient-justice; they completely ignore any right a person might have to give something to someone. Even in exchanges where each party is simultaneously giver and recipient, patterned principles of justice focus only upon the recipient role and its supposed rights. Thus discussions tend to focus on whether people (should) have a right to inherit, rather than on whether people (should) have a right to bequeath or on whether persons who have a right to hold also have a right to choose that others hold in their place. I lack a good explanation of why the usual theories of distributive justice are so recipient-oriented; ignoring givers and trans-ferrers and their rights is of a piece with ignoring producers and their entitlements. But why is it *all* ignored?

Patterned principles of distributive justice necessitate *re*distributive activities. The likelihood is small that any actual freely arrived at set of holdings fits a given pattern; and the likelihood is nil that it will continue to fit the pattern as people exchange and give. From the point of view of an entitlement theory, redistribution is a serious matter indeed, involving, as it does, the violation of people's rights. (An exception is those takings that fall under the principle of the rectification of injustices.) From other points of view, also, it is serious.

Taxation of earnings from labor is on a par with forced labor.[14] Some persons find this claim obviously true: taking the earnings of *n* hours labor is like taking *n* hours from the person; it is like forcing the person to work *n* hours for another's purpose. Others find the claim absurd. But even these, if they object to forced labor, would oppose forcing unem-ployed hippies to work for the benefit of the needy.[15] And they also would object to forcing each person to work five extra hours each week for the benefit of the needy. But a system that takes five hours' wages in taxes does not seem to them like one that forces someone to work five hours, since it offers the forcee a wider range of choice in activities than does taxation in kind with the particular labor specified. (But we can imagine a gradation of systems of forced labor, from one that specifies a particular activity, to one that gives a choice among two activities, to . . . ; and so on up.) Furthermore, people envisage a system with something like a proportional tax on everything above the amount necessary for basic needs. Some think this does not force someone to work extra hours, since there is no fixed number of extra hours he is forced to work, and since he can avoid the tax entirely by earning only enough to cover his basic needs. This is a very uncharacteristic view of forcing for those who *also* think people are forced to do something *whenever* the alternatives they face are considerably worse. However, *neither* view is correct. The fact that others intentionally intervene, in violation of a side-constraint against aggression, to threaten force to limit the alternatives, in this case to paying taxes or (presumably the worse alternative) bare subsistence, makes the taxation system one of forced labor, and distinguishes it from other cases of limited choices which are not forcings.[16]

The man who chooses to work longer to gain an income more than sufficient for his basic needs prefers some extra goods or services to the leisure and activities he could perform during the possible nonworking hours; whereas the man who chooses not to work the extra time prefers the leisure activities to the extra goods or services he could acquire by working more. Given this, if it would be illegitimate for a tax system to seize some of a man's leisure (forced labor) for the purpose of serving the needy, how can it be legitimate for a tax system to seize some of a man's goods for that purpose? Why should we treat the man whose happiness requires certain material goods or services differently from the man whose preferences and desires make such goods unnecessary for his happiness? Why should the man who prefers seeing a movie (and who has to earn money for a ticket) be open to the required call to aid the needy, while the person who prefers looking at a sunset (and hence need earn no extra money) is not? Indeed, isn't it surprising that redistributionists choose to ignore the man whose pleasures are so easily attainable without extra labor, while adding yet another burden to the poor unfortunate who must work for his pleasures? If anything, one would have expected the reverse. Why is the person with the nonmaterial or nonconsumption desire allowed to proceed unimpeded to his most favored feasible alternative, whereas the man whose pleasures or desires involve material things and who must work for extra money (thereby serving whoever considers his activities valuable enough to pay him) is constrained in what he can realize? Perhaps there is no difference in principle. And perhaps some think the answer concerns merely administrative convenience. (These questions and issues will not disturb those who think forced labor to serve the needy or realize some favored endstate pattern acceptable.) In a fuller discussion we would have (and want) to extend our argument to include interest, entrepreneurial profits, and so on. Those who doubt that this extension can be carried through, and who draw the line here at taxation of income from labor, will have to state rather complicated patterned *historical* principles of distributive justice, since end-state principles would not distinguish *sources* of income in any way. It is enough for now to get away from end-state principles and to make clear how various patterned principles are dependent upon particular views about the sources or the illegitimacy or the lesser legitimacy of profits, interest, and so on, which particular views may well be mistaken.

What sort of right over others does a legally institutionalized end-state pattern give one? The central core of the notion of a property right in X, relative to which other parts of the notion are to be explained, is the right to determine what shall be done with X; the right to choose which of the constrained set of options concerning X shall be realized or attempted.[17] The constraints are set by other principles or laws operating in the society; in our theory by the Lockean rights people possess (under the minimal state). My property rights in my knife allow me to leave it where I will, but not in your chest. I may choose which of the acceptable options involving the knife is to be realized. This notion of property helps us to understand why earlier theorists spoke of people as having property in themselves and their labor. They viewed each person as having a right to decide what would become of himself and what he would do, and as having a right to reap the benefits of what he did.

This right of selecting the alternative to be realized from the constrained set of alternatives may be held by an *individual* or by a *group* with some procedure for reaching a joint decision; or the right may be passed back and forth, so that one year I decide what's to become of X, and the next year you do (with the alternative of destruction, perhaps, being excluded). Or, during the same time period, some types of decisions about X may be made by me, and others by you. And so on. We lack an adequate, fruitful, analytical apparatus for classifying the *types* of constraints on the set of options among which choices are to be made, and the *types* of ways decision powers can be held, divided, and amalgamated. A *theory* of property would, among other things, contain such a classification of constraints and decision modes, and from a small number of principles would follow a host of interesting statements about the *consequences* and effects of certain combinations of constraints and modes of decision.

When end-result principles of distributive justice are built into the legal structure of a society, they (as do most patterned principles) give each citizen an enforcible claim to some portion of the total social product; that is, to some portion of the sum total of the individually and jointly made products. This total product is produced by individuals laboring, using means of production others have saved to bring into existence, by people organizing production or creating means to produce new things or things in a new way. It is on this batch of individual activities that patterned distributional principles give each individual an enforcible claim. Each person has a claim to the activities and the products of other persons, independently of whether the other persons enter into particular relationships that give rise to these claims, and independently of whether they voluntarily take these claims upon themselves, in charity or in exchange for something.

Whether it is done through taxation on wages or on wages over a certain amount, or through seizure of profits, or through there being a big *social pot* so that it's not clear what's coming from where and what's going where, patterned principles of distributive justice involve appropriating the actions of other persons. Seizing the results of someone's labor is equivalent to seizing hours from him and directing him to carry on various activities. If people force you to do certain work, or unrewarded work, for a certain period of time, they decide what you are to do and what purposes your work is to serve apart from your decisions. This process whereby they take this decision from you makes them a *part owner* of you; it gives them a property right in you. Just as having such partial control and power of decision, by right, over an animal or inanimate object would be to have a property right in it.

End-state and most patterned principles of distributive justice institute (partial) ownership by others of people and their actions and labor. These principles involve a shift from the classical liberals' notion of self-ownership to a notion of (partial) property rights in *other* people.

Considerations such as these confront end-state and other patterned conceptions of justice with the question of whether the actions necessary to achieve the selected pattern don't themselves violate moral side-constraints. Any view holding that there are moral side-constraints on actions, that not all moral considerations can be built into end-states that are to be achieved,[18] must face the possibility that some of its goals are not achievable by any morally permissible available means. An entitlement theorist will face such conflicts in a society that deviates from the principles of justice for the generation of holdings, if and only if the only actions available to realize the principles themselves violate some moral constraints. Since deviation from the first two principles of justice (in acquisition and transfer) will involve other persons' direct and aggressive intervention to violate rights, and since moral constraints will not exclude defensive or retributive action in such cases, the entitlement theorist's problem rarely will be pressing. And whatever difficulties he has in applying the principle of rectification to persons who did not themselves violate the first two principles, are difficulties in balancing the conflicting considerations so as correctly to formulate the complex principle of rectification itself; he will not violate moral side-constraints by applying the principle. Proponents of patterned conceptions of justice, however, often will face head-on clashes (and poignant ones if they cherish each party to the clash) between moral side-constraints on how individuals may be treated on the one hand and, on the other, their patterned conception of justice that presents an end-state or other pattern that *must* be realized.

May a person emigrate from a nation that has institutionalized some end-state or patterned distributional principle? For some principles (e.g., Hayek's) emigration presents no theoretical problem. But for others it is a tricky matter. Consider a nation having a compulsory scheme of minimal social provision to aid the neediest (or one organized so as to maximize the position of the worst off group); no one may opt out of participating in it. (None may say, "Don't compel me to contribute to others and don't provide for me via this compulsory mechanism if I am in need.") Everyone above a certain level is forced to contribute to aid the needy. But if emigration from the country were allowed, anyone could choose to move to another country that did not have compulsory social provision but otherwise was (as much as possible) identical. In such a case, the person's only motive for leaving would be to avoid participating in the compulsory scheme of social provision. And if he does leave, the needy in his initial country will receive no (compelled) help from him. What rationale yields the result that the person be permitted to emigrate, yet forbidden to stay and opt out of the compulsory scheme of social provision? If providing for the needy is of overriding importance, this does militate against allowing internal opting out; but it also speaks against allowing external emigration. (Would it also support, to some extent, the kidnapping of persons living in a place without compulsory social provision, who could be forced to make a contribution to the needy in your community?) Perhaps the crucial component of the position that allows emigration solely to avoid certain arrangements, while not allowing anyone internally to opt out of them, is a concern for fraternal feelings within the country. "We don't want anyone here who doesn't contribute, who doesn't care enough about the others to contribute." That concern, in this case, would have to be tied to the view that forced aiding tends to produce fraternal feelings between the aided and the aider (or perhaps merely to the view that the knowledge that someone or other voluntarily is not aiding produces unfraternal feelings).

N O T E S

1. Since the second part of this essay [not included here] discusses Rawls' theory, the reader mistakenly may think that every remark or argument in the first part against alternative theories of justice is meant to apply to or anticipate a criticism of his theory. This is not so; there are other theories also worth criticizing.

2. Applications of the principle of justice in acquisition may also occur as part of the move from one distribution to another. You may find an unheld thing now, and appropriate it. Acquisitions also are to be understood as included when, to simplify, I speak only of transitions by transfers.

3. If the principle of rectification of violations of the first two principles yields more than one description of holdings, then some choice must be made as to which of these is to be realized. Perhaps the sort of considerations about distributive justice and equality I argue against play a legitimate role in *this* subsidiary choice. Similarly, there may be room for such considerations in deciding which otherwise arbitrary features a statute will embody, when such features are unavoidable because other considerations do not specify a precise line, yet one must be drawn.

4. One might try to squeeze a patterned conception of distributive justice from the framework of the entitlement conception, by formulating a gimmicky obligatory "principle of transfer" that would lead to the pattern. For example, the principle that if one has more than the mean income, one must transfer everything one holds

above the mean to persons below the mean so as to bring them up to (but not over) the mean. We can formulate a criterion for a "principle of transfer" to rule out such obligatory transfers, or we can say that no common principle of transfer, no principle of transfer in a free society will be like this. The former is probably the better course, though the latter also is true.

Alternatively, one might think to make the entitlement conception instantiate a pattern, by using matrix entries that express the relative strength of a person's entitlements as measured by some real-valued function. But even if the limitation to natural dimensions failed to exclude this function, the resulting edifice would *not* capture our system of entitlements to *particular* things.

5. F. A. Hayek, *The Constitution of Liberty* (Chicago: Henry Co., 1972), chap. 6: "Equality, Value, and Merit," p. 87.

6. This question does not imply that they will tolerate any and every patterned distribution. In discussing Hayek's views, Irving Kristol has recently speculated that people will not long tolerate a system that yields distributions patterned in accordance with value rather than merit. (" 'When Virtue Loses All Her Loveliness'—Some Reflections on Capitalism and 'The Free Society,' " *The Public Interest,* Fall 1970, pp. 3–15.) Kristol, following some remarks of Hayek's, equates the latter with justice. Since some case can be made for the external standard of distribution in accordance with benefit to others, we ask about a weaker (and therefore more plausible) hypothesis.

7. Varying situations continuously from that limit situation to our own would force us to consider whether entitlement considerations lexicographically precede the considerations of the usual theories of distributive justice, so that the *slightest* strand of entitlement outweighs the considerations of the usual theories of distributive justice.

8. Might not a transfer have instrumental effects on a third party, changing his feasible options? (But what if the two parties to the transfer independently had used their holdings in this fashion?) I discuss this question elsewhere, but note here that this question concedes the point for distributions of ultimate intrinsic noninstrumental goods (pure utility experiences, so to speak) that are transferrable. It also might be objected that the transfer might make a third party more envious because it worsens his position relative to someone else. I find it incomprehensible how it can be thought that this involves a claim of justice. On envy, see *Anarchy, State, and Utopia* (New York: Basic Books, 1974), chap. 8.

Here and elsewhere in this essay, a theory which incorporates elements of pure procedural justice might find what I say acceptable, *if* kept in its proper place; that is, if background institutions exist to ensure the satisfaction of certain conditions on distributive shares. But if these institutions are not themselves the sum or invisible-hand result of people's voluntary (nonaggressive) actions, the constraints they impose require justification. At no point does our argument assume any background institutions more extensive than those of the minimal night-watchman state, limited to protecting persons against murder, assault, theft, fraud, and so on.

9. See the selection from John Henry MacKay's novel, *The Anarchists,* reprinted in Leonard Krimmerman and Lewis Perry, eds., *Patterns of Anarchy* (New York: Doubleday, 1966), pp. 16–33, in which an individualist anarchist presses upon a communist anarchist the question: "Would you, in the system of society which you call 'free Communism' prevent individuals from exchanging their labor among themselves by means of their own medium of exchange? And further: Would you prevent them from occupying land for the purpose of personal use?" The novel continues: "[the] question was not to be escaped; if he answered 'Yes!' he admitted that society had the right of control over the individual and threw overboard the autonomy of

the individual which he had always zealously defended; if on the other hand, he answered 'No!' he admitted the right of private property which he had just denied so emphatically. . . . Then he answered 'In Anarchy any number of men must have the right of forming a voluntary association, and so realizing their ideas in practice. Nor can I understand how any one could justly be driven from the land and house which he uses and occupies . . . every serious man must declare himself: for Socialism, and thereby for force and against liberty, or for Anarchism, and thereby for liberty and against force.'" In contrast, we find Noam Chomsky writing, "Any consistent anarchist must oppose private ownership of the means of production," and "the consistent anarchist then . . . will be a socialist . . . of a particular sort" (Introducation to Daniel Guerin, *Anarchism: From Theory to Practice*, trans. Mary Klooper [New York: Monthly Review Press, 1970], pp. xiii and xv).

10. Is the patterned principle stable that requires merely that a distribution be Pareto-optimal? One person might give another a gift or bequest that the second could exchange with a third to their mutual benefit. Before the second makes this exchange, there is not Pareto-optimality. Is a stable pattern presented by a principle choosing that among the Pareto-optimal positions that satisfies some further condition *C*? It may seem there cannot be a counterexample, for won't any voluntary exchange made away from a situation show that the first situation wasn't Pareto-optimal? (Ignore the implausibility of this last claim for the case of bequests.) But principles are to be satisfied over time, during which new possibilities arise. A distribution that at one time satisfies the criterion of Pareto-optimality might not do so when some new possibilities arise (Wilt Chamberlain grows up and starts playing basketball); and though people's activities will tend to move then to a new Pareto-optimal position, *this* new one need not satisfy the contentful condition *C*. Continual interference will be needed to insure the continual satisfaction of *C*. (The theoretical possibility should be investigated of a pattern's being maintained by some invisible-hand process that brings it back to an equilibrium that fits the pattern when deviations occur.)

11. *Collective Choice and Social Welfare* (San Francisco: Holden–Day, Inc., 1970), chaps. 5 and 6.

12. Oppression will be less noticeable if the background institutions do not prohibit certain actions that upset the patterning (various exchanges or transfers of entitlement), but rather prevent them from being done, by nullifying them.

13. One indication of the stringency of Rawls's difference principle is its inappropriateness as a governing principle even within a family of individuals who love one another. Should a family devote its resources to maximizing the position of its least well off and talented child, holding back the other children or using resources for their education and development only if they will follow a policy throughout their lifetimes of maximizing the position of their least fortunate sibling? Surely not. How then can this even be considered as the appropriate policy for enforcement in the wider society?

14. I am unsure as to whether the arguments I present below show that such taxation just *is* forced labor; so that "is on a par with" means "is one kind of." Or alternatively, whether the arguments emphasize the great similarities between such taxation and forced labor, to show it is plausible and illuminating to view such taxation in the light of forced labor. This latter approach would remind one of how John Wisdom conceives of the claims of metaphysicians.

15. Nothing hangs on the fact that here and elsewhere I speak loosely of *needs*, since I go on, each time, to reject the criterion of justice which includes it. If, however, something did depend upon the notion, one would want to examine it more carefully. For a skeptical view, see Kenneth Minogue, *The Liberal Mind* (New York: Methuen S. Company, Ltd., 1963), pp. 103–112.

16. Further details that this statement should include are contained in my essay, "Coercion," in *Philosophy, Science, and Method*, eds. S. Morgenbesser, P. Suppes, and M. White (New York: St. Martin's Press, Inc., 1969).

17. On the themes in this and the next paragraph, see the writings of Armen Alchian.

18. See Nozick, *Anarchy, State, and Utopia*, chap. 3.

IV

Conclusions

(13)

Economic Justice:
Controversies and
Policies

Mary Jo Bane

"INEQUALITY"—the notion, not the book—is many faceted. It has been commented on by students of philosophy, economics, social stratification, and public policy; few of the commentaries agree on the appropriate phrasing of questions, not to mention methodology or value premises. *Inequality*—the book by Jencks and friends—spoke to only a small part of the general notion. The book presented data on the process of social stratification in the context of a policy argument. The policy question posed, and I think answered, in *Inequality* was quite modest: to what extent can income inequality in the United States be reduced by equalizing education, family background, and IQ? Public interest in that question was, however, also quite modest. Consequently many people read into the data in *Inequality*, often incorrectly, answers to their own quite different questions; others castigated the authors for not dealing with different questions, whatever the data; while still others criticized the data independent of the policy issues.

Subsequent—and, indeed, prior, as those who are familiar with the research know—empirical studies of the process of social stratification and the determination of income suggest that the numbers presented in *Inequality* are pretty much correct.[1] The effect of schooling was probably slightly underestimated as a result of random measurement error in the census data used for the basic analyses. The mistakes, at least as re-

Several people made helpful comments on an earlier draft of this piece and I am grateful to them: Christopher Jencks, Michael Olneck, Philip Selznick, and Kenneth Winston.

vealed by more sophisticated analyses of considerably better data,[2] were, however, quite small and did not distort in any important ways the estimates of the relative importance of family background, schooling, and other factors in the determination of income.

The policy implications of the data were, however, only partly explored in *Inequality*. This paper attempts to explore a bit more. I will look at the *Inequality* data with a view toward developing a notion of economic justice, evaluating the American economic structure against the standard of justice, and suggesting some policy directions.

Fairness, Equality, and Equal Opportunity

Almost no one advocates strict income equality per se. Even the most egalitarian argue that people ought to be able to make some choices about how they spend their time. They ought to be able, for example, to work less rather than more or to choose a pleasant rather than a disagreeable job if they are willing to sacrifice other benefits. All of these choices would lead to a certain amount of inequality which almost everyone is willing to accept. Most people, from Daniel Bell to the person in the street, go much farther than this in the amount of inequality they prefer. They seem to think that strict equality would be boring, repressive, and generally unpleasant.

An interesting study of people's attitudes toward equality of income has recently been done by Lee Rainwater (1974b). Most of his respondents did not find the idea of equal distribution at all attractive; as one woman said:

It's communism—everybody is the same and they all share. I wouldn't want it. If I work harder than somebody else, why shouldn't I be able to get more and live better than somebody else.

Instead, they defined desirable equality in two ways: as equal treatment and as equality of opportunity. Rainwater's respondents argued that everyone should be treated alike, no matter how much or how little money he or she has. One person said:

Treat everybody like you treat yourself. If you get down to the working people, they treat everybody the same—hello Joe, how are you? Colored people, whatever. The upper class is *stuck-up*.

Another said: "Equality is fairness. Everybody being treated fairly. The law looking at everybody equally." They seem to be suggesting that everyone, no matter of what status, is entitled to equal respect and equal treatment in certain areas. People with more money ought to be able to buy more material goods, but they ought not be able to buy the right to degrade others or the power to live outside the law.

Rainwater's respondents also emphasized the importance of equal opportunity. Everyone should have the chance to be as successful as he or she can be and wants to be. Everyone should have a chance at an education. People should be considered for jobs on the basis of their abilities, not on the basis of race or social background. Equal opportunity implies unequal results. The realization of this showed up when Rainwater asked his respondents about fair salaries for different types of workers: top management, middle management and professional, average white collar, average working man, lower skilled. The answers included quite substantial differentials. On the average, a fair salary for a lower-skilled person was set at about two-thirds the mean, while a fair salary for top management was about two and a half times the mean.[3] These earnings differentials were justified by the different amounts of training and different responsibilities of the jobs. Interestingly, survey respondents were willing to make some judgments about the fairness of the distribution of results per se. They formulated the notion of a minimum wage, about two-thirds of the average, which anyone who worked full time ought to receive. About half the sample also thought that it was possible for someone to make "too much." Their maximum wage, about $50,000, was defined as "an absolutely top salary—one that even the most highly paid man can't exceed."

The feelings about equality which Rainwater's sample expressed are similar to those articulated in other studies.[4] They are, of course, quite vague. But they also suggest some underlying principles of economic justice.[5] These principles include equal opportunity, fair procedures for rewarding special contributions, and a minimum wage. People in the survey argued that everyone ought to have a chance to succeed. They argued that differential rewards to jobs were justified because of the differential training required and the greater contributions made by people in positions of responsibility or positions requiring great technical competence. They also argued that people should not receive incomes which are "too low," and that something should be done to prevent this from happening.

These are not the only principles, of course, which could be used to assess the fairness of an economic system. I think it can be argued that principles of fairness or brotherhood ought to be used to judge individual cases as well as procedures, and that equality of results ought to be more of a concern. But they are not, and most people seem to think that they should not be. Since practical public policy must start with people's ideas as they are rather than as they perhaps should be, I will use the three principles rather than a more unitary definition of equality in examining the actual distribution of income.

Equal Opportunity

Equal opportunity is hard to get a handle on, as the concept is used to describe and evaluate a wide variety of situations. Even when discussion is limited to economic success, as it is here (ignoring questions of whether people have equal opportunities to gain respect and esteem, improve their minds, express themselves, and so on), the notion is elusive, sometimes applied quite narrowly to specific hiring decisions, sometimes used much more broadly to evaluate whole systems of allocating rewards and punishments.

A narrow definition of equal opportunity is perhaps the most common, finding expression in, for example, the Equal Employment Opportunity Act. Equal opportunity in the narrow sense is said to exist if the decisions which directly determine a person's chances for economic success—hiring, layoffs, promotions, and wages—are made without regard for those characteristics specified by law—race, color, religion, sex, or national origin.[6] Equal opportunity is violated if an employer in effect says, "I'm not hiring you (promoting you, giving you a decent wage) because you're black (Jewish, female)." Equal opportunity extends, in law and in most people's thinking, to the formal prerequisites for economic success —public education, job training programs, labor union membership. When a person is refused admission to a school, a training program, or a union because of race, national origin, or sex, equal opportunity is denied.

Focusing on specific hiring or admission decisions and on specific ascriptive characteristics is the most common way of formulating the notion of equal opportunity. But broader formulations are possible and may in fact be necessary to satisfy standards of economic justice. The Supreme Court, in *Griggs* v. *Duke Power Company*,[7] has suggested one direction which a broader formulation might take. In *Griggs*, black employees challenged Duke Power Company's requirement of a high school education or passing a standardized general intelligence test as a condition of employment or promotion, arguing that the requirements were not related to the jobs. The company had a history of racial discrimination, the requirements were established to circumvent prohibitions of discrimination in the Civil Rights Act, and the effect of the education and test score standards was to confine blacks to the lowest-paid, most unpleasant dead-end jobs. The court in deciding the case forbade the use of criteria which had the effect of discriminating unless the criteria could be proven relevant to job performance, as they were not at Duke Power Company:

The objective of Congress in the enactment of Title VII is plain from the language of the statute. It was to achieve equality of employment opportunities and remove barriers that have operated in the past to favor an identifiable group of white employees over other employees. Under the Act, practices, procedures, or tests neutral on their face, and even neutral in terms of intent, cannot be maintained if they operate to "freeze" the status quo of prior discrimination.

Though subsequent decisions have interpreted *Griggs* quite narrowly, requiring historical support of the intent to discriminate and accepting "statistical significance" as proof of relevance, the potential for a broader conception of equal opportunity exists.[8] Rather than focusing on individual hiring and firing decisions, the focus would be on the total structure of opportunities. Not only would employers be forbidden to say "I'm not hiring you because you're black," they could also be challenged for saying "I'm not hiring you because you're uneducated, which may be because you're black." The formulation of equal opportunity intimated in *Griggs* would look at the workings of prerequisites and criteria in the system of economic statuses. A system which worked in such a way as to have the effect of producing between-group differences in economic success would automatically raise a question of equal opportunity, no matter how nondiscriminatory specific decisions seemed.

Opportunity and Results

Equality of opportunity and equality of results are conceptually distinguishable.[9] In fact, however, equality of opportunity is difficult to assess independently, and researchers must rely on more or less sophisticated analyses of results. Using results to estimate equality of opportunity assumes that if all other relevant differences between groups were taken into account and controlled, then equality of opportunity would lead to equal average results. Inequality of results, conversely, would imply inequality of opportunity, if everything else were controlled.

The difficulties of measuring and taking account of "everything else" are obviously formidable. The notion, though, seems to embody common-sense conceptions. Most people are willing to make some inferences about denial of equal opportunity even in the absence of "No Irish Need Apply" signs or a personnel manager who says "I'm not hiring you because you're black." Instead we assume, partly because of the long history of discrimination in America, that the choice of a white over an equally qualified black is usually an indication of denial of equal opportunity.

Many people are, of course, reluctant to make such a judgment in an individual case. Suppose we watched a personnel manager interviewing and hiring people. If we saw the personnel manager hire a white rather than what seemed to be an equally qualified black for one position, we would probably be willing to excuse the action on the basis of characteristics unknown to us, or even simple idiosyncrasy. But if we saw the personnel manager make the same decision in 100 cases, hiring 100 whites over 100 equally qualified blacks, we would pretty surely charge him or her with discriminatory practices. We would not even need to have seen 100 equally qualified pairs of applicants to make such a judgment. If the average qualifications of the blacks were equal to the average qualifications of the whites, a final hiring roster which deviated substantially from a 50–50 racial mix would be considered by most people, I think, as evidence of a denial of equal opportunity. More generally, if the qualifications of two groups are equal or controlled statistically, inequality of results is a measure of the denial of equal opportunity in the narrow, common usage of the term.

Defining equal opportunity in the broader sense, applying the concept to the total structure of opportunities, would require relaxing the requirement that "other things" be equal or controlled statistically when results were examined. "Other things" may be unequal because of discrimination earlier in life, or because the system works in such a way as to deprive some groups of chances to develop skills, competencies, motivation, and other job-related qualifications. Defining equal opportunity more broadly requires looking at results in a different light. If access to education is influenced by race, then education should not be held constant in evaluating results. If motivation among blacks is low because of an accurate perception that they cannot ever be successful, then motivation should not be held constant in evaluating results. Under the broadest formulation of equal opportunity, nothing should be held constant, because if the system itself is being evaluated, unequal results are themselves evidence of a failure somewhere.

The broad definition of equal opportunity is both unfamiliar and difficult to formulate practically. The following sections examine the notion further and look at empirical research relevant to both the narrow and broad definitions.

Discrimination

A good deal of research is available to estimate the extent to which race and sex are actually used in the allocation of economic success. The research uses statistical techniques to hold other variables constant.[10] If this were done completely, if all relevant variables really were held constant, then a strong inference could be drawn that the remaining race or sex differences in results attested to discriminatory hiring, promotion, or wage decisions.

The research studies show that pure discrimination almost certainly still exists. Studies have been done of the wage and occupation gaps between men and women and between blacks and whites which control for education, work experience, and test scores. These studies show that about one-quarter to one-half of the gap between blacks and whites and between 17 and 40 percent of the gap between men and women are not explained by differences in measurable qualifications.[11] Most social scientists consider the residual gap after qualifications have been controlled a measure of discrimination, even though only a finite number of measurable qualifications were controlled in the equations. It is possible that unmeasured motivational and skill differences between the groups also contribute to the unexplained gap. These unmeasured differences would have to be very large to account for the resulting gaps, and the sheer size of the gap deters most researchers from a benign interpretation. Moreover, what research has been done suggests that the kinds of motivation which can be measured explain almost nothing.[12] More precise estimates of discrimination could presumably be obtained if motivation could be accurately measured and controlled. I suspect that including these variables would reduce somewhat the unexplained gap between men and women, and might also reduce slightly the unexplained gap between blacks and whites.

The size of the unexplained gap between groups after controlling all other relevant personal, motivational, and training characteristics is the cleanest indicator of the extent of equal opportunity. It is not clear, though, that this clean indicator is really the appropriate one, even if it were attainable. The unexplained gap may not define the only area of concern. Using statistical techniques to make other things equal may make the concept of equal opportunity overly narrow. If other things are unequal because of discrimination earlier in life, it would seem reasonable to expand the notion of equal opportunity to encompass opportunities to acquire the prerequisites for jobs as well as jobs themselves. Suppose, for example, that racial discrimination kept blacks from getting as much education as whites of comparable talent and motivation. To that extent, education should not be held constant in analyses of economic success. The amount of discrimination in education should be added to the amount of discrimination in hiring to give an overall estimate of the denial of equal opportunity.

But the problem is more complicated still. The research reported in *Inequality* suggests that blacks do get as much education as whites of comparable family incomes and scores on standardized tests. There is no discernible effect of race on education once these other factors are controlled. But does this mean the educational system is not discriminatory? Parental income and standardized test scores do affect access to education, and both of these are related to race. Should they be considered irrelevant criteria, just as race is?

Family Background

There are no existing laws which prohibit discrimination against people whose parents were poor. Indeed, our laws of inheritance are set up to ensure that, to some extent at least, parents are allowed if not encouraged to pass on their property and privileges to their children. Parents are encouraged to provide for their children to the extent that they are able, to buy them food and clothing and bicycles and TVs and education. Parents' abilities to provide all these things obviously depend on their income. Children's access to all of them (except TV—94 percent of homes have one!) is highly unequal.

To limit the discussion of equal opportunity to race and sex without considering parental income seems, however, somewhat odd. One problem is that the substitution of one form of discrimination for another does not seem like progress. If we heard a personnel manager say to an applicant, "I'm not refusing to hire you because you're black, I'm refusing to hire you because you're poor," we would not be likely to applaud. Moreover, there is at least some sentiment that discrimination on the basis of social background is itself wrong. There is a longstanding American concern for social mobility, for equality of opportunity between the children of the rich and the children of the poor. Parental income is no more "relevant" to job performance than is race. People ought to have equal access to jobs regardless of their parents' income. They should also, presumably, have equal access to the prerequisites for jobs, specifically education.

The importance of thinking about the prerequisites as well as about the jobs is evident in the empirical data. Regression analyses show that parental social class, however measured, has very little direct effect on jobs or earnings, once other things are held constant.[13] One interpretation of this finding is that the ideal of social mobility has really been achieved in America, and that we need not worry about discrimination on the basis of parental economic class since it has already been eliminated. But another interpretation is suggested by another fact: parental income is quite strongly related to the amount of education which people get.[14] This interpretation argues that the "other things" which are not equal but instead extremely unequal create a system in which parents' social class is still quite important in determining their children's chances.

Interpretation of data on the relationships between family background and later outcomes is more difficult than interpretation of data on racial differences in outcomes. Unequal results by race raise a strong presumption of actual discrimination, which has historical precedents in more blatant forms. Social class, in contrast, has no such history of blatant use as a discriminatory criterion. Nonetheless, I think that inequality of results in this area is also evidence of a denial of equal opportunity. When they think about racial discrimination, most people are not concerned with the concrete motivations of individual personnel managers. It does not much matter whether the person doing hiring discriminates consciously by race, discriminates unconsciously, or participates in a system which has developed substitute discriminatory criteria; the results are telling. Similarly, it is discriminatory results which are the test of denial of equal opportunity by social class, whether the actual mechanisms involve specific individual discrimination or an elaborate stratification system based on more subtle criteria.

The measure of unequal results in the case of family background is the existence of a positive correlation between a measure of family background, such as parental income, and an outcome measure.[15] At this point it may clarify the issue to look at a simplified hypothetical path diagram (Figure 13–1). (This and later diagrams are hypothetical in that they assume that all the relevant variables can be defined and measured. Actual path diagrams using empirical data can, however, be examined as attempts to approximate the ideal research situation represented by the hypothetical diagrams.) Suppose we are concerned with the effects of family income on occupation, and suppose that the only important intervening variable is education. This model assumes that parental income can influence occupation in only one of two ways, either directly or by influencing education, which in turn influences occupation. Everything else, including intellectual talent and motivation, is assumed to be equally distributed between the categories of parental income. Thus by controlling all other relevant variables, it assumes that equal opportunity implies equal results. To the extent that results are not equal, a denial of equal opportunity is assumed to exist.

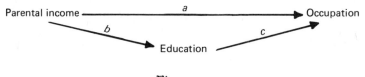

Fig. 13–1.

The path coefficients, represented in Figure 13–1 by letters above the paths, are numbers obtained from regression analyses which express the strength of the relationship between the two variables connected by the path (represented by the arrows). Path coefficients normally fall between 0 and 1. A coefficient of 0 means that there is no relationship between the two variables; a coefficient of 1 (or −1) means that there is a perfect relationship. Intermediate values are harder to interpret, and are not really critical to the present discussion. In general, though, a coefficient of .7 or .8 might be evidence for a strong relationship between the variables; a coefficient of .4 or .5 a modest relationship; and a coefficient of .1 a weak relationship.

Equal opportunity would presumably require that paths *a* and *b* be equal to 0, since that would represent a situation in which neither access to education nor hiring depended on parental income.[16] Path *c* could be greater than 0 in a fair situation, to the extent that education is considered a reasonable criterion to use in allocating status. Demanding that path *b* be zero, while it seems crucial to a sensible definition of equal opportunity, does of course infringe on the "right" of parents to buy education for their children. This is a real problem, since more realistic path models which use real data find that their equivalent of coefficient *b* is generally quite high. It is also a real conflict of principles—and a conflict which becomes even more difficult when the model is expanded.

Let us complicate the model by introducing two more intervening variables, intellectual skill and motivation, and one more background variable, genetic endowment or genotype (Figure 13–2). Again, this is a hypothetical model. Real data suggest that parental income does influence intellectual skills as measured by standardized tests.[17] Nothing is really known about motivation, even though it is always assumed to be an important intervening variable. To make the argument simpler (though some readers may, of course, think it more complicated) I have omitted from Figure 13–2 and the discussion many of the possible paths, such as a direct path from genotype to education. Some I have

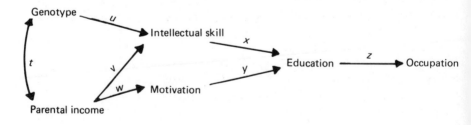

Fig. 13–2.

eliminated because the evidence suggests that they are very small; others because they are of little interest for the argument. For example, I have left out the direct paths from parental income to education and occupation because I assume that most people would agree that equal opportunity would require them to be 0.

Following the logic of the previous argument would seem to require that paths v and w in this diagram from parental income to intellectual skill and motivation be 0, just as it demanded that path b in the previous diagram be 0. It would also seem to require that the correlation t, between parental income and genotype, be 0. But these sorts of requirements seem bizarre.

Motivation does not seem like something which someone is kept from having because of parental income; the lack of motivation cannot, presumably, be traced back to discrimination. But of course in a sense it can. Motivation is influenced by expectations about the future. Expectations, in turn, are shaped by what children see around them, most concretely the successes or failures of their parents. In this sense, parental economic and social circumstances can, albeit indirectly, deprive a child of exposure to those motivational characteristics which in turn influence access to education. Parental income affects intellectual skills similarly. Low parental income is associated with low parental education, which affects the quality of the intellectual environments parents provide for children. Children of high-income parents have two sorts of advantages. They are normally provided with more books, educational toys, travel, and other materials which enhance their intellectual skills. More important, they are usually provided with more intellectual stimulation, more talk, more explanation, more direct and indirect teaching. In these ways, children of low-income parents can be said to be deprived of intellectual skills.

It can be argued then, and often has been by advocates of compensatory education, that equal opportunity demands that there be no relationship between race or parental income and education, despite the variables which intervene to define the relationship. In this view, society has an obligation to compensate for motivational and intellectual differences related to race or class. Unfortunately, the rather limited experiments in compensatory education which have been tried have not been very successful in eliminating these differences. Experience suggests that full compensation would require either massive interventions in the home [18] or measures to retard the progress of the well off. Equality could be achieved, for example, if bright, motivated children were kept out of school for a few years. Neither of these alternatives is particularly appealing to Americans today; [19] both conflict with other important values. The dilemma is a real one.

Genetic Potential

The relationship between parental income and genetic potential also raises difficult questions. Parental income is weakly associated with children's IQ genes,[20] in a kind of circular way. Both children's genetic potential and parental income are related to parental genetic potential. The relationship between parents' and children's genes is obviously quite high; that between parents' genes and parental income is rather weak. Genetic potential seems to have a substantial effect on intellectual skills, though the data is far from conclusive. Intellectual skills, in turn, affect both success in school and the length of time people stay in school. Genetic potential may also affect other characteristics which are conceivably related to economic success: physical appearance and competence, perhaps emotions.

With such a long chain of variables and with the weakness of the relationships at various points in the chain, it is tempting to ignore the whole issue as trivial. The overall connections between beginning and end variables in the chain can be no stronger than the weakest link;[21] the connection between parental income and children's income through genotype, intellectual skills, and education is almost infinitesimal. For public policy purposes the problem is best ignored.

The issues, however, are quite interesting, and a foray into them may illuminate more general notions. Suppose we question why we think economic success can legitimately be denied to people on the basis of their parents' genetic potential, or indeed their own genetic potential. Most people would answer, I am guessing, that the intellectual skills influenced by genetic potential are relevant to job performance and productivity, and are thus legitimate screening devices for schools and employers to use. But are they? The existence of "intellectual skills" as an intervening variable in the path models describing the stratification system in the United States does not mean that the variable is intermediate in any rational way. Imagine, for example, a stratification system which could be diagramed with the variable "height" in the place of intellectual skill. (In fact, relationships involving height do exist in the stratification system and work much the same as intellectual skills. Height is largely determined by genes, is positively related to social class, and is associated, though much less strongly than intellectual skills, with staying in school and getting a good job.) If height were being used as a selection mechanism in schools, we might suspect that it was being used because of its relationship through genotype to parental income, as a not too subtle way of implementing social class discrimination. We would argue that it was irrelevant to success in school and also irrelevant to later jobs, and that this irrelevance, especially in view of its relationship to social class, made it unfair. We would presumably make the argument even if the school system were set up in such a way that height became very important: if, for example, basketball were an important subject, if blackboards were all very high, or if people were seated in such a way that short people's vision was blocked by tall people.

Intellectual skill is probably more legitimately relevant than height in school and in later life. But the relationship is worth exploring. The school system is set up in such a way that quick children succeed. Employers sometimes use standardized mental tests, which essentially measure mental quickness, in hiring. More generally, to the extent that educational credentials are considered in hiring, mental quickness becomes a hiring criterion. Most studies which have been done, however, suggest that there are very few jobs in which intellectual skill as measured by standard tests is related to job performance.[22] These studies raise serious questions about the use of intellectual quickness as a criterion for hiring in most jobs. Literacy and common sense are probably more important, and less dependent on genetic potential. Perhaps both the school system and the hiring system should place more emphasis on these more widely distributed and easily acquired characteristics.

This argument suggests that we ought to consider genetic potential an attribute, like family background, which is essentially irrelevant to performance, and which therefore ought to be ignored as a rationing mechanism. Even more than family background, genetic potential is an attribute over which an individual has no control: a person cannot improve his or her genetic potential by diligence or desire. Like family background, its relevance to performance is limited. Family background and genetic potential might be thought of as lying on a continuum of "relevance." Family background is only slightly relevant, though one can think of jobs in which family background affects performance to some extent; genetic potential is slightly more relevant but by no means determinant in any job and of only modest relevance in most; training is more relevant and its acquisition is more under individual control.

Notions of equal opportunity should probably consider both the relevance of the criteria to the performance of tasks associated with the status and the degree to which the criteria are under individual control. There are, of course, clear cases in which talent is relevant to performance and also partly determined by genetic ability—in dancers, baseball players, musicians, and the like. In these cases, I think most people would consider talent the relevant criterion for selection. In other cases, however, the relevance of talent versus training or motivation is less clear. Managers, for example, can be made as well as born; the kinds of intellectual talents which can be measured by standardized tests

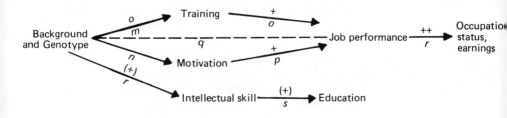

Fig. 13–3.

are relevant but not very relevant. In these fuzzy cases, selection procedures should perhaps give more weight to those qualities over which individuals have some control. Another diagram can illustrate this (Figure 13–3).

Equal opportunity would seem to demand that the relationships between background and genotype and the prerequisites for job performance, hypothesized here to be training and motivation (paths m and n), be o. Training and motivation are expected to influence performance, though not to determine it (thus one plus sign [+] on paths o and p). The dotted line, q, represents an area of uncertainty, where equal opportunity might be defined as demanding careful weighing of the relevance of criteria. Performance under equal opportunity would be the only determinant of occupational status, and would thus show an almost perfect relationship (++ on path r). The only way I can see of reconciling this notion of equal opportunity with the idea that people ought to be able to develop their own talents is to separate education from the status allocation procedures. This separation appears in the lower half of Figure 13–3, which expresses a legitimate relationship among background, genetic potential, intellectual skill, and education.

America today cannot be represented by such a model because the school system's function as a job-training mechanism is not separable from its educational function, and because attempts to measure job performance are seldom made even on the job, not to mention before hiring. One would guess, though, on the basis of other data, that the present relationship between job performance and rewards is not near perfect but indeed quite modest, and that the relationships between background and job prerequisites are not near zero but substantially positive. If this guess is true, bringing about equal opportunity in the broad sense would require dramatic changes in the practices of employers and probably massive public intervention in the family as well. The difficulties are clear.

Fair Procedures

In both philosophical discussions of economic justice and the expressed opinions of ordinary people there is concern about the overall structure of economic positions and statuses. Rainwater's (1974a) respondents, for example, seemed to think that wages could be "too low," were divided on whether income could be "too high," and regarded occupational differentials as fair because of differences in the requirements and the responsibilities of jobs. Their ideas were not tied together in any coherent way, however, and were occasionally inconsistent.

The structural aspects of economic justice are more difficult to deal with conceptually and empirically than equal opportunity. People's standards for evaluating the overall system involve both fair results and fair procedures, qualities which are difficult to disentangle. The problem is further complicated by the acceptance by almost everyone—economist, philosopher, and lay observer alike—of a set of assumptions which are almost surely wrong about how the economic system operates.

Standard economic theory assumes that in a perfectly competitive market economy, people's wages are equal to their "marginal productivity": their wages are equal to the value of what their labor adds to the production of goods. Supply and demand produce an equilibrium in which everyone receives wages precisely equal to what he or she contributes to production. What workers "deserve" is defined very simply as the value of their contribution; under perfect competition workers get what they deserve. The determination of wages under perfect competition is assumed to be fair because it is efficient; a different system would result in lower productivity and lower overall—and average—levels of well-being.

Although the income distribution which results from perfect competition is assumed to be fair in the sense that all workers get what they deserve, welfare economists admit that the distribution may offend our sense of justice in other ways. What a person "deserves" on the basis of his or her economic contribution may not be enough to provide what the community considers a decent standard of living. Through the political process, the society may decide to reallocate some resources, altering the distribution to obtain justice in this other sense, presumably at the cost of some economic efficiency. The society must also decide on a procedure for assessing taxes to finance public spending even in the absence of a transfer program. Tax and transfer decisions are considered essentially political decisions which can be illuminated but never resolved by economic analysis.

The philosopher John Rawls (1971) follows a basically similar line of argument. His formulation of principles of justice seems at first glance quite different from those used by economists:

Social and economic inequalities are to be arranged so that they are . . . attached to offices and positions open to all under conditions of fair equality of opportunity. (p. 302)

Social and economic inequalities are to be arranged so that they are . . . to the greatest benefit of the least advantaged, consistent with the just savings principle (p. 302)

But in later discussions Rawls uses his criterion of benefiting the least advantaged only at the stage of tax and transfer policy, not as a standard for evaluating the initial distribution of goods.[23] Rawls, like traditional economists, assumes that a perfectly competitive market economy will allocate wages as they are deserved in terms of productive contributions. He apparently believes that equality of opportunity will guarantee fairness in the competitive system: Since people's abilities to contribute will be made equal, wage differentials will reflect differences in experience, motivation, hard work, willingness to do disagreeable work, and willingness to engage in long or difficult training—all reasonable criteria, to be sure. This procedurally "fair" distribution can then be modified in Rawls' just society by tax and transfer policies designed in accordance with the principle of benefiting the least advantaged. He argues that a tax and transfer system designed to benefit the least advantaged will probably not involve a large proportion of total resources, since this would destroy the incentive structure and presumably work to the ultimate disadvantage of the least advantaged.

The analyses of both the welfare economists and Rawls have the advantage, perhaps also implicit in the judgments of Rainwater's sample, of focusing on procedures rather than on individual cases. It would be close to impossible to formulate and apply a comprehensive set of principles for judging whether or not each particular wage of each particular worker in each particular industry and region of the country were fair. A wage determination system based on a simple procedure like the competitive market and then tinkered with to produce ultimately just results is conceptually and politically simpler, and thus preferable to one which must deal with innumerable substantive principles and idiosyncratic cases.

Unfortunately there is no reason to believe that the competitive market procedures beloved of economists bear any resemblance to the actual procedures which determine wages in our own society or in any society conceivable in the reasonably near future. America does not and probably will not have free competitive markets for labor. This situation may not always have been so. In the nineteenth and early twentieth century, when much economic analysis was developed, a large proportion of the work force was engaged either in farming or in small business or trade. In these economic arenas, competition is important and incomes can be said to reflect productivity in some broad sense.

Today's economy is, however, quite different, with the majority of workers' wages set by other than competitive processes. Ninety percent of all workers are on nonagricultural payrolls, neither farmers nor self-employed businessmen. Almost a fifth are employed by the government, with earnings prescribed by civil service rules. A quarter are union members, whose wages are bargained and set by contract. How the wages of the other 55 percent are set is not so easily discovered. It seems reasonable to argue, though, that union wage contracts influence wages of nonunion workers as well, and that the conventional standards for an occupation or industry reflect one or another bargained scale. It is difficult to think of situations in which wages directly reflect productivity in a competitive market. The wages of salespeople on commission or assembly workers paid by the piece are among the few examples which come readily to mind. Even these examples are not clear-cut, however, since the basic piece work or commission rates are determined by other procedures.

Pure market determination of wages is hard to imagine in a modern society. It is difficult to conceive of work today as a process of selling labor to the highest bidder. Not is it clear that we consider such contracts fair. Notions of fair labor practices which limit contract rights have developed through collective bargaining and have been embodied in labor law.[24] Employers are effectively prohibited from cutting wages arbitrarily, just as they are effectively prohibited from laying people off without good reason and without some regard for agreed-upon principles of fairness in determining who is to be laid off. Similarly, workers are effectively prohibited from negotiating individual wage contracts which undercut the position of their fellow workers. Thus employers and workers are considered in both law and practice not as parties negotiating individual contracts but as members of institutions defined in part by negotiated procedures and standards of fair practice.

In institutions where wages are not determined by individual contracts in a competitive market, it becomes quite difficult to describe a procedure for establishing wage differentials which people would agree was fair. One possibly appropriate approach would be to apply to wage determination procedures the standards used to evaluate the fairness of governmental administrative decisions. The American economy is largely controlled by corporations and unions large enough to be aptly described as "private governments." To some extent the notion that economic institutions have a governmental character is already implicit in labor law: management is expected to specify clear rules of conduct and to enforce them equally, to give notice of changes in rules, to incorporate some due process standards into disciplinary and dismissal hearings, and so on.[25] Analogously, wage scales can be judged as to whether they are clear, public, nonarbitrary, and applied consistently to individual workers. Pushing the analogy between governmental and economic institutions one step further raises questions of economic democracy as well as economic fairness. Wage scales might be evaluated according to the democracy of the procedure by which they were determined: the degree of participation, responsiveness of representatives, accountability, equality of bargaining power.

Needless to say, political standards are not easy to apply. The proper scale of the bargaining unit and the rights of management must be determined. Moreover, the question of what is to be bargained must be raised: is the object to be bargained the total wage package (as it is now), specific wage differentials (which would seem necessary for economic fairness), or the definition of jobs? In a political procedure, questions of the rights which accrue to people because of their ownership of capital become crucial. To what extent does the ownership of capital which is necessary for production give the owner rights over the workers as well? And are there rights of workers which ought to be kept out of the bargaining process, rights which they ought not be able to bargain away?

Empirical data for assessing how well wage determination procedures meet fair political standards are even harder to get than definitions of the standards themselves. One method of investigation would involve descriptive studies of bargaining procedures, with close attention to power relationships, representativeness, and so on. Other hints come from examining criteria which bargained contracts now incorporate or on which a fair political procedure might be assumed to rely. Bargained contracts, for example, incorporate criteria which are objective and public, and which can be applied to individual cases relatively straightforwardly—e.g., experience. A fair contract could also, presumably, define fair procedures for the application of more subjective criteria. For example, the parties to the agreement might want to reward good work with higher wages. Since good work is a subjective evaluation, they would presumably specify clear procedures for making the evaluation, such as demanding two or more independent evaluations, a peer review board, a grievance procedure, or other such procedures. (The reluctance of teachers' organizations even to entertain the idea of merit pay suggests that agreement on these principles would be very hard to reach.)

Taking this argument, tenuous though it is, one step further, one can examine the extent to which the criteria which would presumably be agreed upon in a fair political procedure actually determine the existing wage structure. It seems probable that job title, competence as evaluated by a peer or supervisor review committee, training, and experience would be agreed-on relevant criteria for assessing the fairness of earnings differentials. It might also be argued that need should affect overall income, though it might not enter wage negotiations (see Figure 13–4). In a fair situation we would expect all the paths in Figure 13–4 to have quite large coefficients; i.e., for all the relationships to be strong. Moreover, we would expect all the variables taken together to account for income almost completely. Other influences on income would be presumed to be either irrelevant or random.

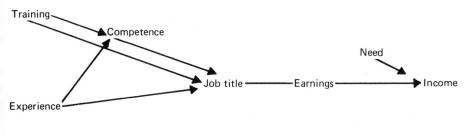

Fig. 13–4.

Data is not available to evaluate Figure 13–4 precisely. The available evidence suggests that training, experience, and job title are to some extent associated with earnings. Need, as estimated by number of people in the family, has a slightly negative rather than positive relation to income. Competence is very difficult to measure, so no trustworthy relationships have been established.[26] None of the research succeeds in explaining very much of the variation in income using variables similar to the ones in the model. Studies which include background variables as well as the variables in the above model tend to explain somewhere between 23 (Jencks, 1972) and 43 (Morgan et al., 1974) percent of the variance in earnings. Part of the residual can undoubtedly be explained by measurement error, but it still appears that the relatively modest coefficients on what we consider relevant variables indicate that the existing system departs considerably from standards of fairness.

Mary Jo Bane

Economic Justice and Public Policy

Perhaps the only conclusion which can be drawn from the above analysis is that complete economic justice is an unattainable goal, at least in the foreseeable future. Equality of opportunity, defined broadly, can only be obtained if society is prepared to advocate massive intrusion into the private lives of its citizens: to manipulate genes, or raise children apart from their parents, or prohibit talented children from going to school, or completely restructure training, credentialing, and job allocation procedures.

Justice in wage determination procedures is equally elusive. A market system, even if it were compatible with a modern economy, would only be fair if capital were owned very broadly and if access to ownership of capital were equal. There are obvious conflicts between these principles of capital dispersion and rights of ownership. But independent of any conflicts of principle, the just situation seems so far from our present society as to make speculation about it fanciful.

A political view of the wage determination process also runs into problems arising from the ownership of capital. Political bargaining processes in economic life, moreover, have all the inherent pitfalls of bargaining and voting procedures in political life. Participation is hard to define and even harder to achieve. The appropriate decision-making unit is hard to define. Since bargaining would presumably take place in rather small units—often individual firms—all the problems of external effects with which we are familiar from the operation of local governments would arise.

We are clearly doomed to a world of imperfect economic institutions. An important implication of this fact is that political institutions for redistribution are not a temporary remedial necessity but a vital part of a fair system. The system, even if made considerably more fair than it now is, has no inherent guarantee of producing a distribution which people would characterize as just. There are serious conflicts between equal opportunity and individual freedom and between procedural justice and ownership of property which preclude full realization of what we would call a fair system.

Unfortunately, there is no consensus and precious little informed argument on what to do in the absence of equal opportunity and fair procedures. A few things do seem to be clear, however. There is very little sentiment in American public opinion for expropriating the wealth of the rich to redistribute to the poor. In one sense, the absence of such a sentiment is strange. Under democratic majority rule procedures a coalition of low- and middle-income people could presumably band

296

together and agree to expropriate for common use the resources of the rich. If money were taken from the top 40 percent, say, and given to the lower 60 percent, a majority of Americans would benefit. Under most proposed redistribution schemes, in fact, the majority of Americans would benefit. A scheme like McGovern's $1,000 a year credit tax would have benefited the lower 85 percent of American families. Only a small proportion would have been hurt.

Yet public opinion polls usually reveal opposition to guaranteed income plans. A recent poll (Rodgers, 1974) which assessed sentiment for a guaranteed income found that only about 30 percent of the respondents favored a guarantee of $3,200. Only 43 percent of respondents with incomes less than $3,000—people who would certainly benefit under such a plan—favored it (Rodgers, 1974, p. 192). This suggests that people either don't understand their self-interest very well or are taking other things into account. There is little evidence on what these other things might be, but a number of possible explanations come to mind. One seems to be the name of the scheme and the character of the person espousing the plan. The above poll was taken when McGovern was advocating a guaranteed income. When Nixon proposed FAP, support for the proposal rose. There may also be more substantial reasons for opposition. People may think a guaranteed income wouldn't work; that the rich have too much power to ever let it happen. Or they may aspire for themselves and their children to be rich and may not want to destroy their own chances, however remote. Or they may think that the rich deserve their money by having worked hard to get it; taking it away would not be fair. Whatever the reasons, and however false the assumptions on which they are based, it seems that Americans are largely unenthusiastic about a purely political redistribution from rich to poor.[27]

It seems equally clear that there are some redistributive actions which Americans feel ought to be taken. A large majority approves of public provision of jobs: 79 percent in one poll favored a program "that would guarantee enough work to families with employable wage earners that a yearly income of $3200 could be earned" (Rodgers, 1974, p. 196). Americans also seem to approve of providing necessary goods to the poor. About two-thirds of the respondents in yet another poll approved of a proposal to expand the food stamp program (Rodgers, 1974, p. 195). Although it is economically more efficient to provide relief in the form of money rather than goods, Americans seem much more willing to go the latter route. Perhaps giving food is seen as an acceptable form of public charity which is still consistent with the general principle that people should receive money only if they work.

To the extent that redistribution means self-interested political action against the rich, then, Americans seem to oppose it. To the extent that redistribution is charity, Americans seem to favor it only to the very limited extent of providing some support to those unable to work. There is a third way of looking at redistribution which may ultimately prove more productive, both conceptually and politically. This is a view of redistribution as a kind of insurance.[28] The insurance notion is embodied in social security and unemployment compensation programs, both of which have widespread support. Presumably the insurance notion could be extended to other sorts of economic difficulties, including low income. Approval of an insurance scheme can surely be imagined in a Rawls-like "original situation" in which no one knows what his or her own position in society will be or what catastrophes he or she may face. Unless people are greater gamblers than I think they are, people in an original situation would presumably agree to insure themselves to some extent against misfortune, with those who are economically lucky at any given time paying into a fund to support the unlucky at a decent level.

An insurance scheme could probably only be implemented in the real, nonoriginal situation, if there were substantially more intergenerational and intrapersonal economic mobility than there appears to be now. An insurance scheme rests on self-interested cushioning against risks, not on charity. People's self-interest characteristically extends only to themselves and their children. Those who are assured of their own positions and those of their children have no incentive for supporting an insurance scheme. Perhaps the real importance of continual pressure for equality of opportunity and fair procedures lies in this area: if people come to believe their places are not secure they will develop more comprehensive procedures for insuring themselves and their kind against disaster. Though this kind of road to economic justice seems convoluted and messy, perhaps it is the best we can do.

NOTES

1. Most of the earlier literature was reviewed in *Inequality* and is cited in footnotes and references. Data on income is published annually, cross-tabulated in useful ways, by the Current Population Survey (e.g., U.S. Bureau of the Census, 1973b). Data from the 1970 census is published, for example in *Sources and Structure of Family Income* (U.S. Bureau of the Census, 1973a), and is also available on magnetic tape. A useful book, relying also on cross-tabulations, is Bluestone et al. (1973). However, analyses of the determinants of economic success cannot proceed

ECONOMIC JUSTICE: CONTROVERSIES AND POLICIES

very far using only census data. Estimating models of wage determination and social stratification requires data sets which include measures not only of current status but also of education, parental background, and, preferably, test scores. Only a few data sets meet these requirements; several were used in *Inequality*, and there is one important new one.

The analyses in *Inequality*, as in Blau and Duncan (1967), relied heavily on the 1962 census survey, "Occupational Change in a Generation." Further work with this data set is reported in Duncan et al. (1972). A second important data set is the longitudinal study of Wisconsin high school seniors, begun in 1957 and followed up in 1964. A complete report on analysis of this data, reaching conclusions similar to those in *Inequality* and Blau and Duncan, is Sewell and Hauser (1975). A sample of veterans born between 1927 and 1934 and tested on the AFQT between 1949 and 1953 was followed up in 1964 through social security records. Results are reported in Cutright (1972). A series of articles by economists on "Investment in Education" was carried by the *Journal of Political Economy* in May/June 1972. Of special interest in that issue is Griliches and Mason, who analyze the determinants of economic success among veterans. Taubman and Wales, in the 1973 May/June issue of the *Journal of Political Economy* report on a different sample of veterans (volunteers who took the Aviation Cadet Qualifying Test in 1943) with similar results. An interesting look at the relationship between schooling and early occupational status is provided by Alexander and Eckland (1973). A good summary of much of the previous research, and comparable results from a large sample surveyed by Melvin Kohn for the National Institute of Mental Health, are reported in Spaeth (1974). Interestingly, similar coefficients are found in analysis of an excellent Swedish longitudinal data set (original data from 1,500 Malmo third-graders in 1938, with a 98 percent follow-up rate) reported in Bulcock et al. (1974).

A new data set, the Panel Study of Income Dynamics conducted by the Survey Research Center of the University of Michigan, is now being used in some of the most interesting current work on social stratification and the determinants of income. The Panel Study followed a sample of households over five years and collected an enormous amount of information on demographic and background characteristics, attitudes, income, and consumption. Analyses of this data done by the Michigan group are reported in Morgan et al. (1974). The Panel Study has also been analyzed by Rainwater (1974b) in an unpublished manuscript. Since Rainwater's analysis of the Panel Study is comparable to the analysis of the OCG reported in *Inequality*, I cite it quite often in this paper as a source of estimates of the effects of background and schooling variables. Since the Panel Study data is not only more recent but also better in many respects than the OCG data, I consider Rainwater's estimates more accurate than those in *Inequality*. Jencks and Rainwater are currently reanalyzing the Panel Study data and several other data sources. Preliminary results from their project on "The Determinants of Economic Success" should be available in 1975.

2. Rainwater (1974b) and Morgan et al. (1974), using data from the five-year Michigan Panel Study of Income Dynamics.

3. Working-class, lower-middle-class, and upper-middle-class respondents gave similar answers. There were, however, large differences of opinion among the respondents, as indicated by the size of the standard deviations around the mean. Means and standard deviations for the hypothetical occupation groups were as follows: 150 at lower skill levels, mean = $6,865, s.d. = (3,010); 400 at average working man level, 8,194 (2,563); 250 at white-collar level, 9,838 (3,230); 150 at middle management and professional level, $15,812 (7,890); 50 at top management level, 32,258 (31,352).

4. See for example, Lane (1962). Similar ideas about fairness, though not with regard to income, were expressed in a survey of employees reported in Selznick

299

Mary Jo Bane

(1969). For example, respondents were asked to check the phrase which seemed to them to describe best the meaning of fair treatment. Forty-one percent checked "getting the same treatment that other employees get—no favoritism"; 53 percent checked "having one's abilities recognized by management"; 14 percent said "having management live up to its promises"; and 2 percent checked other reasons. Justice is not an easy notion to define.

5. These principles are consistent, I think, with the difference principle proposed by John Rawls (1971) and discussed later in the paper.

6. Title VII of the Civil Rights Act as amended by the Equal Employment Opportunity Act of 1972.

7. 401 U.S. 424 (1971).

8. For a good discussion of the case and its implications, see Huff (1974).

9. For some interesting manipulations with these concepts, see Boudon (1973).

10. Technically, there are two ways of doing this. One procedure is to enter dummy variables for race and sex in the overall regression equations. The coefficient of the dummy variable is an estimate of racial discrimination. The other procedure is to run separate equations for races or sexes, substitute the means for one group in the equation for the other, and estimate discrimination from the residual. This second technique allows for the possibility that the relationships between variables as well as the variable levels may differ by race. Whether the relationships actually do vary is not clear. Duncan (1968) and Jencks (1972) found different equations; Rainwater (1974b), using the Michigan data and log income as the dependent variable, did not.

11. Studies of the black-white gap include Duncan (1968) and Masters (1974). The size of the gap varies considerably with the particular samples studied. Studies of young men using the Parnes National Longitudinal Survey data, for example Freeman (1974) and Griliches (1974), have found no racial gap for young, non-southern men. My estimates for the male-female earnings gap come from an excellent unpublished (and untitled) review of the literature by Mary Corcoran, Center for the Study of Public Policy, Cambridge, Mass. A good recent review is Sawhill (1973).

12. See, for example, Morgan et al. (1974) and Duncan et al. (1972).

13. The direct effect is measured by the coefficient of the direct path from parental income, occupation, or education to occupation or earnings. Some representative paths are as follows: .085 from father's occupation to respondent's occupation in Jencks et al. (1972, p. 346); .117 from family background (a measure which included race) to income in Rainwater (1974b, p. 40); .07 from father's education to respondent's wage rate in Morgan et al. (1974), p. 130.

14. The size of the effect is measured by the path coefficient from parental background to education. Jencks et al. (1972) estimated the path from "family background," a hypothetical construct, to education as between .566 and .604. Rainwater (1974) estimates a path coefficient of .578 from family background to schooling. These are large coefficients by anybody's estimate. It should perhaps be noted here that this discussion looks at individual coefficients rather than at overall variance, which was the concern of *Inequality*. At this point I am trying to use the *Inequality* data to speak to the opportunity issue, not to estimate the importance of doing so. The overall variance is, I think, relevant to a somewhat different conception of economic fairness which is discussed later in the paper.

15. In the case of race, simple percentage differences between groups can be looked at, a procedure which could also be used to look at differences between categories of parental income. Since categories distort the reality, which is continuous rather than categorical, the correlation coefficient is a better measure.

16. In this case, of course, the correlation coefficient would also be 0.

17. Jencks et al. (1972) suggested that the path from the hypothetical family

background variable to IQ had a coefficient of .348. The compound path from background to education through IQ was estimated at about .1. Thus the influence of background on education through IQ is considerably less important than the direct influence of background on education.

18. Heber and Garber (1970), for example, seem to have been successful in compensating for the deficiencies of deprived children. Unfortunately, their program requires taking children away from parents and providing them with full-time intensive professional caretakers. Doing this on a large scale would certainly be expensive and probably would not be tolerated.

19. Including myself, to be honest about my preferences. The argument can be made on the grounds of practicality, however, without getting into the strengths and defects of the family.

20. Jencks et al. (1972) estimate the coefficient at about .15.

21. In calculating compound paths, the coefficients of the component paths, for example u, x, and z in Figure 13-2, are multiplied. Jencks et al. (1972, p. 350) estimate the compound paths from children's genotype to eventual income as somewhere between .14 and .18. These are small numbers, and they are made smaller yet when the parental paths are multiplied in as well. Taubman (1974), analyzing a large and previously unexplored twin sample, estimated that genetic endowments of all sorts explain about 20 percent of the variance in earnings. His is the highest estimate I have seen, except for Herrnstein's (1973), which is almost surely wrong.

22. The best compendium of research on this subject is the Labor Department's report on validation studies with its General Aptitude Test Battery (U.S. Dept. of Labor, 1967). Several hundred studies are reported. There are few correlations in the book higher than .3. See also Ghiselli (1966) and Huff (1974).

23. See primarily Chap. 5, "Distributive Shares" (Rawls, 1971).

24. Philip Selznick's book, *Law, Society and Industrial Justice* (1969), describes what he calls the change from contract-based to status-based notions of fair labor practices. He argues that the status notion is an old one, replaced for only a brief time by the rampant economic contractualism of the late nineteenth century. Though Selznick does not discuss wage determination, his notions of industrial justice are extremely relevant to a discussion of fair labor standards for wage determination procedures.

25. A good deal of data on these practices, as seen by employers, employees, and labor lawyers, is presented in Selznick (1969).

26. The best attempt to examine the role of noncognitive worker characteristics is contained in Edwards (1972). He found positive relationships among wages, supervisors' ratings and peer ratings of dependability, rule orientation, and internalization of enterprise goals.

27. This entire discussion borrows ideas and data from Rodgers (1974).

28. For discussions of this notion, see Rodgers (1974) and also Zeckhauser (1974) and Polinsky (1974).

REFERENCES

Alexander, Karl, and Ekland, Bruce. *Effects of Education on the Social Mobility of High School Sophomores Fifteen Years Later (1955–1970)*. Institute for Research in Social Science, University of North Carolina, 1973.

Mary Jo Bane

Blau, Peter, and Duncan, Otis Dudley. *The American Occupational Structure.* New York: Wiley, 1967.

Bluestone, Barry; Murphy, William M.; and Stevenson, Mary. *Low Wages and the Working Poor.* Policy Papers on Human Resources and Industrial Relations 22. Ann Arbor, Mich.: Institute of Labor and Industrial Relations, 1973.

Boudon, Raymond. *Education, Opportunity and Social Inequality.* New York: Wiley, 1973.

Bulcock, Jeffrey W.; Fagerlind, Ingemar; and Emanuelsson, Ingemar. "Research Notes on the Resource Conversion Properties of Family, School-Occupational Environments in Models of the Socioeconomic Career." Mimeographed. University of Stockholm, 1974.

Cutright, Phillips. "Achievement, Mobility and the Draft: Their Impact on the Earnings of Men." HEW Social Security Administration Staff Paper #14, 1972.

Duncan, Otis Dudley. "Inheritance of Poverty or Inheritance of Race." In *On Understanding Poverty,* edited by Daniel P. Moynihan. New York: Basic Books, 1968.

———; Featherman, David; and Duncan, Beverly. *Socioeconomic Background and Achievement.* New York: Seminar Press, 1972.

Edwards, Richard C. "Alienation and Inequality: Capitalist Relations of Production in Bureaucratic Enterprises." Ph.D. dissertation, Harvard University, 1972.

Freeman, R. B. "Social Mobility in the 'New Market' for Black Labor." Unpublished paper. Harvard University, 1974.

Ghiselli, Edwin E. *The Validity of Occupational Tests.* New York: Wiley, 1966.

Griliches, Zvi. "Wages and Earnings of Very Young Men: A Preliminary Report." Unpublished paper, Harvard University, 1974.

———, and Mason, William M. "Education, Income and Ability." *Journal of Political Economy* 80, no. 3, pt. II (1972).

Heber, Rich., and Garber, H. "An Experiment in the Prevention of Cultural-familial Mental Retardation," 1, 2, 3. Grant No. 16-P 56811/5-06 from the Rehabilitation Services Administration of HEW, Washington, D.C., 1970.

Herrnstein, R. J. *IQ in the Meritocracy.* Boston: Atlantic–Little, Brown, 1973.

Huff, Sheila. "Credentialing by Tests or by Degrees: Title VII of the Civil Rights Act and Griggs v. Duke Power Company." *Harvard Educational Review* 44, no. 2 (1974): 246–269.

Jencks, Christopher, et al. *Inequality: A Reassessment of the Effects of Family and Schooling in America.* New York: Basic Books, 1972.

Lane, Robert E. *Political Ideology.* New York: The Free Press, 1962.

Masters, Stanley H. "The Effect of Educational Differences and Labor-Market Discrimination on the Relative Earnings of Black Males." *Journal of Human Resources* 9, no. 3 (1974): 376–389.

Morgan, James N., et al. *Five Thousand American Families—Patterns of Economic Progress,* vols. I and II. Ann Arbor, Mich.: Survey Research Center, Institute for Social Research, University of Michigan, 1974.

Polinsky, A. Mitchell. "Imperfect Capital Markets, Intertemporal Redistribution and Progressive Taxation." In *Redistribution Through Public Choice,* edited by Harold M. Hochman and George Peterson. New York: Columbia University Press, 1974.

Rainwater, Lee. *What Money Buys: Inequality and the Social Meaning of Income.* New York: Basic Books, 1974a.

———. "A Model of Household Heads' Income: 1967–1971." Mimeographed. 1974b.

Rawls, John. *A Theory of Justice.* Cambridge, Mass.: Harvard University Press, 1971.

Rodgers, James D. "Explaining Income Redistribution." In *Redistribution Through Public Choice,* edited by Harold M. Hochman and George Peterson. New York: Columbia University Press, 1974.

Sawhill, Isabel. "The Economics of Discrimination Against Women: Some New Findings." *Journal of Human Resources*, Summer 1973.

Selznick, Philip. *Law, Society and Industrial Justice*. New York: Russell Sage Foundation, 1969.

Sewell, William H., and Hauser, Robert M. *Education, Occupation, and Earnings: Achievement in Early Career*. New York: Academic Press, 1975.

Spaeth, Joe L. "Characteristics of the Work Setting and the Job as Determinants of Income." Mimeographed. Survey Research Laboratory, University of Illinois at Urbana-Champaign, 1974.

Taubman, Paul. "The Determinants of Earnings: A Study of White Male Twins." Unpublished paper, University of Pennsylvania, 1974.

———, and Wales, Terence J. "Higher Education, Mental Ability and Screening." *Journal of Political Economy* 81, no. 1 (1973): 28–55.

U.S. Bureau of the Census. Census of Population: 1970, Subject Reports, Final Report PC(2)-8A, *Sources and Structure of Family Income*. Washington, D.C.: U.S. Government Printing Office, 1973a.

U.S. Bureau of the Census. *Current Population Reports*. Series P-60, No. 90, "Money Income in 1972 of Families and Persons in the United States." Washington, D.C.: U.S. Government Printing Office, 1973b.

United States Department of Labor. *Manual for the General Aptitude Test Battery*. Washington, D.C.: U.S. Government Printing Office, 1967.

Zeckhauser, Richard. "Risk Spreading and Distribution." In *Redistribution Through Public Choice*, edited by Harold M. Hochman and George Peterson. New York: Columbia University Press, 1974.

(14)

"Inequality"
and the Analysis of
Educational Policy

Donald M. Levine

BECAUSE it seeks to make a comprehensive assessment of the causes of inequality in America, *Inequality* has important implications for the policy maker in education. For educational policy, the most relevant of Jencks' conclusions is that "Equalizing opportunity is almost impossible without greatly reducing the absolute level of inequality, and the same is true of eliminating deprivation." [1] Part of the reason for this statement is that background factors are much more important to cognitive development than school resources. Part of it is that, judged by the standard of more equal results, equal opportunity is irrelevant; results are a consequence of luck and peculiar competence unrelated to skill or training. For those concerned with allocating educational resources, the lesson is that school resources have only small, inconsistent effects on cognitive development, and even less significant effects on a person's income. Consequently, analyzing education in terms of the "factory model" that underlies input-output studies is a mistake. Rather, policy makers in the future should think in terms of the "internal life" of schools. The major criterion for school effectiveness should become the quality of school life, and the major goal of educational policy should be an equal distribution of those resources that contribute to the pleasantness of schooling.

These are radical conclusions, and they entail enormous changes in the ways that we look at schooling and formulate policy. They merit

An earlier version of this paper appeared in the *Teachers College Record*, December 1973.

close examination. It is the purpose of this paper to scrutinize the analyses and interpretations that appear in *Inequality* and thereby to indicate profitable directions for future educational policy and policy analysis. Specifically, the paper will first assess *Inequality's* approach to educational goals and the methodological consequences of that approach. Then it will comment on the book's analysis of school effectiveness. Third, it will deal with its account of the social utility of education. Finally, it will bring together the conclusions of the preceding sections and attempt to make some recommendations for the future.

The Goals of Schooling

Inequality's mission is to demonstrate that in the search for economic equality, schooling is a red herring. It only diverts attention from the real issue of direct income redistribution. As Jencks summarized it, "*Inequality* is a short book (192 pages of text) with quite limited objectives. It sought to show that equalizing opportunity, especially educational opportunity, would not do much to reduce economic inequality or reduce poverty."[2] Jencks and his associates decide to show this by criticizing a national policy—waging a war on poverty through education—for which they reconstruct and then disprove the rationale. Briefly, *Inequality's* version of the rationale proposes that:

1. Eliminating poverty is largely a matter of helping children born into poverty rise out of it.
2. Poor children do not escape from poverty [because] they do not acquire basic cognitive skills. . . . Lacking these skills, they cannot get or keep a well-paid job.
3. The best mechanism for breaking the vicious circle is educational reform. Since children born into poor homes do not acquire the skills they need from their parents, they must be taught these skills in schools. . . .[3]

This policy is something of a straw man, and the reconstructed rationale confuses two themes in the evolution of national educational policy.

With the goal of reducing poverty, the federal government in the 1960s expanded a variety of old programs and introduced a number of new ones, only some of which were school programs. The government's commitment to increasing cognitive—and, ostensibly, economic—equality through school reform was much lower than its commitment to alternative schemes. As Alice Rivlin has remarked:

Donald M. Levine

It is not my perception that education reform directed at reducing inequality has been a national policy commanding wide support or substantial resources. . . . [*Inequality's*] contention is that . . . inequality in cognitive achievement has remained the same. This would be surprising only if appreciable resources had been devoted to bringing about some other result and no evidence is presented to show this is so.[4]

Rivlin's perception draws support from an analysis of the federal budget, 40 percent of which goes for transfers and only 2 percent for education.[5] Indeed, the priorities of the Great Society and those of succeeding administrations consistently have emphasized transfers in cash and in kind as the primary tool for reducing economic inequality. In 1963, older income maintenance programs (social security and retirement programs, cash public assistance, veterans' benefits, and unemployment benefits) were budgeted at $28.4 billion, or 25 percent of all federal expenditures, and Great Society programs at $1.7 billion, or 2 percent of total federal expenditures. In the same year education claimed only $5.23 million of the federal budget, less than one-tenth of 1 percent. Federal budget projections for 1973 indicated that older income maintenance programs would account for $74.9 billion, or 29 percent of all federal expenditures, and Great Society transfer programs (housing subsidies, Medicare, Medicaid, food stamps, school lunches, and direct student loans and scholarships) would account for $20 billion, or about 8 percent.[6] In the same year educational programs were budgeted at $4.8 billion, or something less than 2 percent of the total.[7] This ordering of priorities is different from the one *Inequality* implies, and it seems to show more progress toward socialism—that is, income redistribution —than the book notes.

More important is the confusion between equality of opportunity and equality of results that is exemplified in the reconstructed rationale, which assumes economic equality as the goal of educational policy. As Jencks recounts the objectives of the Great Society programs:

During the 1960's, reformers devoted enormous effort to equalizing opportunity. More specifically, they tried to eliminate inequalities based on skin color, and to a lesser extent on economic background. They also wanted to eliminate absolute deprivation: "poverty," "ignorance," "powerlessness," and so forth.[8]

Most of these programs sought to increase mobility by removing the artificial barriers that seemed to hold back particular groups like blacks, other ethnic minorities, and in some cases, the poor. Since poverty was thought to be a problem of "pockets"—of ethnically or geographically defined groups with an isolated, self-renewing culture of poverty—attainment of equal opportunity as well as the solution to poverty seemed linked to increased mobility, which by definition would eliminate poverty pockets. The problem was not seen as structural, so it did not call for a basic rearrangement of society; it was thought to be secular, and therefore capable of being solved by the elimination of barriers to mobility. It is important to note that the concepts of equal opportunity and of eliminating absolute deprivation were different. The former had roots in the notion of a basic freedom that forbids arbitrary distinctions among persons; the latter referred more to an ideal of social justice that finds deprivation morally unacceptable. The two concepts were related, but not in a causal and sufficient way.

Inequality attempts to show that equality of results is the prerequisite for equality of opportunity. But this argument is problematical, especially if the issue is equality of educational opportunity. The prior problem is that of defining equal opportunity. As Jencks and his associates note:

Most Americans . . . believe in what they often call "equal opportunity." By this they mean that the rules determining who succeeds and who fails should be fair. . . . The general principle of fair competition is almost universally endorsed.[9]

Equal opportunity, then, ensures *unequal* results, which proceed from competition. Through inherited advantage, those unequal results may limit the opportunity of succeeding generations. But the first and most relevant question is *why* those results are unequal. Are they unequal even though the rules are fair, or because arbitrary distinctions among persons are involved? This is a question of values. If legislation is any guide, Americans obviously feel that racial rules are unfair. The same cannot be said for rules relating to competence, seniority, or inherited wealth.[10]

The problem for policy makers addressing the goal of equal educational opportunity is further complicated by the evolution of that special concept. From the first, it had a mixed rationale. As James Coleman has noted:

The actual decision of the Court [in *Brown*] was in fact a confusion of two unrelated premises: this new concept, which looked at results of schooling, and the legal premise that the use of race as a basis for school assignment violates fundamental freedoms. . . . I believe the decision would have been more soundly based had it not depended on the effects of schooling, but only on the violation of freedom; but by introducing the question of the effects of schooling, the Court brought into the open the implicit goals of equality of educational opportunity—that is, goals having to do with the *results* of school. . . .[11]

In time, the concept of "*effective* equality of opportunity, that is, equality in those elements that are effective for learning,"[12] came to dominate the definition so completely that it led to the concept of compensatory education, i.e., unequal resource allocation for the sake of more equal school results. The idea of fundamental freedoms seemed to have taken second place.

Underlying this evolution was a concern for more equal occupational opportunity and, ultimately, more equal results in terms of income and occupational status. But in line with earlier ideas about deprivation, this concern was basically negative and related to the plight of minority groups: it sought to help those groups hurdle occupational barriers more easily, not to influence directly the distributions of income and occupational status. Again, the goal of equal educational opportunity must be seen in the context of American attitudes toward opportunity; our society "values self-reliance and eschews doles for the able-bodied and government intervention in the wage system." [13]

More formally expressed, concern with effective equality of educational opportunity as measured by cognitive achievement grew from the perception that such equality might be a necessary—but by no means a sufficient—condition for equality of results.[14] Thus it is a mistake to assume, as *Inequality*'s version of the liberal rhetoric does, that equality of educational opportunity should be judged by equality of results; equality of educational opportunity, like general equality of opportunity, hopes to ensure that whatever inequalities do result from success or failure in educational and job competition actually relate to competence or some other desired quality rather than to arbitrary qualities, such as skin color, or qualities for which a person is not responsible, such as family background.

The issue of how equality of opportunity is related to equality of results is crucial because it determines *Inequality*'s analytical method, which focuses on *intragroup* rather than *intergroup* differences. Jencks and his associates warn that:

This accounts for much of the discrepancy between our conclusions and those of others who have examined the same data. There is always far more in equality between individuals than between groups. It follows that when we compare the degree of inequality between groups to the degree of inequality between individuals, inequality between groups often seems relatively unimportant.[15]

Clearly, concentration on intragroup differentials lies at the heart of *Inequality*'s findings. But it is a direct consequence of the mistaken view that equality of opportunity should be measured by equality of results. It seems to ignore the reason for which Americans first became concerned with equality of opportunity—that is, the perception of systematic discrimination based on obvious group characteristics. Concern with intergroup differences does not exclude concern with intragroup differences, but it probably takes precedence, especially since those differences still are so prevalent. As Beverly Duncan has summarized it:

Whenever we define groups in terms of a characteristic which we believe should be unrelated to economic success and find an appreciable between-group difference in income, there is cause for concern. I am inclined to think that our concern should be no less whatever the degree of income inequality among all individuals. As a national goal, reducing differences among groups may well take priority over reducing differences among individuals.[16]

When Jencks observes that the 50 percent difference in the income of black and white workers is less disturbing than a 600 percent difference between the best- and worst-paid fifths of all workers,[17] he is speaking in a strictly quantitative sense. The *reasons* for those two differences, insofar as we know them, make the first and smaller one much more disturbing, for it proceeds from a denial of basic freedoms. Thus when we speak of equality of opportunity and consider the greater equality of results to which it may lead, we think primarily in terms of intergroup equality, of the elimination of arbitrary and unconstitutional barriers. Until those barriers have been removed, intragroup differences will remain secondary.

The Effects of Schooling

Using intragroup differences based on data from three large-scale surveys, Jencks and his associates develop two central conclusions about the effects of schooling: first, no measurable school resource or policy shows a consistent relationship to a school's effectiveness in boosting achievement; second, the gains associated with any given resource are almost always small. In other words, nothing we do in schools seems to make much difference to the cognitive development of students. The only possible exceptions appear to have little to do with school resources; they are racial and socioeconomic integration and length of schooling.[18] Because these conclusions have obvious policy implications, it is important to understand their limitations.

Generally, the input-output approach—which *Inequality* uses and later repudiates—cannot tell us for certain that nothing makes a difference. It cannot prove the absence of positive relationships between school inputs and outputs, but only that no such relationships have been discovered,

Donald M. Levine

for they probably are sufficiently complicated to have eluded the researcher's mathematical inventiveness, at least at the first cut. As Averch and his colleagues caution:

These results should not be interpreted as indicating that school resources *do not* affect student outcomes. We can only observe that these studies have failed to show that school resources do affect student outcomes. The difference between these two points is a reflection of the problems encountered in doing research in the input-output approach.[19]

These problems are rooted in the fact that input-output analyses deal not with controlled experiments to which a production function might be fitted, but with more or less uncontrolled situations whose data deficiencies limit the studies' comparability and validity. The most important data problem is the great aggregation of inputs. In seeking to establish reliable input-output relationships, we must concentrate on the resources which actually do affect individual outputs. These are the direct costs of production. In schooling, the resources most directly related to a student's outputs are those he actually uses. Unfortunately, collecting such data is almost impossible and would probably require tracking each student through his "resource-using day." Given the impossibility of student-by-student input breakdowns, we then turn to classroom-by-classroom or class-by-class aggregations. If even these data prove impossible to collect, we may turn to school-by-school aggregations and, eventually, to district-by-district data. But the higher this aggregation, the less meaningful the phrase "per pupil expenditure" becomes. Districts do not allocate funds equally, and neither do schools or classroom teachers. Differences in resources devoted to a particular student may be significant within the same school, depending on the student's curriculum, his claims on the teacher's time, his absences, and many other factors. Unfortunately, the EEOS data which Jencks and his associates use are mainly for districts, and the school-by-school data they do have relate to high school, where differential expenditures per pupil are likely to have much less effect than in the earlier years.

Another aggregation problem with the input data is that they can tell us what is being done in the classroom only in a general sense—so much for salaries, so much for materials and equipment, and so on. They ignore *how* the resources are used. We usually do not know, for example, what teachers and students are doing with the 1,500 books the school's library recently acquired. Because of this difficulty, *Inequality* concludes "that if schools continue to use their resources as they now do, giving them more resources will not change children's test scores. If schools used their resources differently, however, additional resources might conceivably have higher payoffs." [20]

310

Despite the problems with input data, most debate has centered on output measurement. One reason for disagreement there is that the ways in which outputs are measured depend on the goals of schooling, and people differ greatly over those goals. Because they are widely available, scores on standardized achievement tests usually serve as proxies for output. The narrowness of such scores, their tenuous relationship to student development, and their inadequacy as a summary measure of school effectiveness impress the authors of *Inequality* as much as they have other researchers, but there are no alternatives. As a result, *Inequality* is forced to ignore both noncognitive outcomes and measures of what teachers actually seem to do with their students.

In addition, the goals and goal-related activities of teachers may differ widely from the kinds of performance standardized achievement tests are designed to measure. *Inequality* speculates that teachers seek first to make children behave, and secondly to teach the kinds of skills measured on standardized tests.[21] This view may not match reality, for teachers frequently specialize in subject matter only indirectly related to "standardized skills," and schools often are organized in the same way. Writing of the output data in the EEOS, Henry Dyer has noted:

A serious weakness in the Coleman analysis is just this point: its criterion of academic achievement is almost exclusively a measure of verbal ability which has long been known to be a slow-developing function that for obvious reasons is likely to be far more a product of a child's home than of his school experience. The Coleman study pays scant attention to the kinds of achievement on which the schools have traditionally focused . . . and it is precisely in these subjects that there appear to be substantial differential effects among schools *even when differences in socioeconomic levels have been accounted for.* The other two earlier studies tend to reinforce this finding.[22]

Though parents, administrators, and teachers frequently voice their concern about improving children's scores on standardized achievement tests, we have no proof that raising scores on such tests is even a tertiary goal for teachers. Indeed, it seems possible that these tests have been widely accepted not because they represent school goals accurately, but because parents easily understand the grade level equivalents into which achievement test scores are translated, and the tests are general enough to short-circuit debate about the appropriate ends of schooling.[23] Before using standardized tests as summary measures of school effectiveness, we must discover how congruent they are with teacher goals.[24]

A final difficulty with the data for input-output analyses is that the "natural experiments" which might furnish exceptions to the average school are poorly controlled, if at all, and often do not attempt innovation. The prime example is Title I of the Elementary and Secondary Education Act of 1965, the mismanagement of which was notorious.[25] The unfortunate result is that most input-output analyses, like *Inequality*, must confine themselves to the average school and thereby diminish the chances of discovering significant input-output relationships.

Even if we found significant input-output relationships in education, how would we judge the desirability of spending money for programs whose results might be only incrementally different from the results of existing school programs? The answer to this question largely depends on the costs of achieving incremental effectiveness. Developing such cost-effectiveness calculations requires much closer attention to the causes of variations in school effectiveness and their replicability. It is remarkable that almost all studies of school effectiveness ignore the problem of developing cost-effectiveness calculations for whatever school effects are discovered. This deficiency is important both at the school level—for determining preferred alternatives to achieve limited educational objectives—and at the social policy level—for determining preferred alternatives to achieve broader societal objectives. Without such calculations, we have little quantitative basis for saying whether a school is unusually effective and worth studying or for concluding that the schools, as marginal institutions, have a very small role in any program to reduce inequality. In simplistic terms, the significance of differences and the marginality of institutions are questions of alternative policies and their relative cost-effectiveness. Jencks and his associates, for example, compare the influence of schooling in reducing inequality to that of background and unexplained factors and find it negligible. But in thinking about policy, we must examine the available options in terms of cost, immediate and long-range impacts, and feasibility. Cost-effectiveness comparisons of different methods for reducing inequality encourage evaluating the utility of education relative to that of other approaches. Without cost comparisons, assertions of education's insignificant effects do not effectively eliminate its utility as an instrument of social policy. As Moynihan observed of the war on poverty: "While the differential effects of state intervention may be small, they may be no less crucial for that reason." [26]

The Utility of Schooling

Having sought to show that variations in the quality of schooling have only small, inconsistent effects on cognitive achievement, *Inequality* addresses the long-term effects of schooling, and thus the question of its ultimate social and economic utility. The question of utility is first a question of goals. Because goals differ for different people and interests at different policy-making levels, there are numerous ways to judge the utility of education. Some people may have an economic goal and use the criteria of labor productivity and returns to educational investment. Goals related to the quality of life may use criteria such as the external benefits to society of an educated citizenry. People concerned with the structure of society may concentrate on the criteria of increased social mobility or more equality of results. All of these criteria relate to goals which may be achieved through alternative means, one of which is education. The utility of education therefore depends on how well schooling achieves these goals in comparison with other approaches. And because these goals are usually interrelated, we should measure the utility of education along a number of parameters simultaneously.

Inequality concentrates on only one of those parameters. Following the dictates of the original argument, it seeks to evaluate education in terms of its effects on inequality, as indicated by the degree and type of variation in occupational status, income, and job satisfaction that can be attributed to education. Because the effect of education on occupational status is circular—one of the two ways in which people define an occupation's status is the amount of education it requires—and because job satisfaction appears to be more a matter of how well your occupational neighbor is doing than of how much education helped you get the job you wanted, the most meaningful criterion is income. Thus the first reduction of *Inequality*'s general question is, "What effects does education have on income?"

There is a further reduction. The book's previous conclusion that differences in the quality of schooling have relatively unimportant effects on cognitive skills causes this section to treat education not in terms of any changes it may have fostered in students, but primarily in terms of the number of years a person has attended school. Since cognitive development does not seem to vary much with variations in school quality, any impact that education may have on income will proceed from the cognitive development that length of schooling (rather than quality) induces. So the second reduction of the question reads, "What effects do years of schooling have on income?" [27] *Inequality* then defines income as annual earnings.

Trends in income inequality which might relate to trends in educational attainment depend on a vast number of factors other than wage returns to years of schooling (and the immediate future of such trends is obscure).[28] Jencks and his associates note that these trends depend on the degree of inequality in individual incomes, differences between families in the number of people with incomes, and the correlation between incomes of different persons in the same family.[29] They then decide to concentrate only on individual earnings and present a table of the annual earnings of full-time, year-round workers in 1968. This is not a sound approach to the general question of income inequality. As the authors point out, it excludes individuals who did not work all year, individuals who worked less than full time, and such "unearned" incomes as dividends, rent, welfare, and social security.[30] It also excludes noncash income and transfers (e.g., food stamps, jobs with room and board), private transfers (e.g., employer's contributions to pension funds, families' support of individuals who are counted as separate households), the value of nonmarket activities (e.g., housekeeping, child care), and the income value of public services such as garbage collection and even public education. These exclusions are matters of more than academic interest because they limit exploration of the ways in which years of schooling may influence income inequality. There is evidence, for example, that mothers with more years of schooling contribute more valuable child care than less educated mothers.[31] Moreover, educational attainment may have particularly large effects on an individual's ability to obtain *any* employment during periods of business contraction, but the data cited prevent exploration of this possibility. There also is evidence that a very important factor in income inequality is the number of weeks worked,[32] and educational attainment may help to determine the frequency of a person's unemployment and the time it takes him to search for another job. Finally, by ignoring the number of workers in families and family size, *Inequality* also ignores the possibilities that better-educated wives have higher chances of employment, or that families with higher educational attainment have fewer children, and therefore higher per capita income.

Inequality posits two types of income inequality: that between occupational categories (intergroup), and that for all individuals, which can be seen by proxy in the income inequality within occupations (intragroup). The book's basic conclusion is that the additional earnings which result from extra schooling are quite low and mainly artificial:

Rate-of-return estimates do tell us that efforts to keep everyone in school longer make little economic sense. . . . Efforts to get everyone to finish high school and attend college must, therefore, be justified primarily on noneconomic grounds. Otherwise they probably cannot be justified at all.

This conclusion seems particularly persuasive when we recall that the financial return to schooling derives almost exclusively from the fact that schooling provides men with access to highly paid occupations, not from the fact that it enables men in a given occupation to earn more. Giving everyone credentials cannot provide everyone with access to the best-paid occupations. It can only raise earnings if it makes people more productive within various occupations. There is little evidence that it will do this.[33]

In short, education is not a very profitable investment, and whatever profits it does show are the result of job market irrationality. The basis for the second part of this assertion is small. Examining the question of whether employers' preference for educated workers is actually related to the higher productivity of the educated or is an arbitrary rationing system, *Inequality* concludes that "There is something to be said for both theories and very little evidence that allows us to choose between them. . . . The data do not . . . allow us to say whether employers' preference for educated workers is rational or irrational." [34] The main argument for the rationing or credentials view of education advanced in *Inequality* is that, once people enter a particular occupation, those with additional education do not make appreciably more money than others in the occupation.[35] But this line of reasoning is questionable. In many occupations, schooling levels will be fairly homogeneous, so income variations because of education will be understated. As the authors note, it also is possible that employers are rational because those with less education may have compensating qualities that bring their productivity and earnings to the levels of those with more education. Most importantly, this analysis ignores postschool investments in training and experience. There is growing evidence to indicate that postschool investment increments explain much of the variation in men's incomes; that although those with more schooling tend to make more postschool investments, the dispersion of these investments increases with age, and their rates of return decline; and that employers are rational even when they use education as a credential because the more highly educated may be easier (and therefore cheaper) to train once they are on the job.[36]

Despite *Inequality*'s contention that education does not lead to productivity gains, there is strong contrary evidence. The basis of the human capital approach is that economic development has proceeded at a pace faster than growth in the traditional factors of production can explain; the residual is attributed to growth in human capital. One persuasive indication that education does lead to increased productivity is that the rate of return to secondary education has risen sharply in this century and does not seem about to decline, despite huge increases in the percentage of Americans who have completed high school.[37] Certain groups —blacks, women, and others—have had depressed rates because of discrimination, but not because of lower productivity. As Mincer puts it:

When we look at the massive trends in schooling in this century and in the past decades and years we wonder whether we have not been overschooling our children. Certainly, there are signals of distress coming from the young and from many concerned parents and educators.

Yet, if we view schooling as an investment process, there is no evidence that the profitability of that investment has declined as numbers of students have grown. The private rate of return to schooling has remained roughly constant around a respectable 10 percent figure (with deviations depending on data and analysis) in the past three decades.[38]

It appears, then, that education is not as poor an investment as *Inequality* would have us believe. It is true that certain minority groups do not benefit as highly as their productive capacity warrants, but that is because of job discrimination, a factor that has been changing slowly. As it has, rates of return to minority groups have risen.[39] Returns to college and graduate education have been neither as high nor as consistent as returns to lower levels of education, but errors in estimating the foregone earnings of higher education students and the high segmentation of the job market for college graduates may be partly responsible. For white males, then, finishing high school is an attractive investment; for others, returns are improving. Moreover, to suggest, as *Inequality* does, that educational attainment has such small and artificial returns that it cannot be economically justified as a national policy is not egalitarian. A diminution of support for efforts to get everyone to finish high school can easily lead to greater intergroup inequality. It would add to existing barriers in the labor market at least the barrier of reduced job access, and most probably the barrier of lower productive capacity.[40]

Despite the apparently satisfactory returns to education, we must remember that income is only a partial criterion for evaluating the utility of education, and economic analysis is only one of several ways to examine educational policy. There are noneconomic criteria—such as the creation of knowledge or the growth of self-esteem—and noneconomic analyses—such as the study of socialization processes—that should enter into any comprehensive attempt to assess the utility of schooling. Stating educational outputs only in terms of dollar benefits ascribes to those outputs a solidity they do not possess and places crippling restrictions on the framework for policy analysis. Similarly, income is only a partial criterion for evaluating policies designed to reduce inequality. Jencks and his associates suggest that inequality consists of people's differential abilities to participate in a social system, and that these abilities depend on how much a person can spend relative to other people.[41] Thus, income differentials constitute inequality. Yet participation in a social system also depends on capacities other than that of spending: awareness of power and information networks, articulateness, and cultural knowledge. Without income differentials, there would still be inequality unless efforts were made to distribute these other goods equally.

Finally, we must recognize that, even if educational attainment does have attractive economic returns and we try to equalize educational attainment, the result may be increased mobility and less inequality among groups but no change in economic inequality among individuals. More equal educational attainment can remove the barriers to advancement that hinder many groups, and it can produce more equal average lifetime earnings streams, but it cannot insure that a person's progress after he has passed those barriers will be basically the same as his neighbor's, or that every individual will get the same returns to schooling. These latter objectives depend more on changing the economic and social structure of America than on interventions such as education and quota hiring (or even increased redistribution of income).[42] Once again, policies for reducing intergroup inequality will not do much to reduce intragroup inequality, and it becomes necessary to decide which kind of inequality is most pressing: that which involves arbitrary denial of basic freedoms (intergroup), or that which involves relative deprivation (intragroup). On that decision rests the validity of recommendations for both educational and economic policy.

Educational Policy

Inequality makes two recommendations for educational policy. First, we should abandon the factory metaphor for education in favor of a family model. Like families, individual schools will be quite diverse and should be judged according to very different standards. The only common criterion should be whether teachers and students find the school a pleasant and rewarding place to be; otherwise, a particular school's objectives and performance should reflect the values of the parents who send their children to it. Second, we should equalize access to school resources, although there is little we can do to equalize utilization of those resources, which depends on family-determined attitudes toward education.[43]

The basis for these recommendations is that: None of the evidence we have reviewed suggests that school reform can be expected to bring about significant social changes outside the schools. More specifically, the evidence suggests that equalizing educational opportunity would do very little to make adults more equal.[44]

There are three reasons for the evident ineffectiveness and inutility of schooling:

First, children seem to be far more influenced by what happens at home than by what happens in school. They may also be more influenced by what happens

Donald M. Levine

on the streets and by what they see on television. Sceond, reformers have
very little control over those aspects of school life that affect children. Real-
locating resources, reassigning pupils, and rewriting the curriculum seldom
change the way teachers and students actually treat each other minute by
minute. Third, even when a school exerts an unusual influence on children,
the resulting changes are not likely to persist into adulthood. . . .[45]

In other words, because schooling can do little to reduce intragroup
inequality, we must view it as an end in itself rather than as a means
to some other end. We are forced to view schooling as an end in itself
because schooling has relatively few effects on children; policy makers
have few effects on schools; and whatever effects school does have are
short-lived.

We have seen that these conclusions do not follow necessarily from the
evidence. At the outset of this paper, we saw that schooling has not
been a primary tool for reducing inequality of results and that equal
opportunity—to which the schools looked—is a concept functionally distinct from equal results. Judging education by its ability to equalize
results is inappropriate. Such judgment also imposes a single criterion
on an institution with multiple goals.[46] Also, intergroup rather than
intragroup comparisons may be more relevant to the question of equal
opportunity. In the second section we saw that Inequality's analysis of
school effectiveness is limited by methodology and data; that it considers a limited number of inputs and outputs despite recognition that
alternatives may be more significant; and that without introducing cost
considerations, it is difficult to judge the relative utility of education.
In the third section, we saw that the analysis of the long-term effects
of education is qualified by a narrow definition of income and by certain
technical problems, and that there is substantial evidence to support
the economic utility of educational investment. For these reasons, Inequality's policy recommendations seem at least premature.

In some ways, those recommendations are large steps backward. While
the family metaphor may be an accurate reflection of the passivity of
schools, it fails to take account of a basic objective of universal, publicly
supported education: the desire to provide a common experience, to
socialize children according to common norms and processes.[47] And the
family metaphor sounds like a concession to irrationality, since it eliminates opportunities for more rational allocation of educational resources
by preventing interschool and interprogram comparisons according to
criteria more concrete than the quality of school life. This limitation
is especially deleterious for the educational policy maker if the family
metaphor is extended down from the school to the classroom level,
where interprogram and intraprogram decisions must be implemented.
Inequality's other recommendation for educational policy—that access to

318

school resources be equalized—involves a return to the less problematic aspect of the 1954 Supreme Court decision, i.e., that discriminatory access violates fundamental freedoms. But it also may encourage a regression of emphasis from the effectiveness of educational resources and the cost of producing educational outputs to an archaic concept of equal educational opportunity that concentrates on inputs only.

In light of these difficulties, what is to be done? Where should we direct our attention in the effort to formulate educational policy? How can we provide more convincing and useful analyses of educational policy?

1. We must try to establish more clearly the hierarchy of goals which structures educational policy. A prerequisite for this effort is analyzing more carefully the hierarchy of social goals which educational goals are supposed to serve. Analyzing social and educational goals is a somewhat nebulous task. It consists mainly in formalizing and making explicit values and their interrelations. Values change, and policy must keep pace with those changes.

Inequality, for example, is only one of several recently published works that express a growing concern with equality of results.[48] As we have seen, the goal of equal results is distinct from and partially conflicts with the goal of equal opportunity, for the individual outcomes of a competitive system that includes equal opportunity will be unequal. Part of the problem in reconciling equal results with equal opportunity is empirical and calls for finding out whether or not the barriers that comprise unequal opportunity have been so thoroughly eliminated that the rules of competition—if not its outcomes—are fair. Only when these barriers have diminished to insignificance will intragroup differences and equality of results take precedence over intergroup differences and equality of opportunity. But a more thorny part of the problem is philosophical and requires an understanding of basic American values:

What is at stake today is the redefinition of equality. A principle which was the weapon for changing a vast social system, the principle of equality of opportunity, is now seen as leading to a new hierarchy, and the current demand is that the "just precedence" of society, in Locke's phrase, requires the reduction of all inequality, or the creation of *equality of results*—in income, status, and power—for all men in society. This issue is the central problem of post-industrial society.[49]

The difficulties of this value shift are not to be minimized. At the least, they include basic revisions in the concepts of individual merit, the social basis of reward systems, and deserving.[50]

Within a revised hierarchy of social goals, we will have to clarify the meaning of equal educational opportunity by reconciling the goals of

Donald M. Levine

equal access to educational resources and of effective equality of opportunity, i.e., more equal educational results. Although equality of educational opportunity is a concept whose "definition will be the outcome of a variety of interests and will certainly differ from time to time as those interests differ,"[51] the notion that schools have obligations to develop fully the potential of their students and to bring all of them to a certain level of cognitive ability seems unlikely to vanish. Thus concern with the outcomes of schooling, as well as its inputs, will persist, as will output-oriented objectives for education.

2. Our means of analyzing educational policies must be revised. It is here that *Inequality* provides the most guidance, by demonstrating that for many observers, the failure of the search for educational production functions means that there are no ways in which variations in educational inputs affect variations in educational outputs. Yet a production function is a very limited way of looking at resource-effectiveness relationships. The production function's view of resources is confined to highly aggregated inputs undifferentiated as to quality or application. Its view of effectiveness usually is limited to only one outcome of schooling—cognitive development. So it is presumptuous to say that school policies and resources make no difference; we have yet to examine what school inputs do and how they do it, to scrutinize the process and interaction variables of resource-effectiveness relationships.

Clearly, we need approaches other than traditional input-output analyses that look to establishing reliable production functions. A prime requirement of any new approach will be a systems orientation. Policy analysis for education must consider not just the inputs, processes, and outputs of schooling, but their interaction with other educational processes that occur before, during, and after schooling. These processes include the family experiences to which *Inequality* gives so much weight and the postschool investments that Mincer finds important. Because a systems orientation emphasizes the role of schooling in a broader educational system, it leads us both to consider the dynamic relationship of schooling with other systems that, by plan or not, influence educational outcomes, and to compare the preferredness of schooling with that of nonschool alternatives. By focusing our attention in these ways, a systems orientation permits us to assess the educational effectiveness of schooling relative to other institutions and systems, to isolate new opportunities for intervention within and without the school system, and to weigh the ultimate—rather than proximate—utility of schooling for the social system.

One type of analysis that can include a systems orientation and incorporate observations of processes and interactions is *cost-effectiveness analysis in a programmatic setting*. Analysis of this sort concentrates on a range of resources (not just costs) at the school and program levels and relates these resources directly to program objectives and student outcomes measured along multiple parameters. Thus it permits us to examine fine breakdowns of resources actually applied to students; to evaluate school programs according to the outputs they are intended—rather than assumed—to produce; and to study effectiveness at a disaggregated, relatively microscopic level that helps to dispel the mystery of the "black box" of input-output analysis.

The two greatest attractions of cost-effectiveness analysis in a programmatic context are: (1) that it includes observations and measures of the process and interaction variables that condition individual cost-effectiveness relationships; and (2) that it can reconcile the need for experimentation in the schools with the requirements of management, thereby encouraging innovative applications of school resources. The several advantages of this mode of analysis are sufficiently clear to have evoked a detailed implementation strategy [52] and suggestions for its extension to the broader realm of social policy analysis.[53] Clarification of social and educational goals and adoption of a new mode of analysis cannot guarantee an antidote to the disappointment with schooling that has characterized recent years. It is possible that attempts to analyze the educational goal hierarchy will fail repeatedly and force us to conclude that because educational goals are undefinable, "it is inappropriate to adopt the standard rationalist approach of first defining goals then seeking means to achieve them efficiently." [54] Schools may indeed function like families and call for other than rationalist approaches to evaluation and policy making. Or cost-effectiveness analysis with a systems orientation may indicate that schools and school effects are so much the results of contiguous systems that it makes more sense to invest in nonschool policies. But unless we take these new approaches to policy analysis, we will be unable—like *Inequality*—to provide a convincing analytical basis for better educational policies.

NOTES

1. Christopher Jencks, Marshall Smith, Henry Acland, Mary Jo Bane, David Cohen, Herbert Gintis, Barbara Heyns, Stephen Michelson, *Inequality: A Reassessment of the Effect of Family and Schooling in America* (New York: Basic Books, 1972), p. 5.
2. Christopher Jencks, "*Inequality* in Retrospect," *Harvard Educational Review* 43, no. 1 (1973): 138.
3. Jencks et al., *Inequality*, p. 7.

Donald M. Levine

4. Alice M. Rivlin, "Forensic Social Science," *Harvard Educational Review* 43, no. 1 (1973): 64–65.

5. Ibid.

6. Charles L. Schultz, Edward R. Fried, Alice M. Rivlin, and Nancy H. Teeters, *Setting National Priorities for the 1973 Budget* (Washington, D.C.: The Brookings Institution, 1972), p. 11.

7. Ibid., p. 320.

8. Jencks et al., *Inequality*, p. 3.

9. Ibid.

10. *Inequality* uses a very broad definition of fairness in examining equality of opportunity. It seems to imply that competitive advantages—no matter what their source—are unfair. This broad definition leads to apparent absurdities. It eliminates the notion of deserving on which the idea of equal opportunity seems to be based. As Stuart Hampshire, "A New Philosophy of the Just Society," *The New York Review of Books* 18, no. 3 (1972): 36, has observed of John Rawls' idea of fairness: Is there anything at all that, strictly speaking, a man can claim credit for, or he can properly be said to deserve, with the implication that it can be attributed to him, the ultimate subject, as contrasted with the natural forces that formed him? In the last analysis, are not all advantages and disadvantages distributed by natural causes, even when they are the effects of human agency? And if we are not strict theists, we will surely not suppose that there is cosmic justice in these distributions . . . the fairness aimed at is not only the negation of aristocracy but of meritocracy. Secondly, such a broad view eliminates—by definition—any distinction between equal opportunity and equal results. Opportunities become results as people age, and any inequality of result can be said to limit a person's next opportunity. Even with parity at the outset of job competition, the results of a person's first job competition will affect his opportunities in successive competitions; equality of opportunity is determined by equality of results of the person's last competitive experience, and this holds from preschool to retirement. And as *Inequality* seems to recognize, this effect is as much an intergenerational as a lifetime one: parents' results determine children's opportunities, just as adolescents' results determine adults' opportunities.

11. James Coleman, "The Concept of Equality of Educational Opportunity," *Harvard Educational Review* 38, no. 1 (1968): 15.

12. Ibid., p. 18.

13. Rivlin, "Forensic Social Science," p. 74.

14. In a technical note, Jencks and his associates offer tentative confirmation of the reasonableness of this view: "When we predict occupational status from AFQT scores, the errors in prediction are larger for men with high scores than for men with low scores. This suggests that cognitive skills may be a necessary but not sufficient condition for advancement." Jencks et al., *Inequality*, app. B, p. 337.

15. Ibid., p. 14.

16. Beverly Duncan, "Comments on *Inequality*," *Harvard Educational Review* 43, no. 1 (1973): p. 126.

17. Jencks et al., *Inequality*, p. 14.

18. Ibid., p. 109, estimates that both types of integration would reduce cognitive inequality between black and white children and between rich and poor by 10 to 20 percent; equalizing length of schooling might reduce cognitive inequality another 5 to 15 percent. This conclusion is interesting because equality of educational opportunity was early defined as equality of exposure to schooling. See Edmund W. Gordon, "Toward Defining Equality of Educational Opportunity," in *On Equality*

of Educational Opportunity, ed. Frederick Mosteller and Daniel P. Moynihan (New York: Random House, 1970).

19. See Harvey A. Averch, Stephen J. Carroll, Theodore S. Donaldson, Herbert J. Kiesling, and John Pincus, "How Effective Is Schooling? A Critical Review and Synthesis of Research Findings," pp. 63–97 of this book.

20. Jencks et al., *Inequality*, p. 97.

21. Ibid., p. 95.

22. Henry Dyer, "School Factors," *Harvard Educational Review* 38, no. 1 (1968): 46. Dyer is speaking here of Marion F. Shaycoft, *The High School Years: Growth in Cognitive Skills* (Pittsburgh, Pa.: American Institutes of Research and School of Education, University of Pittsburgh, 1967); of William G. Mollenkopf and S. Donald Melville, *A Study of Secondary School Characteristics as Related to Test Scores* (Princeton, N.J.: Educational Testing Service, 1956); and of Samuel M. Goodman, *The Assessment of School Quality* (Albany, N.Y.: New York State Education Department, 1959).

23. See Roger T. Lennon, "Accountability and Performance Contracting" (paper presented at the Annual Meeting of the American Educational Research Association, February 1971).

24. "It is becoming increasingly clear that different educational objectives and values exist as well as individual differences in types and levels of ability. We must therefore realize that research based on limited measures, and accounting for relatively few objectives, cannot lead to conclusive generalizations about educational outcomes." Averch et al., "How Effective is Schooling?"

25. With Title I programs, "the equality of a child's experience is seldom changed, so we should not expect the results to change." Jencks et al., *Inequality*, pp. 126–127, n. 107.

26. Daniel P. Moynihan, "Equalizing Education: In Whose Benefit?," pp. 98–117.

27. This restatement is somewhat simplified. The mode of analysis used in *Inequality* organizes the book to use at the same time a number of variables that may explain variation in income. Again, though, the relevant question for educational policy makers is how education might make a difference in income. Chapter 7 of *Inequality*—"Income Inequality"—discusses four types of variables: background, cognitive skills, occupational status, and educational attainment. Educational policy makers can do little to change background factors (though they can try to compensate for them). Preceding sections of *Inequality* imply that policy makers can do little to alter the level of cognitive skills beyond increasing educational attainment. Occupational status is partly defined by educational attainment. So education attainment is the relevant question here.

28. Jencks et al., *Inequality*, p. 234, n. 9: "The coefficient [of variation in income] declined slightly from 1961 to 1968, but the long-term trend is unclear. . . ." Not only is the trend hazy but also the level of income inequality in the United States is a matter of debate because the underlying concepts are unclear. See, especially, Herman P. Miller, *Income Distribution in the United States*, A 1960 Census Monograph (Washington, D.C.: U.S. Government Printing Office, 1966); and Roger A. Herriot and Herman P. Miller, "The Taxes We Pay: An Analysis of the Tax Burden at Each Income Level," *The Conference Board Record* 8, no. 5 (1971).

29. Jencks et al., *Inequality*, p. 211.

30. Ibid., p. 212.

31. See Arlene Leibowitz, *Education and Allocation of Women's Time* (New York: National Bureau of Economic Research, 1972). This is one of the few pieces of research, but the basic concept has been put forth by several students of human

capital, especially Gary Becker, "A Theory of the Allocation of Time," *Economic Journal* 75 (1975).

32. See T. Paul Schultz, "Long-term Change in Personal Income Distribution," pp. 147–169 of this book.

33. Jencks et al., *Inequality*, p. 224.

34. Ibid., pp. 182, 183.

35. Ibid., p. 182.

36. See Jacob Mincer, *Schooling, Experience and Earnings* (New York: National Bureau of Economic Research, 1974); also Burton Weisbrod, "Education and Investment in Human Capital," *Journal of Political Economy* 70 (October 1972): supplement.

37. Attempting to explain this phenomenon, Finis Welch, "Education in Production," *Journal of Political Economy* 78, no. 1 (1970), has provided some evidence to show that the educated have improved entrepreneurial and allocative abilities that allow them to allocate production factors more rationally.

38. See Jacob Mincer, "Youth, Education, and Work," pp. 185–194 of this book.

39. See Schultz, "Long-term Change in Personal Income Distribution."

40. Despite the evidence from economics, the education-income relationship is hotly contested. See, for example, Ivar Berg, *Education and Jobs: The Great Training Robbery* (New York: Praeger, 1970). In part, Berg argues that employers' preferences for educated workers are irrational because workers with high school diplomas are not more productive in certain occupations than those without. But if a diploma is simply a license, as Berg contends, then the returns to schooling should not be continuous. One of the most convincing demonstrations that this rate *is* continuous comes from a study of veterans' school investments made after separation from the services; in that case, each additional year of school—and not just a degree or diploma—was strongly associated with increased earnings, even with background and ability held constant. See Zvi Griliches and William Mason, "Education, Income and Ability," *Journal of Political Economy* 80, no. 3, pt. II (1972). Jerald G. Bachman, reporting on the Youth in Transition study of the University of Michigan's Institute for Social Research, asserts that the weekly wages of dropouts and high school graduates are nearly identical, but he admits that his sample is very young and differences may show up later. If Mincer's notion that it takes some years for the earnings of the educated to overtake those of the less educated but more experienced is correct, the differences Bachman refers to are probable. Jerald G. Bachman, "Comment: Anti-Dropout Campaign and Other Misanthropies," *Transaction* 9, no. 5 (1972); and Mincer, *Schooling, Experience, and Earnings*.

41. Jencks et al., *Inequality*, pp. 5–6.

42. Ibid., pp. 195–196.

43. Ibid., pp. 256–258.

44. Ibid., p. 255.

45. Ibid., pp. 255–256.

46. Jencks seems to have recognized this problem in an interview printed in the *Phi Delta Kappan*, December 1972, p. 257: "We don't talk at all about some other kinds of outcomes of schooling that I think are important. . . . So we can't say what kind of impact schooling makes in many areas of life, or whether kinds of differences between schools play a major role in the development of many traits." It is difficult, then, to see how Jencks feels able to make broad policy recommendations for education.

47. See Gordon, "Toward Defining Equality of Educational Opportunity"; James A. Coleman, "The Concept of Equality of Educational Opportunity," pp. 199–213 of this book.

48. See John Rawls, *A Theory of Justice* (Cambridge, Mass.: Harvard University

Press, 1971); and S. M. Miller and Pamela A. Roby, *The Future of Inequality* (New York: Basic Books, 1970).

49. Daniel Bell, "On Meritocracy and Equality," *The Public Interest* 29 (Fall 1972): 40.

50. Both Jencks and Bell seem to recognize the ambiguity introduced by these problems:

> But if those with low incomes are mostly being punished for failings they can remedy, such as not wanting to work, the case for redistribution is more problematic. This is also true if most of the poor are being punished for making the "wrong" choice at some time in the past, such as dropping out of school. Society has a stake in discouraging certain kinds of antisocial behavior, and if dropping out of school reduces an individual's capacity to contribute to the general welfare, it may make sense to punish this decision by paying dropouts less. . . . It is not clear, however, how much of the variation in people's incomes derives from factors they could change, how much from factors they could once have changed, and how much from factors that have always been completely beyond their control. . . . Until we know what the relevant factors are, the question remains opaque. (Jencks, "*Inequality* in Retrospect," p. 156.)
>
> What if the "least fortunate" are there by their own choice? . . . If individuals—for cultural or psychological reasons—do not avail themselves of opportunities, is it the society's responsibility, as the prior obligation, to devote resources to them? But if not, how does one distinguish between the genuinely disadvantaged and those who are not? (Bell, "On Meritocracy and Equality," p. 60, n. 15.)

51. From an internal momorandum circulated prior to the EEOS; Coleman, "The Concept of Equality of Educational Opportunity."

52. See Sue A. Haggart, Arthur J. Alexander, and Polly Carpenter, *Relating School Resources to Educational Outcomes: A Research Strategy* (Santa Monica, Calif.: The Rand Corporation, 1972).

53. Erich Jantsch, "Forecasting and the Systems Approach: A Critical Survey," *Policy Sciences* 3, no. 4 (1972): 497, has suggested that cost effectiveness ". . . can go further in expressing and measuring also the effectiveness of attaining a specified target or contributing to a goal which may, for example, be determined by different probability distributions for different alternatives. The development of a generalized social cost-effectiveness concept would constitute considerable improvement over the present state in which cost-benefit still rules."

54. John Pincus, *Incentives for Innovation in the Public Schools* (Santa Monica, Calif.: The Rand Corporation, 1973), p. 22.

INDEX